Forensic Anthropology

Forensic Anthropology
Current Methods and Practice

Angi M. Christensen

Nicholas V. Passalacqua

Eric J. Bartelink

AMSTERDAM • BOSTON • HEIDELBERG • LONDON
NEW YORK • OXFORD • PARIS • SAN DIEGO
SAN FRANCISCO • SINGAPORE • SYDNEY • TOKYO

ELSEVIER

Academic Press is an imprint of Elsevier

Academic Press is an imprint of Elsevier
The Boulevard, Langford Lane, Kidlington, Oxford, OX5 1GB
525 B Street, Suite 1800, San Diego, CA 92101-4495, USA

First published 2014

British Library Cataloguing in Publication Data
A catalogue record for this book is available from the British Library

Library of Congress Cataloging-in-Publication Data
A catalog record for this book is available from the Library of Congress

ISBN: 978-0-12-418671-2

For information on all Academic Press publications visit
our website at store.elsevier.com

Contents

Foreword

Forensic anthropology represents a complex and rapidly evolving field of science. Case applications are diverse, including evidence recovery, estimating the biological profile, evaluating time since death, reporting evidence of foul play, and contributing to positive identification. Each of these many specialized areas has its own methodology, supporting scientific literature, and limitations. Such diversity can prove challenging both to those entering the field and established practitioners who must defend their interpretations in the legal arena.

This textbook represents a welcomed and much needed addition to the supporting literature in forensic anthropology. Written by three experienced forensic anthropologists working in different laboratory settings, the volume places the practice of forensic anthropology within the context of contemporary forensic science and the scientific principles of modern physical anthropology and biology. Explanations of the science involved are accompanied by case examples, profiles of some current practitioners, and information on the training required. The volume offers not only a detailed presentation of the many techniques involved in the practice of forensic anthropology, but also a sense of the underlying science. Such perspective offers readers a vital understanding of this rapidly changing field, as well as a comprehensive view of its content.

Douglas H. Ubelaker

Preface

The principle rationale for writing this textbook was the perceived need for a comprehensive introductory text that approaches forensic anthropology as a modern and well-developed science. This effort includes consideration of forensic anthropology within the broader forensic science community, extensive use of case studies, and discussion of the most recent research, technology, and challenges in the field.

We approached this through an innovative style, using ground truths and case experience from our varied backgrounds and current practices as working forensic anthropologists. This book is not intended as a technical manual, but as a scientific text designed to guide the reader through the various components of forensic anthropology. We present principles at a level that is appropriate for those new to the field, while at the same time incorporating evolutionary, biomechanical, and other theoretical explanations for the features and phenomena observed. We believe that the student or aspiring practitioner should not only be able to detect, measure, and evaluate relevant features of the skeleton, but should also appreciate the scientific principles that underpin them and their variants. This text is also distinctive for its inclusion of topics such as requirements for practicing forensic anthropology, the types of jobs that are available to the aspiring practitioner, and how students can become more involved in the field.

In addition, this text presents current perspectives and developments, including the incorporation of "best practices" as identified by the Scientific Working Group for Forensic Anthropology (SWGANTH). Although seminal works are noted, attention is given primarily to the most recent and most scientifically valid applications commonly employed by working forensic anthropologists. Some of these new techniques are significantly more complex than traditional forensic anthropological approaches, but we believe that their inclusion is important, so that the student is aware of the breadth and scope of the field, is informed about innovative techniques in the discipline, and is prepared by understanding the necessary background of those who practice in the field today (for example, a strong background in metric analysis and statistics).

This text is well-suited for introductory or upper level courses in forensic anthropology, including courses taught in anthropology programs as well as those taught in the growing number of forensic science programs. This text can stand alone in a forensic anthropology course. It would also serve as an appropriate supplemental reference for other courses involving human identification or skeletal biology, or as a supplemental text for a human osteology course. Although we do not see this text as a primary professional reference for practicing forensic anthropologists, it could serve as a general reference for professionals with little or no training in forensic anthropology, including physical anthropologists trained in other areas of the field (such as paleoanthropology or primatology), archaeologists, forensic scientists, dentists, pathologists, crime and death scene investigators, law enforcement, and legal professionals.

This text is applicable to coursework in forensic anthropology and archaeology internationally. Although some aspects are US-specific (e.g., the US legal system), the vast majority of the material in the text is internationally applicable and is therefore suitable for a forensic anthropology course in countries outside the United States. Further, this text addresses issues of international forensic anthropological relevance including armed conflict and human rights investigations.

We thoroughly enjoyed collaborating on this text, and feel that the use of multiple authors working in different settings to write a textbook helps mitigate the biases, errors, and misconceptions that may result from a single-authored text or those originating from authors from the same institution. We believe that instructors and students will find this text comprehensive, practical, and relevant to current practices in the discipline of forensic anthropology. While we strived to keep the cost of this text down by printing all figures in black and white, we appreciate the value of color images for both instruction and comprehension. We have therefore made all images available in color (where applicable) at the following website: http://booksite.elsevier.com/9780124186712/.

We would like our readers to know that we welcome any comments, feedback, or suggestions from our colleagues as well as students utilizing this text. It is clear that the field of forensic anthropology is dynamic, and like all good sciences, is in a constant state of revision and advancement. We also appreciate that backgrounds and views differ, and that understanding and teaching the principles of forensic anthropology is improved through sharing and discussing different perspectives. We welcome such discourse from any source.

There are many whose assistance and contributions we would like to acknowledge. The following individuals and institutions provided access to specimens and/or contributed figures, images, or case material which was incorporated throughout the text: Bradley Adams and the Office of the Chief Medical Examiner – New York City; Bruce Anderson and the Pima County Office of Medical Examiner; Gail Anderson, Lynne Bell, and the Victoria Experimental Network Under the Sea (VENUS); Lisa Bright; Craig Brodfuehrer; Gil Brogdon; Nicole Burt; Cristina Cattaneo; Karen Cebra; Christian Crowder and Amy Beresheim; Dennis Dirkmaat; Shuala Drawdy and the International Committee of the Red Cross; Todd Fenton; Karen Gardner; Rich Graf; Gary Hatch and the Radiology-Pathology Center for Forensic Imaging, University of New Mexico School of Medicine; Joe Hefner; Kevin Horn; David Hunt and the National Museum of Natural History; Rebecca Hurst; Richard Jantz, Lee Jantz and the University of Tennessee Forensic Anthropology Center; the Joint POW/MIA Accounting Command Central Identification Laboratory; Elias Kontanis and the National Transportation Safety Board; Thomas Lera and the National Postal Museum; Jennifer Love, Jason Wiersema, and the Harris County Institute of Forensic Sciences; Audrey Meehan; Rebecca Meeusen; Diana Messer and Valerie Andrushko; Frank Bayham, Kevin Dalton, Turhon Murad, Colleen Milligan, P. Willey, and the Department of Anthropology at California State University, Chico; Amy Mundorff; Elayne Pope; Rich Press; Chris Rainwater; Garrett Reismann; Paul Sledzik; Brian Spatola and the National Museum of Health and Medicine; Kate Spradley and Texas State University – San Marcos; Mikylee Vaughan; Virginia Office of the Chief Medical Examiner; Roland Wessling; and Yolo County Sheriff's Office.

We would also like to express our appreciation for our great many other colleagues, friends, and family members who provided valuable reviews, guidance, and support for this work. Thank you.

Author Biographies

Angi M. Christensen, PhD, D-ABFA

Angi M. Christensen is a Forensic Anthropologist with the Federal Bureau of Investigation (FBI) Laboratory in Quantico, Virginia. Her primary responsibilities include conducting forensic anthropological casework and providing training for FBI agents and other law enforcement personnel, and she facilitated the development of the FBI's Forensic Anthropology Program. She is also an Adjunct Professor in the Forensic Science Program at George Mason University.

Angi received her BA in Anthropology at the University of Washington in Seattle, WA (1997), and her MA and PhD in Anthropology at the University of Tennessee in Knoxville, TN (2000 and 2003). Her research interests include methods of personal identification, trauma analysis, elemental analysis, and underwater taphonomy. She has published articles in *Journal of Forensic Sciences, American Journal of Physical Anthropology, Forensic Science International, Journal of Anatomy,* and *Forensic Science Communications.*

Angi is a board certified Diplomate of the American Board of Forensic Anthropology, a Fellow in the Physical Anthropology Section of the American Academy of Forensic Sciences, and currently serves as the Vice-Chair of the Scientific Working Group for Forensic Anthropology.

Nicholas V. Passalacqua, PhD

Nick Passalacqua is a deploying Forensic Anthropologist with the Joint POW/MIA Accounting Command's Central Identification Laboratory (JPAC CIL). Nick received his BA in Anthropology at Michigan State University in 2005, his MS in Anthropology from Mercyhurst College (now Mercyhurst University) in 2007, another MA in Anthropology from Michigan State University in 2011, and his PhD in Anthropology from Michigan State in 2012.

Prior to his work at the JPAC CIL, Nick served as a visiting scientist at the National Institute of Legal Medicine – North Branch (Porto, Portugal); worked as a bioarchaeologist for the Medieval Spanish archaeological sites of the Castro de Chao Samartín, Iglesia de El Salvador, and San Julian de Viñon; instructed mass fatality incident response courses for the Pennsylvania Emergency Management Agency (PEMA); assisted for numerous years in Mercyhurst University's summer short courses in forensic anthropology; and instructed for three semesters of anthropology courses as adjunct faculty at Lansing Community College.

Nick's research interests include age-at-death estimation, skeletal trauma and taphonomy, paleodemography, and paleopathology. His bioarchaeological dissertation research focused on issues of health and demography in Medieval Asturias, Spain. Nick has publications in such journals as *Journal of Forensic Sciences*, *International Journal of Osteoarchaeology*, and *American Journal of Physical Anthropology*. He has also contributed chapters in such books as: *The analysis of burned human remains, Age estimation of the human skeleton*, and *A companion to forensic anthropology*.

Eric J. Bartelink, PhD, D-ABFA

Eric J. Bartelink is an Associate Professor in the Department of Anthropology and Director of the Human Identification Laboratory at California State University, Chico. He received his BS in Anthropology at Central Michigan University (1995), his MA in Anthropology at California State University, Chico (2001), and his PhD in Anthropology at Texas A&M University (2006). He became the 89th Diplomate of the American Board of Forensic Anthropology in 2012. Eric's interests are in forensic anthropology and bioarchaeology, and he has conducted research focused on skeletal trauma, taphonomy, paleopathology, and stable isotope analysis. He has conducted an extensive research program focused on central California bioarchaeology, and also conducted work in American Samoa. In 2000, he assisted with the excavation of mass graves in Bosnia-Herzegovina through the United Nations International Criminal Tribunal for the Former Yugoslavia, and also assisted in the identification of victims from the World Trade Center 9/11 disaster in 2002 and 2003. He has published articles in *Journal of Forensic Sciences, American Journal of Physical Anthropology, Journal of Archaeological Science, International Journal of Osteoarchaeology, Journal of Archaeological Method and Theory, Archaeometry*, and *California Archaeology*.

Eric teaches courses in introductory physical anthropology, human osteology, forensic anthropology, bioarchaeology, forensic science, and statistics. He is Fellow of the American Academy of Forensic Sciences, and a member of the American Association of Physical Anthropologists, Society of American Archaeology, Paleopathology Association, and the Society for California Archaeology. He is a current board member of the Scientific Working Group for Forensic Anthropology and the American Board of Forensic Anthropology.

Introduction

A human skeleton is discovered by hikers in the woods. A body that is burned beyond recognition is delivered to the morgue. Fractures found on the bones of an accident victim are inconsistent with witness accounts of the event. An airline disaster has resulted in the fragmentation and dispersion of numerous body parts. Victims of a war crime are discovered in a clandestine grave. These diverse and challenging cases all have something in common: they are all within the purview of *forensic anthropology*. This chapter introduces the field of forensic anthropology, and highlights the roles and responsibilities of working forensic anthropologists today.

1.1 Forensic anthropology

Anthropology is a broad field, defined as the study of humankind (from the Greek *anthropos* "man" and *logia* "study"). Anthropology is generally considered to consist of four primary subdisciplines: **cultural anthropology**, **linguistic anthropology**, **archaeology**, and **physical anthropology**. Cultural (also referred to as socio-cultural or social) anthropology is the study of human cultural variation, including aspects of social organization, subsistence practices, economics, politics, conflict, technology, and religion, among others. Linguistic anthropology is the study of human communication, including differences across time and space, and how language systems affect human culture and behavior. Archaeology is the study of past human cultures through the materials left behind. Material culture can include **artifacts** (e.g., tools), **ecofacts** (e.g., skeletal remains, food refuse), and **features** (e.g., remains of buildings and other structures). Archaeologists often use cultural and evolutionary theories to test hypotheses against the archaeological record.

Physical (or biological) anthropology is the study of the **evolution** and diversity of **primates**, especially the **human lineage**. This is accomplished through the study of **comparative anatomy**, and the study of human and non-human primate variation (e.g., morphology and genetics) and behavior. Many physical anthropologists focus specifically on **skeletal biology**, or the study of the anatomy and biology of the skeleton (which includes the bones and teeth). Skeletal biologists often specialize in broad areas such as **functional morphology**, **bioarchaeology**, **paleopathology**, and **forensic anthropology**.

Forensic Anthropology. http://dx.doi.org/10.1016/B978-0-12-418671-2.00001-X

Forensic anthropology is considered to be an applied subfield of physical anthropology and can be defined as the application of anthropological method and theory to matters of legal concern, particularly those that relate to the recovery and analysis of the skeleton. The practice of forensic anthropology often involves estimating the sex, ancestry, age, and stature from skeletal material from unknown individuals. This summary of estimated biological parameters is referred to as the **biological profile**, which is compared to missing persons records in an attempt to identify the person to whom the skeletal remains belong. Forensic anthropologists also specialize in the search for and recovery of human remains, the analysis of skeletal trauma and other alterations which may be relevant to the individual's cause and manner of death, and the facilitation of personal identification through the recognition of traits and features that may be associated with a particular individual.

1.2 History of forensic anthropology

Forensic anthropology is still considered to be a relatively young scientific discipline, with four temporal eras that are generally recognized to mark certain periods of development (Stewart, 1979; Thompson, 1982; Sledzik et al., 2007). Prior to the 1940s, the practice of forensic anthropology was limited to anatomists, physicians, and some physical anthropologists who worked primarily as university professors or museum curators and occasionally consulted on skeletonized remains cases for law enforcement. During this formative period, there was no formal instruction in forensic applications of physical anthropology and little published research. With regard to medicolegal applications of the discipline, practitioners were either informally trained or self-taught, and played only a limited role in cases of **medicolegal significance**. It was during this time that Thomas Dwight (1843–1911), a Harvard anatomy professor, became the first to extensively publish works on topics that would become the foundation of forensic anthropology, including methods of estimating sex, age, and stature from the skeleton. His award-winning essay, *The Identification of the Human Skeleton: A Medicolegal Study* (1878), along with many other publications related to human anatomy and forensic anthropology, helped earn Thomas Dwight the title of "Father of Forensic Anthropology in the United States."

From the 1940s to the early 1970s, attention from medicolegal and military agencies increased, with recognition of the utility of forensic anthropology in the identification of deceased service members from WWII and the Korean War. Important anthropological events of this time included two works by Wilton Marion Krogman (1903–1987): *Guide to the Identification of Human Skeletal Material* (1939) and *The Human Skeleton in Forensic Medicine* (1962). This period also saw an increase in development of forensic anthropological methods based on the skeletal remains of deceased soldiers. Many of these early studies form the basis of methods still in use today.

From the 1970s to 1990s, the field became increasingly professionalized, particularly with the establishment of the Physical Anthropology section of the American Academy of Forensic Sciences in 1972 (see Box 1.1), and the creation of the American Board of Forensic Anthropology in 1977 (see Box 1.2). Another

> ## BOX 1.1 THE AMERICAN ACADEMY OF FORENSIC SCIENCES
>
> Founded in 1948, the American Academy of Forensic Sciences (AAFS) is a professional society dedicated to the application of science to the law, the promotion of education, and the elevation of accuracy, precision and specificity in the forensic sciences (American Academy of Forensic Sciences, 2012). As of the time of this writing, the AAFS membership includes more than 6000 members representing all 50 United States and more than 60 other countries worldwide. Members are divided into eleven sections representing the scientific disciplines of Criminalistics, Digital and Multimedia Sciences, Engineering Sciences, General, Jurisprudence, Odontology, Pathology/Biology, Physical Anthropology, Psychiatry and Behavioral Science, Questioned Documents, and Toxicology. The AAFS holds annual meetings each February and has its own internationally recognized journal, *The Journal of Forensic Sciences.*
>
> The Physical Anthropology section was added to the AAFS membership in 1972, when interest among physical anthropologists was sufficient to meet the minimum membership requirements. More information about AAFS including membership can be found at www.aafs.org.

> ## BOX 1.2 THE AMERICAN BOARD OF FORENSIC ANTHROPOLOGY
>
> The American Board of Forensic Anthropology (ABFA) was incorporated in 1977 as a non-profit organization to provide a program of certification in forensic anthropology, recognizing certified Diplomates for their qualifications and for meeting standards set forth by the ABFA (American Board of Forensic Anthropology, 2012). As of the time of this writing, 99 forensic anthropologists have been board certified, with approximately 70 being currently active. More information about the ABFA including certification requirements can be found at www.theabfa.org.

significant work, *Essentials of Forensic Anthropology* (1979) by T. Dale Stewart (1901–1997), was one of a growing number of publications in the field. There was also a significant increase in research, employment, acceptance by the forensic community, and establishment of graduate programs that specialize in forensic anthropology.

1.3 Forensic anthropology today

Today, forensic anthropology is a well-established forensic discipline that has experienced a recent and significant expansion in attention and breadth, facilitated in large part by increased public, media, and professional interest (see Box 1.3). There has been an enormous increase in research and publications in the field, coupled with the development of numerous graduate programs with curricula specifically tailored to prepare students for careers in forensic anthropology. The formation of the Scientific Working Group for Forensic Anthropology in 2008 marked the discipline's recognition of the need to formulate and codify standard practices (Box 1.4).

BOX 1.3 TV'S "BONES"

Already gaining massively in popularity, the field of forensic anthropology was launched into the public spotlight with the FOX TV series *Bones* which premiered in 2005. Featuring Dr. Temperance Brennan as a brilliant but socially-challenged forensic anthropologist, the show is based on the fictional writings of Board Certified Forensic Anthropologist Dr. Kathy Reichs. There is some artistic license involved, of course, and in the spirit of many other popular TV crime shows, bone-related mysteries are solved in short order with the help of Brennan's cocksure FBI agent sidekick. Her high-tech toys at the fictitious "Jeffersonian Institute" are the envy of even the most sophisticated forensic anthropology laboratories in existence today.

BONES

BOX 1.4 THE SCIENTIFIC WORKING GROUP FOR FORENSIC ANTHROPOLOGY

In the 1990s, the Federal Bureau of Investigation (FBI) Laboratory began sponsoring Scientific Working Groups (SWG) in partnership with the National Institute of Justice (NIJ) to improve practices and build consensus with their federal, state, and local forensic community partners (Adams and Lothridge, 2000). Scientific working groups consist of representatives from forensic, industrial, commercial, and academic communities, including international participants, who assist in the development of standards and guidelines and improve communications throughout their respective disciplines (NIJ, 2012).

The Scientific Working Group for Forensic Anthropology (SWGANTH) was formed in 2008 under the joint sponsorship of the FBI Laboratory and the Department of Defense Central Identification Laboratory. Like many of the other SWGs, the primary objectives of SWGANTH are to develop and disseminate best practice guidelines and standards for the discipline. SWGANTH's guidelines are currently published on their website, www.swganth.org, where one can also learn about current activities, upcoming meetings, and other relevant matters. Although voluntary in most cases, following SWG guidelines is generally considered best practice, and SWG guidelines are increasingly recognized and considered by courts. Many of the techniques and approaches described in this book follow guidelines promulgated by SWGANTH. The administrative oversight and future role of the SWGs are currently matters under consideration by NIJ.

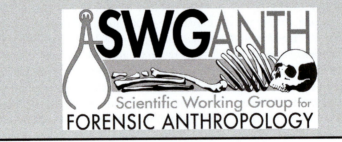

Historically, forensic anthropologists were only consulted to estimate a biological profile when remains were nearly or completely skeletonized and a standard soft tissue **autopsy** could not be performed. Today, the increased breadth and scope of the field includes not only these traditional analyses, but also personal identification, trauma analysis, taphonomic analysis, estimating the postmortem interval, and the application of anthropological knowledge to the investigation of **mass disasters** and violations of international law. In addition, forensic anthropologists are increasingly involved in the analysis of recently deceased individuals and investigations involving the living.

Especially in the current era of forensic anthropology, a forensic anthropologist needs to have a specialized and advanced education. In order to interpret findings from the study of skeletal material, a forensic anthropologist must understand how and why humans vary throughout history, across geography, between the sexes, during an individual's lifetime, and between individuals. It is therefore important to understand not only the technical aspects of performing a forensic anthropological examination, but also the evolutionary, biological, **biomechanical**, and cultural underpinnings of skeletal variation in order to understand and interpret findings. This typically involves a broad education in anthropology as well as the physical and natural sciences.

Experience ideally includes working with skeletal collections, mentorship with a practicing forensic anthropologist, and hands-on experience with forensic cases. Forensic anthropologists often collaborate with professionals from other disciplines, so it is important to understand how anthropological analyses integrate with and affect other forensic examinations, including **molecular biology**, **pathology**, **entomology**, chemistry, archaeology, **geology**, and **botany**. It is also becoming increasingly important to understand the legal, cultural, and scientific challenges related to various forensic anthropological analyses.

1.4 Careers in forensic anthropology

Due to both the increasing appreciation for the utility of forensic anthropology as well as the expanding scope of the field, forensic anthropologists are now employed in a wide variety of professional settings. The majority of forensic anthropologists are still university professors who provide forensic anthropological consultations as a matter of public service. These services, however, have become increasingly frequent and integrated into the university structure. Over the past few decades, several university anthropology programs have developed laboratories where practitioners perform casework as well as train and mentor students. Examples include the Forensic Anthropology Center at the University of Tennessee, the C.A. Pound Human Identification Laboratory at the University of Florida, the Forensic Anthropology Center at Texas State University (see Box 1.5), and the Human Identification Laboratory at California State University, Chico.

BOX 1.5 DR. KATE SPRADLEY, TEXAS STATE UNIVERSITY

Dr. Kate Spradley is an Associate Professor in the Department of Anthropology at Texas State University in San Marcos, Texas. Like many university professors, the primary duties of her job include teaching, research, and service. Courses taught by Dr. Spradley include forensic anthropology, biological anthropological theory, human biological variation, and growth and development. Dr. Spradley's research interests include human variation, specifically the use of craniometric data to understand biological relationships among geographic groups. Her current research focuses on developing new methods of sex estimation and improved ancestry estimation for Hispanic individuals. As part of her service work, she provides forensic anthropological consulting services for both archaeological and clandestine settings. She also serves as the laboratory's case manager for NamUs (see Chapter 14). Dr. Spradley received her BA and MA in Anthropology from the University of Arkansas and her PhD in Anthropology from the University of Tennessee.

Photo courtesy of Texas State University

Medical examiners' offices are increasingly employing forensic anthropologists to not only assist with skeletal remains cases, but also to apply their expertise to recently deceased individuals, especially in regard to the analysis of skeletal trauma. In larger jurisdictions, there may be full-time work for a forensic anthropologist (see Box 1.6). As of the time of this writing, for example, the New York Office of Chief Medical Examiner (see Box 1.7) and the Harris County (Texas) Institute of Forensic Science each have multiple full-time forensic anthropologists. In other jurisdictions, anthropologists in medical examiner's offices may perform forensic anthropological analyses as one of their roles, and may also fill additional roles such as medicolegal investigator or fingerprint examiner.

Museums continue to employ forensic anthropologists, and some also provide forensic anthropological services as consultants. The Smithsonian Institution's National Museum of Natural History (NMNH), for example, has a long history of providing forensic anthropological services, including to the FBI (Ubelaker, 2000),

BOX 1.6 DR. BRUCE E. ANDERSON, PIMA COUNTY OFFICE OF THE MEDICAL EXAMINER

Dr. Bruce E. Anderson is the Forensic Anthropologist for the Pima County Office of the Medical Examiner (PCOME) in Tucson, Arizona. Dr. Anderson's principal duties include conducting postmortem forensic anthropology examinations for the purposes of effecting identification, constructing biological profiles, describing perimortem trauma, and comparing the results of examinations to missing persons reports, many of which are entered into NamUs. Because of the high volume of casework due to the many foreign national migrants that cross through southern Arizona, Dr. Anderson encourages and facilitates anthropological research on these skeletal cases. Dr. Anderson is an Adjunct Assistant Professor of Anthropology at the University of Arizona, where he occasionally teaches an introductory course in forensic anthropology. He also mentors anthropology students in the Forensic Anthropology Internship Program and oversees the Postdoctoral Fellowship Program at the PCOME. Dr. Anderson received his BA degree from Arizona State University and his Master's and Doctoral degrees from the University of Arizona.

Photo by Matt Nager

and several of the anthropologists employed by the NMNH continue to provide this public service. The National Museum of Health and Medicine (NMHM) employs forensic anthropologists in various roles who also provide their services on casework (see Box 1.8).

Forensic anthropologists have also found employment in the growing number of federal laboratories that recover and analyze skeletal remains for identification as part of their primary mission. The Joint POW/MIA Accounting Command – Central Identification Laboratory (JPAC-CIL) in Hawaii was initially established to assist in the identification of deceased military personnel in the Pacific region. Today, the laboratory is congressionally mandated to identify a minimum number

BOX 1.7 DR. BRADLEY ADAMS, OFFICE OF CHIEF MEDICAL EXAMINER, NEW YORK

Dr. Bradley Adams is the Director of the Forensic Anthropology Unit at the Office of Chief Medical Examiner in New York City. In this role, Dr. Adams and his team are responsible for all forensic anthropology casework in the five boroughs of New York City (Manhattan, Brooklyn, Queens, the Bronx, and Staten Island). The typical types of cases may involve estimation of the biological profile and analysis of skeletal trauma. In addition to laboratory analysis of skeletal remains, members of the Forensic Anthropology Unit also assist with certain types of scene recoveries such as buried bodies or scattered remains. Dr. Adams and his team are also integral players in the ongoing work related to identification efforts for 9/11 victims of the World Trade Center attacks, and they serve as critical members of the agency's disaster response team. Dr. Adams received a dual undergraduate degree from the University of Kansas in Anthropology and in Spanish. For graduate school he attended the University of Tennessee and received a MA and PhD in Physical Anthropology with a focus on forensic anthropology.

Photo courtesy of Bradley Adams

of service members annually, and employs numerous full-time forensic anthropologists and archaeologists (see Box 1.9). The laboratory also assists in a small number of local recent forensic cases. The Armed Forces Medical Examiner System (AFMES), which is responsible for the examination and identification of recently deceased military personnel, as well as US citizens who died abroad, has forensic anthropologists who assist with morgue operations, particularly in cases involving fragmentary remains. The FBI Laboratory employs anthropologists who assist in the detection, recovery, and analysis of skeletal material in support of federal, state, and local investigations.

BOX 1.8 MR. BRIAN F. SPATOLA, NATIONAL MUSEUM OF HEALTH AND MEDICINE

Mr. Brian F. Spatola is the Collections Manager of the Anatomical Division of the National Museum of Health and Medicine (NMHM) in Silver Spring, Maryland. His responsibilities involve caring for over 20,000 preserved anatomical specimens in the museum, which include a skeletal pathology collection ranging from historic Civil War surgery specimens to modern forensic material, as well as promoting and facilitating research and educational use of the collections. As the anatomy lab manager, Mr. Spatola oversees the preparation and conservation of specimens using various preservation techniques. A substantial amount of his time involves care of the collections and rectifying historical issues. He also provides forensic anthropology support to the Office of the Armed Forces Medical Examiner and the Virginia Office of the Chief Medical Examiner. Mr. Spatola received his BA from the University of North Texas, and his graduate training consisted of laboratory and field work with the Forensic Anthropology and Computer Enhancement Services Lab (FACES) at Louisiana State University where he received his MA.

Photo courtesy of National Museum of Health and Medicine

Forensic anthropologists have taken on important roles in the identification of victims of mass disasters. Many forensic anthropologists are members of the Disaster Mortuary Operation Response Team (DMORT), a federal response team of numerous specialists that assists local jurisdictions (e.g., coroners, medical examiners, and law enforcement) in the event of a mass disaster. Such work is typically

BOX 1.9 DR. JOSEPH T. HEFNER, JOINT POW/MIA ACCOUNTING COMMAND, CENTRAL IDENTIFICATION LABORATORY

Dr. Joseph T. Hefner is a Forensic Anthropologist and Laboratory Manager for the Joint POW/MIA Accounting Command, Central Identification Laboratory in Honolulu, Hawaii. As part of the JPAC-CIL mission, Dr. Hefner is actively involved in the recovery and identification of US service members lost in past wars. Traveling to Southeast Asia, the Pacific theater, Europe, and Korea, the anthropologists and archaeologists from the CIL spend weeks (and often months) in the field searching for fallen soldiers. In the laboratory, Dr. Hefner uses his knowledge of skeletal biology and forensic anthropology to build a biological profile, make chest radiograph comparisons, and perform histological analyses. This information is provided to the JPAC-CIL's Scientific Director, who determines whether an identification can be made. Dr. Hefner received his undergraduate degree from a small liberal arts college in North Carolina (Western Carolina University, Cullowhee, NC), a post-baccalaureate from Mercyhurst College (Erie, PA), and his Master's and PhD from the University of Florida (Gainesville, FL).

Photo by Dr. Derek Benedix

sporadic and rarely a career in and of itself. Forensic anthropologists may, however, serve in mass disaster roles as part of their other responsibilities, such as being the mass fatality planner/coordinator in a medical examiner's office. The National Transportation Safety Board (NTSB) is charged with investigating civil aviation accidents as well as certain highway, pipeline, marine, and rail incidents. The NTSB employs several forensic anthropologists to assist with mass fatality medicolegal operations (see Box 1.10).

BOX 1.10 DR. ELIAS J. KONTANIS, NATIONAL TRANSPORTATION SAFETY BOARD

Dr. Elias J. Kontanis is the Coordinator for Medicolegal Operations for the National Transportation Safety Board (NTSB). His principal duties include interacting with federal, state, and local agencies regarding victim recovery, examination, identification, and related medicolegal matters following major transportation accidents. Dr. Kontanis is also responsible for communicating with family members of victims and accident survivors regarding the NTSB investigation and other medicolegal concerns. A major component of his position is to create and deliver training programs to medical examiners, coroners, police and fire agencies, other federal, state, and local agencies, and the transportation industry on the role of the NTSB and management of mass fatality medicolegal operations. Dr. Kontanis earned a PhD in biology from Cornell University in 2005 and is a Registered Medicolegal Death Investigator. He is also a Federal Aviation Administration Certificated Flight Instructor and Advanced Ground Instructor, and holds a commercial certificate for single-engine fixed wing aircraft with an instrument rating.

Photo courtesy of Elias Kontanis

Anthropologists have become increasingly involved in humanitarian, human rights, and armed conflict investigations abroad. Among the first was the use of forensic anthropology to investigate conflicts in Latin America (especially Argentina) in the 1970s and 1980s. Many forensic anthropologists have also assisted in the excavation and analysis of skeletal remains in the Balkans since the 1990s. Such investigations continue today, and forensic anthropologists can find work in association with these investigations with organizations like Physicians for Human Rights (PHR), the International Commission on Missing Persons (ICMP), and the International Committee for the Red Cross (ICRC) (see Box 1.11).

In looking for careers in forensic anthropology, students and aspiring practitioners should bear in mind that actual position titles are most often not "Forensic

---

BOX 1.11 MS. SHUALA DRAWDY, INTERNATIONAL COMMITTEE OF THE RED CROSS

Ms. Shuala Drawdy is a Forensic Advisor for the International Committee of the Red Cross (ICRC) in Geneva, Switzerland. Her primary duties include teaching and advising on the recovery and analysis of skeletal remains, as well as advising governmental authorities and forensic experts on strategies to address large numbers of missing persons and unidentified remains. She works with authorities on the collection of information from family members pertinent to resolving the fate of missing persons, and in the proper and dignified management of human remains following disaster situations. In collaboration with her colleagues at the ICRC, Ms. Drawdy also provides guidance on legal issues related to humanitarian efforts, including domestic legislative reform related to forensic investigations of unidentified human remains. Ms. Drawdy received her BA and MA in Anthropology from the University of Florida, and also pursued additional graduate studies in international issues related to forensic anthropology including human rights and humanitarian law, humanitarian assistance, political science, and international relations.

Photo by Marko Kokic

Anthropologist," as can be seen in the various job titles of anthropologists shown in Boxes 1.5–1.11. Effectively, the roles often involve performing forensic anthropological analyses, but job titles might be "Professor," "Criminalist," "Physical Scientist," "Curator," "Collections Manager," "Death Scene Investigator," "Autopsy Technician," or "Independent Contractor." Regardless of the job title or office of employment, there will always be some connection to a relevant legal system. This may be through a direct link to local or federal law enforcement, medicolegal authority, or international councils. Regardless of the setting, practicing forensic anthropologists must maintain high ethical standards, and keep not only the goal of the analysis (e.g., identification or trauma analysis) in mind, but also the client (e.g., law enforcement or medical examiner), since different audiences or customers may request or focus on different aspects of an analysis. Even if not performing skeletal examination casework, many have found that the forensic anthropologist's skill set is well-suited to other positions within the medical, legal, forensic science, or crime scene disciplines. Examples include roles in laboratory management, biomechanical engineering, and crime scene investigation.

Many job positions in forensic anthropology, such as those at most universities, require a doctoral degree. A PhD in anthropology or closely-related field such as human biology is currently required to achieve board certification through the ABFA. There are, however, an increasing number of positions available to those holding a Master's degree. While there is currently no official certification for forensic anthropologists with Master's degrees, it is recommended that at least a Master's degree is achieved before independently conducting forensic anthropological casework (SWGANTH, 2010).

1.5 **Layout of this book**

Forensic anthropology is a continually evolving discipline that can no longer be characterized simply by the occasional consultation with law enforcement by someone trained in physical anthropology. As part of the professionalization of the field, students are expected to receive formal coursework and training in forensic anthropology, and to have a high level of expertise in human skeletal anatomy, skeletal variation, biomechanics, taphonomy, and archaeology, as well as a general understanding of the forensic sciences. The aim of this text is to provide a holistic introduction to the topics relevant to the modern practice of forensic anthropology, emphasizing new approaches and research directions. Case studies are heavily emphasized to provide a sense of the real challenges encountered in conducting forensic anthropology casework.

This book is organized to guide the beginning student through basic human osteology and odontology, followed by field and laboratory methods used in estimating the biological profile, performing trauma analysis, and facilitating personal identification. Chapter 2 emphasizes key anatomical terms and directions, the growth and development of skeletal and dental tissues, and the names and major features of individual bones and teeth which comprise the human skeleton. Chapter 3 outlines skeletal examination methods, including osteometric analysis, radiography, and histology, as well as chain-of-custody of evidence, quality assurance, case documentation, and report writing. This chapter demonstrates how forensic anthropological examinations are conducted and reported, noting inherent limitations to skeletal analysis.

With this information as a baseline, Chapter 4 discusses the medicolegal context, including the differentiation of skeletal from non-skeletal material, human from non-human remains, and contemporary from non-contemporary remains. This chapter outlines the various types of cases that may be sent to a forensic anthropologist for examination, noting that not all may be of true medicolegal significance.

An important component of skeletal analysis is the recognition and identification of postmortem alterations to human remains and the taphonomic agents that cause them. Chapter 5 explores the role of taphonomy in detail, including the typical stages of decomposition, factors that influence the rate of decay, the signatures left on remains by various taphonomic agents, and estimations of the postmortem interval or time since death. This is followed by a discussion of method and theory in forensic archaeology, with an emphasis on appropriate techniques used to detect, recover, and document human remains from buried and surface contexts (Chapter 6).

The following chapters shift focus to the laboratory, starting with a brief introduction to the methods used to process and prepare skeletal materials for analysis (Chapter 7). The advantages and disadvantages of different processing methods are discussed, followed by methods for skeletal reconstruction and estimation of the number of individuals represented. The following four chapters review methods used to estimate aspects of the biological profile, including sex, ancestry, age, and stature (Chapters 8–11, respectively). Each chapter addresses skeletal variation from an evolutionary and biomechanical framework, emphasizing principles such as sexual dimorphism and population variation, as well as growth, development, and the eventual deterioration of the skeleton with advancing age. Because the biological profile often comprises the first phase of the identification process by helping to narrow the pool of possible matches with missing persons, it is critical that estimations are undertaken based on valid reference samples.

Chapter 12 outlines skeletal and dental variants and pathological conditions commonly identified in human skeletal remains, especially those that may have significance for personal identification or population affinity. A framework for conducting a differential diagnosis for pathological conditions, lesions, and anomalies is provided. Chapter 13 focuses on skeletal trauma, emphasizing the differentiation of antemortem and perimortem trauma, and also postmortem damage or taphonomic alterations on skeletal remains. Mechanisms of trauma are presented in light of bone biomechanics (e.g., blunt force, sharp force, and high-velocity projectile trauma), followed by a discussion of trauma analysis in the context of burned remains.

Chapter 14 provides an overview of methods used to facilitate personal identification, including comparisons of antemortem and postmortem records (such as radiographs), DNA testing, and statistically-based comparisons. In addition, the utility of methods such as facial approximation and craniofacial superimposition are discussed in regard to their role in presumptive identifications and exclusion of possible matches.

The final chapter (Chapter 15) discusses forensic anthropology as part of the larger forensic science community. This section focuses on current and future challenges faced by forensic anthropologists, new research directions, and scientific collaborations with other forensic specialties that complement forensic anthropology casework. The chapter will be of interest especially to those students who choose to embark on a career in the forensic sciences, including forensic anthropology.

1.6 Summary

- Anthropology is a broad discipline, encompassing the subfields of cultural anthropology, linguistic anthropology, archaeology, and physical anthropology.
- Forensic anthropology is an applied subfield of physical anthropology, defined as the application of anthropological method and theory to matters of legal concern, particularly those that relate to the study of the skeleton.
- Thomas Dwight is considered "The Father of Forensic Anthropology in the United States" due in part to his influential publication *The Identification of the Human Skeleton: A Medicolegal Study* in 1878.
- Forensic anthropology is a relatively young but well-established discipline that typically involves estimating the "biological profile" (usually sex, age, ancestry, and stature), analyzing skeletal trauma, estimation of the time since death, and facilitating personal identification, though the scope can be considerably broader.
- Although traditionally employed only in academic settings, today forensic anthropologists work in a wide variety of professional settings including universities, museums, medical examiner's offices, federal laboratories, and international organizations.
- Forensic anthropologists should be familiar with related scientific disciplines as well as the legal context of their work.
- Most jobs in forensic anthropology require advanced and specialized education and training, ideally including a broad background in the physical and natural sciences as well as hands-on training and experience in the application of forensic anthropological methods.

1.7 **Test yourself**

- Anthropology is often considered a holistic science. Explain why this is the case and how anthropologists are able to approach the entirety of the human condition.
- Explain what events and developments have shaped forensic anthropology into the science it is today.
- Where do the majority of forensic anthropologists work? What are some of the different roles assumed by forensic anthropologists in these settings? Describe the connection of these workplaces and roles to the legal system.
- What is the role of the American Academy of Forensic Sciences? What is the role of the American Board of Forensic Anthropology? What is the role of the SWGANTH?
- Why is it important for forensic anthropologists to understand the relationship of skeletal analysis to biology, evolution, and biomechanics?

Definitions

Anthropology The study of humankind (from the Greek *anthropos* "man" and *logia* "study")

Archaeology The study of past human culture through material remains left behind

Artifact Any object modified by humans, usually tools, pottery, jewelry, etc.

Autopsy A postmortem examination of the body in order to determine cause and manner of death, typically performed by a forensic pathologist

Bioarchaeology The study of past human lifeways through the analysis of human remains and their archaeological context

Biological profile The summary of various biological parameters estimated from human skeletal material, typically, age, sex, ancestry, and stature

Biomechanical Of or relating to the mechanics of a living body, especially forces exerted on the skeleton

Botany The study of plants; in forensics, the application of botany to gain information about possible crimes

Comparative anatomy The study of similarities and differences in the anatomical structures of different animals

Cultural (or socio-cultural or social) anthropology The study of human cultural variation, including aspects of social organization, subsistence practices, economics, politics, conflict, technology, and religion, among others

Ecofact A natural object with cultural significance, for example, food refuse, skeletal remains, or pollen

Entomology The study of insects; in forensics, the study of those insects that inhabit decomposing remains to aid in legal investigations, usually to estimate time since death

Evolution A process by which organisms develop and diversify from earlier forms

Feature An observable modification to the landscape such as buildings, roads, or pits

Forensic anthropology The application of anthropological method and theory to matters of legal concern, particularly those that relate to the study of the skeleton

Functional morphology The study of the structure and function of the musculoskeletal system

Geology The study of the earth's physical structure and the processes acting upon it; in forensics, the study of potential evidence in the form of earth materials such as minerals and soils

Human lineage The line of descendants leading to modern humans

Linguistic anthropology The study of human communication and language systems, including differences across time and space, and how they affect human culture and behavior

Mass disaster An unexpected man-made or natural event that causes widespread damage, injury, or death

Medicolegal significance Relating to both medicine and law; of interest to the medicolegal death investigation system

Molecular biology A branch of biology concerned with the molecular basis for biological activity

Paleopathology The study of diseases in antiquity

Pathology The study of diseases; in forensics, the use of medical knowledge to determine the cause and manner of death

Physical (or biological) anthropology The study of the evolution and diversity of primates, especially the human lineage

Primates Mammals of the order Primates, which includes prosimians, monkeys, apes, and humans

Skeletal biology The study of the anatomy and biology of the skeleton

References

Adams, D.E., Lothridge, K.L., 2000. Scientific Working Groups. Forensic Sci. Commun. 2 (3).

American Academy of Forensic Sciences. (n.d.) www.aafs.org. Accessed August, 2012.

American Board of Forensic Anthropology. (n.d.) www.theabfa.org. Accessed August, 2012.

Dwight, T., 1878. The identification of the human skeleton: A medico-legal study. Massachusetts Medical Society, Boston.

Krogman, W.M., 1939. Guide to the identification of human skeletal material. FBI Law Enforcement Bull. 8, 3–31.

Krogman, W.M., 1962. The human skeleton in forensic medicine. Charles C Thomas, Springfield.

National Institute of Justice, 2012. http://www.nij.gov/topics/forensics/lab-operations/standards/scientific-working-groups.htm. Accessed September 15, 2012.

Scientific Working Group for Forensic Anthropology, 2010. Qualifications, Revision 0. Retrieved from http://www.swganth.org.

Sledzik, P.S., Fenton, T.W., Warren, M.W., Byrd, J.E., Crowder, C.M., Drawdy, S.M., Dirkmaat, D.C., Galloway, A., Finnegan, M., Fulginiti, L.C., Hartnett, K., Holland, T.D., Marks, M.K., Ousley, S.D., Rogers, T., Sauer, N.J., Simmons, T.L., Symes, S.A., Tidball-Binz, M., Ubelaker, D.H., 2007. The fourth era of forensic anthropology: Examining the future of the discipline. Proceedings of the 59th annual meeting of the American Academy of Forensic Sciences, San Antonio, TX.

Stewart, T.D., 1979. Essentials of Forensic Anthropology. Charles C Thomas, Springfield.

Thompson, D.D., 1982. Forensic Anthropology. In: Spencer, F. (Ed.), A History of Physical Anthropology 1930–1980. Academic Press, New York, pp. 357–369.

Ubelaker, D.H., 2000. A history of Smithsonian-FBI collaboration in forensic anthropology, especially in regard to facial imagery. Forensic Sci. Commun. 2 (4).

Human Osteology and Odontology

2

2.1 Principles of human osteology and odontology

Analyses performed by a forensic anthropologist depend on a thorough knowledge of human **osteology**, which is the study of bones, and **odontology**, the study of teeth. Together, bones and teeth comprise the **skeleton** or skeletal system. In humans (and other vertebrates), the skeleton is a system of mineralized **connective tissue** which serves as a framework for support and attachment for muscles, tendons, and ligaments, and acts as a system of levers operated by muscles used for body movement. Bones also serve to protect organs such as the brain and heart, produce blood cells, and store minerals and fat. Teeth are small mineralized structures that function to **masticate** (chew, or break down) food, and also serve roles in speaking (and in some non-human animals, certain teeth are also used as weapons).

Forensic anthropologists must have an intimate knowledge of the human skeleton, with the ability to recognize and identify not only complete bones, but also fragmentary remains, which are commonly encountered in forensic casework. It is also critically important to understand normal bone biology and anatomy as well as its variants. These variations (some "normal" and some "non-normal") form the principles behind why and how forensic anthropologists are able to differentiate between skeletons of different groups and individuals, and to recognize alterations such as skeletal trauma, damage, and pathological conditions. Although osteology and odontology primarily focus on the study of **morphology** (shape) and rote memorization of the names of bones (as well as their parts and features), related anatomical terminology, internal composition, and the study of growth and development provide the background to understanding why bones are shaped the way that they are.

This chapter serves as a broad introduction to human osteology and odontology, which will supply a foundation of terminology and knowledge to be used for the remainder of the text. To maximize comprehension, this chapter should be paired with hands-on study of skeletal material whenever possible. Aspiring practitioners of forensic anthropology should plan to take multiple advanced courses in human osteology and skeletal variation, and should also consider coursework in **zooarchaeology**, which focuses on the skeletons of non-human animals. Because **dentition**

Forensic Anthropology. http://dx.doi.org/10.1016/B978-0-12-418671-2.00002-1

(which refers to the teeth and their arrangement in the mouth) develops differently than bone and for different functions, it will be addressed in its own section at the end of this chapter.

2.2 Bone biology

The human skeleton can best be appreciated by a thorough understanding of bones at their gross anatomical, microstructural, and molecular levels. Bone is a very strong yet lightweight composite material constructed of both **organic** and **inorganic** components. **Collagen** is a large protein molecule that comprises most of bone's organic content. Collagen occurs as long elastic fibers, and gives bone its flexibility. The inorganic component of bone is **hydroxyapatite** $(Ca_{10}(PO_4)_6 (OH)_2)$ which is a mineral composed of calcium phosphate. This mineral component gives bone its strength and rigidity.

At the microstructural level, there are three types of bone cells which serve to form and maintain the bone tissue. **Osteoblasts** are bone forming cells, which synthesize and deposit bone material. They secrete the **osteoid** which will form the bone matrix and begin the mineralization process. **Osteoclasts** are bone resorbing cells that remove bone tissue. **Osteocytes** are mature living bone cells which no longer secrete osteoid. These cells are surrounded by bony matrix and are responsible for bone tissue maintenance.

Mature bone is very dense and layered and cannot be nourished by surface blood vessels. Bone is therefore organized into **Haversian systems** or **osteons** which allow for the passage of blood, lymph, and nerve fibers. Osteons represent the basic structural unit of compact bone, and are organized parallel to the long axis of the bone. Osteons are roughly cylindrical structures measuring approximately 300 microns in diameter and approximately 3–5 mm in length. Each osteon has a central canal called a **Haversian canal** which contains the blood and nerve supply. This central canal is surrounded by concentric rings called **lamellae**. Perpendicular to the Haversian canal are smaller canals called **Volkmann's canals** which serve as a link between Haversian canals. Located within the lamellae are small cavities called **lacunae** which house the osteocytes. Individual osteocytes are connected by a series of small channels called **canaliculi**. Osteons which are initially formed during growth are referred to as **primary osteons**. Those that are formed later during bone remodeling (see Box 2.1) are referred to as **secondary osteons**.

Histology is the study of the microscopic structures of tissue, and this area of study has numerous applications in forensic anthropology. When bone is examined histologically, it is usually sectioned transversely relative to the orientation of osteons, resulting in the ability to view osteon cross-sections (see Figure 2.1). Most of the structures previously mentioned can be seen in a histological cross-section.

At the gross anatomical level, bone is organized into two different structural types (Figure 2.2). **Compact** or **cortical** bone is dense bone that is typically found on external surfaces of bones, and forms the walls of the shafts of long bones.

Trabecular or **cancellous** bone is porous, spongy bone that is typically found at the ends of long bones as well as in vertebral bodies and flat bones. It is characterized by thin bony spicules called **trabeculae**, and has a porosity of around 50–90% (cortical bone, by comparison, has a porosity of around 5–10%). When located in cranial bones, cancelleous bone is called **diploë**. The hollow inner part of bone shafts is called the **medullary cavity**, which in life contains primarily red marrow during growth and development, and is later replaced by yellow fatty marrow in adulthood. The external surfaces of all bones (except joint surfaces) in life are covered by a thin

---

BOX 2.1 BONE REMODELING

During remodeling, osteoblasts and osteoclasts work together as a **basic multicellular unit**, or BMU. The BMU acts to replace primary osteons with secondary osteons through a six-phase process:

(1) *Activation*, which takes approximately three days, involves the recruitment of the precursor cells necessary to form the BMU.
(2) During *resorption*, osteoclasts secrete demineralizing acids and cut a tunnel that is longitudinal to the bone axis, at a rate of approximately 40–50 μm per day.
(3) The *reversal* phase is the transition between osteoclastic cutting and osteoblastic bone formation.
(4) During *formation*, osteoblasts lay down osteoid for concentric lamellae along the tunnel at a rate of about 1–2 μm per day.
(5) The *mineralization* phase involves mineralization of the osteoid.
(6) During *quiescence*, the secondary osteon is considered mature, and the remaining osteoblasts become osteocytes or are removed.

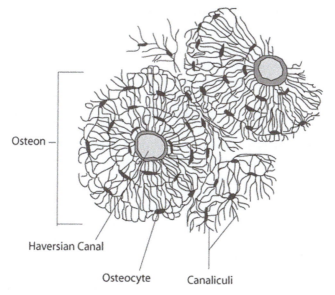

FIGURE 2.1 **Transverse cross-section of osteons**

(Adapted from Gray, 1918)

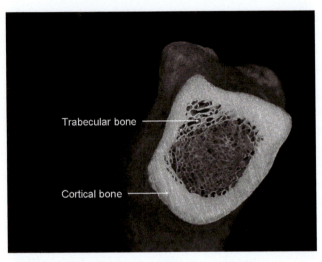

FIGURE 2.2 Cortical and trabecular bone in a femoral cross-section

but relatively tough tissue layer called the **periosteum** (on the skull, this tissue is referred to as the pericranium). The inner surface is covered by a membrane called the **endosteum**. These layers help nourish the bone and are involved in bone repair following trauma (see Chapter 13).

2.3 Bone growth and development

All bones grow by the deposition of bone matrix on a pre-existing surface or precursor, in a process called **osteogenesis**. Some bones, particularly those of the cranial vault, form through **ossification** within a connective tissue membrane. This type of development is called **intramembranous ossification**. Most other bones of the body develop by ossification of cartilage precursors (formed mostly of flexible collagen) in a process called **endochondral ossification**. Although the mechanisms differ slightly, both result in the same type of mature Haversian bone. Immature or **woven** bone forms first in development (and also in fracture repair – see Chapter 13), and is less organized and less dense than mature bone. Woven bone is eventually replaced by mature **lamellar** bone through modeling.

Most bones develop from two or more centers of ossification. The first center to appear is called the **primary ossification center**, and in long bones this is called the **diaphysis** or shaft. Most primary centers have begun to ossify before birth. **Secondary ossification centers** appear later (most forming after birth), and in long bones these are called the **epiphyses**. Between the diaphysis and epiphysis is a cartilaginous layer called the metaphysis or growth plate, which is where bones grow in length. The diaphysis and epiphyses eventually fuse to form the complete bone (Figure 2.3). The appearance and union of ossification centers occurs at relatively predictable times during life and can therefore be a very useful indicator of an individual's age (see Chapter 10).

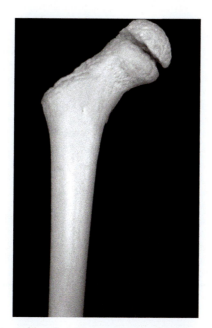

FIGURE 2.3 Subadult femur with unfused femoral head epiphysis

Bone is constantly being altered by osteoclastic and osteoblastic activity, both during development and throughout adulthood. As bone develops, the size as well as the shape is modified. This sculpting of the bone into its final adult shape is called **modeling**. Modeling occurs through continuous action of osteoblasts and osteoclasts in response to changing stresses as the bone matures, and is seen during bone growth and development as well as fracture repair. **Remodeling**, on the other hand, is the continual removal and replacement of existing mature bone. Remodeling occurs primarily to repair normal microdamage to the bone, but can also change the bone shape to some extent as a result of mechanical forces acting on the bone (Box 2.1). Because the process of remodeling replaces existing osteons with new ones and occurs throughout an individual's life, bone remodeling can be used as a means of estimating an individual's age (see Chapter 8).

The study of bone biomechanics involves the use of the laws of physics and the principles of engineering to consider the motions of the skeleton and the forces acting upon it. Forces that can produce bone failures (fractures) are reviewed in more detail in Chapter 13. Everyday forces due to normal use determine how bones grow to fit their functions, and how they adapt and are remodeled during life in response to biomechanical needs. This principle has been referred to as the "law of bone transformation" or "**Wolff's Law**" since the concept was first credited to German anatomist and surgeon Julius Wolff in the 19th century (Wolff, 1892). It has since been refined, however, by the **Utah Paradigm of Skeletal Physiology**, which explains through a number of principal tenets how bone growth and loss is stimulated by local mechanical forces (Box 2.2).

BOX 2.2 THE UTAH PARADIGM

While Wolff's Law stated that mechanical forces can affect bone architecture, it did not propose a mechanism or predict a specific architectural consequence of any specific mechanical influence (Frost, 1998). The Utah Paradigm of Skeletal Physiology represents a supplement to the understanding of skeletal physiology that was initiated in the 1960s, well-established by 1995, and was championed largely by Harold Frost. Part of this paradigm is based on the principle of the "mechanostat," a feedback loop that is proposed to orchestrate adaptations based on mechanical usage. The primary tenets of the Utah Paradigm (from Frost, 1998) are:

- Mechanical forces on skeletons generate signals in skeletal organs that control the biological mechanisms that determine the architecture and strength of those organs
- These occur in ways that let the organs endure their voluntary mechanical usage for life without being hurt or breaking
- To work properly, these mechanisms need non-mechanical factors (hormones, vitamins, calcium, genes, cytokines, etc.)
- Only mechanical factors can guide those mechanisms in time and anatomical space
- This arrangement determines skeletal health and the factors which cause or help to cause numerous disorders of skeletal and extraskeletal organs

---

2.4 Skeletal anatomy

Study of the anatomical features of the skeleton requires the use of standard nomenclature that represents a common language used by anatomists, anthropologists, and medical practitioners. After growth and development is complete and all epiphyses have fused, the mature adult human skeleton consists of approximately 206 bones. All of the bones of the human skeleton (with one exception) **articulate** with at least one other bone of the skeleton, forming the highly integrated system of skeletal structures. Due to the differing positions and relationships of these structures, the terminology used to refer to structures and relative positions should be understood. The following sections outline and define some of the anatomical terms, bone names, and features that are important in forensic anthropological analyses.

Anatomical directions and planes are used in reference to bones, body parts, their portions, and their relative positions. All of these terms are relative to a standard **anatomical position**, which for humans is standing, facing with the feet pointing forward, the palms of the hands facing forward, and the thumbs pointed laterally (see Figure 2.4, Figure 2.5, and Table 2.1). In the anatomical position, none of the bones are crossed when the body is viewed from the front. For some of these terms, bear in mind that they may differ somewhat for humans versus other animals, since humans are **bipeds** while most others are **quadrupeds**, and body parts are therefore in different positions relative to each other. When the terms *left* and *right* are used, they refer to the left and right sides of the individual or bone being studied with respect to anatomical position, not from the perspective of the observer.

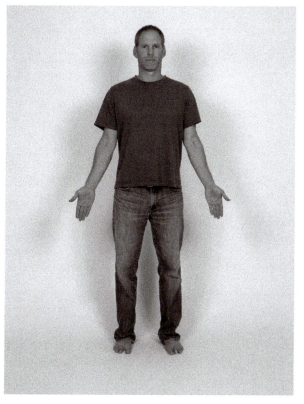

FIGURE 2.4 Standard anatomical position

(Photo by Rebecca Meeusen)

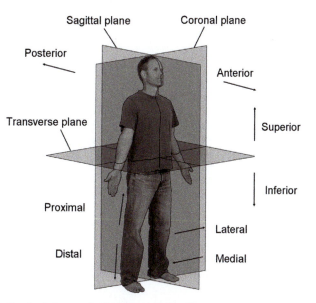

FIGURE 2.5 Anatomical planes of reference and directions

(Photo by Rebecca Meeusen)

Table 2.1 Anatomical planes of reference and directions		
Planes of reference	Sagittal	A plane through the body from front to back that divides the body into left and right halves. Any planar slice through the body that parallels the sagittal plane is called a para-sagittal plane; also called mid-sagittal, median, or midline
	Coronal	A plane at right angles to the sagittal plane that divides the body into front and back halves; also called frontal
	Transverse	A plane that slices through the body perpendicular to the sagittal and frontal planes; also called horizontal
	Frankfort	A plane running through the bottom of the left orbit (orbitale) and the upper margin of the left and right external auditory meati (porion); also called Frankfort Horizontal
Directional terms	Superior	Up, or toward the head; also called cranial for quadrupeds
	Inferior	Down, or away from the head; also called caudal for quadrupeds
	Anterior	Toward the front of the body; also called ventral for quadrupeds
	Posterior	Toward the back of the body; dorsal is used for quadrupeds
	Medial	Toward the midline of the body
	Lateral	Away from the midline of the body
	Proximal	Closest to an articular point; nearest the axial skeleton
	Distal	Farthest from an articular point; away from the axial skeleton
	External	Outer/outside
	Internal	Internal/inside
	Ectocranial	The outer surface of the cranial vault
	Endocranial	The inner surface of the cranial vault
	Superficial	Closest to the surface
	Deep	Farther from the surface
	Subcutaneous	Below the skin
	Palmar	The palm side of the hands
	Plantar	The sole side of the foot
	Dorsal	The top of the foot or back of the hand

(White et al., 2011)

Bones have many generalized external structures and features that are often examined and utilized in forensic anthropological analyses. Bones can be categorized as being **long bones** (which are characterized by being mostly tubular, such as limb bones), **flat bones** (such as those of the cranium), or irregular (such as the bones of the vertebral column, wrist, and ankle). Bones are integrated with the muscular, vascular, nervous, and other bodily systems, and their surface morphology reflects this interconnectivity. This can be seen in their various projections, depressions and foramina which serve as the attachment sites for muscles, the passage of blood vessels and nerves, and other reflections of adjacent anatomy. Some of these general feature terms are defined in Table 2.2.

Table 2.2 Gross anatomical features of bones

Projections	*Articulation*	An area where two bones contact at a joint
	Boss	A smooth, broad eminence
	Condyle	A rounded articular process
	Crest	A prominent, sharp ridge of bone
	Eminence	A bony projection, less prominent than a process
	Epicondyle	A non-articular projection near a condyle
	Facet	A small articular surface
	Hamulus	A hook-shaped projection
	Head	A large rounded articular end of a bone
	Line	A raised linear surface
	Malleolus	A rounded protuberance of the ankle
	Neck	The section of a bone between the head and the shaft
	Process	A bony prominence
	Ridge	A linear bony elevation
	Spine	A long, thin process
	Torus	A bony thickening
	Trochanter	A large blunt process of the femur
	Tuberosity	A large roughened eminence
	Tubercle	A small roughened eminence
Depressions and holes	*Alveolus*	A tooth socket
	Canal	A tunnel-like foramen
	Fontanelle	A cartilaginous space between cranial bones of an infant
	Foramen	A hole through a bone
	Fossa	A broad, shallow depressed area
	Fovea	A pit-like depression
	Groove	A long pit or furrow
	Meatus	A short canal
	Sinus	A cavity within a cranial bone
	Sulcus	A long, wide groove
	Suture	A fibrous, interlocking joint of the cranial bones

(White et al., 2011)

The skeleton can be divided into several major sections. The **cranial skeleton** refers to the bones of the skull, while the **postcranial skeleton** (or **infracranial skeleton**) refers to everything below the skull. The postcranial skeleton can be further subdivided into the **axial skeleton**, which consists of bones along and near the body's midline, and the **appendicular skeleton**, which consists of the bones of the limbs as well as their supporting structures where they connect with the axial skeleton.

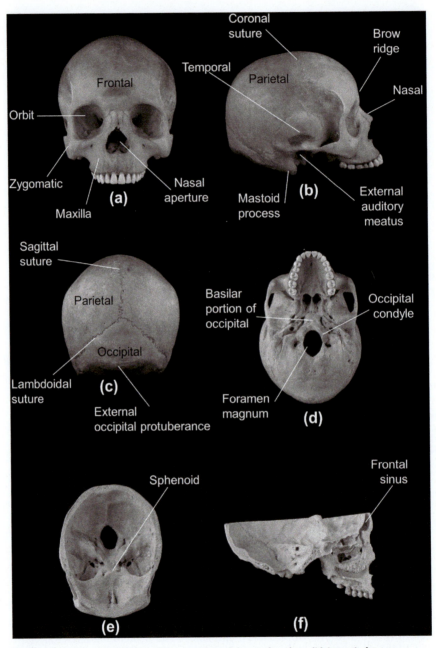

FIGURE 2.6 Bones and features of the cranium: (a) anterior view, (b) lateral view, (c) posterior view, (d) inferior view, (e) superior view, (f) lateral view along mid-sagittal plane

(Photos by Rebecca Meeusen; specimens courtesy of the National Museum of Natural History)

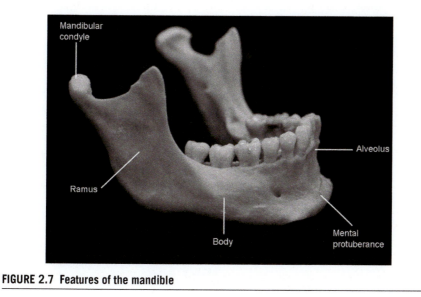

FIGURE 2.7 Features of the mandible

The **skull** consists of the entire bony head including the bones of the *cranium* (Figure 2.6) and the *mandible* (Figure 2.7) for a total of 28 bones. These include the *frontal*, two *parietals*, two *temporals* (each of which contain three auditory ossicles: the *malleus*, *incus*, and *stapes*), the *occipital*, the *sphenoid*, two *maxillae*, two *palatines*, two *inferior nasal conchae*, the *ethmoid*, the *vomer*, two *lacrimals*, two *nasals*, two *zygomatics*, and the mandible. The bones of the cranium can be divided into two groups: the **cranial vault** or **neurocranium**, consisting of the bones that form the sides, top, and back of the brain case, and the **splanchnocranium** or **facial skeleton**, consisting of the bones of the face. Several of the bones of the cranium contain **sinuses** (or paranasal sinuses), which are air pockets that are linked to the nasal cavity. Sinuses can be found in the frontal bone, the maxillae, the ethmoid, and the sphenoid, and the mastoid processes of the temporal bone contain sinus-like air cells. While the functions of the sinuses are not well understood, the frontal and maxillary sinuses have proven useful in anthropological assessments of identification. Tables 2.3–2.4 describe the bones and selected features of the skull.

The axial skeleton refers to bones on or near the body's midline including the skull as well as and the **thorax** or **trunk**. Bones of the thorax include the *hyoid, sternum, vertebrae,* and *ribs,* and these bones and some of their features are described in Table 2.5. The hyoid (Figure 2.8) is the only bone in the body that does not articulate with any other bone. It is located in the anterior neck and serves as a connection point for various structures of the neck and throat. The sternum (or breastbone) (Figure 2.9) anchors the anterior ends of ribs 1–7 and also connects with the shoulder girdle. It consists of three major portions: the *manubrium* (the most superior portion), the *body* (the central portion), and the *xiphoid process* (the most inferior portion).

Table 2.3 Bones and features of the skull

Bones of the skull and associated features	*Frontal bone*	Bone comprising the front-most portion of the neurocranium and the superior portions of the orbits
	Frontal squama	The vertical portion making up the forehead
	Horizontal portion	The portion comprising the orbital roofs
	Superciliary arches	The bony tori over the orbits (also called the brow ridge)
	Parietal bones	Paired bones forming the sides and roof of the cranial vault
	Parietal eminence	The large, rounded eminence in the center of the bone
	Meningeal grooves	Vascular grooves on the endocranial surface from the middle meningeal arteries
	Temporal bones	Paired bones forming the lateral cranial vault and part of the cranial base; also house the auditory ossicles
	Temporal squama	The vertical plate-like portion
	Petrous pyramid	The dense endocranial portion
	External auditory meatus (EAM)	The opening of the ear canal
	Mastoid process	The roughened inferior projection
	Auditory ossicles	Small bones housed in the temporal bone; each side has three – the malleus, incus, and stapes
	Occipital bone	Bone forming the back of the cranial vault and base
	Squamous portion	The vertical portion that is part of the cranial base
	Basilar portion	The thick anterior/inferior projection
	Foramen magnum	The large hole for the passage of the brain stem
	External occipital protuberance	The variably pronounced projection on the posterior ectocranial surface
	Occipital condyles	The articular surfaces for the first cervical vertebra
	Maxillae	Paired bones forming a majority of the face
	Alveolar process	The portion that holds the teeth
	Alveoli	Holes for the roots of the teeth
	Anterior nasal spine	Projection forming the inferior portion of the nasal aperture
	Palatines	Paired L-shaped bones forming the posterior palate
	Vomer	Small thin bone that divides the nasal cavity

Table 2.3 Bones and features of the skull—cont'd

	Inferior nasal conchae	Paired bones forming the lateral walls of the nasal cavity
	Ethmoid	Spongy bone located between the orbits
	Lacrimals	Thin rectangular bones of the medial walls of the orbits
	Nasals	Paired bones that form the bridge of the nose
	Zygomatics	Paired bones of the cheeks
	Sphenoid	Bone situated between the cranial vault and the face
	Body	The robust portion on the midline
	Greater wings	The laterally-extending segments
	Lesser wings	Posterior projections on the endocranial surface
	Mandible	Lower jaw
	Body	Thick anterior portion that holds the teeth
	Ramus	Thin vertical portion that articulates with the cranial base

(White et al., 2011)

Table 2.4 Sutures and other features of the skull

Sutures	Sagittal suture	The articulation between the two parietal bones
	Coronal suture	The articulation between the frontal and parietal bones
	Lambdoidal suture	The articulation between the occipital and the parietals and temporals
	Metopic suture	The articulation between the left and right frontal halves, only occasionally retained into adulthood
	Basilar suture	The articulation between the sphenoid and the basilar portion of the occipital bone; also called the spheno-occipital synchondrosis
	Nasal aperture	The hole for the nose, formed by portions of the nasal bones and maxillae
Other features of the skull	Orbits	The sockets for the eyes, formed by numerous cranial bones
	Sinuses	Air pockets, located in the frontal, maxillae, ethmoid, and sphenoid bones
	Temporal line	Raised line that anchors the temporalis muscle, which crosses the frontal and parietal bones
	Temporomandibular joint	The joint where the temporal bones articulate with the mandible

(White et al., 2011)

Table 2.5 Bones and features of the axial skeleton

Bones of the axial skeleton and associated features	*Hyoid bone*	U-shaped bone of the anterior neck
	Sternum	
	Manubrium	The wide, superior portion of the sternum
	Corpus sterni	The thin central portion of the sternum
	Xiphoid	The variably fused inferior tip of the sternum
	Vertebrae	Bones of the spinal column
	Body	The anterior and primary weight-bearing portion
	Vertebral arch	The posterior portion, enclosing the spinal cord
	Vertebral foramen	The hole through which the spinal cord passes; comprised of the body and the vertebral arch
	Spinous process	The most posterior projection
	Transverse process	The laterally directed projections
	Articular facets	Projections for articulation with adjacent vertebrae
	Cervical vertebrae	The most superior vertebrae in the spinal column, normally seven total
	Atlas	The first (most superior) cervical vertebra, which articulates with the occipital bone
	Axis	The second cervical vertebra, which forms a pivot with the atlas
	Transverse foramen	Foramen through the transverse process
	Thoracic vertebrae	The middle vertebrae in the spinal column, normally 12 total
	Costal fovea	Articular facets for the ribs
	Lumbar vertebra	The most inferior vertebrae in the spinal column, normally five total
	Mammillary process	Superior projection for the articular facets
	Sacrum	The most inferior portion of the spinal column and the posterior portion of the pelvis, formed of 4–6 fused segments
	Coccyx	The variably fused 3–5 segments of the vestigial tail
	Ribs	Long slender bones of the rib cage, normally 12 on each side or 24 total
	Head	The most proximal portion which articulates with the thoracic vertebral body
	Shaft	The curved main part of the rib
	Sternal end	The most anterior portion which articulates with the costal cartilage
Other features of the axial skeleton	*Vertebral column*	Comprised of the cervical, thoracic, and lumbar vertebra as well as the sacrum and coccyx
	Rib cage	The protective structure formed by the 24 ribs

(White et al., 2011)

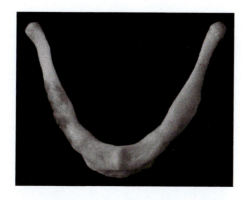

FIGURE 2.8 Hyoid

(Photo by Rebecca Meeusen; specimen courtesy of the National Museum of Natural History)

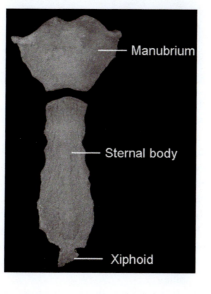

FIGURE 2.9 Sternum

(Photo by Rebecca Meeusen; specimens courtesy of the National Museum of Natural History)

The vertebrae provide support for the central part of the body, anchor various muscles of the back, and serve as a protective passageway for the spinal cord. There are 24 moveable (unfused) vertebrae of three different types in different regions of the *vertebral column* or *spinal column* (Figure 2.10). The seven *cervical vertebrae* are the most superior, forming the neck. The 12 *thoracic vertebrae* make up the middle back, and the five *lumbar vertebrae* make up the lower back. Vertebrae are typically referred to by their type and number counting from superior to inferior. For example, cervical vertebra number 5, or C5, is the fifth of the cervical vertebra from the top; thoracic vertebra number 10, or T10, is the tenth of the thoracic vertebrae;

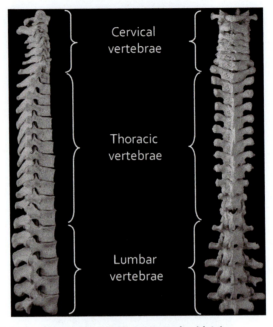

FIGURE 2.10 Vertebral column: lateral (left) and posterior (right)

(Photos by Rebecca Meeusen; specimens courtesy of the National Museum of Natural History)

and lumbar vertebra number 3 is the third of the lumbar vertebrae. All vertebrae have a central foramen called the *vertebral foramen* through which the spinal cord passes.

Cervical vertebrae (Figure 2.11) are the smallest of the vertebrae and are characterized by small *vertebral bodies* and a foramen through each of their *transverse processes* (called the *foramen transversarium*). The first two vertebrae are especially distinctive (Figure 2.12). The *atlas* is ring-shaped, with large superior facets for articulation with the occipital bone. The *axis* is characterized by a superior projection called the *odontoid process* (also called the *dens* or *dens epistropheus*) which allows the head to pivot on the spine.

Thoracic vertebrae make up the middle portion of the spinal column and can be distinguished by their facets for articulation with the ribs, one on each side of the vertebral body, and one on each transverse process (Figure 2.13). Though the typical number of thoracic vertebrae is 12, accessory thoracic vertebrae (usually accompanied by accessory ribs) are not uncommon. Lumbar vertebrae are the most inferior of the moveable vertebra and are characterized by large vertebral bodies due to their greater weight-bearing function (Figure 2.14).

At the distal end of the vertebral column is the *sacrum* which is formed of 4–6 fused vertebral segments (Figure 2.15). This bone also serves as the posterior portion of the pelvis. Inferior to the sacrum is the variably fused *coccyx* which represents the **vestigial** human tail and consists of 3–5 variable fused segments.

There are 12 ribs on each side (24 in total) which form the *rib cage* (Figure 2.16). Each rib articulates posteriorly with the vertebrae, and the first ten ribs (ribs 1–10)

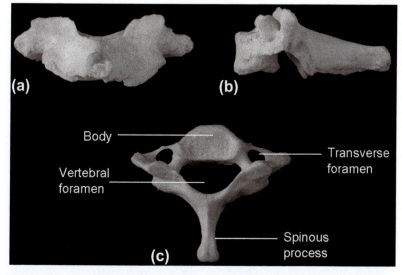

FIGURE 2.11 Cervical vertebrae: (a) posterior, (b) lateral, and (c) superior

(Photos by Rebecca Meeusen; specimens courtesy of the National Museum of Natural History)

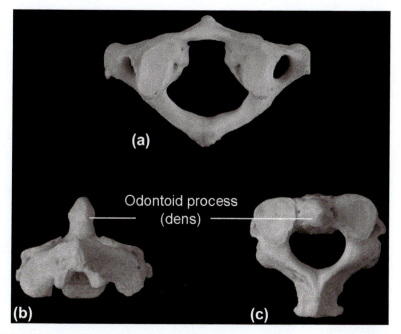

FIGURE 2.12 (a) cervical vertebra 1, (b) cervical vertebra 2 posterior, and (c) superior

(Photos by Rebecca Meeusen; specimens courtesy of the National Museum of Natural History)

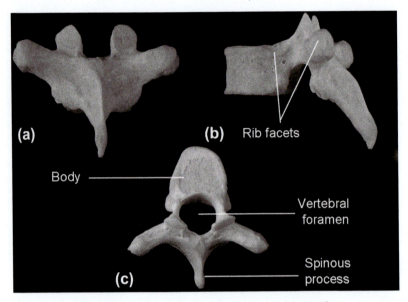

FIGURE 2.13 Thoracic vertebrae: (a) posterior, (b) lateral, and (c) superior

(Photos by Rebecca Meeusen; specimens courtesy of the National Museum of Natural History)

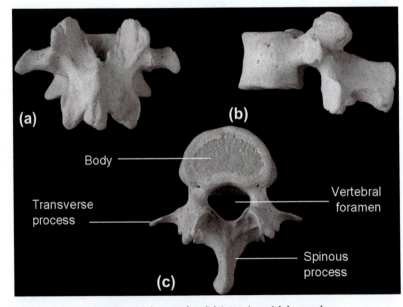

FIGURE 2.14 Lumbar vertebrae: (a) posterior, (b) lateral, and (c) superior

(Photos by Rebecca Meeusen; specimens courtesy of the National Museum of Natural History)

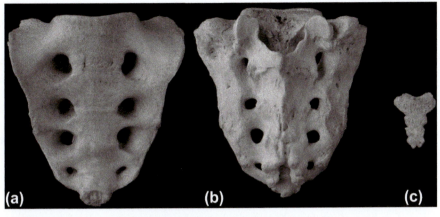

FIGURE 2.15 Sacrum: (a) anterior, (b) posterior; and (c) coccyx

(Photos by Rebecca Meeusen; specimens courtesy of the National Museum of Natural History)

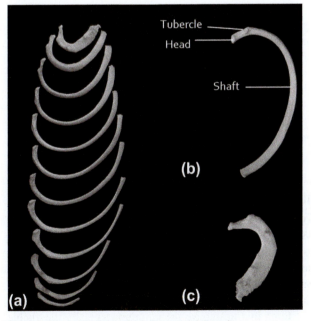

FIGURE 2.16 Ribs: (a) ribs 1–12, (b) typical rib, and (c) first rib

(Photos by Rebecca Meeusen; specimens courtesy of the National Museum of Natural History)

articulate anteriorly with *costal cartilage* connected to the sternum. Ribs 11–12 do not connect to the sternum in this way, and because of this they are called "floating ribs." Most ribs are characterized by being long, slender, and curved bones. Ribs 1 and 2 can be distinguished because they are flatter and more tightly curved. Sequentially, ribs 1–7 increase in length, and then decrease in length from ribs 8–12. Also, with each sequential rib, the angle becomes more obtuse.

The appendicular skeleton consists of the bones of the arms and legs as well as their supporting structures where they articulate with the axial skeleton. The supporting structure of the upper limb is referred to as the *shoulder girdle*, consisting of the *clavicle* and *scapula*, which connects the trunk to the arm (Figure 2.17). The upper limb consists of the arm, wrist, and hand. The bones of the arm include the *humerus* (Figure 2.18), which makes up the upper arm, and the *radius* (Figure 2.19) and *ulna* (Figure 2.20), which make up the lower arm (also called the forearm). The wrist consists of eight small irregular bones called *carpals*. The hand consists of five *metacarpals*, one for each **digit** or **ray**. The metacarpals are numbered 1–5 counting from lateral (the thumb side) toward medial (the little finger side). The fingers consist of bones called *manual phalanges*; the first digit (the thumb) consists of two phalanges (a proximal and a distal), while digits 2–5 each consist of three (a proximal, intermediate and distal) (Figure 2.21). Often, accessory bones of the hand and wrist occur and are called *sesamoid* bones. Some features of the upper limb are described in Table 2.6.

The *pelvic girdle*, consisting of the two *os coxae* or *innominates* along with the sacrum, connects the trunk to the lower limb (Figure 2.22). The os coxae form from three fused portions called the *ilium, ischium,* and *pubis*. The lower limb consists of the leg, ankle, and foot. The bones of the leg include the *femur* (Figure 2.23), which makes up the upper leg, the *patella* or kneecap (Figure 2.24), and the *tibia* (Figure 2.25) and *fibula* (Figure 2.26) which make up the lower leg. The ankle consists of seven irregular bones called *tarsals*. The foot consists of five *metatarsals*, one for each digit. The first toe (the "big toe") consists of two *pedal phalanges*, while digits 2–5 consist of three. Sesamoid bones may also occur in the ankle and foot (Figure 2.27). Some features of the lower limb are described in Table 2.7.

2.5 Dentition

The dentition consists of the teeth of the cranium and the mandible. Teeth articulate with bone via the *alveoli* or tooth sockets. For the upper dentition, the tooth sockets occur in the maxillae; in the lower dentition they are in the mandible. Due to their placement and orientation within the skeletal system, the dentition have their own set of directional terms (Table 2.8 and Figure 2.28).

Teeth have two major portions (Figure 2.29 and Table 2.9). The *crown* is the portion of the tooth that lies above the gumline (typically the visible portion in the mouth), and the *root*, which is the portion below the gumline that anchors the tooth in the alveolus. Like bone, teeth are composed of calcified tissue, though it differs somewhat from bone. Teeth contain three different tissue types. *Dentin* forms the

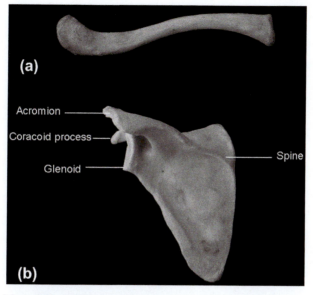

Acromion

Coracoid process

Glenoid

Spine

FIGURE 2.17 (a) clavicle, and (b) scapula

(Photos by Rebecca Meeusen; specimens courtesy of the National Museum of Natural History)

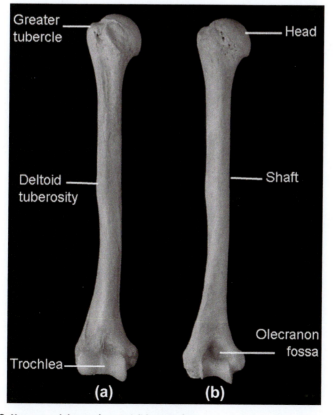

Greater tubercle

Head

Deltoid tuberosity

Shaft

Olecranon fossa

Trochlea

FIGURE 2.18 Humerus: (a) anterior, and (b) posterior

(Photos by Rebecca Meeusen; specimens courtesy of the National Museum of Natural History)

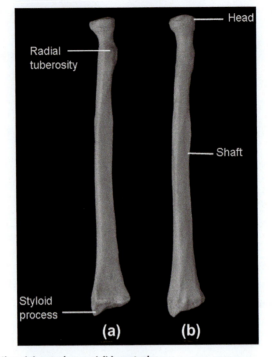

FIGURE 2.19 Radius: (a) anterior, and (b) posterior

(Photos by Rebecca Meeusen; specimens courtesy of the National Museum of Natural History)

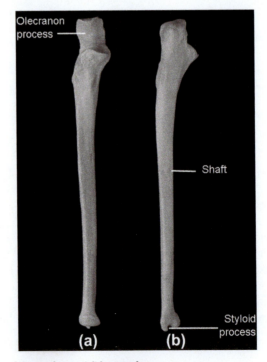

FIGURE 2.20 Ulna: (a) anterior, and (b) posterior

(Photos by Rebecca Meeusen; specimens courtesy of the National Museum of Natural History)

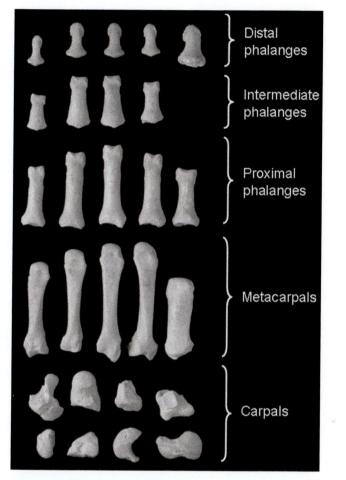

FIGURE 2.21 Bones of the wrist, hand and fingers

(Photos by Rebecca Meeusen; specimens courtesy of the National Museum of Natural History)

main part of the inner tooth. *Enamel* covers the external surface of the *crown*, and is the hardest tissue on the body. Enamel contains no living cells and has no blood supply. *Cementum* covers the external surface of the *root*.

Teeth take four basic forms that are related to their functions. *Incisors* are the blade-like anterior teeth that are used for cutting. *Canines* (sometimes called *eye teeth*) are conical teeth lying just posterior to the incisors and generally function similarly to incisors. *Premolars* (also called *bicuspids*) are two-cusped teeth that are transitional in form and function between the anterior and posterior teeth. *Molars* are the most posterior teeth which are used for grinding. The distal most (third) molars are sometimes called *wisdom teeth*, and are among the most variably present teeth in the human dentition (Box 2.3).

Table 2.6 Bones and features of the upper limb

Bones of the upper limb and associated features	*Clavicle*	S-shaped bone that articulates with the sternum and scapula; also called the collar bone
	Scapula	Flat, triangular-shaped bone; also called the shoulder blade
	Spine	The raised posterior ridge
	Acromion	The lateral most projection of the spine
	Coracoid process	The anterolateral projection
	Glenoid fossa	Shallow cavity that articulates with the humerus
	Humerus	The bone of the upper arm
	Head	Rounded portion that articulates with the scapula
	Greater and lesser tubercles	Blunt eminences on the anterior aspect of the proximal humerus
	Deltoid tuberosity	Eminence on the lateral shaft for insertion of the deltoid muscle
	Trochlea	Spool-shaped distal region, for articulation with the ulna
	Olecranon fossa	Posterior hollow, articulates with the olecranon process
	Radius	The lateral bone of the forearm
	Head	Rounded proximal end, for articulation with the humerus
	Radial tuberosity	Eminence on the proximal anteromedial for insertion of the biceps muscle
	Styloid process	The sharp projection on distal end
	Ulnar notch	Concave articulation with the ulna
	Ulna	The medial bone of the forearm
	Olecranon process	The proximal projection which is the insertion for the triceps muscle
	Styloid process	The sharp projection on the distal end
	Carpals	The eight bones of the wrist, consisting of the scaphoid, lunate, triquetral, pisiform, trapezium, trapezoid, capitate, and hamate
	Metacarpals	The five bones of the hand
	Manual phalanges	The bones of the fingers; on each side there are five proximal phalanges, four intermediate phalanges, and five distal phalanges (singular: phalanx)
Other features of the upper limb	*Shoulder girdle*	Supporting structure of the upper limb, consisting of the clavicle and scapula
	Elbow	The joint between the humerus and the radius/ulna
	Sesamoid bone	Accessory bone of the hand or wrist
	Nutrient foramen	Present on the anterior surfaces the humerus, radius, and ulna; provides passage for vascular supply

(White et al., 2011)

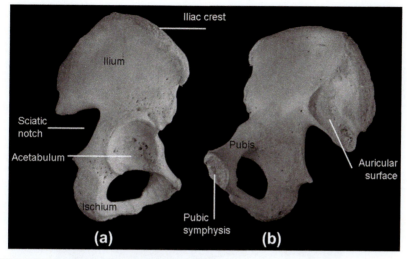

FIGURE 2.22 Os coxa: (a) lateral, and (b) medial

(Photos by Rebecca Meeusen; specimens courtesy of the National Museum of Natural History)

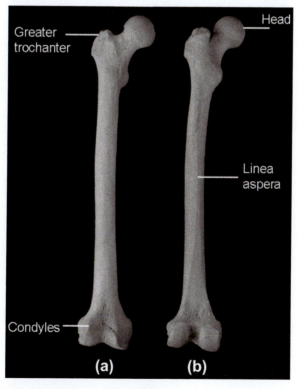

FIGURE 2.23 Femur: (a) anterior, and (b) posterior

(Photos by Rebecca Meeusen; specimens courtesy of the National Museum of Natural History)

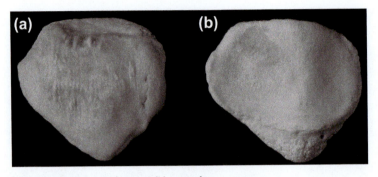

FIGURE 2.24 Patella: (a) anterior, and (b) posterior

(Photos by Rebecca Meeusen; specimens courtesy of the National Museum of Natural History)

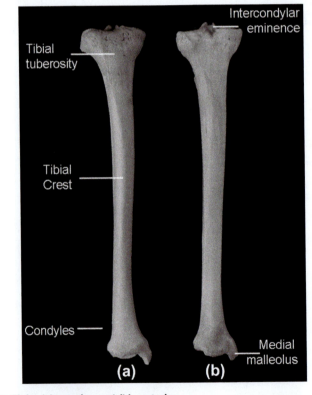

FIGURE 2.25 Tibia: (a) anterior, and (b) posterior

(Photos by Rebecca Meeusen; specimens courtesy of the National Museum of Natural History)

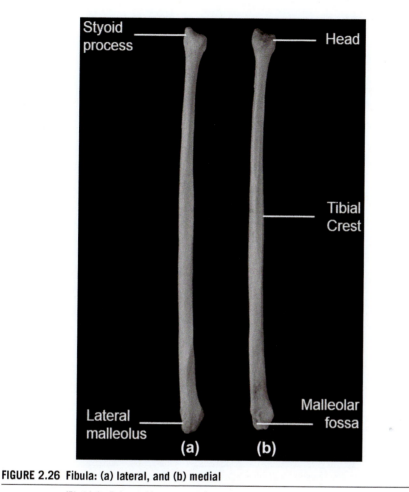

FIGURE 2.26 Fibula: (a) lateral, and (b) medial

(Photos by Rebecca Meeusen; specimens courtesy of the National Museum of Natural History)

Teeth develop in a process called **odontogenesis** within the jaws, in alveolar pockets called *crypts*. Humans, like most other mammals, develop two different sets of dentition called the *deciduous* dentition (or primary dentition, baby teeth, or milk teeth), and the *permanent* dentition (or secondary dentition, or adult teeth). Teeth develop from the crown toward the root. When the crown is complete, the developing tooth will **erupt**, or move into its occlusal position in the mouth. During childhood, the deciduous dentition is shed and replaced by the permanent dentition. The eruption and shedding of the deciduous dentition is important for proper growth and space allocation for the permanent dentition, and the sequence of dental development and eruption is often used in the process of aging subadult individuals (see Chapter 10).

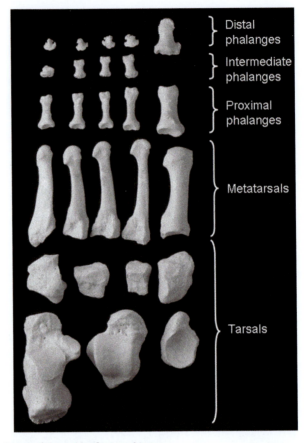

FIGURE 2.27 Bones of the ankle, foot, and toes

(Photos by Rebecca Meeusen; specimens courtesy of the National Museum of Natural History)

A **dental formula** is a system for summarizing the number of each type of tooth (incisor, canine, premolar, molar) in each quadrant of the mouth. Dental formulae show variation between species and may be different for the maxillary and mandibular dentition. For example, the dental formula for a dog is 3142/3143 (upper/lower dentition), indicating that there is an additional molar in the mandible. In humans, the deciduous dentition consists of 20 total teeth, with the dental formula 2102 (or 2102/2102), indicating two incisors, one canine, zero premolars, and two molars in each quadrant. The permanent dentition consists of 32 teeth in total, with the dental formula 2123 (or 2123/2123), indicating two incisors, one canine, two premolars, and three molars in each quadrant.

Table 2.7 Bones and features of the lower limb

Bones of the lower limb and associated features	*Os coxa*	Hip bone; also called the innominate
	Ilium	The blade-like superior portion
	Ischium	The postero-inferior portion
	Pubis	The anterior portion
	Acetabulum	The round hollow which forms the hip socket and articulates with the femoral head
	Greater sciatic notch	Wide notch on the ilium
	Pubic symphysis	The anterior surface where the left and right os coxae meet
	Auricular surface	The posterior surface of the ilium which articulates with the sacrum
	Femur	The bone of the upper leg
	Femoral head	The round proximal part that articulates with the os coxae
	Linea aspera	The raised ridge on the posterior shaft
	Condyles	The large protrusions on the posterior distal portion
	Trochanters	Blunt prominences on the proximal posterior surface
	Patella	The knee cap
	Tibia	The major of the two lower leg bones; also called the shin bone
	Tibial tuberosity	The roughened area on the anterior surface of the proximal end
	Medial malleolus	The projection on the medial surface of the distal end
	Anterior crest	The sharp ridge forming the shin
	Fibula	The smaller, lateral bone of the lower leg
	Malleolus	The projection on the lateral surface of the distal end
	Tarsals	The seven bones of the ankle, consisting of the talus, calcaneus, navicular, cuboid, medial cuneiform, intermediate cuneiform, and lateral cuneiform
	Metatarsals	The five bones of the foot
	Pedal phalanges	The bones of the toes; on each side there are five proximal phalanges, four intermediate phalanges, and five distal phalanges
Other features of the lower limb	*Pelvic girdle*	Supporting structure of the lower limb, consisting of the os coxae
	Knee	The joint between the femur and tibia and also including the patella
	Sesamoid bone	Accessory bone of the foot or ankle
	Nutrient foramen	Present on the posterior surfaces the femur, tibia, and fibula; provides passage for vascular supply

(White et al., 2011)

Table 2.8 Directional terms of the dentition

Dental directional terms	*Mesial*	Toward the point on the midline where the central incisors contact each other
	Distal	Away from the point on the midline where the central incisors contact each other
	Lingual	Toward the tongue
	Labial	Toward the lips (for anterior teeth)
	Buccal	Toward the cheeks (for posterior teeth)
	Interproximal	In contact with adjacent teeth in the same jaw
	Occlusal	Facing the opposite dental arch, usually the chewing surface
	Incisal	The biting or occlusal edge of incisors
	Mesiodistal	Axis running from medial to distal
	Buccolingual	Axis running from buccal or labial to lingual; also called labiolingual

(White et al., 2011)

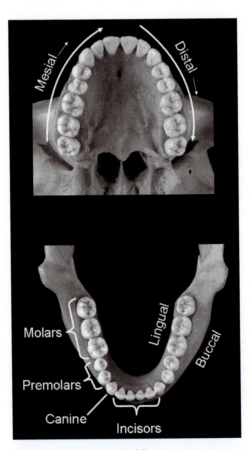

FIGURE 2.28 Features and directions of the dentition

(Photos by Rebecca Meeusen; specimens courtesy of the National Museum of Natural History)

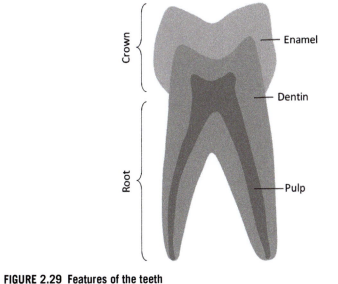

FIGURE 2.29 Features of the teeth

Table 2.9 Teeth and features of the dentition

Tooth types	Incisors	Spatulate teeth of the anterior dentition used for cutting; each jaw contains four
	Canines	Conical teeth distal to the incisors used for grabbing; each jaw contains two
	Premolars	Two-cusped, transitional teeth between the canines and molars; each jaw contains four
	Molars	Four- to five- cusped distal teeth used for grinding; each jaw contains six
Tooth features	Crown	The part of the tooth above the gumline and covered with enamel
	Neck	The junction of the crown and the root
	Root	The part below the gumline that anchors the tooth in the alveolus
	Cusp	A projection on the occlusal surface of a crown
	Enamel	The tissue that covers the crown
	Dentin	The tissue that forms the core of the crown and root
	Cemento-enamel junction	Where the enamel meets the root
	Cementum	The tissue on the external surface of the roots

Table 2.9 Teeth and features of the dentition—cont'd

Other features of the dentition	*Alveoli*	The tooth sockets; where the teeth articulate with the maxillae and the mandible (singular: alveolus)
	Calculus	A calcified deposit resulting from plaque often found on tooth crowns
	Carious lesion	A lesion or hole from tooth decay
	Deciduous dentition	The first set of teeth to develop; also called primary dentition or "baby teeth"
	Permanent dentition	The second set of teeth to develop; also called secondary dentition or adult teeth
	Crypt	Alveolar pocket where tooth development occurs

(White et al., 2011)

BOX 2.3 THIRD MOLAR AGENESIS

The absence or **agenesis** of the third molar is a well-documented phenomenon, with most people exhibiting absence, impaction, or malposition of the third molars. It is also related to agenesis and reduction of size of other molars and other teeth (Garn et al., 1963; Nanda, 1954). Third molar agenesis has been noted to be related to craniofacial morphology (Sanchez et al., 2009), and is evolutionarily hypothesized to be related to an overall reduction in jaw length (and accompanying increase in brain size), with less reliance on the teeth for subsistence and survival (Thompkins, 1996; Anderson, 1975).

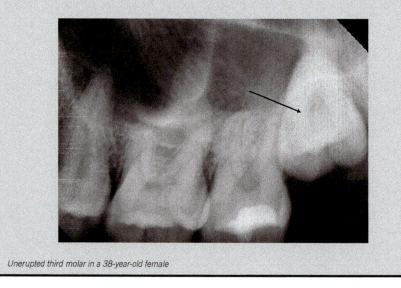

Unerupted third molar in a 38-year-old female

2.6 Summary

- Forensic anthropological analyses depend on a thorough knowledge of human osteology and odontology including bone and tooth morphology, features, related anatomical terminology, internal composition, and growth and development.
- The skeleton serves many functions including support, movement, protection, storage, and blood production.
- Bone is composed of collagen and hydroxyapatite, and is organized into units called osteons. Bone tissue is arranged into cortical (compact) and trabecular (spongy) bone.
- There are three types of bone cells: osteoblasts (bone forming cells), osteoclasts (bone resorbing cells), and osteocytes (mature, non-secreting bone cells). The actions of these cells in sculpting a bone's final form are called modeling; the actions of these cells in repairing microdamage throughout life are called remodeling.
- The adult human skeleton consists of approximately 206 bones including those of the skull (cranium and mandible), axial skeleton (ribs, vertebrae, hyoid, sternum), and the appendicular skeleton (upper limb, lower limb, and supporting structures).
- Teeth are composed of dentin, enamel, and cementum. The dentition erupts in two series – the deciduous dentition and the permanent dentition. The dental formula for adult humans is 2123 indicating two incisors, one canine, two pre-molars, and three molars in each quadrant.

2.7 Test yourself

- Describe the relationship between a Haversian canal, Volkmann's canal, and cannaliculi. Why does bone have this arrangement of passageways?
- What are the three types of bone cells and what is each responsible for?
- How might a thorough knowledge of normal skeletal anatomy help a forensic anthropologist in identifying abnormalities in growth and development?
- Stand (or imagine yourself) in anatomical position. Describe the anatomical directional relationship between the following bones and your sternum: cranium, humerus, T2, patella.
- How many adult teeth do you currently have? Keep in mind the variability of wisdom teeth. How does this relate to the adult human dental formula?
- What is the major difference between intramembranous and endochondral ossification?

Definitions

Agenesis The absence or failure of development of a body part
Anatomical position The standard reference position which for humans is standing, facing with the feet pointing forward, and the palms of the hands forward with the thumbs pointed out
Appendicular skeleton Bones of the limbs

Articulate To fit, join, or unite

Axial skeleton Bones along (or near) the body's midline

Basic multicellular unit (BMU) Osteoblasts and osteoclasts working together in the process of bone remodeling

Biped An animal that moves on two feet

Canaliculi Small channels that connect osteocytes

Collagen A large protein molecule that comprises most of bone's organic content

Connective tissue A class of biological tissue that functions to support, connect, or separate tissues and organs of the body

Cortical bone Dense bone found on external surfaces of bones and the walls of the shafts of long bones; also called compact bone

Cranial skeleton The bones of the skull

Dental formula A system for summarizing the number of each type of tooth in each quadrant of the mouth

Dentition The teeth and their arrangement

Diaphysis The shaft of a long bone; also called the primary ossification center

Digit One of the five segments of the hand or foot; also called a ray

Diploe Trabecular bone within the cranial bones

Endosteum A thin tissue layer lining the interior surface of bones

Epiphysis The end portions of long bones; also called secondary ossification center

Erupt The process of a tooth moving into its occlusal position in the mouth

Flat bones Bones that are characterized by being largely flat, such as those of the cranium

Haversian canal The central passageway of an osteon

Histology The study of tissue microstructure

Hydroxyapatite A mineral composed of calcium phosphate that makes up the inorganic component of bone

Inorganic Not biological in origin and lacking carbon atoms

Lacuna Spaces of a Haversion system in which osteocytes reside

Lamellae Concentric rings of bone around a Haversian canal

Lamellar bone Mature compact bone

Long bones Bones that are characterized by being largely tubular, such as those of the limbs

Masticate Chew; break down

Medullary cavity The hollow inner part of a bone shaft

Metaphysis Growth plate

Modeling The action of osteoblastic and osteoclastic activity to sculpt bone during growth and development (and fracture repair) into its final form

Morphology Shape

Neurocranium Bones forming the sides, top, and back of the brain case; also called the cranial vault

Odontogenesis The process of mineralization of the teeth during development

Odontology The study of teeth

Organic Biological in origin and containing carbon atoms

Osteoblast Bone forming cell

Osteoclast Bone resorbing cell

Osteocyte Mature bone cell

Osteogenesis The process of mineralization of bones during development

Osteoid Unmineralized bone matrix

Osteology The study of bones

Ossification The process of bone formation and mineralization; endochondral ossification refers to bone formation from a cartilaginous precursor, while intramembranous ossification refers to bone formation from a connective tissue membrane

Osteon Also called Haversian system, the basic structural unit of bone; those formed during growth are called *primary osteons* while those that are formed later during bone remodeling are called *secondary osteons*

Periosteum A thin tissue layer lining the exterior surface of bones

Postcranial The skeleton below the cranium; also called infracranial

Quadruped An animal that moves on four feet

Remodeling The action of osteoblastic and osteoclastic activity to repair microdamage throughout life

Sinus An air pocket in the cranium that is continuous with the nasal cavity; also called paranasal sinus

Skeleton System of calcified connective tissue that includes the bones and teeth

Skull The cranium plus the mandible

Splanchnocranium The bones of the face; also called the facial skeleton

Thorax The part of the body between the head and the abdomen, also called the trunk

Trabeculae Thin bony spicules that comprise trabecular bone

Trabecular bone Spongy, porous bone; also called cancellous bone

Utah Paradigm of Skeletal Physiology A refinement of Wolff's Law that explains that bone growth and loss is stimulated by local mechanical forces

Vestigial Pertaining to a vestige or remnant; a rudimentary or degenerate structure

Volkmann's canal Vascular canals that transversely connect Haversian systems

Wolff's Law The principle of bone remodeling to fit its biomechanical function; also called the "law of bone transformation"

Woven bone Unorganized bone formed rapidly during growth and fracture repair

Zooarchaeology The study of non-human animal bones, often those from archaeological sites

References

Anderson, D.L., Thompson, G.W., Popovich, F., 1975. Evolutionary dental changes. Am. J. Phys. Anthropol. 43 (1), 95–102.

Frost, H.M., 1998. Changing concepts in skeletal physiology: Wolff's Law, the mechanostat, and the "Utah Paradigm." Am. J. Human. Biol. 10, 599–605.

Garn, S.M., Lewis, A.B., Kerewsky, R.S., 1963. Third molar agenesis and size reduction of the remaining teeth. Nature 200, 488–489.

Gray, H., 1918. Anatomy of the Human Body. Lea & Febiger, Philadelphia.

Nanda, R.S., 1954. Agenesis of the third molar in man. Am. J. Orthod. 40 (9), 698–706.

Sanchez, M.J., Vicente, A., Bravo, L.A., 2009. Third molar agenesis and craniofacial morphology. Angle Orthod. 79 (3), 473–478.

Thompkins, R.L., 1996. Human population variability in relative dental development. Am. J. Phys. Anthropol. 99, 79–102.

White, T.D., Black, M.T., Folkens, P.A., 2011. Human Osteology, third ed. Academic Press, San Diego.

Wolff, J., 1892. Das Gestez der Transformation der Knochen. Verlag von August Hirschwald, Berlin.

Skeletal Examination and Documentation Methods

3.1 Examination methods

Forensic anthropological analyses involve the application of various examination methods and techniques. Those applied in any particular case are largely dependent on the question being asked, such as: Are the bones human? To whom do the skeletal remains belong? How long have they been here? How did the individual die? The amount and condition of skeletal material present also affects which methods are possible or most appropriate to apply.

Forensic anthropologists can rarely provide definitive answers regarding interpretations of skeletal remains; all methods have inherent limitations (due to, for example, overlap between different biological groups or inherent limits of the observations or techniques). Results of forensic anthropological analyses therefore typically take the form of **assessments** or **estimates**. An assessment usually involves observing morphological traits with no estimable error rates, correct classification rates, or associated statistics. An estimate involves using metric traits which provide an error rate or expected correct classification rate (Spradley and Jantz, 2011), although in some cases, statistics can and should be applied to morphological traits (Hefner, 2009). Common approaches used to make forensic anthropological assessments and estimates from skeletal remains include **macroscopic** (visual) analysis, metric analysis, and **radiology**. In some cases, other specialized techniques or analyses such as **histology** or **elemental analysis** may also be employed.

These analyses should be performed in a forensic anthropology laboratory which has access to some basic examination equipment (Figure 3.1). This should include at least one table large enough to lay out an entire adult skeleton in anatomical order. Large tables are useful for photographing the remains as well as providing a visual inventory. Ideally, the laboratory should be equipped with multiple large tables, especially if more than one case is likely to be examined simultaneously. Since many cases are received with adhering soft tissue that may need to be removed (see Chapter 7), the laboratory should have a processing area with a water source and fume hood as well as any necessary processing tools (such as hotplates, crock pots, scalpels, forceps, and scissors). The laboratory should be equipped with necessary safety supplies (such as gloves and lab coats) and should also be capable of handling and managing biohazardous waste (Warren et al., 2008).

Forensic Anthropology. http://dx.doi.org/10.1016/B978-0-12-418671-2.00003-3

FIGURE 3.1 Forensic anthropology laboratory

(Image courtesy of JPAC/CIL)

For many skeletal examinations, it will be necessary to have at least a low-power microscope, measurement tools, and media for recording notes (such as paper or a computer). The laboratory examination area should also have sufficient lighting. For certain analyses, specialized analytical equipment or instruments may be required. The laboratory should also have sufficient storage for supplies, chemicals, reference materials, case files, and inactive cases (such as those awaiting additional examination). Areas where evidence is examined or stored should be securable, meaning that there is restricted access limited to analysts involved in the case. Specific requirements for particular examination and documentation methods are discussed in the sections below.

Macroscopic analysis

Virtually every anthropological examination involves some form of **macroscopic** or gross visual analysis. Macroscopic analysis is used in conducting an inventory of the remains, assessing the overall condition of the material, describing taphonomic changes, estimating sex, age, and ancestry, and interpreting pathology and trauma. Many conclusions can be drawn based on macroscopic analysis alone, including determining whether bones are human or non-human, and estimating the sex, ancestry, or age of the individual. Macroscopic analyses should be performed using sufficient ambient or overhead lighting, and may also be aided by small light sources that can be used to view within the cranium.

Many macroscopic approaches, especially those relating to estimating aspects of the biological profile (see Chapters 8–10), involve assessing the presence or absence, degree of expression, or overall morphology of skeletal features. Such observations are often scored in some manner or compared to charts or exemplars such as photographs or casts. Traits analyzed in this way have been referred to as **morphoscopic traits** (Ousley and Hefner, 2005). For example, in the assessment of sex, the pelvis may be examined for the presence or absence of a preauricular sulcus. In the assessment of ancestry, the anterior nasal spine may be categorized as slight, intermediate, or marked. In the estimation of age, the morphology of the pubic symphysis can be compared to written descriptions and exemplar casts to determine which of the described phases it most closely resembles. Morphoscopic features are sometimes referred to as **non-metric** traits since they are visually assessed versus measured, but it has been suggested that the term "non-metric trait" be reserved for those morphological features which are non-pathological, epigenetic traits that can be scored as present or absent, such as the presence of a metopic suture (Buikstra and Ubelaker, 1994; Hefner et al., 2012).

While macroscopic analysis has many advantages including ease of application and no need for sophisticated equipment, it also has limitations. It is typically considered more subjective, less standardized, and more prone to bias than some other types of analysis, such as metric analysis (Hefner, 2009) or analyses involving analytical instrumentation. By their nature, macroscopic interpretations are often less amenable to error analysis and sometimes rely heavily upon experience and training. Nonetheless, macroscopic approaches can be highly reliable and valid, and in some cases, may be the only means of analysis possible.

Metric analysis

Metric analysis in forensic anthropological cases involves recording and analyzing skeletal measurements, also referred to as **osteometrics**. Metric analysis can often help to reveal skeletal differences that are difficult to detect and interpret by macroscopic methods alone, such as differences in size between males and females, and differences in cranial shape between ancestral groups. Measurements are also used in the calculation of certain parameters such as stature. Some advantages of metric analyses are that they add statistical weight to estimates and eliminate certain errors associated with more observational methods. Although fairly straightforward in most cases, metric analysis requires knowledge and training in the use of measurement instrumentation, how to locate particular landmarks on the remains, how to perform the relevant calculations, and how to interpret the results.

Sliding calipers, spreading calipers, and osteometric boards (Figure 3.2) are the foundation for most metric analyses in forensic anthropology today, and are used to take two-dimensional, linear skeletal measurements. Calipers measure from one specific point on a bone to another, while the osteometric board is used to measure the maximum lengths or breadths of long bones or to take other larger measurements which would exceed the maximum measuring capacity for standard calipers. Other

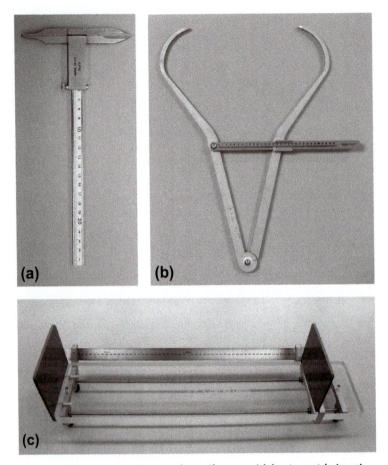

FIGURE 3.2 (a) sliding calipers, (b) spreading calipers, and (c) osteometric board

methods for quantifying human remains, bony features, and human variation exist, including digitizers, laser scanners, and radiographic techniques, some of which can take measurements in three-dimensional space. Calipers and osteometric boards, however, are still the standard because of their wide availability, relatively low cost, and ease of use.

While some measurements are very specialized and tailored to particular types of analyses, many forensic anthropologists employ some or all of a suite of relatively standardized skeletal measurements. Many of these measurements, especially those of the skull, are taken from a set of specified **osteometric landmarks**, which when applied to the skull are called **craniometric landmarks.** A list of these landmarks for the cranium can be found in Table 3.1, with their locations depicted in Figure 3.3. The standard measurements of the cranium and mandible are described in Table 3.2 and Figure 3.4. Abbreviations used in the measurements refer to the landmarks involved (displayed in

Table 3.1 Craniometric landmarks

Landmark (and abbreviation)	Definition
Alare (al)	The most laterally positioned point on the anterior margin of the nasal aperture
Alvelon (alv)	The point where the midline of the palate is intersected by a straight tangent connecting the posterior borders of the alveolar crests
Auriculare (au)	A point on the lateral aspect of the root of the zygomatic process at the deepest incurvature, wherever it may be
Basion (ba)	The point where the anterior margin of the foramen magnum is intersected by the mid-sagittal plane
Bregma (b)	The point where the sagittal and coronal sutures meet
Condylon (cdl)	The most lateral points of the mandibular condyles
Dacryon (d)	The point on the medial border of the orbit at which the frontal, lacrimal, and maxilla intersect
Ectoconchion (ec)	The intersection of the most anterior surface of the lateral border of the orbit and a line bisecting the orbit along its long axis
Ectomolare (ecm)	The most lateral point on the lateral surface of the alveolar crest
Euryon (eu)	The most laterally positioned point on the side of the braincase
Frontomalare temporale (fmt)	The most laterally positioned point on the fronto-malar suture
Frontotemporale (ft)	A point located generally forward and inward on the superior temporal line directly above the zygomatic process of the frontal bone
Glabella (g)	The most forwardly projecting point in the mid-sagittal plane at the lower margin of the frontal bone, which lies above the nasal root and between the superciliary arches
Gnathion (gn)	The lowest point on the inferior margin of the mandibular body in the mid-sagittal plane
Gonion (go)	The point on the mandible where the inferior margin of the mandibular corpus and the posterior margin of the ramus meet
Infradentale (id)	The point between the lower incisor teeth where the anterior margins of the alveolar processes are intersected by the mid-sagittal plane
Lambda (l)	The point where the two branches of the lambdoidal suture meet with the sagittal suture
Nasion (n)	The point of intersection of the naso-frontal suture and the mid-sagittal plane
Nasospinale (ns)	The lowest point on the inferior margin of the nasal aperture as projected in the mid-sagittal plane
Opisthocranion (op)	The most posteriorly protruding point on the back of the braincase, located in the mid-sagittal plane
Opisthion (o)	The point at which the mid-sagittal plane intersects the posterior margin of the foramen magnum
Prosthion (pr)	The most anterior point on the alveolar border of the maxilla between the central incisors in the mid-sagittal plane; note that this point is anteriorly located on the alveolar process for measurements 6 and 8, and inferiorly located for measurement 10
Zygion (zy)	The most laterally positioned point on the zygomatic arches

(Modified from Moore-Jansen et al., 1994)

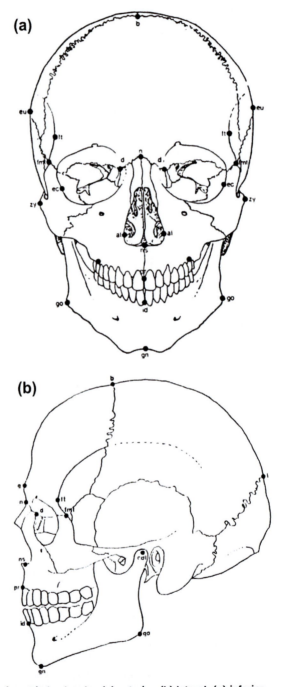

FIGURE 3.3 Craniometric landmarks: (a) anterior, (b) lateral, (c) inferior

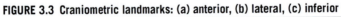

(from Moore-Jansen et al., 1994)

(c)

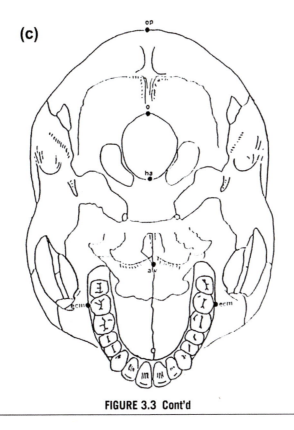

FIGURE 3.3 Cont'd

lower case), or the abbreviated measurement (displayed in upper case). Standard measurements for postcranial elements are shown in Table 3.3 and Figure 3.5. Many guides, including *Data Collection Procedures for Forensic Skeletal Material* (Moore-Jansen et al., 1994) and *Standards for Data Collection from Human Skeletal Remains* (Buikstra and Ubelaker, 2004), offer more detailed definitions, considerations, and recommendations for which instruments are most appropriate for each measurement. It is recommended that this suite of standard measurements be recorded in all applicable cases.

Skeletal measurements can be analyzed and interpreted using **statistics** much more readily than most macroscopic methods, and the use of statistical analysis in conjunction with qualitative descriptions in forensic anthropological casework is recommended (SWGANTH, Statistical Methods, 2012). In order to select and apply appropriate statistical models in casework and research, it is important that forensic anthropologists have a strong background in statistics and quantitative methods of data analysis. Definitions of various basic statistical terms that are commonly used in forensic anthropological analyses can be found in Table 3.4.

Two of the more commonly employed statistical analyses in forensic anthropology are regression analysis and discriminant function analysis. **Regression analysis**

Table 3.2 Measurements of the cranium and mandible

Measurement (and abbreviations)	Definition
1. Maximum Cranial Length (g-op, GOL)	The distance of glabella (g) from opisthocranion (op) in the mid-sagittal plane measured in a straight line
2. Maximum Cranial Breadth (eu-eu, XCB)	The maximum width of the skull perpendicular to the mid-sagittal plane wherever it is located
3. Bizygomtic Breadth (zy-zy, ZYB)	The direct distance between both zygia (zy) located at their most lateral points of the zygomatic arches
4. Basion-Bregma Height (ba-b, BBH)	The direct distance from the lowest point on the anterior margin of the foramen magnum, basion (ba), to bregma
5. Cranial Base Length (ba-n, BNL)	The direct distance from nasion (n) to basion (ba)
6. Basion-Prosthion Length (ba-pr, BPL)	The direct distance from basion (ba) to prosthion (pr)
7. Maxillo-Alveolar Breadth (ecm-ecm, MAB)	The maximum breadth across the alveolar borders of the maxilla measured on the lateral surfaces at the location of the second maxillary molars
8. Maxillo-Alveolar Length (pr-avl, MAL)	The direct distance from prosthion (Hrdlicka's prealveolar point) to alveolon (alv)
9. Biauricular Breadth (au-au, AUB)	The least exterior breadth across the roots of the zygomatic processes, wherever found
10. Upper Facial Height (n-pr)	The direct distance from nasion (n) to prosthion (pr)
11. Minimum Frontal Breadth (ft-ft, WFB)	The direct distance between the two frontotemporale
12. Upper Facial Breadth (fmt-fmt)	The direct distance between the two frontomalare temporalia
13. Nasal Height (n-ns, NLH)	The direct distance from nasion (n) to nasospinale (ns)
14. Nasal Breadth (al-al, NLB)	The maximum breadth of the nasal aperture
15. Orbital Breadth (d-ec, OBB)	The laterally sloping distance from dacryon (d) to ectoconchion (ec)
16. Orbital Height (OBH)	The direct distance between the superior and inferior orbital margins
17. Biorbital Breadth (ec-ec, EKB)	The direct distance from one ectoconchion (ec) to the other
18. Interorbital Breadth (d-d, DKB)	The direct distance between right and left dacryon
19. Frontal Chord (n-b, FRC)	The direct distance from nasion (n) to bregma (b) taken in the mid-sagittal plane
20. Parietal Chord (b-l, PAC)	The direct distance from bregma (b) to lambda (l) taken in the mid-sagittal plane
21. Occipital Chord (l-o, OCC)	The direct distance from lambda (l) to opisthion (o) taken in the mid-sagittal plane

Table 3.2 Measurements of the cranium and mandible—cont'd

Measurement (and abbreviations)	Definition
22. Foramen Magnum Length (ba-o, FOL)	The direct distance of basion (b) from opisthion (o)
23. Foramen Magnum Breadth (FOB)	The distance between the lateral margins of the foramen magnum at the point of greatest lateral curvature
24. Mastoid Length (MDH)	The projection of the mastoid process below, and perpendicular to, the eye-ear plane in the vertical plane
25. Chin Height (id-gn)	The direct distance from infradentale (id) to gnathion (gn)
26. Height of Mandibular Body	The direct distance from the alveolar process to the inferior border of the mandible perpendicular to the base at the level of the mental foramen
27. Breadth of Mandibular Body	The maximum breadth measured in the region of the mental foramen perpendicular to the long axis of the mandibular body
28. Bigonial Width (go-go)	The direct distance between both gonia (go)
29. Bicondylar Breadth (cdl-cdl)	The direct distance between the most lateral points on the two condyles (cdl)
30. Minimum Ramus Breadth	The least breadth of the mandibular ramus measured perpendicular to the height of the ramus
31. Maximum Ramus Breadth	The distance between the most anterior point on the mandibular ramus and line connecting the most posterior point on the condyle and the angle of the jaw
32. Maximum Ramus Height	The direct distance from the highest point on the mandibular condyle to gonion
33. Mandibular Length	The distance of the anterior margin of the chin from a center point on a projected straight line placed along the posterior border of the two mandibular angles
34. Mandibular Angle	The angle formed by the inferior border of the corpus and the posterior border of the ramus

(Modified from Moore-Jansen et al., 1994)

is a statistical approach that assesses the relationship between two or more variables. The simplest form of regression analysis is a linear, bivariate (two-variable) regression that describes the relationship between the two variables of interest. Such analyses are often used in forensic anthropology, for example when determining the relationship between the length of a bone and an individual's known stature (see, for example, Figure 11.3). This mathematical relationship then allows for the estimation of an unknown stature based on a known bone length (or vice versa).

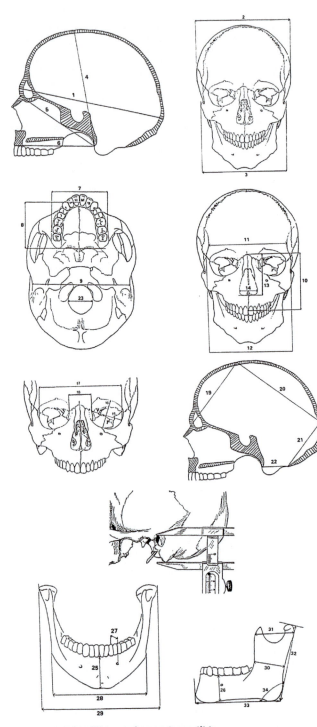

FIGURE 3.4 Measurements of the cranium and mandible

(From Moore-Jansen et al., 1994)

Table 3.3 Measurements of the postcranial skeleton

Measurement	Definition
35. Maximum Length of Clavicle	The maximum distance between the most extreme ends of the clavicle
36. Sagittal Diameter of the Clavicle at Midshaft	The anterio-posterior distance from the surface of the midshaft
37. Vertical Diameter of the Clavicle at Midshaft	The distance from the cranial to the caudal surface of the midshaft
38. Height of the Scapula	The direct distance from the most superior point of the cranial angle to the most inferior point on the caudal angle
39. Breadth of the Scapula	The distance from the midpoint on the dorsal border of the glenoid fossa to midway between the two ridges of the scapular spine on the vertebral border
40. Maximum Length of the Humerus	The direct distance from the most superior point on the head of the humerus to the most inferior point on the trochlea
41. Epicondylar Breadth of the Humerus	The distance of the most laterally protruding point on the lateral epicondyle from the corresponding projection of the medial epicondyle
42. Maximum Vertical Diameter of the Head of the Humerus	The direct distance between the most superior and inferior points on the border of the articular surface
43. Maximum Diameter of the Humerus at Midshaft	The maximum diameter that can be found at the humeral midshaft
44. Minimum Diameter of the Humerus at Midshaft	The minimum diameter that can be found at the humeral midshaft
45. Maximum Length of the Radius	The distance from the most proximally positioned point on the head of the radius to the tip of the styloid process without regard to the long axis of the bone
46. Sagittal Diameter of the Radius at Midshaft	The anterio-posterior diameter of the midshaft
47. Transverse Diameter of the Radius at Midshaft	The distance between the maximum medial and lateral bone surfaces at the midshaft
48. Maximum Length of the Ulna	The distance between the most superior point on the olecranon and the most inferior point on the styloid process
49. Dorso-Volar Diameter of the Ulna	The maximum diameter of the diaphysis where the crest exhibits the greatest development
50. Transverse Diameter of the Ulna	The diameter measured perpendicular to the Dorso-Volar diameter at the level of greatest crest development
51. Physiological Length of the Ulna	The distance between the deepest point on the surface of the coronoid process and the lowest point on the inferior surface of the distal head of the ulna

Continued

Table 3.3 Measurements of the postcranial skeleton—cont'd

Measurement	Definition
52. Minimum Circumference of the Ulna	The least circumference near the distal end of the bone
53. Anterior Height of the Sacrum	The distance from a point on the promontory in the mid-sagittal plane to a point on the anterior border of the tip of the sacrum measured in the mid-sagittal plane
54. Anterior Breadth of the Sacrum	The maximum transverse breadth of the sacrum at the level of the anterior projection of the auricular surfaces
55. Transverse Diameter of the Sacral Segment 1	The distance between the two most lateral points on the superior articular surface measured perpendicular to the mid-sagittal plane
56. Height of the Innominate	The distance from the most superior point on the iliac crest to the most inferior point on the ischial tuberosity
57. Iliac Breadth	The distance from the anterior superior iliac spine to the posterior superior iliac spine
58. Pubis Length	This distance from the point in the acetabulum where the three elements of the innominate meet to the upper end of the pubic symphysis
59. Ischium Length	The distance from the point in the acetabulum where the three elements forming the innominate meet to the deepest point on the ischial tuberosity
60. Maximum Length of the Femur	The distance from the most superior point on the head of the femur to the most inferior point on the distal condyles, located by raising the bone up and down and shifting sideways until the maximum length is obtained
61. Bicondylar Length of the Femur	The distance from the most superior point on the head of the femur to a plane drawn along the inferior surfaces of the distal condyles
62. Epicondylar Breadth of the Femur	The distance between the two most laterally projecting points on the epicondyles
63. Maximum Diameter of the Femoral Head	The maximum diameter of the femur head measured on the border of the articular surface
64. Anterio-posterior Subtrochantic Diameter of the Femur	The anterio-posterior diameter of the proximal end of the diaphysis measured perpendicular to the transverse diameter at the point of the greatest lateral expansion of the femur below the lesser trochanter
65. Transverse Subtrochanteric Diameter of the Femur	The transverse diameter of the proximal portion of the diaphysis at the point of its greatest lateral expansion below the base of the lesser trochanter
66. Anterio-posterior Diameter of the Femur at Midshaft	The anterio-posterior diameter measured approximately at the midpoint of the diaphysis, at the highest elevation of the linea aspera

Table 3.3 Measurements of the postcranial skeleton—cont'd

Measurement	Definition
67. Transverse Diameter of the Femur at Midshaft	The distance between the medial and lateral margins of the femur from one another measured perpendicular to and at the same level as the sagittal diameter
68. Circumference of the Femur at Midshaft	The circumference measured at the midshaft at the same level of the sagittal and transverse diameters
69. Length of the Tibia	The distance from the superior articular surface of the lateral condyle of the tibia to the tip of the medial malleolus
70. Maximum Epiphyseal Breadth of the Proximal Tibia	The maximum distance between the two most laterally projecting points on the medial and lateral condyles of the proximal epiphysis
71. Epiphyseal Breadth of the Distal Tibia	The distance between the most medial point on the medial malleolus and the lateral surface of the distal epiphysis
72. Maximum Diameter of the Tibia at the Nutrient Foramen	The maximum distance between the anterior crest and the posterior surface at the level of the nutrient foramen
73. Transverse Diameter of the Tibia at the Nutrient Foramen	The straight line distance from the medial margin to the interosseous crest, perpendicular to # 72
74. Circumference of the Tibia at the Nutrient Foramen	The circumference measured at the level of the nutrient foramen
75. Maximum Length of the Fibula	The maximum distance between the most superior point on the fibular head and the most inferior point on the lateral malleolus
76. Maximum Diameter of the Fibula at Midshaft	The maximum diameter at the midshaft
77. Maximum Length of the Calcaneus	The distance between the most posteriorly projecting point on the tuberosity and the most anterior point on the superior margin of the articular facet for the cuboid measured in the sagittal plane and projected onto the underlying surface
78. Middle Breadth of the Calcaneus	The distance between the most laterally projecting point on the dorsal articular facet and the most medial point on the sustentaculum tali

(Modified from Moore-Jansen et al., 1994)

Discriminant function analysis is a statistical approach that is used to predict group membership based on a set of variables. In forensic anthropology, this type of analysis is often used to estimate ancestry and sex based on a series of cranial and post-cranial measurements. Discriminant function analysis proceeds by inserting the appropriate measurements into discriminant function equations, and assessing where the resulting calculation falls with respect to various sectioning points which are developed

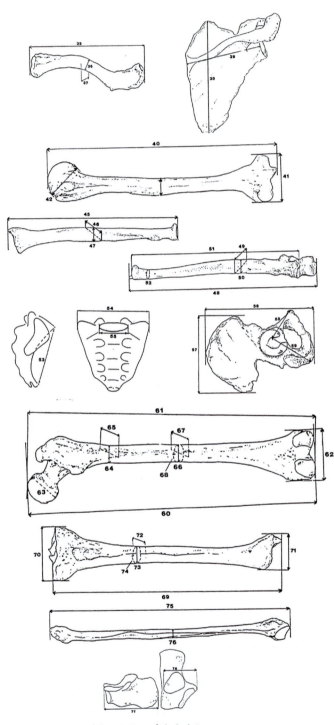

FIGURE 3.5 Measurements of the postcranial skeleton

(From Moore-Jansen et al., 1994)

Table 3.4 Basic statistical terms

Term	Definition
	Measures of Central Tendency
Mean	The arithmetic average of all values
Median	A numerical value that separates the lower half from the upper half of the distribution; for an odd number of values, it is the middle value; for an even number of values, it is the mean of the two middle values
Mode	The most common value represented in a data set
	Measures of Variation
Variance	A measure of the spread of values in a data set
Standard Deviation	A measure of how much variation exists in a range of values, expressed in the same unit of measurement as the mean
Range	The difference between the highest and lowest value of a given set of values
Standard Error	The standard deviation of a distribution of samples, used to measure uncertainty of the true population mean and standard deviation
	Measures of Sources of Error
Error	The difference between an estimated quantity and its true value
Precision	The degree of accuracy with which a parameter is estimated by an estimator, usually measured by the standard deviation of the estimator and known as the standard error
Reliability	The ability to obtain the same result using the same methods and instrument
Validity	The degree to which an observation or result reflects empirical reality
Bias	A systematic (not random) deviation from the true value

based on a reference sample of individuals of known sex and ancestry. Discriminant function analyses were first used in forensic anthropology in the 1960s (Giles, 1964; Giles and Elliot, 1962; Hanihara et al., 1964). These early applications involved a degree of manual calculation and required a certain suite of measurements to be used, which required that all of the necessary landmarks were present in the skeletal remains.

In the 1990s, the procedure for performing discriminant function analysis was considerably simplified and statistically augmented by the development of Fordisc Personal Computer Forensic Discriminant Functions (or more commonly, simply "Fordisc"), an interactive computer program that calculates custom discriminant function analyses (Jantz and Ousley, 2005). Fordisc is built on a large database of individuals of known sex and ancestry including the Howells data set (Howells, 1973; Howells, 1989) and a growing Forensic Anthropology Data Bank (Jantz and Moore-Jansen, 1988) (see Box 3.1). Unlike previous discriminant function approaches, Fordisc performs automated (as opposed to manual) calculations, and can provide classifications based on any combination of standard measurements (as opposed to needing certain measurements to be available). The standard measurements described in the previous tables and figures are included in (and can be contributed to) Fordisc

---

BOX 3.1 THE FORENSIC ANTHROPOLOGY DATA BANK (FDB)

Many forensic anthropological methods are based on studies of known reference material (i.e., skeletons of individuals of known sex, age, stature, and ancestry). Most skeletal collections available for study (at least within the United States) are composed largely of individuals born in the 19th century. These older skeletal collections may not be the most appropriate reference sample for modern forensic casework, however, since they may not resemble modern populations due to **secular changes** in size, morphology, and proportions.

The Forensic Anthropology Data Bank (FDB) was developed in 1986 due largely to the efforts of Dr. Richard Jantz with the assistance of the National Institute of Justice, as a repository of data collected from contemporary known skeletons. Today, data is contributed by forensic anthropology practitioners, and has grown to include skeletal information on more than 3400 individuals. The skeletal information submitted for cases includes cranial and postcranial measurements, scores for various aging methods, non-metric cranial information, details of trauma, congenital traits, and dental observations. In some cases, the FDB also contains demographic information such as place of birth, medical history, occupation, stature, and weight (Ousley and Jantz, 1998).

---

and the Forensic Anthropology Data Bank – another reason that collecting this information in casework is recommended. It is important to note that while Fordisc will always provide a classification, there is significant responsibility on the user. The data must be properly collected and entered, the program must be properly run, and the results must be properly interpreted.

When using Fordisc, the available measurements are recorded and entered into an electronic form, and then a series of skeletal populations to be included in the discriminant function analysis is selected (Ousley and Jantz, 2012) (Figure 3.6). After selecting the "Process" button, Fordisc uses linear discriminant function analysis to classify group membership by maximizing between-group differences using the sum of the numerical weights (i.e., factor) calculated for each measurement (Ousley and Jantz, 2012). These factors enable the classification of unknown skeletons, provided that the unknown individual belongs to a group represented in the reference samples. This is an important point, because Fordisc will always classify the measurements of the skeleton into the closest selected group, even if the individual belongs to a group that is not selected (or may not even exist within the reference database). Interpretation of the results is therefore critical and is described in the following in more detail.

Fordisc uses **Mahalanobis's D^2**, a multivariate measure of the difference between groups, to measure the average differences between groups for each analysis. Fordisc's output provides the D^2 values (labeled as "Distance from") for the unknown set of measurements relative to all groups used in the analysis, with the smallest D^2 value representing the group most similar to the measurements of the unknown skeleton (Figure 3.7). The unknown individual will always be classified into the population with the smallest Mahalanobis distance. In some instances, a few of the selected populations will have very similar Mahalanobis distances, requiring close examination by the analyst to interpret the results.

Next in the output is the **posterior probability** value, which provides a measure of the *relative* distance of the unknown skeleton to each group, compared to the other

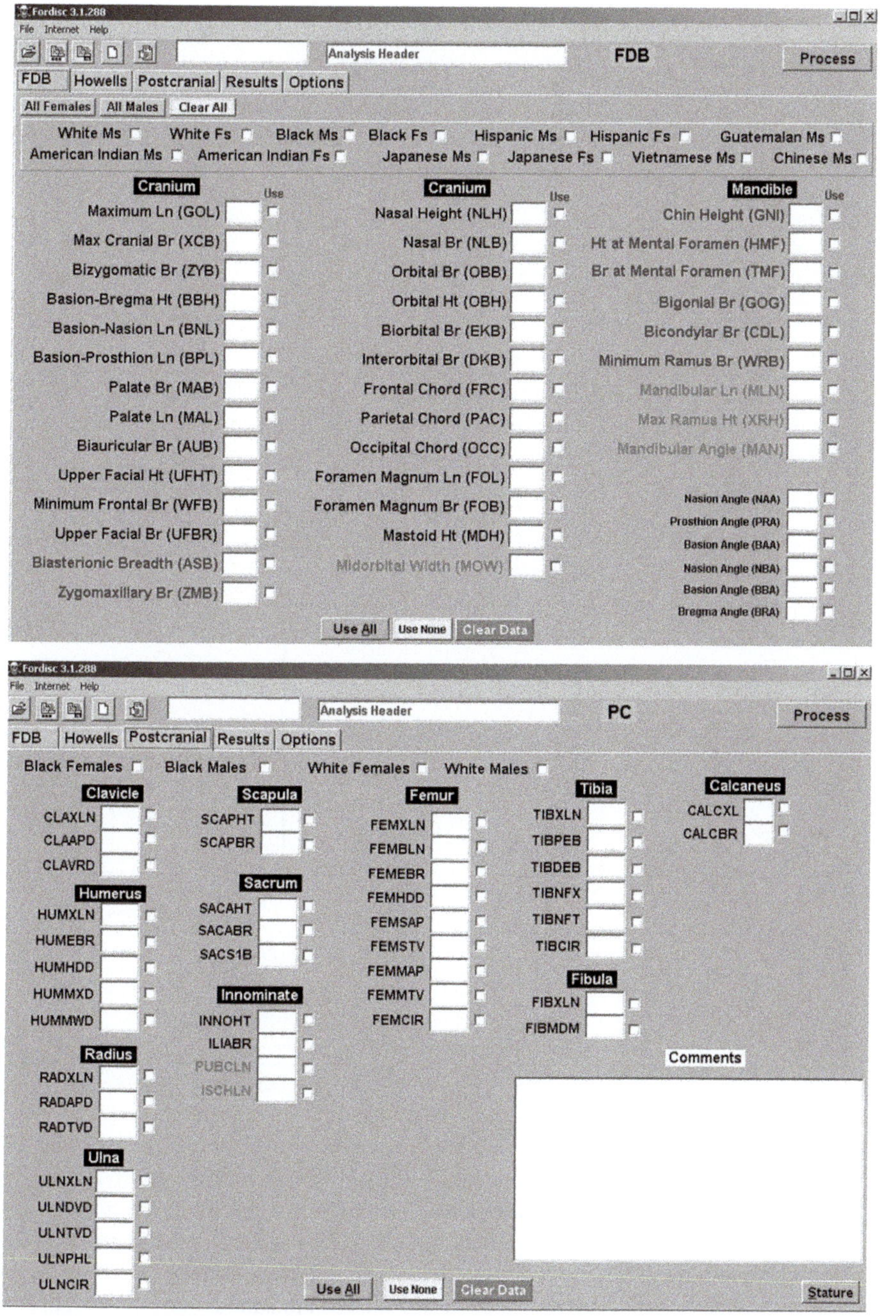

FIGURE 3.6 Fordisc electronic forms

(Jantz and Ousley, 2005)

Multigroup Classification of Current Case

Group	Classified into	Distance from	Probabilities Posterior	Typ F	Typ Chi	Typ R
WF	**WF**	5.5	0.990	0.915	0.905	0.851 (38/249)
AF		15.9	0.005	0.497	0.144	0.226 (25/31)
HF		17.7	0.002	0.230	0.089	0.123 (51/57)
BF		18.4	0.002	0.161	0.072	0.143 (67/77)
JF		19.3	0.001	0.160	0.056	0.063 (60/63)

Current Case is closest to WFs

FIGURE 3.7 Fordisc ancestry results for a white female skull

Note that the posterior probability of 0.990 indicates that the skull is more similar to White Females than any of the other groups selected, and the typicality of 0.915 indicates that the skull is highly typical of other White Female skulls.

(Ousley and Jantz, 2005)

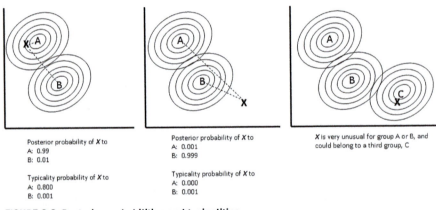

FIGURE 3.8 Posterior probabilities and typicalities

(Adapted from Ousley and Jantz, 2012)

groups selected for comparison. Note that all posterior probabilities will always sum to 1.0 (with the probabilities ranked from highest to lowest for each group included in the analysis), and that the unknown skeleton is assumed to belong to one of the groups selected. Groups with posterior probabilities less than 0.1 can usually be excluded. After posterior probability is the **typicality** value (labeled as "Typ F"), which is a measure of the *absolute* distance of the unknown skeleton to each group centroid, or how "typical" the skeleton is of each group (Figure 3.8). High typicality values suggest that the skeleton is similar to the other skeletons in that reference group, while low values suggest that it is atypical. Groups with typicality probabilities less than 0.01 can

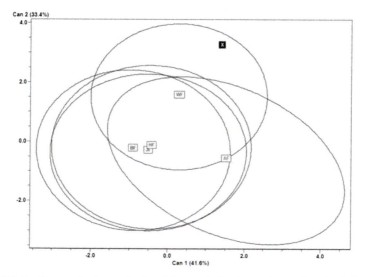

FIGURE 3.9 Fordisc graph of canonical variates analysis of an unknown female skull

Note the X is the unknown individual, which falls within the ellipse of the White Female (WF) group and outside of the ellipses for the other selected groups.

(Jantz and Ousley, 2005)

usually be excluded. Fordisc also generates two- and three-dimensional graphical representations of the results, which can assist the analyst in interpretation (Figure 3.9).

Fordisc analyses can be run initially by choosing to include all measurements and all groups. Fordisc will notify the user if any measurements seem especially atypical (too large or too small), which may be the result of measurement or recording errors that can be caught and fixed early in the analysis.

Analyses should be repeated, typically eliminating groups with posterior probabilities of less than 0.1 and typicality probabilities of less than 0.01. Analyses ideally result in two to four remaining classification groups. The user should also ensure that all selected populations have large enough samples based on the number of variables selected. If the sample sizes are too small, a large number of variables will overfit the model, resulting in potential misclassifications. A general rule is to have one variable (measurement) for every three individuals in the smallest population; for example, in an analysis with multiple populations where the smallest population has a sample size of 45, the maximum amount of variables should be 15. Overfitting can be avoided using stepwise variable selection (available under "Options") and/or by removing measurements.

Fordisc's primary reference samples are based on modern human skeletons and thus are not appropriate for classifying archaeological material (Ousley et al., 2009). Fordisc does, however, include W.W. Howells' craniometric database, consisting of measurements of historic and prehistoric crania from various parts of the world (Ousley and Jantz, 2012). This may be applicable for comparisons with historic or

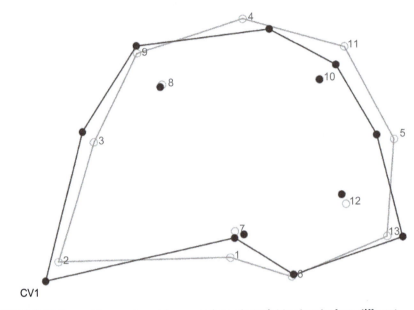

FIGURE 3.10 Geometric morphometric comparison of cranial landmarks from different populations

(Image courtesy of Kate Spradley)

prehistoric skulls for remains which may be of questionable medicolegal significance, but should be used cautiously due to the large number of groups represented. Specific applications of Fordisc can be found in this text in the chapters on sex estimation (Chapter 8), ancestry estimation (Chapter 9), and stature estimation (Chapter 11).

Geometric morphometrics (GM) is an approach involving the multivariate (multiple-variable) statistical analysis of **Cartesian** coordinate data using landmark point locations, and is becoming widely used in forensic anthropology (Slice, 2007). This type of analysis preserves information about the relative spatial arrangement of data points such as cranial landmarks, allowing for visualization of group and individual differences (see Figure 3.10). Typically, GM data are collected using a digitizer, which records three-dimensional point data (i.e., an x-, y- and z-coordinate for each point), usually from a defined skeletal landmark (e.g., bregma, prosthion, basion, etc.). This data can then be used to analyze linear distances between the landmarks or overall shapes. While currently used primarily in research applications in the study of group and individual differences (e.g., Kimmerle et al., 2008), it may also be used as an analytical tool in forensic casework.

Radiology

Radiology is the study of high-energy radiation used to examine and diagnose internal structures. The process of using radiology to make images is called **radiography.**

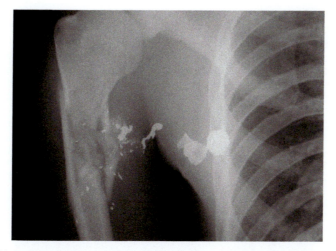

FIGURE 3.11 Radiograph showing fractured humerus and projectile fragments

(Image courtesy of B.G. Brogdon, M.D.)

Radiography in forensic anthropology is useful for documentation as well as detection and diagnostic applications. It can be used to produce a record of the condition of the remains at the time of examination, detect the presence of foreign material such as a bullet (Figure 3.11), and visualize internal skeletal structures that are not visible to the naked eye such as paranasal sinuses or developing dentition. It can also be used to diagnose conditions such as antemortem fractures or pathological conditions, or to see the placement of surgical implants.

Taking and examining radiographs requires some knowledge of the relative **radiodensities** of various materials. Keeping thickness as well as other technical parameters constant, the radiographic appearance of materials will vary as a function of their **attenuation** properties. This explains, for example, why it is possible to detect foreign material such as projectiles within bone using radiography – bullet lead attenuates more X-rays (i.e., it is more radiopaque) than bone, making it appear distinct from bone (which attenuates more X-rays than soft tissues but less than lead) in a radiograph.

The radiographic investigation of human remains began soon after the discovery of X-rays (see Box 3.2) as investigators came to realize that X-rays provided a nondestructive means of examining human remains. Today, the value of radiography is well established in criminal and medicolegal work, and it is considered to be a standard component of most forensic anthropological analyses. One advantage of radiography in the analysis of skeletal remains is that because there is no concern regarding health hazards of the decedent due to X-ray exposure, skeletal remains can be radiographed numerous times and using varying parameters that would probably be considered unhealthy for live individuals. Not all forensic anthropologists have received formal training in radiology or the use of radiographic equipment, however,

BOX 3.2 DISCOVERY OF X-RAYS

On Friday afternoon, November 8, 1895, the German physicist Wilhelm Conrad Roentgen, working in his Worzburg physics laboratory, made a serendipitous and monumental discovery. When he filled a vacuum tube with a special gas and passed electric voltage through it, it produced a fluorescent glow, and Roentgen realized that a previously unknown ray (termed X-ray) was being emitted from the tube (Roentgen, 1895; English translation in Pais, 1986). Roentgen also reported that the materials containing atoms with a high atomic number (Z), notably lead, attenuated these rays much more readily than atoms with few protons in the nucleus such as hydrogen and many other atoms in soft tissues. One of the first medical photographs (the first roentgenogram or radiograph) is of the hand of Roentgen's wife, made on December 22, 1895. As usual, she was wearing her wedding ring, and its image showed up clearly on the radiograph (see photo: Wilhelm Roentgen ca. 1895, and inset, radiograph of Frau Roentgen's hand). For his discovery of X-rays, Roentgen received the first Nobel Prize in physics in 1901.

(Image from http://www.xtal.iqfr.csic.es/Cristalografia/parte_02-en.html, accessed August, 2012)

so collaboration with a radiologist or technician with experience in this area may be required. Although radiography units can be expensive, they have become commonplace in hospitals, morgues, and crime labs, and are therefore often accessible to a forensic anthropologist.

Histology

Histology is the study of the microscopic structure of tissues. A histological analysis of skeletal material can be used in forensic anthropological examinations to determine whether unknown material is bone, and whether or not the bone can be excluded as being human in origin (see Chapter 4). It can also be used in the assessment of skeletal age on the basis of bone remodeling (see Chapter 10). In addition, it can be useful in the diagnosis of disease or recognizing the early stages of bone healing (Barbian and Sledzik, 2008; Schenk, 2003) (see Chapter 13).

Histological analysis requires some specialized equipment and training which may not be available in all forensic anthropology laboratories. In order to observe the microscopic structures of osseous tissue, the bone must be prepared as thin sections (50–100 **micrometers** thick). This is typically accomplished by cutting sections of the bone into ~1 mm wafers using a sectioning saw, and then grinding and polishing the wafer until it is suitably thin for microscopic examination (which means that it must transmit light, and that there ideally are few if any overlapping structures). In some cases, particularly if bone fragments are very small or taphonomically compromised (e.g., burned, ancient, or highly weathered), the bone may need to be embedded in resin to stabilize it during cutting. This requires additional supplies, such as the chemicals needed to prepare the resin as well as a vacuum pump to ensure that the resin completely penetrates the bone sample and that all air bubbles are removed.

The thin section is then mounted on a glass microscope slide and examined using **light microscopy**, sometimes with the aid of tissue staining and/or polarized light. Using this approach, the microstructure of the bone can be visualized, imaged, measured, and interpreted. Because histological examination is a destructive process, it should only be used when necessary and should follow thorough macroscopic and other non-destructive analyses.

Elemental analysis

Elemental analysis is the analysis of a material for its elemental or isotopic composition. In anthropological examinations, elemental analysis is useful in two particular areas. First, it may be used in the determination of whether a material is bone or some other material (see Chapter 4) based on whether or not it contains bone's signature levels of calcium and phosphorus. This approach is especially useful when pieces of unknown (but suspected to be skeletal) material are very fragmented and/or taphonomically compromised (Christensen et al., 2012). This technique may also be used to determine whether bone (especially cremated bone) is mixed or contaminated with other material (Gilpin, 2013).

Elemental analysis may also be used in stable isotopic profiling of human tissues such as bones, teeth, hair, and fingernails as a means of identifying an individual's likely dietary or residence pattern based on food and water consumed. **Isotopes** are variants of an element which share the same number of protons, but differ in the number of neutrons. *Stable isotopes* are those isotopes which do not spontaneously decay over time (as compared to *radioactive isotopes*, which decay into other forms over time). Organisms incorporate different relative abundances of stable isotopes (e.g., $^{13}C/^{12}C$) into their tissues from food and drink consumed during life. In certain

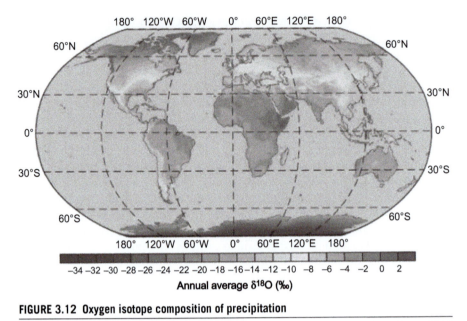

FIGURE 3.12 Oxygen isotope composition of precipitation

(From Bowen, 2010)

cases, stable isotope analysis can provide information on dietary patterns, such as whether an individual was vegan or had a diet that was high in corn (because corn is a plant that is enriched in the heavy isotope ^{13}C).

More importantly, stable isotope analysis, especially of incremental tissues such as teeth, hair, and nails, can be used to track an individual's migration history and residence patterns based on signatures that reflect a particular drinking water source or geological region where food is grown (Meier-Augenstein, 2006, 2010; Bartelink et al., 2013). Figure 3.12 shows the geographic oxygen isotope composition of precipitation which represents oxygen isotopes present in water that is ingested. Comparison of the oxygen isotope profile of an individual's tissues to this known distribution can suggest previous patterns of residence. For example, oxygen isotope values in teeth record the drinking water source at the time of tooth formation, whereas hair and nails provide a more recent record. This information can be particularly useful in cases where a body is recovered a significant distance from where the individual last resided.

Elemental analysis requires the use of specialized equipment such as scanning electron microscopy/energy dispersive spectroscopy (SEM/EDS), X-ray fluorescence spectrometry (XRF), or X-ray diffraction (XRD) (Figure 3.13). These instruments are quite expensive and require extensive training, and therefore elemental analysis is only performed in a few anthropology laboratories. This equipment, however, is generally available in analytical chemistry and biology laboratories, as well as in many major crime laboratories.

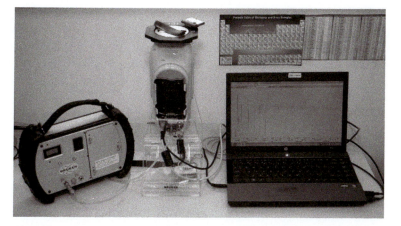

FIGURE 3.13 X-ray fluorescence spectrometer being used to analyze a possible bone fragment

(Image courtesy of Thomas Lera, Smithsonian National Postal Museum)

3.2 Skeletal remains as evidence

When analyzing forensic skeletal material, it is important to remember that the skeleton represents **evidence**. The results of the analysis may be used to make legal determinations such as identity and cause of death, or possibly convict a perpetrator of a crime. Skeletal remains therefore need to be handled, stored, and tracked in a way that protects them from loss, contamination, or damage. All skeletal material should be labeled with a unique item number, often on the skeletal elements themselves using a waterproof indelible marker. In some cases (due to bone surface preservation or characteristics), it may be necessary to treat the bone surface with another material or substance (such as a thin layer of adhesive) prior to labeling so that the label can be seen and read. This labeling system should be tied to the case documentation, and will facilitate evidence tracking as well as help with certain parts of the anthropological examination process, such as inventory and estimation of the number of individuals present (Chapter 7).

The forensic anthropology laboratory should have and follow documented **standard operating procedures**, or SOPs. These procedures should detail standard laboratory practices for evidence examination as well as describe how to document the chain-of-custody of evidence and provide guidelines for the proper handling of skeletal material. If remains will be stored over the long term or curated (such as in museums), other considerations should include the storage conditions and storage medium (see Chapter 7). It is important that all laboratory staff, including students and interns, follow these laboratory procedures to ensure the integrity of the evidence (Warren et al., 2008).

Anthropological examinations also involve potential exposure to safety concerns, including biological hazards associated with working with human remains, physical hazards associated with equipment such as saws and scalpels, radiological hazards associated with X-rays, and chemical hazards associated with certain examinations (such as histological or isotopic sample preparation). When working with human remains, anthropologists should follow **universal precautions** and wear at least a laboratory coat and protective gloves, and they should adopt all safety precautions associated with examination equipment and materials.

Quality assurance

Forensic anthropology practitioners (whether they are associated with a large laboratory, medical examiner's office, or university) should have a quality assurance system (SWGANTH, Laboratory Management and Quality Assurance, 2011). **Quality assurance** refers to planned and systematic actions necessary to provide adequate confidence that an entity will fulfill requirements for quality (International Organization for Standardization, 2005). In other words, quality assurance involves taking proactive steps to ensure the consistency and quality of the product – in this case, of forensic anthropological examination results. Quality assurance typically includes measures that ensure the safety of personnel, adherence to SOPs, maintenance of equipment, evidence security, and maintenance of practitioner ability and skill.

Many laboratories demonstrate meeting professional and regulatory standards by seeking **accreditation**. There are various accrediting bodies and guidelines that exist to promote and ensure the quality of evidence and of the conclusions reached from the examination of that evidence. For crime laboratories, accrediting bodies currently include the American Society of Crime Laboratory Directors/Laboratory Accreditation Board (ASCLD/LAB), Forensic Quality Services (FQS), and the American Association for Laboratory Accreditation (A2LA). No organization currently offers accreditation in the discipline of forensic anthropology, though as of the time of this writing, this is currently being discussed among the forensic anthropological community and accreditation providers. Forensic anthropology laboratories wishing to seek accreditation can apply under an alternative discipline (such as trace evidence or crime scene investigation).

Case documentation

Case documentation typically includes notes, maps and diagrams, and images, and should be prepared in a manner conducive to authentication, verification, and traceability (SWGANTH, Documentation, Reporting and Testimony, 2012). Case notes should accurately describe the entire evidence analysis process, and should document all techniques used including citations for references and methods used, as well as instruments and their parameters and settings. Calculations should be included in the notes as well as all significant observations leading to and supporting the report's conclusions. This may include the methods and standards used, a selected phase, or category based on observations, estimations, statistical results, and any other supporting data.

Images may include photography, radiography, or instrument data output such as charts or graphs. At a minimum, skeletal remains should be photographed prior to any alteration (including processing or destructive analyses) to record the initial

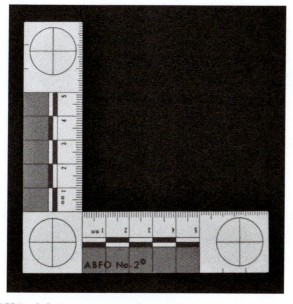

FIGURE 3.14 ABFO No.2 © photomacrographic scale

(Image courtesy of JPAC/CIL)

condition of the remains, and to document evidence of trauma or features that may be useful for identification. Thorough photo-documentation is also useful in recollecting details about a case that may be forgotten if, for example, a case goes to trial many years after the examination was performed.

Photographs should include a scale, preferably a photomacrographic scale, such as the American Board of Forensic Odontology (ABFO) No. 2 © photomacrographic scale (see Figure 3.14) that includes circles which are useful in identifying and compensating for distortion that results from taking photographs at oblique angles. When possible, the camera should be directed perpendicular to the subject or target area of the photograph. A contrasting background helps to enhance the images, and for bones, a backing of black fabric usually works quite well. Radiopaque rulers are available for inclusion in radiographs. Since it is not always possible to discern side from a radiograph, radiographs should also include a radiopaque marker indicating side (typically an "L" or "R" marker placed on the left or right side) (see Figure 3.15).

The selection of the photographs needed to document a case will vary depending on a number of factors, but there are some views which are considered standard. For example, the skull should ideally be photographed from six views in order to document it completely: anterior, posterior, superior, inferior, and left and right lateral views. An overall view of the available skeletal elements in roughly anatomical position is also useful. Individual bones or regions should be photographed close-up in order to document specific features or observations such as trauma.

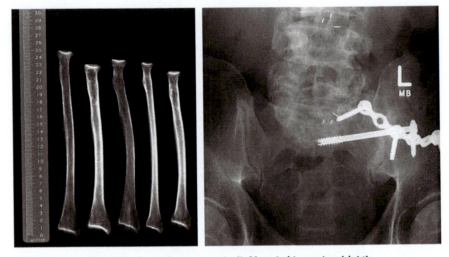

FIGURE 3.15 Radiograph with radiopaque scale (left) and side marker (right)

(Left image courtesy of JPAC/CIL; right image from Christensen and Anderson, 2013)

Reporting and report writing

While it is recognized that forensic anthropologists may have varying needs and constraints based on the laboratory in which they work, as well as different writing and reporting styles, an anthropological report should contain certain basic components such as the name and address of the laboratory where the work was performed, a case identification number, and the name and signature of the person who performed the work. The report should contain the examination results in an organized and clearly-stated fashion, keeping the audience (often law enforcement) in mind. Reports should also contain information regarding the strength of conclusions or possible limitations where applicable. For example, if a significance level or a confidence interval can be calculated (such as with Fordisc results or regression methods for stature estimation), these should be included in the report. If a comparison is made (such as between an antemortem and postmortem record), the strength of the association or "match" between the two records should also be communicated in the report. In some cases, this may be quantitative (such as if population frequencies are known), while in other cases it may be more qualitative (see Chapter 14). If appropriate, the report should also note whether results were inconclusive.

When an examination is performed and a report is issued, it is possible that a forensic anthropologist may be called to testify in court regarding his or her results and/or his or her role in the analysis. Testifying is relatively rare for most forensic anthropologists, particularly those who are primarily employed by higher learning institutions and only occasionally consult on cases. The infrequency of testifying is also due in part to the fact that many forensic anthropological reports are biological profiles that provide lead information for investigators, and such information is rarely if ever the subject of a trial. Most courtroom testimony by forensic anthropologists focuses on trauma, recovery and scene investigation, and estimation of the postmortem interval (Murray and Anderson, 2007). Court testimony will be based on the findings and wording used in the final forensic anthropology report. Caution must be used in testimony to avoid speculation or claims which cannot be justified by the evidence available.

3.3 **Case studies**

While it is recognized that individuals will have different writing styles and organizations will have different reporting requirements, the following two samples represent examples of anthropological reports.

Skeletons, Inc. Forensic Anthropology Laboratory
123 Osteon Drive
Biomechanicsburg, VA 12345
777-555-4321

FORENSIC ANTHROPOLOGY REPORT

Case Number: 999-55444

12 June 2013

To: Sheriff John Johnson
        456 Main Street
        Springfield, CA 67890

Examination Results

A small fragment of suspected human bone was submitted to the laboratory on 1 June 2013. The item was examined visually and using low-powered microscopy, but no features or characteristics indicative of origin were observed.

The item was examined using X-ray fluorescence spectrometry (XRF). Results indicate levels of calcium and phosphorus consistent with skeletal tissue.

The item was then sectioned for histological analysis and examined using polarized light microscopy. The results indicate the presence of plexiform bone which is inconsistent with the microstructure of human bone.

Human origin can therefore be excluded for this item.

If you have any questions about the content of this report, please contact me at 777-555-4321.

Oz Teology
Oz Teology, PhD, D-ABFA
Forensic Anthropologist

Skeletons, Inc. Forensic Anthropology Laboratory
123 Osteon Drive
Biomechanicsburg, VA 12345
777-555-4321

FORENSIC ANTHROPOLOGY REPORT

Case Number: 999-55777

29 July 2013

To: Mr. David Davidson
      100 First Street
      Newtown, IL 90123

Examination Results

Skeletal remains suspected to be those of Sally Smith were submitted to the laboratory on 30 June 2013. Specifically, the skeletal items consist of the following elements:

Cranium	Left *os coxa*
Mandible	Right *os coxa*
Right femur	Sacrum
Left tibia	Left clavicle
Left fibula	Right clavicle
Left humerus	Right scapula
Right humerus	

Prior to analysis, the skeletal remains were cleaned with soft bristle brushes and cold water to remove adhering sediment.

Minimum Number of Individuals

One. The remains are consistent in anatomical representation, taphonomic features, and biological indicators with originating from one (1) individual.

Sex

Female. Morphoscopic analysis of the left and right *os coxae* following the criteria of Phenice (1979) indicate that the remains are most likely those of a female.

Ancestry

European (White). Metric analysis of the cranium using Fordisc 3.0 (Jantz and Ousley 2005) indicates the measurements of the remains most closely resemble those of individuals of White ancestry using a three group comparison of White Females, Black Females and Hispanic Females (posterior probability of WF 0.925, BF 0.050, HF 0.025).

Age

24-29 years. Skeletal development, specifically the complete fusion of the epiphyses of the long bones with incomplete fusion of the epiphysis of the clavicle, indicates an age 24-29 years (McKern and Stewart, 1957).

Stature

5'1"-5'9". Metric analysis of the maximum length of the right femur (448 mm) using Fordisc 3.0 for White females (95% confidence interval) results in an estimate of 65.1 +/- 4 inches.

Trauma and Other Alterations

No evidence of antemortem or perimortem trauma was noted. Many of the skeletal elements present display pitting and scoring consistent with postmortem carnivore scavenging.

Identification Comparison

This biological profile is consist with that of Sally Smith, reported to be a female of European ancestry, 28 years of age, with a height of 5'4". If antemortem records of Smith (such as radiographic medical or dental records) become available for comparison, these may be helpful in confirming whether the remains are those of Sally Smith.

If you have any questions about the content of this report, please contact me at 777-555-4321.

Oz Teology

Oz Teology, PhD, D-ABFA
Forensic Anthropologist

3.4 Summary

- A variety of methods are used in skeletal analysis, including macroscopic (visual) observation, metric analysis, radiography, histology, and elemental analyses. The most appropriate method selected for a particular case depends on a number of factors including what is being asked and the type and amount of material present.
- In most cases, metric analysis and instrumental methods are more objective and more easily quantified than macroscopic methods.
- Statistical analysis forms the basis of many interpretations in forensic anthropology, including the biological profile and personal identification. Measures of central tendency and variation form the foundation of skeletal estimations based on metric data.
- Modern human skeletal samples, such as those represented in the Forensic Anthropology DataBank, are essential for forensic casework. Changes in size, morphology, and proportions over time make it important to use modern reference samples when possible.
- Radiography is useful as a method of documentation, and is an essential tool for the analysis of trauma and pathology, and for assessing features that are useful for personal identification.
- Skeletal remains represent evidence, and should be handled, stored, and analyzed in a way that maintains the integrity of the evidence. Quality assurance measures can help ensure the consistency and quality of the examination process.
- Conclusions stated in reports and provided as testimony in court should be organized and clear, and avoid speculation that is not supported by the evidence.

3.5 Test yourself

- Discuss some of the advantages and disadvantages of macroscopic versus metric analysis. When should specialized destructive methods such as histology or elemental analysis be used? If you needed to perform destructive analysis, how would you justify this to law enforcement?
- Why is it important to have modern documented human skeletal collections available for study? How would using data from earlier collections possibly affect your results?
- What information can be discovered through the use of radiography? How might this information be used in a court trial?
- Why should forensic scientists avoid speculation in their reports and when testifying in court? Can you think of an example of a speculative statement that would be difficult to support scientifically?
- What is the purpose of accreditation and why is it important?
- Why is the chain-of-custody of evidence important? If you were a defense attorney cross-examining a forensic anthropologist, what questions would you ask about his or her laboratory's operating procedures?

Definitions

Accreditation A process (usually voluntary) of displaying competency and credibility, usually in testing laboratory practices

Assessment An evaluation based on the nature or quality of something that is not amenable to the calculation of classification rates or statistical analysis

Attenuation The reduction in energy of a beam of radiation when passed through a material

Cartesian A coordinate system that specifies the position of a point in space

Craniometric landmarks Osteometric landmarks applied to the skull

Discriminant function analysis A statistical analysis used to predict category or group membership

Elemental analysis The process of analyzing a material for its elemental and sometimes isotopic composition

Estimate An evaluation based on value or quantity which can be used to calculate classification rates or perform statistical analysis, usually involving the use of metrics or quantifiable traits

Evidence Facts or information that indicate whether a particular hypothesis or proposition is true; in the legal sense, information that bears on the truth or falsity of an assertion made in litigation

Grave Goods Artifacts placed with a decedent's remains by other individuals

Histology The study of the microscopic structure of tissues

Isotope A variant of an element which shares the same number of protons, but differs in the number of neutrons; radioactive isotopes spontaneously decay over time while stable isotopes do not

Light (or optical) microscopy The use of microscopes and transmitted light to observe structures that cannot be seen with the naked eye

Macroscopic Of a size that is measurable, assessable, or visible with the naked eye

Mahalanobis D^2 A multivariate measure of the difference between groups

Micrometer (or micron, μm) One millionth of a meter (1×10^{-6} m); or one thousandth of a millimeter (0.0001 mm)

Morphoscopic Trait Traits that are assessed based on presence or absence, degree of expression, or overall morphology

Non-metric trait Dichotomous, discontinuous, epigenetic skeletal variant that can be classified as present or absent (also called discrete trait)

Osteometric landmarks A standardized set of skeletal locations from which measurements are taken

Osteometrics The practice of recording and analyzing skeletal measurements

Personal Effects Artifacts that belonged to an individual in life and are found with the decedent's remains

Posterior probability In Fordisc, a measure of the *relative* similarity of an unknown skeleton to the groups selected for comparison

Quality assurance Planned and systematic actions necessary to provide adequate confidence that an entity will fulfill requirements for quality; taking proactive steps to ensure the consistency and quality of the product

Radiodensity The relative ability of substances to resist the passage of radiant energy; those substances that are more resistant (attenuate more) are *radiopaque* while those that are less resistant (attenuate less) are *radiolucent*

Radiography The use of radiology to make images (radiographs)

Radiology The use of high-energy radiation (such as X-rays) in the imaging, examination, and study of internal structures, and in the diagnosis and treatment of disease

Regression analysis A statistical analysis used to measure the relationship between two variables

Secular change Temporal or long term trends

Standard Operating Procedures (SOPs) A codified set of guidelines for practice

Statistics The science of collecting, organizing, and interpreting numerical data

Typicality In Fordisc, a measure of the *absolute* similarity of an unknown skeleton to the groups selected for comparison

Universal precautions The practice of avoiding contact with biological hazards (such as bodily fluids) by wearing protective attire such as gloves and goggles

References

Barbian, L.T., Sledzik, P.S., 2008. Healing following cranial trauma. J. Forensic Sci. 53, 263–268.

Bartelink, E.J., Berry, R., Chesson, L.A., 2013. Stable isotopes and human provenancing, and case review. In: Mallett, X., Blythe, T. (Eds.), Advances in Forensic Human Identification. Taylor & Francis, Boca Raton, pp. 157–184.

Bowen, G.J., 2010. Isoscapes: Spatial pattern in isotopic biogeochemistry. Annu. Rev. Earth. Planet. Sci. 38, 161–187.

Buikstra, J.E., Ubelaker, D.H., 2004. Standards for Data Collection from Human Skeletal Remains. Archaeological Survey Research Seminar Series 44, Fayetteville.

Christensen, A.M., Anderson, B.E., 2013. Personal identification. In: Tersigni-Tarrant, M.T., Shirley, N. (Eds.), Forensic Anthropology: An Introduction. CRC Press, Boca Raton, pp. 397–420.

Christensen, A.M., Smith, M.A., Thomas, R.M., 2012. Validation of X-ray fluorescence spectrometry for determining osseous or dental origin of unknown material. J. Forensic Sci. 57 (1), 6–11.

Giles, E., 1964. Sex determination by discriminant function analysis of the mandible. Am. J. Phys. Anthropol. 22 (2), 129–135.

Giles, E., Elliot, O., 1962. Race identification from cranial measurements. J. Forensic Sci. 7 (2), 147–157.

Gilpin, M., 2013. Elemental analysis of variably contaminated remains using X-ray fluorescence spectrometry [MA Thesis]. George Mason University, Fairfax.

Hanihara, K., Kimura, K., Minamidate, T., 1964. The sexing of Japanese skeleton by means of discriminant function. Nihon Hôigaku Zassi [Japanese Journal of Forensic Medicine] 18, 107–114.

Hefner, J.T., 2009. Cranial nonmetric variation and estimating ancestry. J. Forensic Sci. 54 (5), 985–995.

Hefner, J.T., Ousley, S.D., Dirkmaat, D.C., 2012. Morphoscopic traits and the assessment of ancestry. In: Dirkmaat, D.C. (Ed.), A Companion to Forensic Anthropology. Wiley-Blackwell, Chichester, pp. 287–310.

Howells, W.W., 1973. Cranial variation in man. In: Papers of the Peabody Museum. Peabody Museum of Archeology and Ethnology, vol. 67. Harvard University, Cambridge.

Howells, W.W., 1989. Skull shapes and the map. In: Papers of the Peabody Museum. Peabody Museum of Archeology and Ethnology, vol. 78. Harvard University, Cambridge.

International Organization for Standardization, 2005. General Requirements for the Competence of Testing and Calibration Laboratories. ISO/IEC 17025 2005(E). 2nd ed. [4.0].

Jantz, R.L., Moore-Jansen, P.H., 1988. A database for forensic anthropology: Structure, content and analysis. In: Report of Investigations No. 47. Department of Anthropology, University of Tennessee, Knoxville.

Jantz, R.L., Ousley, S.D., 2005. FORDISC 3.0: Personal computer forensic discriminant functions. The University of Tennessee, Knoxville.

Kimmerle, E.H., Ross, A., Slice, D., 2008. Sexual dimorphism in America: Geometric morphometric analysis of the craniofacial region. J. Forensic Sci. 53 (1), 54–57.

Meier-Augenstein, W., 2006. Stable isotope fingerprinting: chemical element "DNA." In: Thompson, T., Black, S. (Eds.), Forensic Human Identification: An Introduction. Taylor & Francis, Boca Raton, pp. 29–53.

Meier-Augenstein, W., 2010. Stable Isotope Forensics: An Introduction to the Forensic Applications of Stable Isotope Analysis. Wiley, Wiltshire.

Moore-Jansen, P.M., Ousley, S.D., Jantz, R.L., 1994. Data Collection Procedures for Forensic Skeletal Material. Report of Investigations No. 48. Department of Anthropology, University of Tennessee, Knoxville.

Murray, B.A., Anderson, B.E., 2007. Forensic anthropology in the court room: Trends in testimony. In: Proceedings of the 59th annual meeting of the American Academy of Forensic Sciences. San Antonio, TX.

Ousley, S.D., Hefner, J.T., 2005. The statistical determination of ancestry. In: Proceedings of the 57th Annual Meeting of the American Academy of Forensic Sciences; Feb 21–26. New Orleans, LA.

Ousley, S.D., Jantz, R.L., 1998. The Forensic Data Bank: Documenting skeletal trends in the United States. In: Reichs, K.J. (Ed.), Forensic Osteology: Advances in the identification of human remains. CC Thomas Press, Springfield, pp. 441–458.

Ousley, S.D., Jantz, R.L., 2012. Fordisc 3 and statistical methods for estimating sex and ancestry. In: Dirkmaat, D.C. (Ed.), A Companion to Forensic Anthropology. Wiley-Blackwell, Chichester, pp. 311–329.

Ousley, S.D., Jantz, J.T., Fried, D.L., 2009. Understanding race and human variation: Why forensic anthropologists are good at identifying race. J. Forensic Anthropol. 139 (1), 68–76.

Pais, A., 1986. Inward bound: Of matter and forces in the physical world. Clarendon Press, Oxford, pp. 37–38.

Rontgen, W.C., 1895. Uber eine neue art von strahlen. Sitzungsberichte der physikalisch-medizinischen gesellschaft zu Wiurzburg, 137.

Schenk, R.K., 2003. The biology of fracture repair. In: Browner, B.D., Jupiter, J.B., Levine, A.M., Trafton, P.G. (Eds.), Skeletal Trauma: Basic Science, Management, and Reconstruction, third ed. Saunders, Philadelphia, pp. 29–319.

Scientific Working Group on Forensic Anthropology, 2011. Laboratory Management and Quality Assurance, Rev 1.

Scientific Working Group on Forensic Anthropology, 2012. Documentation, Reporting and Testimony, Rev 0.

Scientific Working Group on Forensic Anthropology, 2012. Statistical Methods, Rev 0.

Slice, D.E., 2007. Geometric morphometrics. Annu. Rev. Anthropol. 36, 266–281.

Spradley, M.K., Jantz, R.L., 2011. Sex estimation in forensic anthropology: Skull versus postcranial elements. J. Forensic Sci. 56 (2), 289–296.

Warren, M.W., Walsh-Haney, H.A., Freas, L., 2008. The Forensic Anthropology Laboratory. CRC Press, Boca Raton.

Medicolegal Significance

4.1 The medicolegal context

While the scope of forensic anthropology can be defined rather broadly, it most frequently involves the laboratory analysis of recent human skeletal remains. Although it may seem intuitive and obvious, it is sometimes necessary for a forensic anthropologist to first determine whether remains or items in question actually fit the criteria of being recent human skeletal material. This is typically referred to as determining the **medicolegal significance**, or whether the material is of interest to the medicolegal death investigation system. Cases relevant to the medicolegal system are typically those involving the identification of the deceased, and often the investigation of unnatural or unattended deaths. As a rule, in terms of handling, chain-of-custody, etc. (see Chapter 3) potential remains should be considered to be potentially significant until determined otherwise (SWGANTH, 2011). In order to be considered of medicolegal significance to a forensic anthropologist, three questions must be answered in the affirmative:

- Is the material skeletal (bone or tooth) versus some other material?
- Is the skeletal material human versus non-human in origin?
- Is the human skeletal material **contemporary** (recent) versus non-contemporary (historic or prehistoric)?

Note that non-skeletal materials, as well as non-human bones and ancient human remains may be of **forensic** interest. For example, non-skeletal materials may still be relevant to an investigation, possibly representing case-related evidence. Non-human animal bones may be relevant to cases of illegal wildlife trade (e.g., a **wildlife forensics** case) or animal abuse. Ancient human remains may be the subject of modern forensic investigations including looting or grave robbing, or pertaining to legal matters involving tribal affiliation and repatriation. While not all human remains are within the purview of the medicolegal system, the possession and treatment of human remains always falls under state or federal laws in the United States. In most instances, however, these items and materials are not of *medicolegal* concern. While forensic anthropologists may occasionally become involved in cases that have forensic but not medicolegal significance, it is far more common for anthropologists to be involved in medicolegal cases. Here, medicolegal simply refers to the need for

Forensic Anthropology. http://dx.doi.org/10.1016/B978-0-12-418671-2.00004-5

human remains to be processed through the medicolegal system for identification and/or criminal prosecution. This chapter therefore focuses on these more typical forensic anthropological examinations, and the term "medicolegal significance" is used.

Investigations conducted by law enforcement or medicolegal investigators often depend on this initial determination of medicolegal significance to decide how to proceed. Naturally, the determination that material *is* recent human skeletal remains has a substantial influence on the direction of the investigation, but the forensic anthropologist's expertise may also have a considerable impact if it can be determined early in the investigation that material is *not* of medicolegal significance. The determination that a bone discovered in a wooded area is from a deer rather than a human may save local investigators from investing in an unnecessary large-scale search and recovery effort followed by needlessly gathering, packaging, and delivering a collection of deer bones to the medical examiner or forensic anthropologist. In many cases, the determination is also relevant to forensic analyses subsequent to anthropological examinations. For example, bones or teeth determined to be non-human in origin do not need to submitted for DNA analysis, saving time and expense.

It should now be apparent that recognizing the medicolegal significance of questioned items or materials is an important first step in a forensic anthropological analysis. It is recommended that, where feasible, forensic anthropologists are involved early in the investigation so that these determinations can be made accurately and as early as possible. The following sections describe how these determinations are typically made.

4.2 Skeletal versus non-skeletal material

When suspected skeletal material is complete and in good condition, the determination of whether it is bone or tooth versus some other material is often straightforward. This is usually accomplished by gross visual examination of the questioned material and surrounding context, and recognizing whether or not it possesses features diagnostic of osseous and dental tissue such as osteological and dental landmarks, or other biological structures. Sometimes, however, this determination can be made difficult due to fragmentation or **taphonomic** processes that may destroy or obscure many of the gross morphological features that normally make bones and teeth readily recognizable. These processes may be deliberate, as in cases where perpetrators of a crime try to eliminate evidence by physical, chemical, or thermal destruction. Natural taphonomic processes may also be responsible, including weathering, sun bleaching, animal scavenging, soil and water chemistry (**diagenesis**), and root etching.

In some cases, skeletal material may at first be difficult to differentiate from other material (such as wood, mineral, plastic, shell or metal), especially to the untrained observer, but sometimes to a skilled anthropologist as well. The most commonly encountered context in which skeletal material and other materials may be initially confused is in cases of burning, especially within structures (e.g., house fires), where fragments of burned bone may be intermixed with various other burned, melted, and fragmented materials such as building components, furniture, and appliances (Figure 4.1). Examples of this were frequently encountered in the analysis of materials recovered following the World Trade Center attack of September 11, 2001 (MacKinnon and Mundorff, 2006) (see Box 4.1). Another context that may make this

FIGURE 4.1 Examples of materials that may initially be mistaken for bone

From top left to bottom right: lava rock, ceramic, tubing, and drywall.

BOX 4.1 NON-SKELETAL MATERIAL RECOVERED FROM THE WORLD TRADE CENTER

The terrorist attacks of September 11, 2001 resulted in the deaths of 2,792 people at the World Trade Center in New York City. During the long recovery effort, thousands of non-skeletal materials and non-human bone samples were collected as possible human remains. An anthropological review process helped to exclude many samples from genetic testing, although some samples were processed for DNA prior to anthropological assessment. Two examples are featured. The item pictured on the left is a metal hinge shaped very much like a human metatarsal, and the item on the right is a piece of plastic that looked so much like bone that it was sampled for DNA.

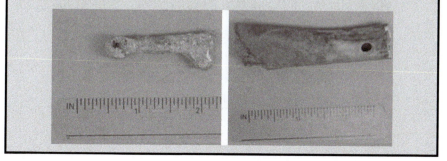

determination more challenging is the deliberate contamination of cremated remains (**cremains**), such as when non-skeletal material is added to the cremated skeletal material for the purpose of disguising improper cremation practices (Figure 4.2).

The type of analysis selected will depend on the size and condition of the material in question, but if a determination cannot be made based on a visual analysis, other methods typically include radiography, microscopy (including histological analysis), and elemental analysis. Radiographically, osseous and dental tissues are typically more **radiopaque** due to their mineral content (see Chapter 3), which may readily differentiate them from other commonly encountered non-mineralized materials. Internal structures such as trabeculae and tooth pulp chambers may also be identifiable. Radiography is a technique that can be used to quickly and easily determine whether skeletal material is present among a collection of other debris such as leaves, sticks, and rocks.

Microscopic or **histological analysis** may reveal microstructures indicative of osseous or dental tissue such as Haversian systems, trabecular bone, enamel prisms, or cement layers. Microscopically, bone also has a compact and sometimes grainy surface that is distinctive and unlike that of many other materials (Ubelaker, 1998). It is recommended that microscopy begin at lower magnification, progressing to higher magnification, leaving the material intact. This use of sectioning and histological examination should only be employed when necessary since it is a form of destructive analysis.

Recent studies have demonstrated the utility of **elemental analysis** in the determination of skeletal or non-skeletal origin. The basis for this approach is that bones and teeth possess a specific elemental composition that includes both calcium and phosphorus (as discussed in Chapter 2). Other biominerals such as gastropod shells

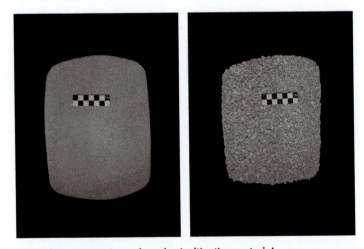

FIGURE 4.2 Possible cremated remains mixed with other material

The left image consists of non-osseous material that was separated from the cremains shown in the right image.

and corals, for example, contain only calcium and no phosphorus. One method of elemental analysis involves using scanning electron microscopy and energy dispersive X-ray spectroscopy (SEM/EDS) in conjunction with a Federal Bureau of Investigation (FBI) developed spectral database (Ubelaker et al., 2002; Ward, 2000). The database includes X-ray spectra for various materials (including bones and teeth), and unknown materials can be compared to the spectra in the database to determine consistency with known materials. The technique can successfully identify skeletal material, but involves the destruction of a small sample and considerable preparation.

Skeletal material may also be identified using an alternate light source (ALS). ALS, usually involving the use of shortwave light, is frequently used in forensic searches and analyses as a means of identifying forensically significant items such as bodily fluids, impressions, and fingerprints. The utility of ALS in these cases is due to the phenomenon of fluorescence. Fluorescence occurs when a molecule absorbs a photon of radiant energy at a particular wavelength and then quickly re-emits the energy at a slightly longer wavelength. When used with an appropriate filter, light of a certain wavelength can cause certain objects or substances to appear remarkably more visible (brighter). In forensics, a fact of particular significance is that many body secretions such as semen, saliva, and sweat contain various fluorescent enzymes and proteins. Bone also fluoresces under shortwave light, and although the apatite component can fluoresce under certain conditions, it is the collagen component of bone that contributes most significantly to its fluorescent properties (Bachman and Ellis, 1965). One study found that using appropriate parameters, skeletal material can be differentiated from other substances, including other biominerals such as seashells, on the basis of its fluorescence (Christensen et al., in press).

Another method uses X-ray fluorescence spectrometry (XRF) to determine the elemental composition of possible skeletal material (Christensen et al., 2012). XRF is a non-destructive, routine, and reliable method of elemental analysis of unknown material and is commonly employed in mineralogical and metallurgical studies. Bones and teeth have a characteristic calcium and phosphorus XRF profile that is not found in other materials, with few exceptions (Figure 4.3). Bones and teeth can be identified using this technique regardless of size, antiquity, or state of presentation. One advantage of this method is that it requires no sample destruction or preparation, though for highly surface-contaminated specimens it may be beneficial to remove adhering substances, exposing a clean surface of the questioned material.

Portable XRF units are available and are sometimes used as tools at crime scenes. They have been suggested as a possible means of field screening and sorting skeletal from non-skeletal material, especially at fire scenes (Trombka et al., 2002; Schweitzer et al., 2005; Byrnes and Bush, 2009). Currently available portable units, however, may not be able to detect elements of low atomic number, and given that the detection of phosphorus plays a key role in the identification of osseous and dental tissue, these instruments are likely to yield false negatives in the field. In these types of analyses, the use of laboratory-based instrumentation capable of effectively detecting phosphorus is highly recommended (Christensen et al., 2012).

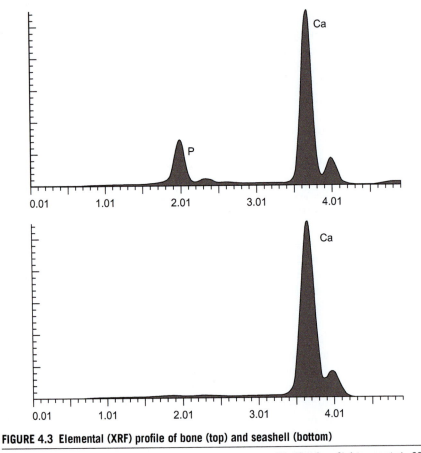

FIGURE 4.3 Elemental (XRF) profile of bone (top) and seashell (bottom)

(Modified from Christensen et al., 2012)

While the use of these advanced techniques for determining the skeletal or non-skeletal origin of material is seldom necessary, it may have a significant impact on an investigation. In these cases, it is especially important to consider issues of evidence handling and preservation – items that are already very small and fragile may be susceptible to loss or additional destruction.

4.3 Human versus non-human skeletal material

Approximately 20–30% of cases examined by forensic anthropologists are determined to be of non-human origin (Bass, 2005; Klepinger, 2006). In many of these instances, partial or nearly complete skeletons, entire bones, or large fragments are submitted to a medical examiner or forensic anthropologist for identification. Due to differences in locomotion, growth and development, biomechanics, and diet, numerous differences exist between the skeletons of different animal species. Naturally, the

FIGURE 4.4 Metapodials (metacarpus and metatarsus) of a mule deer *(Odocoileus hemionus)*

presence of elements not found in human remains such as tails, claws, horns, **bacula**, or metapodials (Figure 4.4) can make the determination of non-human origin rather obvious. If a skull is present, even most untrained investigators can typically determine whether or not it is human in origin. For post-cranial elements, however, especially those of similarly-sized animals, more advanced training is typically required to make the correct determination. Sometimes, even seemingly well-trained professionals (such as physicians and medical examiners) may incorrectly identify non-human bones as human, possibly leading to unnecessary additional investigation by law enforcement. The detailed knowledge that forensic anthropologists have of the human skeleton allows the rapid identification of non-human bones in most cases.

Many forensic anthropologists also have additional training in vertebrate comparative anatomy or **zooarchaeology**, permitting a more specific level of taxonomic identification. In most cases, investigators are primarily interested in whether the remains in question are human, but a more specific identification such as to class, family, genus, or species provides an additional degree of certainty. There are a number of detailed atlases and reference guides to non-human bone identification (for example, Adams and Crabtree, 2008; Cornwall, 1956; France, 2009, 2011;

Gilbert, 1973, 1980; Gilbert et al., 1981; Schmid, 1972), but no resource can substitute for years of training in comparative skeletal anatomy and access to a comparative vertebrate skeletal collection. Assessment of human versus non-human can be undertaken at three fundamental levels: macroscopic, microscopic, and biochemical.

Macroscopic methods involve visual or radiographic assessment of skeletal and dental morphology, with particular attention to the bone architecture (shape) but also with consideration of size as well as stage of growth and development (i.e., immature versus skeletally mature adult). A skilled human osteologist will usually have no problem in differentiating human from non-human remains when the bones are relatively complete, because the overall shapes of the bones and their features are rather distinct. Even for human osteologists not well-versed in non-human osteology, their intimate knowledge of human skeletal anatomy allows for clear recognition of when something is *not* human. The major differences between the human and non-human mammal vertebrate skeleton are related to differences in locomotion – humans are **bipeds** (walking on two legs) and most other land mammals are **quadrupeds** (walking on four legs). These differences in locomotion are reflected in almost every aspect of skeletal anatomy (see Figures 4.5–4.7 and Box 4.2).

Although vertebrates of other taxonomic classes can also be confused with human remains (e.g., birds, reptiles including turtles, amphibians, fishes, and sea mammals), misidentifications involving terrestrial mammals such as bear, deer, pig, or raccoon are more likely due to their greater similarity in bone size and morphology (see Figure 4.8). An additional source of confusion sometimes involves growth and developmental stages of the human skeleton compared to non-human animals, but a skilled forensic anthropologist will readily recognize features attributable to bone maturity (or immaturity). For example, a 6cm humerus with fused epiphyses clearly represents a mature non-human animal that is small in size overall, and not a human infant (Figure 4.9). Knowledge of the stages of bone and tooth development and epiphyseal union sequences gained through careful study of subadult skeletons is an important component of forensic anthropological training. Yet another feature that could initially confuse investigators is the presence of surgical hardware (typically associated with human remains) found associated with non-human remains (see Box 4.3).

At the macrostructural level, non-human trabecular mammalian bone is more homogenously distributed than human bone (Chilvarquer et al., 1987). Additionally, the boundary between cortical bone and trabecular bone is more apparent in non-human mammals, and is less well-defined in humans. There are several sources that provide detailed summaries of general anatomical differences between the human and non-human mammal skeleton (Mulhern, 2009; Adams and Crabtree, 2008; France 2009, 2011).

In cases of fragmented, weathered, or burned bone fragments, it may be more difficult to determine whether the remains are human or non-human. For these cases, microscopy may be useful for comparing the microstructure of bones, although histological approaches should be employed with caution in the case of burned bone, since heat may alter some of the microscopic structures (Nelson, 1992). As discussed in Chapter 2, human bone is arranged in Haversian systems (secondary osteons), which are composed of concentric rings oriented along the long axis of the bone.

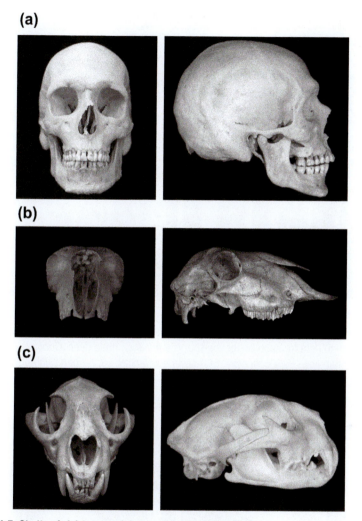

FIGURE 4.5 Skulls of: (a) human, (b) deer, and (c) mountain lion

Non-human bone, in contrast, is primarily non-Haversian (fibrolamellar, laminar, and plexiform) bone, usually arranged in a more linear pattern (Figure 4.10). Fibrolamellar bone, however, is also found in human fetal skeletons and pathological bone (Hillier and Bell, 2007; Mulhern, 2009) so its presence is not sufficient to determine non-human origin. Moreover, although non-human bone is primarily fibrolamellar, Haversian systems may appear, especially near muscle attachment sites (entheses) in larger mammals, such as horses, cows, sheep, pigs, and goats (Mulhern, 2009). Alternating osteon and lamellar banding patterns may occur in non-human mammalian bone, and only rarely in human bone (Ubelaker, 1989; Mulhern and Ubelaker, 2001, 2012). For readers interested in this and other applications of bone histology, see *Bone Histology* by Crowder and Stout (2012).

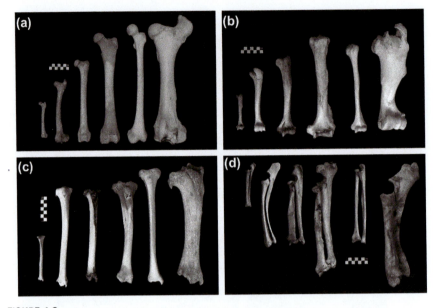

FIGURE 4.6

(a) Left femur, (b) right humerus, (c) right tibia, and (d) right radius and ulna of various species. Left to right for each bone: dog (*Canis familiaris*), mule deer (*Odocoileus hemionus*), mountain lion (*Felis concolor*), bear (*Ursus americanus*), human (*Homo sapiens*), and Cow (*Bos taurus*).

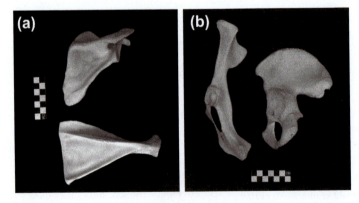

FIGURE 4.7

(a) Right scapula of human (*Homo sapiens*) (top), and mule deer (*Odocoileus hemionus*) (bottom), and (b) left innominate of mule deer (*Odocoileus hemionus*) (left) and human (*Homo sapiens*) (right).

BOX 4.2 DIFFERENCES BETWEEN HUMAN AND NON-HUMAN SKELETONS

Skull: The human skull is rounded and globular, with a small, non-projecting (**orthognathic**) face. The foramen magnum is anteriorly located to balance the head over the spinal column. Due to this configuration, muscle attachment sites on the inferior surface of the human skull are relatively gracile. This differs from the non-human skull, which is elongated front to back, with a projecting (**prognathic**) snout, posteriorly positioned foramen magnum, and several prominent crests to anchor large muscles.

Dentition: There are few animals with similar dentition to humans. Like apes, humans have low, rounded molar cusps (bunodont), reflecting an omnivorous diet. Of note is that other omnivores share gross similarities in their molar patterns to humans, including raccoons, bears, and pigs. Although there are clear differences, fragmentary dental remains have the greatest chance of misidentification. Humans also have vertically implanted anterior teeth and small canines that lack a **diastema** (gap).

Vertebral column: Human bipedality requires an unusual configuration of the vertebral column, which resembles an s-shaped curve that forms along the cervical, thoracic, and lumbar spine. Human vertebrae increase in size from the neck to the lower back due to increased weight bearing. Spinous processes show little variation in length, are often bifurcated in cervical vertebrae, and tend to be sharp and point inferiorly in thoracic vertebrae. Among quadrupeds, there is little variation in vertebrae size, as body weight is distributed more evenly along the length of the spinal column. Some mammals have very elongated spinous processes on their thoracic vertebrae, which form the shoulder "hump."

Thorax: The thorax in humans is broad and shallow, and is much narrower and deeper in quadrupeds. Due to these differences, there is a greater degree of curvature to the human thorax, which allows for easier seriation of the twelve rib pairs. A well-defined costal groove, located on the internal and inferior aspect of most humans ribs, is absent in non-human mammals.

Shoulder girdle: The clavicle (collarbone) is elongated in humans and is often reduced or absent in non-human mammals. The scapula (shoulder blade) in humans is triangular and elongated supero-inferiorly, whereas the non-human mammal scapula is longest medio-laterally. The acromian and coracoid processes are also more well-defined and show a greater degree of projection in humans.

Pelvic girdle: The human pelvis is wide and broad, forming a basin to hold the internal organs. The ilium is short and flaring (curving medially), compared with the more narrow and elongated ilium of non-human mammals. These differences reflect the adaptation for bipedality in humans versus quadrupedalism in non-human animals, as well as the requisite human compromise between efficient locomotion and safe childbirth for humans' relatively massive heads. The human pelvis connects through a fibrocartilaginous joint along the pubic symphysis, whereas in some non-human mammals, the pelvis is fused along the pubic symphysis.

Long bones: In general, human long bones are more gracile and have smoother, less complex joint surfaces than non-human long bones. The more defined morphology of non-human mammal joint surfaces reflects more specialized adaptations for specific forms of quadrapedal locomotion, and in many cases, reflects the need for high joint stability. The shoulder joint in humans, on the other hand, freed from locomotion, has increased mobility at the expense of stability. The femoral and humeral heads are more rounded and enlarged relative to overall size in humans than in non-human mammals. The human femoral neck is also elongated to position the legs under the body's center of gravity. The knee joint in humans is **valgus** (medially oriented), reflecting the angle where the distal femur and proximal tibia intersect. For this reason, a human distal femur will appear

Continued

> ### BOX 4.2 DIFFERENCES BETWEEN HUMAN AND NON-HUMAN SKELETONS—cont'd
>
> to lean when the condyles are placed on a table. In contrast, a non-human mammal femur will stand vertically when placed on a table. In many non-human mammals, the radius and ulna and/or the tibia and fibula are fused together instead of being separate elements.
>
> *Hands and feet:* The hands and feet of humans are very distinct relative to non-primate mammals, and have nails instead of claws on the terminal digits. The human hand is grasping, similar to all other primates, but has a precision grip and very sensitive tactile pads (fingertips). The proximal and intermediate hand phalanges are flattened anteriorly and rounded posteriorly. The foot phalanges are smaller and shorter (except the hallux) and rounded in cross-section. The elongated human hand and foot are distinctive, and are rarely confused with non-human remains. One of the more commonly cited examples of misidentification is bear paws (minus fur and claws), which show general similarities with human hands (Stewart 1979; Hoffman 1984), especially between the metapodials (metatarsals and metacarpals) and phalanges of bear paws and the human hand. In bears, the navicular and lunate are fused and the metapodials have a ridge on the distal articular surface.

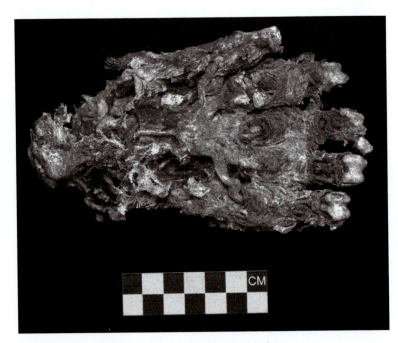

FIGURE 4.8 Bear paw, commonly mistaken for a human hand

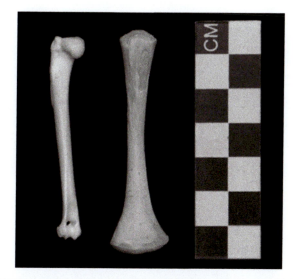

FIGURE 4.9 Mature non-human humerus (left) and infant human humerus (right)

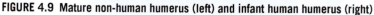

BOX 4.3

In 2008, this bone was discovered when a homeowner's dog brought it to their residence. The bone was turned in to a local sheriff's office, who believed it to be human. Comparison with non-human bones suggested it belonged to a canid (dog), most likely a family pet that had undergone surgery. This case highlights a potential area of confusion, as investigators may initially expect skeletal material with orthopedic devices to be human remains. It is evident that the plate was surgically implanted into the animal long before death, as new bone has grown around some of the plate screws.

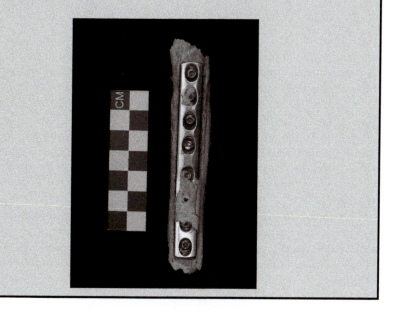

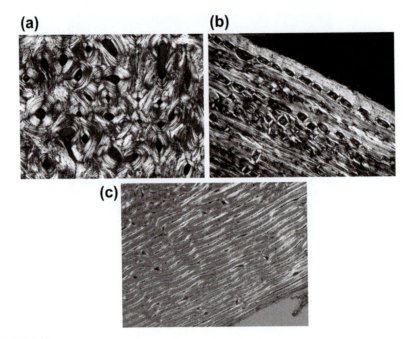

FIGURE 4.10

(a) Human femur, showing Haversian bone (100x, polarized light), (b) non-human (horse) femur showing multiple rows of secondary osteon "banding" (40x, polarized light), and (c) non-human (pig) humerus showing fibrolamellar bone with the organization pattern typically classified as "plexiform" bone (40x, semi-polarized light).

(Images courtesy of C. Crowder and A. Berensheim)

Protein-based methods, such as radioimmunoassay (pRIA), have been successfully applied to human versus non-human assessments. Solid-phase double-antibody radioimmunoassay can be used to determine whether extracted protein is from a human or non-human bone (Ubelaker et al, 2004). The extracted protein is combined with rabbit antisera which have been exposed to albumins or sera of select animal species (e.g., human, bison, bear, rat, elephant, elk, goat, pig or dog). Species-specific antibodies are then combined with the protein and antisera to observe antibody-antigen reactions. Finally, radioactive antibodies are combined with each sample to determine the strongest antibody-antigen reactions, which are species-specific. This method provides a robust test of species identification that can be used when macroscopic and microscopic methods fail to yield conclusive results.

DNA may also be used to determine human or non-human origin, though other techniques are typically equally effective and more economical. Note, moreover, that most microscopic and protein-based methods should be utilized as a last resort after macroscopic analysis since they typically involve sample alteration and/or destruction.

4.4 Contemporary versus non-contemporary human skeletal remains

Once skeletal remains have been determined to be human in origin, the final question relevant to medicolegal significance is whether the remains belong to a contemporary individual whose identity needs to be established for legal reasons. Contemporary, in the medicolegal context, is typically defined as having died within the last 50 years or so. If the remains are not contemporary, then they likely fall outside of the purview of the medicolegal system, either because identification of the individual is not possible or necessary to establish, or because the individual has already been previously processed through the medicolegal system. Examples of non-medicolegally significant human remains include those from archaeological contexts, disturbed cemeteries, anatomical teaching specimens, and "**trophy skulls**" (SWGANTH, 2011).

In most cases, the determination of whether remains are contemporary can be accomplished simply by examining the amount of soft tissue present. One case has been described, however, in which the presence and quality of soft tissue suggested a recent death although the remains were actually historic in nature (Bass, 1984) (Box 4.4). In general, the primary indicators used to assess whether human remains are contemporary are **taphonomic**, **contextual**, and **biocultural**.

Taphonomic indicators are those that affect the appearance, quality, and preservation of the remains. In most instances, recent remains will be more well-preserved than remains that are older, especially if they buried. If most of the soft tissue and viscera are still present, the remains are likely to be very recent, though intentional preservation practices should also be considered. Even when soft tissues have decomposed, well-preserved bone, such as bone that is still hydrated or greasy, is more likely to be recent than poorly preserved bone, such as bone that is highly weathered, dried, decalcified, or friable. Bone is naturally a white to yellowish color, but over time and in the absence of surrounding soft tissues, it will begin to take on the color of the soil or environment in which it is deposited (Huculak and Rogers, 2009). Further, the exposure to the environment and microorganisms in the surrounding soil will influence the degree of diagenesis of skeletal remains. Taphonomic indicators that suggest an extended burial period, such as soil color absorption and deterioration in bone quality, are likely indicators of a non-contemporary burial (Willey and Leach, 2009; Huculak and Rogers, 2009).

Deliberate postmortem treatment of the remains such as embalming, autopsy, or processing for skeletal curation or analysis may also give indications regarding medicolegal significance. For example, the presence of anatomical hardware or associated drill holes may be indicators that remains were specially prepared and used as teaching skeletons before being rediscovered (Figure 4.11). Embalming and postmortem grooming practices have changed over the years, including variation in the procedures, the chemicals used, and associated cultural and religious

BOX 4.4 THE CASE OF COLONEL WILLIAM SHY

In the late 1970s, Dr. William M. Bass was asked to examine and estimate the postmortem interval of remains disinterred on property that formerly belonged to the family of Confederate Colonel William Shy. Although little was known about time since death estimation at that time, the presence and quality of soft tissue led Dr. Bass to estimate the postmortem interval to be around one year. Some of the flesh was still pink, and there were still remnants of internal organs including the brain. The remains turned out to be those of Colonel Shy himself who was buried in 1864. Interestingly, Shy was embalmed with arsenic and buried in a cast iron coffin. These practices, which are relatively uncommon, resulted in the unexpected state of soft tissue preservation, causing Dr. Bass to conclude that the remains were much more recent than they actually were. This case clearly demonstrated the need to study postmortem changes and decomposition, and paved the way for decades of subsequent and ongoing taphonomic research (Bass, 1984).

(Photo: Colonel William Shy, killed in the battle of Nashville, December 16, 1864)

customs (Mayer, 2000). These too may be indicators of the contemporaneity of the remains.

Context refers to where something was found, where it was found in relation to other artifacts, when in time it was found, and when it was originally deposited (Thomas, 1979; Dirkmaat and Adovasio, 1997). Understanding the context in which the remains were found is often the key to determining the medicolegal significance. For example, remains scattered in a remote wooded area are likely to be medicolegally significant, while those discovered in a known cemetery are likely to be non-significant. **Artifacts** associated with remains often provide contextual evidence of when the remains were deposited. Artifacts are of two basic types: **personal effects**, which are artifacts that belonged to the individual in life and are found with the decedent's remains, and **grave goods**, which are artifacts placed with a decedent's remains by other individuals. Personal effects typically include the individual's clothing, jewelry, wallet, and other belongings directly associated with their person. Grave goods are often items placed by friends and family

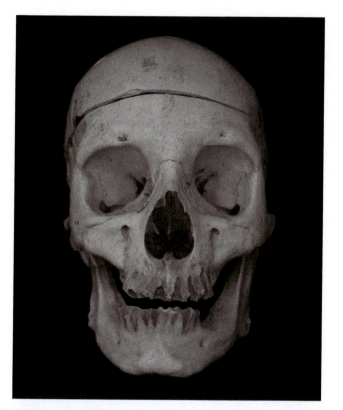

FIGURE 4.11 Anatomical teaching specimen initially submitted as a medicolegal case by law enforcement

members of the decedent and may include artifacts associated with the burial itself, such as coffin hardware (e.g., nails or hinges) (Bell, 1990). Grave goods may also be deposited by individuals who disposed of the body. In some cases, artifacts may include currency or other modern and directly dateable items that may provide clues to contemporaneity.

Artifacts may also include materials such as stone tools and pottery which are likely indications of a non-contemporary burial. Note that artifacts may contain information regarding not only the medicolegal significance of the remains, but also the identity of the decedent (such as a driver's license or jewelry), the identity of those involved with the decedent's disappearance (such as a perpetrator's DNA on a discarded cigarette), or evidence relating to the death event (such as a bullet recovered underneath the body).

Biocultural factors may also assist in the determination of medicolegal significance. For example, diet and food preparation practices have changed dramatically in the last several hundred years, and as a result, non-contemporary individuals may exhibit dental or skeletal adaptations or modifications that are not typically seen in modern populations. Notably, prehistoric Native Americans can often be distinguished from contemporary Americans by the dramatic degree of occlusal attrition on their dentition (Figure 4.12), which resulted from the introduction of grit into the diet from food grinding implements, as well as use of the dentition in the processing of hides and basketry. Certain cultural modifications such as cranial deformation and dental mutilation may also be clues to the cultural affiliation and contemporaneity of the remains (Velasco-Suarez et al., 1992).

Interment conditions may also provide contextual clues to contemporaneity. For example, **clandestine** burial or body disposal is more likely to lack any pretreatment or care typically seen in normal burial circumstances. Certain cultural burial arrangements, such as flexed and semi-flexed positions, were used by some prehistoric societies, whereas modern day burials are most often in an extended position.

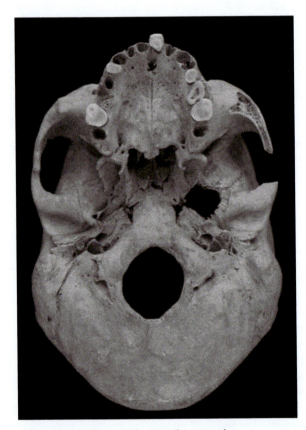

FIGURE 4.12 Dental occlusal wear on Native American remains

Medical and dental care and treatment have changed significantly over the years and may present a quick and obvious way to determine whether human remains are contemporary. The presence of modern surgical devices such as hip replacements or sternotomy wires and dental treatments such as restorations, bridges, and crowns are evidence that the remains are contemporary (Figure 4.13). It may even be possible in many cases to more precisely date certain appliances or techniques based on their known time of manufacture or implementation. On the other hand, evidence of **trephination** (cranial surgery) or other ancient medical practices are indicative of a non-contemporary origin (Figure 4.14).

Burials are sometimes accidentally disturbed during construction projects or through cultural resource management (CRM) archaeological projects. In these situations, a forensic anthropologist may be able to assist investigators in determining whether the remains are contemporary or not. In the case of prehistoric Native Americans or other indigenous ancient burials, these remains are of academic interest but not within the purview of the medicolegal system, and in any case cannot be positively identified because there will be no antemortem skeletal information with which to compare to establish identity. Often in these cases in the United States, the Native American remains will be turned over to either the state archaeologist or local tribe for re-burial depending on laws and jurisdiction (Ousley and Hollinger, 2009). Federal laws, such as the Native American Graves Protection and Repatriation Act (NAGPRA), may dictate the disposition of Native American remains.

Another common example of the discovery of non-contemporary remains is the accidental uncovering of historic cemetery burials that have lost their grave markers, for example during routine construction and roadwork (Berryman et al., 1997). These remains, however, are not considered medicolegally significant, as the individual's death would have been investigated previously and the individual already identified. These investigations are then primarily concerned with re-associating the remains to the burial plot and potentially contacting any living relatives depending on the date of the burial.

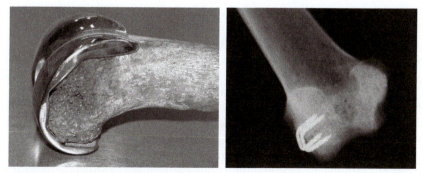

FIGURE 4.13 Surgically-implanted devices

Knee replacement (left) and Anterior cruciate ligament (ACL) surgery (right).

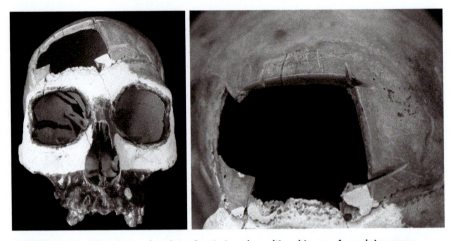

FIGURE 4.14 Prehistoric cranium from South America with evidence of cranial surgery (trephination)

While the technology is not yet widely available due to the need for more research as well as high equipment and processing costs, it may soon be more practical to date human remains using the "bomb curve" radiocarbon method (Taylor et al., 1989; Ubelaker, 2001; Ubelaker and Houck, 2002; Ubelaker and Buchholz, 2006; Wild et al., 2000; Ubelaker and Parra, 2011; Cardoso et al., 2012). Preliminary studies suggest that radiocarbon dating techniques can provide valuable data and may become practical in the future of forensic death investigation. Radiocarbon dating is based on the principle that ^{14}C (or carbon-14), an unstable radiometric isotope of ^{12}C, is produced in the earth's upper atmosphere due to cosmic ray bombardment (Libby et al., 1949). The ^{14}C is then distributed throughout the atmosphere as carbon dioxide ($^{14}CO_2$) and taken in by organisms. At death, organisms stop taking in carbon, and the ^{14}C begins radioactive decay, via the half-life of ^{14}C (5,730 years). Measuring the remaining ^{14}C using an accelerator mass spectrometer allows calculation of the date at which the organism stopped taking in carbon (Ubelaker, 2001).

Currently, the best-established methods are those relating to artificial radiocarbon dating with special reference to the modern bomb curve (Ubelaker et al., 2006). Between 1950 and 1963, atmospheric thermonuclear testing resulted in artificially elevated levels of carbon-14 in terrestrial organisms, including humans (Figure 4.15). Analysis of radiocarbon values in bones and teeth can distinguish whether an individual died before or after 1950. Expanding on this research, recent radiocarbon studies of human teeth indicate that they can be used to estimate the date of birth of an unidentified decedent using the bomb curve (Buchholz and Spalding, 2010). Combined with standard age at death estimation methods, radiocarbon dating utilizing the bomb curve may hold significant promise for facilitating identification as well as determining contemporaneity (Alkass et al., 2010).

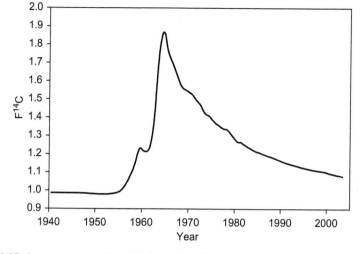

FIGURE 4.15 Average annual atmospheric carbon-14

(From Ubelaker et al., 2006)

4.5 **Other considerations in medicolegal significance**

While direct examination of questioned material is typically preferable and some-times necessary, forensic anthropologists can often make the determination of medi-colegal significance, especially between human and non-human bones, on the basis of high-quality photographs that include a scale. In this manner, anthropologists can provide real-time or expedient answers even if they cannot be present at the scene. Specimens determined *not* to be of medicolegal significance may be returned to investigators, curated as comparative material, or discarded depending on the poli-cies and needs of the investigators and forensic anthropology laboratory. Such items, however, should still be collected and removed from the scene and not left in place to be inadvertently rediscovered at a later time.

4.6 **Case study: human or non-human?**

A partially skeletonized leg was discovered along a river in northern California (Figure 4.16). Local law enforcement was contacted, and they submitted the leg for identification to an archaeologist, a pathologist, and a veterinarian. The archaeologist and pathologist identified the remains as being from a human right leg. The veteri-narian suggested that the remains may in fact be non-human in origin. Of particular interest was the fact that the lower leg had been severed with a saw, indicating dis-memberment. Believing the remains to be a human leg, law enforcement assembled a team including search and rescue personnel, detectives, and several sheriffs' office staff members. A three-day search failed to yield additional remains.

FIGURE 4.16 Case study: Human or non-human leg?

Because of the conflicting opinions by the three experts who examined the remains, law enforcement contacted forensic anthropologists for another opinion. The remains were concluded to consist of a complete left femur and proximal two-thirds of a tibia and fibula, which were still articulated due to the presence of desiccated tissue. The remains were additionally immediately identified as belonging to a black bear, and therefore not of medicolegal significance. In this case, much time and expense could have been saved had the agency contacted a forensic anthropologist at the beginning. This case also underscores the potential limitations of utilizing specialists who do not routinely examine skeletal remains.

4.7 Summary

- The recognition of the medicolegal significance of material to a forensic anthropologist includes determining whether the material is skeletal versus some other material, whether skeletal material is human or non-human, and whether human skeletal material is contemporary or non-contemporary.
- The determination of skeletal or non-skeletal origin is typically accomplished by gross visual examination, but when material is small and/or taphonomically compromised, this may be accomplished by using radiography, microscopy, or elemental analysis.
- A recently developed method of elemental analysis for determining skeletal or non-skeletal origin involves the use of X-ray fluorescence spectrometry (XRF) to determine the presence of calcium and phosphorus. The approach is reliable and non-destructive.
- Differences between human and non-human skeletal remains are primarily differences in architecture (shape) as a result of differences in locomotion (bipedalism versus quadrupedalism).

- The determination of human or non-human origin is typically accomplished by gross visual examination, but other techniques that may be employed include histology or protein-based methods such as protein radioimmunoassay (pRIA).
- The determination of contemporary or non-contemporary is typically based on observations of taphonomy, context, and biocultural information. Radiocarbon dating may also be useful.
- Artifacts are an example of contextual information that may provide clues regarding whether remains are contemporary or non-contemporary. Artifacts include personal effects (items belonging to the deceased individual) and grave goods (items deposited with the deceased individual by other persons).

4.8 Test yourself

- Describe how you would approach the determination of medicolegal significance during the laboratory analysis of small, fragmentary pieces of material suspected to be possible human remains. What methods would aid in your assessment?
- Given that analyses should proceed from least destructive to most destructive, list the order of approaches you would use to determine whether a bone is human or non-human in origin.
- Why do differences in locomotion affect bone architecture? Describe how forensic anthropologists use this information in determining whether remains are human or non-human.
- You are presented with a small femur (15 cm in length) with fused epiphyses. Discuss whether this bone is likely to be human or non-human based on this information.
- You are presented with a partially skeletonized bear paw initially suspected to be a human hand. In what ways does a bear paw differ from a human hand? What information would you provide investigators to demonstrate that the remains are non-human?
- You are presented with two isolated human molar teeth. Both appear in similar states of preservation (soiled and discolored, but otherwise in good condition), but one has extremely worn cusps, and the other has an apparent restoration. What can you say about their likely medicolegal significance?
- For each of the following scenarios, describe some of the indicators that may help to determine the medicolegal significance of the discovery:
  - Skeletal remains from an accidentally disturbed prehistoric burial.
  - Materials misplaced from an anatomical teaching collection.
  - A human cranium (an apparent "trophy skull") found in an attic.
  - Human skeletal remains from an accidentally disturbed historic grave.
  - An apparent human skeleton found in a ditch along a highway.

Definitions

Artifact Any object created or modified by humans, including, for example, clay pots, clothing, or a driver's license

Baculum A bone that supports the penis in many mammals including rodents, carnivores, and primates, but not humans (plural: bacula, also called os priapi)

Biocultural The relationship between human biology and culture

Biped A two-footed animal

Clandestine Done secretly or kept secret, especially in relation to illegal activities

Contemporary Of the present time; recent; modern

Context The relationship of something to space and time; for an artifact, where it was found on earth, where it was found in relation to other artifacts, when in time it was found, and when it was originally deposited

Cremains Cremated remains; the ashes or remains of a cremated body

Decedent A person who has died

Diagenesis Physical and chemical changes occurring to a deposited material

Diastema A gap or space between teeth

Elemental analysis The process of analyzing a material for its elemental and sometimes isotopic composition

Forensic Pertaining to laws or the legal system

Histological analysis (histology) The study of the microscopic structure of tissues

Medicolegal Significance Relating to both medicine and law; of interest to the medicolegal death investigation system

Orthognathic Having a non-projecting lower facial skeleton

Plexiform Rapidly forming bone common to non-human mammals, human infants, and human pathological bone, and appearing as a series of brick-like structures

Prognathic Having a projecting lower facial skeleton

Quadruped A four-footed animal

Radiopaque (or radiodense) Obstructing the path of X-rays, and therefore appearing lighter in radiographs

Taphonomy The "laws of burial," typically referring to the state of preservation and modification of remains (adj: taphonomic)

Trephination The surgical opening of the cranium, often performed in prehistory using rudimentary tools to saw through the cranium for therapeutic or spiritual reasons

Trophy skull A human skull or cranium which is not of medicolegal significance due to its context. Typically, trophy skulls are human remains which were taken as trophies, keepsakes, or memorabilia from foreign victims during past wars, often WWII, the Korean War, or the Vietnam War.

Valgus Oblique displacement from the body's midline

Wildlife forensics The use of scientific procedures to investigate crimes in which the victim is a non-human animal (wildlife)

Zooarchaeology The study of non-human animal remains at archaeological sites, usually consisting of hard tissues such as bones, teeth, and shells

References

Adams, B.J., Crabtree, P.J., 2008. Comparative skeletal anatomy: A photographic atlas for medical examiners, coroners, forensic anthropologists, and archaeologists. Human Press, Totowa.

Alkass, K., Buchholz, B.A., Ohtani, S., Yamamoto, T., Druid, H., Spalding, K.L., 2010. Age estimation in forensic sciences. Mol. Cell. Proteomics 9 (5), 1022–1030.

Bachman, C.H., Ellis, E.H., 1965. Fluorescence of bone. Nature 206, 1328–1331.

Bass, W.M., 1984. Time interval since death: A difficult decision. In: Rathbun, T.A., Buikstra, J.E. (Eds.), Human identification: Case studies in forensic anthropology. Charles C Thomas, Springfield, pp. 136–147.

Bass, W.M., 2005. Human Osteology: A Laboratory and field manual of the human skeleton, 3rd ed. Missouri Archaeological Society, Columbia.

Bell, E.L., 1990. The historical archaeology of mortuary behavior: Coffin hardware from Uxbridge, Massachusetts. Hist. Archaeol. 24, 54–78.

Berryman, H.E., Bass, W.M., Symes, S.A., Smith, O.C., 1997. Recognition of cemetery remains in the forensic setting. In: Haglund, W.D., Sorg, M.H. (Eds.), Forensic taphonomy: the postmortem fate of human remains. CRC Press, Boca Raton, pp. 165–170.

Buchholz, B.A., Spalding, K.L., 2010. Year of birth determination using radiocarbon dating of dental enamel. Surface Interface Anal. 42 (5), 398–401.

Byrnes, J.F., Bush, P.J., 2009. Practical considerations in trace element analysis of bone by portable x-ray fluorescence. Proceedings of the 61st Annual Meeting of the American Academy of Forensic Sciences; 2009 February 16–21; Denver, CO. American Academy of Forensic Sciences, Colorado Springs.

Cardoso, H.F.V., Puentes, K., Monge Soares, A., Santos, A., Magalhaes, T., 2012. The value of radiocarbon analysis in determining the forensic interest of human skeletal remains found in unusual circumstances. J. Forensic Leg. Med. 19 (2), 97–100.

Chilvarquer, I., Katz, J.O., Glassman, D.M., Prihoda, T.J., Cottone, J.A., 1987. Comparative radiographic study of human and animal long bone patterns. J. Forensic Sci. 32, 1645–1654.

Christensen, A.M., Horn, K.J., Smith, V.A., In press. The use of an alternate light source for detecting bones underwater. Journal of Forensic Sciences.

Christensen, A.M., Smith, M.A., Thomas, R.M., 2012. Validation of X-ray fluorescence spectrometry for determining osseous or dental origin of unknown material. J. Forensic Sci. 57 (1), 6–11.

Cornwall, I.W., 1956. Bones for the Archaeologist. Phoenix House, London.

Crowder, C.M., Stout, S., 2012. Bone histology: An anthropological perspective. CRC Press, Boca Raton.

Dirkmaat, D.C., Adovasio, J.M., 1997. The role or archaeology in the recovery and interpretation of human remains from an outdoor forensic setting. In: Haglund, W.D., Sorg, M.H. (Eds.), Forensic Taphonomy: The Postmortem Fate of Human Remains. CRC Press, Boca Raton, pp. 39–64.

France, D.L., 2009. Human and non-human bone identification: A color atlas. CRC Press, Boca Raton.

France, D.L., 2011. Human and non-human bone identification: A concise field guide. CRC Press, Boca Raton.

Gilbert, B.M., 1973. Mammalian osteo-archaeology: North America. Missouri Archaeological Society, Springfield.

Gilbert, B.M., 1980. Mammalian osteology. Modern Printing Company, Laramie.

Gilbert, B.M., Martin, L.D., Savage, H.G., 1981. Avian osteology. Modern Printing Company, Laramie.

Hillier, M.L., Bell, L.S., 2007. Differentiating human bone from animal bone: A review of histological methods. J. Forensic Sci. 54, 249–263.

Hoffman, M., 1984. Identification of non-skeletonized bear paws and human feet. In: Rathbun, R.A., Buikstra, J.E. (Eds.), Human Identification: Case Studies in Forensic Anthropology. Charles C. Thomas, Springfield, pp. 96–106.

Huculak, M.A., Rogers, T.L., 2009. Reconstructing the sequence of events surrounding body disposition based on color staining of bone. J. Forensic Sci. 54 (5), 979–984.

Klepinger, L.L., 2006. Fundamentals of forensic anthropology. Wiley-Liss, Hobokan.

Libby, W.F., Anderson, E.C., Arnold, J.R., 1949. Age determination by radiocarbon content: world-wide assay of natural radiocarbon. Science 109, 227–228.

MacKinnon, G., Mundorff, A.Z., 2006. The World Trade Center: September 11th, 2001. In: Thompson, T., Black, S. (Eds.), Forensic Human Identification: An Introduction. CRC Press, Boca Raton, pp. 485–499.

Mayer, R.G., 2000. Embalming: History, Theory, and Practice. McGraw-Hill, New York.

Mulhern, D.M., 2009. Differentiating human from non-human skeletal remains. In: Blau, S., Ubelaker, D.H. (Eds.), Handbook of Forensic Anthropology and Archaeology. Left Coast Press, Walnut Creek, pp. 96–106.

Mulhern, D.M., Ubelaker, D.H., 2001. Differences in osteon banding between human and non-human bone. J. Forensic Sci. 46, 220–222.

Mulhern, D.M., Ubelaker, D.H., 2012. Differentiating human from non-human bone microstructure. In: Crowder, C., Stout, S. (Eds.), Bone Histology: An Anthropological Perspective. CRC Press, Boca Raton, pp. 109–134.

Nelson, R., 1992. A microscopic comparison of fresh and burned bone. J. Forensic Sci. 37 (4), 1055–1060.

Ousley, S., Hollinger, R.E., 2009. A forensic analysis of human remains from a historic conflict in North Dakota. In: Steadman, D.W. (Ed.), Hard Evidence: Case Studies in Forensic Anthropology, second ed. Prentice Hall, Upper Saddle River, pp. 91–101.

Schmid, E., 1972. Atlas of Animal Bones: For Prehistorians, Archaeologists and Quaternary Geologists. Elsevier Publishing Company, Amsterdam.

Schweitzer, J.S., Trombka, J.I., Floyd, S., Selavka, C., Zeosky, J., Gahn, N., McClanahan, T., Burbibe, T., 2005. Portable, generator-based XRF instruments for non-destructive analysis at crime scenes. Nuclear Instruments and Methods in Physics Research Section A: Accelerators, Spectrometers, Detectors and Associated Equipment 52, 816–819.

Scientific Working Group for Forensic Anthropology, 2011. Determination of medicolegal significance from suspected osseous and dental remains (Revision 2). Retrieved from, http://www.swganth.org.

Stewart, T.D., 1979. Essentials of forensic anthropology. Charles. C. Thomas, Springfield.

Taylor, R.E., Suchey, J.M., Payen, L.A., Slota, P.J., 1989. The use of radiocarbon (14C) to identify human skeletal materials of forensic science interest. J. Forensic Sci. 34, 1196–1205.

Thomas, D.H., 1979. Archaeology. Holt, Rinehart and Winston, New York.

Trombka, J.I., Schweitzer, J., Selavka, C., Dale, M., Gahn, N., Floyd, S., Marie, J., Hobson, M., Zeosky, J., Martin, K., McClannahan, T., Solomon, P., Gottschang, E., 2002. Crime scene investigations using portable, non-destructive space exploration technology. Forensic Sci. Int. 52, 1–9.

Ubelaker, D.H., 1989. Human skeletal remains: Excavation, analysis, interpretation, 2nd ed. Taraxacum, Washington, DC.

Ubelaker, D.H., 1998. The evolving role of the microscope in forensic anthropology. In: Reichs, K.J. (Ed.), Forensic osteology: Advances in the identification of human remains, 2nd ed. Charles C Thomas, Springfield, pp 514–532.

Ubelaker, D.H., 2001. Artificial radiocarbon as an indicator of recent origin of organic remains in forensic cases. J. Forensic Sci. 46, 1285–1287.

Ubelaker, D.H., Buchholz, B.A., 2006. Complexities in the use of bomb-curve radiocarbon to determine time since death of human skeletal remains. Forensic Sci. Commun. 8.

Ubelaker, D.H., Houck, M.M., 2002. Using radiocarbon dating and paleontological extraction techniques in the analysis of a human skull in an unusual context. Forensic Sci. Commun. 4.

Ubelaker, D.H., Parra, R.C., 2001. Radiocarbon analysis of dental enamel and bone to evaluate date of birth and death: Perspective from the southern hemisphere. Forensic Sci. Int. 208, 103–107.

Ubelaker, D.H., Buchholz, B.A., Stewart, J.E.B., 2006. Analysis of artificial radiocarbon in different skeletal and dental tissue types to evaluate date of death. J. Forensic Sci. 51 (3), 484–488.

Ubelaker, D.H., Lowenstein, J.M., Hood, D.G., 2004. Use of solid-phase double-antibody radioimmunoassay to identify species from small skeletal fragments. J. Forensic Sci. 49, 924–929.

Ubelaker, D.H., Ward, D.C., Braz, V.S., Stewart, J., 2002. The use of SEM/EDS analysis to distinguish dental and osseous tissue from other materials. J. Forensic Sci. 47, 940–943.

Velasco-Suarez, M., Martinez, B.A., Oliveros, R.G., Weinstein, P.R., 1992. Archaeological origins of cranial surgery: Trephination in Mexico. Neurosurgery 31 (2), 313–319.

Ward, D.C., 2000. Use of an X-ray spectral database in forensic science. Forensic Sci. Commun. 2 (3).

Wild, E.M., Arlamovsky, K.A., Golser, R., Kutschera, W., Priller, A., Puchegger, S., Rom, W., Steier, P., Vycudilik, W., 2000. ^{14}C dating with the bomb peak: An application to forensic medicine. Nuclear Instruments and Methods in Physics Research Section B: Beam Interactions with Materials and Atoms 172, 944–950.

Willey, P., Leach, P., 2009. The skull on the lawn: Trophies, taphonomy, and forensic anthropology. In: Steadman, D.W. (Ed.), Hard Evidence: Case studies in forensic anthropology. Prentice Hall, New Jersey, pp. 179–189.

Forensic Taphonomy

5

5.1 Principles of forensic taphonomy

The term **taphonomy** is broadly defined as the laws of burial, derived from the Greek *taphos*, meaning burial and *onomy*, meaning law. The term was first coined by Ivan Efremov, a Russian paleontologist and science fiction author in the 1940s, in order to explain the process of "the transition (in all its details) of animal remains from the biosphere into the lithosphere" (Efremov, 1940:92). The study of taphonomy originated as a way to explain how and why skeletal elements or portions of skeletal assemblages ended up in the context in which they were found, as understanding taphonomic processes helps to explain why the paleontological record differs from the biological community from which it is derived (Beary and Lyman, 2012). Taphonomy is now understood to refer to the study of everything that happens to biological organisms from the time of death to the time of discovery.

Since its inception, the study of taphonomy has become incorporated into various sub-disciplines of anthropology, including paleoanthropology, archaeology, and more recently, forensic anthropology (Lyman, 1994; Haglund and Sorg, 1997; Haglund and Sorg, 2002; Dirkmaat and Passalacqua, 2012). In each of these areas, an understanding of taphonomy helps to reconstruct and interpret the events associated with the deposition, dispersion, and modification of human remains. In a medicolegal context, the term **forensic taphonomy** is often used, referring to the study of postmortem processes which affect the preservation and recovery of human remains, which helps in reconstructing the circumstances surrounding the death event (Haglund and Sorg, 1997:13). Forensic taphonomy is therefore essentially the study and interpretation of postmortem modifications to the body. A detailed understanding of taphonomy can facilitate the reconstruction of events that occurred between the deposition of the remains and their recovery (Ubelaker, 1997). It can aid in differentiating taphonomic events from antemortem and perimortem events (such as trauma), and estimating the time since death or **postmortem interval** (PMI). In addition, a thorough understanding of taphonomic processes in local environments (including the terrain and scavenger species present) can aid in searches for human remains and the context of their discovery.

Much of what is known about forensic taphonomy has been gained from observational studies on decomposition and postmortem modification of humans and

BOX 5.1 TAPHONOMIC RESEARCH FACILITIES

The University of Tennessee's Anthropological Research Facility (often referred to as "The Body Farm") (see also Box 4.4) was a pioneering addition to forensic anthropological research, involving the direct study of donated, decomposing human bodies in order to better understand forensic taphonomic processes. While these studies have yielded excellent data on postmortem changes in eastern Tennessee, it is widely recognized that such changes are highly dependent on environment and climatic factors, especially temperature. More recently, several other institutions have developed similar facilities including: the Forensic Anthropology Center at Texas State (FACTS), located at Texas State University, San Marcos, TX; the Southeast Texas Applied Forensic Science Facility (STAFS), located at Sam Houston State University, Huntsville, TX; the Forensic Osteology Research Station (FOREST), located at Western Carolina University, Cullowhee, NC; and most recently, the Forensic Investigation Research Station (FIRS), located at Colorado Mesa University, Grand Junction, CO. The development of multiple decomposition research facilities provides new avenues for research on human decomposition in different environments and also provides opportunities for training courses for forensic scientists and law enforcement personnel.

Taphonomic research at Texas State University, San Marcos (Photo courtesy of Kate Spradley)

non-human animals. These studies are primarily conducted at outdoor field laboratories associated with universities, which have increased in number over the last several years (Box 5.1). There are few such research facilities dedicated to aquatic decomposition, although some work has been done recently in British Columbia, Canada (Box 5.2). The following sections describe some of the taphonomic processes known to affect human remains, how and why these processes may vary, and how they can be interpreted in forensic contexts.

BOX 5.2 THE VICTORIA EXPERIMENTAL NETWORK UNDER THE SEA

The Victoria Experimental Network under the Sea (VENUS) is an underwater cabled laboratory at the University of Victoria, British Columbia (venus.uvic.ca). VENUS involves an array of remotely operated fiber optic cables linked to cameras, instruments, and sensors on the sea floor, and live data can be viewed from anywhere in the world. Research at VENUS includes the collection of oceanic data on physical, biological, and chemical conditions, including the study of the postmortem fate of animal remains on the ocean floor. Marine taphonomy is little understood, as conducting research under the ocean is extremely difficult. VENUS offers a unique opportunity for researchers to study decomposition in real time. Dr. Gail Anderson and Dr. Lynne Bell (School of Criminology, Simon Fraser University) are conducting a series of experiments in a variety of depths, habitats, and seasons to develop an understanding of faunal colonization, artifacts caused by **abiotic** and **biotic** factors, and effect of submergence on skeletal elements (Anderson, 2010).

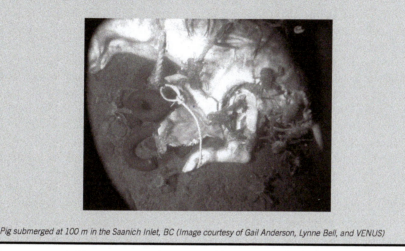

Pig submerged at 100 m in the Saanich Inlet, BC (Image courtesy of Gail Anderson, Lynne Bell, and VENUS)

5.2 **Decomposition and postmortem soft tissue changes**

The soft tissues of the body are the first to become modified after death. Early visible postmortem changes to the soft tissues include *algor mortis, livor mortis,* and *rigor mortis,* stages which are typically assessed by investigators and the medical examiner at autopsy. **Algor mortis** is the cooling of the body after death (Knight, 2002). During life, the body maintains a temperature of approximately 98.6°F, which is an optimum operating temperature for many of the body's chemical reactions. After death, the body no longer maintains this temperature, so it begins to cool and equilibrate to the ambient temperature. The rate at which this cooling occurs depends on the temperature differential between the body and the environment (elevated body temperatures and cool ambient temperatures will increase this rate), but as a general rule, the body cools at a rate of about one degree per hour during the first twelve hours.

Livor mortis (also called hypostasis) is the pooling of the blood in the body due to gravity and the lack of blood circulation as a result of the cessation of cardiac activity (Knight, 2002). These factors cause the blood to pool in the lowest points of the body, giving the skin a purplish-red discoloration. Livor mortis typically begins around thirty minutes to four hours after death, and is most pronounced approximately twelve hours after death. There are two recognized stages of livor mortis, which are a function of whether the blood has begun to coagulate. Prior to blood coagulation, livor is "unfixed"; if the body is moved, the blood will re-pool in whichever part of the body is closest to the ground in the new position. Livor becomes "fixed" when the blood coagulates, preventing the blood from re-pooling if the body is moved into another position.

Rigor mortis is muscle stiffening caused by the binding together of muscle fibers. Muscles require a molecule called adenosine triphosphate (ATP) in order to release from a contracted state (Knight, 2002); after death, the body's ATP reserves are quickly exhausted and muscles remain contracted until the muscle fibers themselves start to decompose. Rigor mortis is typically seen first in the small muscles of the face and jaw. Rigor generally begins to set in several hours after death, peaks around twelve hours after death, and then subsides over the next day or so with decomposition of the muscle fibers (Knight, 2002). The timing of rigor mortis is dependent on environmental conditions such as temperature, as well as the physical activity of the decedent around the time of death.

Decomposition is the process by which organic material is broken down into simpler forms. It occurs systematically in all biological organisms with the cessation of normal life functions (Gill-King, 1997; Marks et al., 2009), and begins immediately following death. Decomposition (also sometimes called postmortem decay) results in many physical and biochemical changes that can be observed macroscopically and microscopically. Decomposition occurs through two primary chemical processes: *autolysis* and *putrefaction*. They often occur in tandem, but one may predominate in certain conditions.

Autolysis (or "self-digestion") is the destruction of cells through the action of their own enzymes. Autolysis typically occurs most rapidly in the pancreas and stomach, and may be the predominant decomposition process in more arid environments.

Putrefaction is the microbial deterioration of tissues caused by the proliferation of bacteria associated with the digestive system. Putrefaction causes color changes in the body including various shades of green, purple, and brown due to the release of pigments from the breakdown of internal structures. In a process called **intravascular hemolysis**, bacteria increases throughout the circulatory system, resulting in a significant darkening of the vessels, a process often referred to as **marbling**.

Also associated with putrefaction is the production of gases. These gases, primarily located in the abdomen, cause the body to bloat. This bloating can cause the affected areas of the body to expand dramatically. Over time the affected areas may rupture or the gas will subside naturally. **Skin slippage**, or shedding of the epidermis from the body caused by the deterioration of the junction between the dermis and epidermis, is also associated with early decomposition processes. Many local environmental factors affect the decomposition process, including temperature, moisture, and soil chemistry, but the processes of autolysis and putrefaction are still responsible for the chemical breakdown of tissues (Knight, 2002).

In some cases, conditions may prevent or significantly delay the complete decomposition of remains. **Artifactual preservation** refers to the preservation of a body or tissues by natural processes, chemical substances, or by the destruction of bacteria which may significantly alter normal decomposition processes. Such preservation may be related to the environment (such as aridity, moisture, or extremely cold temperatures), or the depositional substrate (such as being in contact with preservative compounds in tree bark, pine needles, or decomposing leaves). Preservation may also be facilitated by body coverings including clothing (especially leather such as boots and jackets), plastic, or airtight caskets. The use of chemicals such as embalming compounds will also significantly delay decomposition.

Mummification is the preservation of remains by desiccation or drying out (Figure 5.1). The process of mummification requires relatively low humidity, and is more likely to occur in individuals who have a low amount of body fat. Although it can occur naturally, some ancient cultures, such as the societies of ancient Egypt, practiced deliberate mummification of bodies. In a forensic context, mummification is likely to occur in arid areas (whether hot or cold). The skin may turn a dark brown color and become leathery in texture (Galloway, 1997). Despite the dried nature of the outer tissue layers, there may continue to be insect activity (e.g., maggots and carrion beetles) occurring below the skin, especially if the remains contain moisture from bodily fluids and remaining soft tissues (Galloway, 1997). Tannic acids such as those found in peat bogs also tend to facilitate natural mummification (Box 5.3).

FIGURE 5.1 Mummified human remains

BOX 5.3 BOG BODIES

Bodies that have become mummified in a peat bog have been called "bog bodies" or "bog people." Most of these specimens have been discovered in northwestern Europe, including many that are estimated to be thousands of years old. It is believed that many of the individuals were killed and deposited into the peat bogs as part of cultural practices which may have included human sacrifice (Fischer, 1998). The conditions in peat bogs that facilitate this degree of preservation include having low oxygen, low temperature, and high acidity. The soft tissues such as the skin and organs are often well preserved while the bones and teeth are often decalcified due to the acidity (Brothwell and Gill-Robinson, 2002). The most famous bog body is that of "Grauballe Man," a very well-preserved body discovered in 1952 in Denmark. It is estimated to date from the 3rd century BC.

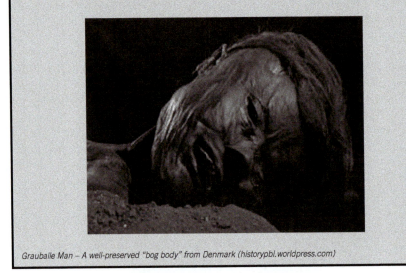

Grauballe Man – A well-preserved "bog body" from Denmark (historypbl.worldpress.com)

Saponification is the process of the conversion of fatty tissue to **adipocere** (Gill-King, 1997; Clark et al., 1997; Ubelaker and Zarenko, 2011). Saponification usually occurs in unoxygenated, alkaline, semi-moist to wet environments, and is therefore more likely to occur in remains deposited in water. Saponification can also occur in remains from moist, airtight crypts or burials, and may be accelerated by bacteria. Adipocere, sometimes referred to as "grave wax," is typically white in color and waxy in consistency, but can vary from white to grey or tan to black, and can be semi-soft to hard in consistency (Figure 5.2). Once formed, adipocere is relatively resistant to subsequent change, and can preserve many of the soft tissues. Saponification can occur in as little as three weeks, but onset takes place typically at one to two months.

Differential decomposition refers to the premature, irregular, or disproportional decomposition in an area or areas of the body. One of three causes is usually responsible: an injury that exposes blood and tissues and provides a portal for scavengers, exposure to physical or chemical agents such as heat or corrosive acids, or prior local bacterial infection such as an abscess or cellulitis. In a forensic context, differential decomposition is important to detect and document if present, since it may provide

FIGURE 5.2 Adipocere on saponified human remains

information about an individual's health just prior to death, or it may suggest trauma or foul play. For example, if a body that is otherwise fairly well preserved shows significant decomposition in the area of the neck, that region should be carefully examined for evidence of possible injury since it is not an area that would normally be expected to decompose at a faster rate.

The bones and teeth of the skeleton are much more durable and take longer to decompose than soft tissues. **Skeletonization** refers to the completion of soft tissue decomposition, where only the hard tissues of the skeleton remain. The skeleton also undergoes postmortem changes, which are discussed in the following section.

5.3 **Postmortem skeletal changes**

Once the soft tissues have decomposed, the skeleton is subject to modification and degradation by a number of factors that are largely dependent on the depositional environment. In the context of taphonomy, **diagenesis** is the term used to refer to any chemical, physical, or biological change to a bone after its initial deposition. (Note that the term "diagenesis" has been adopted from the science of geology, where it is used to refer to the changes that sediment undergoes as it converts to rock; when used in the geological context, it does not refer to surface changes such as weathering.) Many factors related to the depositional environment can be responsible for bone diagenesis. Postmortem changes to bones and teeth typically include those due to interaction with ground water and sediment, soil pH, as well as weathering, transport by natural or physical forces, plant growth through bones, and microbes, which can also cause structural damage to bones (Nielsen-Marsh and Hedges, 2000).

FIGURE 5.3 Sun bleached mandibles of an artiodactyl

Weathering is a postmortem modification process of hard tissues as a response to natural agents in their immediate environment over time. While a number of factors are involved in this complex process, sun exposure, wet/dry and freeze/thaw cycles are primarily responsible for physical changes to skeletal material. Weathering of bones and teeth can appear as bleaching from exposure to sun, cracking, flaking, warping, and erosion (Figure 5.3). Other factors that play a role in the progression of bone weathering include microenvironment, weather extremes, bone density, and **taxon**. Proper analysis of the context in which the remains are discovered is therefore necessary in order to interpret weathering patterns (Lyman and Fox, 1997). The degree and condition of weathering can be documented through detailed descriptions, and is often described using stages such as those in Table 5.1 (Behrensmeyer, 1978; Lyman and Fox, 1997).

Various other factors can result in skeletal modification. Movement of bones due to recovery, bioturbation, or transport can lead to breakage or abrasion. Bones will also become discolored and stained by their immediate environment, including sediments transported via groundwater into the pore spaces of bone. Soil is commonly responsible for bone staining, but it can also result from prolonged contact with decomposition fluids, leaves, algae, or metal objects such as zippers or buttons. Bodies deposited (especially buried) in areas with trees and plants may also be affected by roots, which can adhere to and even etch and degrade the bone surface (Figure 5.4).

Table 5.1 Stages of bone weathering

Stage	Description
0	Bone surface shows no sign of cracking or flaking due to weathering
1	Bone shows cracking, normally parallel to the fiber structure (e.g., longitudinal in long bones), articular surfaces may show mosaic cracking of covering tissue as well as in the bone itself
2	Outermost concentric thin layers of bone show flaking, usually associated with cracks
3	Bone surface is characterized by patches of rough, homogeneously weathered compact bone, resulting in a fibrous structure, all lamellar bone is absent from these patches
4	The bone surface is coarsely fibrous and rough in texture
5	Bone is falling apart in situ

(From Behrensmeyer, 1978)

FIGURE 5.4 Damage on a cranium due to invasion of cheatgrass

5.4 Scavenging

Scavenging refers to the consumption and associated modification of remains by other animals. Understanding scavenging is important for distinguishing non-human modification from other modifications of soft tissue and bone. Knowledge of which non-human animal has modified the remains may also lead to a more successful recovery effort, by helping to determine where additional remains might be located.

Scavengers of human remains are many, but the most prominent are insects, carnivores, and rodents, and it is not uncommon for there to be evidence of multiple scavenger types. The damage to the bone, the pattern of damage, and the environmental context can all help identify which scavenger may be responsible.

Insects are almost always the first scavengers to arrive at a deceased body. **Forensic entomology** is the study of arthropods (order Arthropoda), which includes scavenging insects, arachnids, centipedes, millipedes, and even crustaceans associated with forensic contexts (Houck and Siegel, 2010). Forensic entomology casework can include insect infestations of buildings, food products, or even living persons (for example, cases of neglect in which insects are found associated with bedsores of rest home patients). Most of the emphasis of forensic entomology, however, is on the use of insects to aid in the estimation of time since death, season of death, geographic origins of remains, the determination of whether remains have been moved following death, the identification of possible evidence of trauma, and the detection of the presence of drugs (Haskell et al., 1997). The presence of fly maggots, as well as other **necrophagous** (scavenging) insects, on decomposing human remains is a common finding, and entomologists are able to use arthropod life cycles and **succession** (the order in which different arthropods arrive at a corpse) of various species to estimate time since death.

Fly species in the families calliphoridae (blow flies) and muscidae (house flies), as well as sarcophagidae (flesh flies) are often early arrivals to a corpse, and usually begin to deposit either egg masses (**oviposit**) or live maggots (**larvaposit**) within the first few minutes to hours following death (Haskell et al., 1997). The eggs or larvae go through a series of developmental stages called instars, and then transition into a pupal stage. The adult fly will eventually emerge out of the pupa casing or puparium. Forensic entomologists collect insects such as adult flies and maggots that are in various stages of development to study the insects on a corpse (Figure 5.5).

Entomological evidence typically is most useful in the early stages of decomposition. Other insects, such as dermestid beetles, are commonly found in the later stages of decay when fly activity is diminished, often preferring to consume the more dried out soft tissues of the body (Haskell et al., 1997). Although a more complete discussion of entomology is beyond the scope of this chapter, it is important to note that forensic anthropologists and forensic entomologists commonly collaborate on both casework and research related to human decomposition and estimates of the postmortem interval. It is also beneficial for forensic anthropologists to be familiar with basic procedures for collecting entomological evidence from decomposing human remains (Catts and Haskell, 1990).

Many animals of the order Carnivora ("meat eating" mammals) will scavenge human remains, as will a number of omnivores. Carnivorous scavengers of human remains primarily include canids such as wolves, coyotes, foxes, domesticated dogs, cats, as well as omnivores such as bears and pigs (Carson et al, 2000; Rippley et al., 2012; Berryman, 2002). Scavengers will modify, consume, disarticulate, and disperse soft and bony tissue during the scavenging process (Haglund, 1997a).

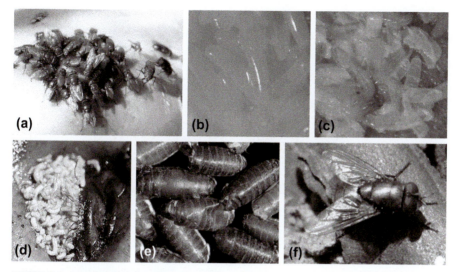

FIGURE 5.5 Insect development on a corpse

(a) Flies arriving at a corpse, (b) eggs, (c) newly-hatched instars, (d) maggots feeding on remains, (e) pupa cases, and (f) adult calliphoridae fly

(Images courtesy of Rebecca Hurst)

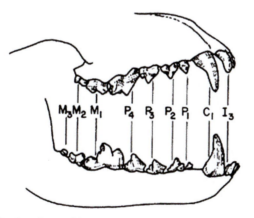

FIGURE 5.6 Generalized canid dentition

(From Haglund, 1997a)

The dentition of carnivores is specialized for gripping and tearing soft tissue, and much of the dentition is therefore sharp and pointed, including the canine and carnassial teeth (Figure 5.6). Canines are long pointed teeth lateral to the incisors and are used for holding and tearing food (and are occasionally used as weapons). **Carnassials** are modified last upper premolars and first lower molar teeth found in carnivores and are used for shearing.

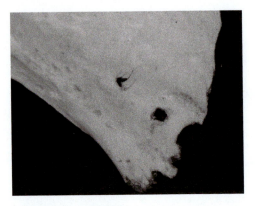

FIGURE 5.7 Carnivore punctures on a scapula

Table 5.2 Stages of carnivore scavenging	
Stage	**Condition of remains**
0	Early scavenging of soft tissue with no body unit removal
1	Destruction of the ventral thorax accompanied by evisceration and removal of one or both upper extremities including scapulae and partial or complete clavicles
2	Lower extremities fully or partially removed
3	All skeletal elements disarticulated except for segments of the vertebral column
4	Total disarticulation with only cranium and other assorted skeletal elements or fragments recovered
(Adapted from Haglund, 1997a)	

Carnivore scavenging often leaves characteristic marks on bone (Figure 5.7). Punctures are the most diagnostic feature of carnivore scavenging and are produced when the points of the canine and carnassial teeth penetrate bone and result in small perforations. Other types of carnivore tooth marks include pits, scoring, and furrows (Haynes, 1980; Haglund, 1997a). Pits are non-perforating indentations caused by the tips of teeth. Scoring refers to linear, parallel scratches produced when teeth slip and drag over cortical bone. Furrows are channels in bone, usually produced by cusps of cheek teeth and often extend from the ends of long bones longitudinally into the marrow cavity (Haglund, 1997a). The overall pattern of missing bone resulting from carnivore scavenging is also usually distinctive. The internal viscera and ends of long bones provide the most nutrition (especially in terms of fat content) and are also often the easiest to access and grasp, and hence tend to be consumed first. It is therefore common to see missing sternal ends of ribs, and long bones from which the proximal and distal ends have been consumed. Scoring systems such as the one in Table 5.2 can help document the general pattern of scavenging.

FIGURE 5.8 Bear scavenging a pig's carcass

(Image courtesy of Lisa Bright)

Although they primarily eat grasses, berries, and other vegetation, bears' diet varies depending on season and location, and they will occasionally eat meat (Figure 5.8), including human remains. Bears are more likely than canids to exploit the axial skeleton, and have been noted to consume, remove, and damage the vertebral column, ribs, and sternum (Carson et al., 2000). There are also a number of scavenging birds, such as vultures, that will consume and alter human remains. Vultures will often arrive to scavenge shortly after remains have begun to decompose, and have been observed to completely skeletonize animal carcasses within 3–24 hours (Reeves, 2009). The voraciousness of vulture scavenging, however, may vary significantly depending on region and climate (Dabbs and Martin, 2013). Marks left on bones by vultures are minimal, primarily including shallow, linear scratches, and damage to the small and delicate bones of the face, especially those of the eye orbit (Reeves, 2009).

Rodents (order Rodentia) such as rats, mice, squirrels, and porcupines have been associated with human bone modification and accumulation (Haglund, 1997b). The incisors of the rodent dentition are specialized, continue to grow throughout life, and sharpen each other during gnawing (Moore, 1981) (Figure 5.9). Rodents gnaw on bone (and many other substances) in order to provide attrition for their constantly growing anterior dentition. This gnawing action typically results in parallel striae in cortical bone (Figure 5.10). The pattern of rodent gnawing can vary with a number of factors, including the species of rodent, size of the incisors, amount of gnawing, and shape of the bone surface. Rodents tend to gnaw on the ends of long bones or bony surfaces where one jaw can easily lock, such as muscle attachments and other bony processes. The preference for bone densities and fat content varies by rodent species (Klippel and Synstelien, 2007).

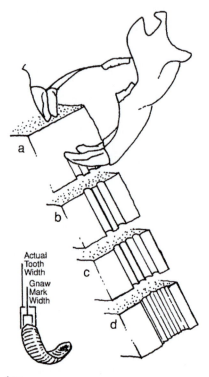

FIGURE 5.9 Rodent gnawing

(From Haglund, 1997)

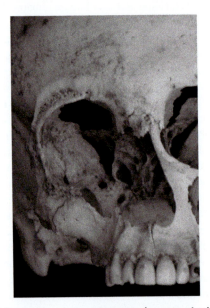

FIGURE 5.10 Parallel striae on bone from rodent gnawing around orbit

In aquatic environments, the scavenging populations are significantly different (Sorg et al., 1997). Fishes and sharks will typically tear open the skin, and fish gnaw especially at ears, lips and other soft tissues of the face. Crustaceans such as large shrimp, lobsters, and crabs will tear through muscle leaving crater-like pits of varying size. Microscavengers such as beach flies, sea lice, and small shrimp may occur at a body in large numbers, and may enter the mouth and pass into the lungs and stomach. Gastropod mollusks such as chitons, snails, and abalones also feed on decaying flesh and adipocere, and will scrape algae and microbes from bone surfaces. Echinoderms such as sea stars and sand dollars have scavenging species that may utilize human remains as a food source. There are no aquatic insects with specialized necrophagous feeding habits to parallel blow flies and carrion beetles on land, but some aquatic insects can be useful in estimating time since death and will typically be found in the facial area and body cavities. Floating remains are often subject to aquatic scavengers as well as some terrestrial scavengers such as flies and birds.

5.5 Body movement and disarticulation patterns

Particularly for surface or submerged remains (i.e., those that are not buried or otherwise confined), bodies are seldom recovered intact and in anatomical position. Rather, remains tend to be disturbed, and become disarticulated and dispersed over time. The decomposition of soft tissues will eventually result in the disarticulation of all skeletal elements, as the connective tissues that hold the joints together decompose. Transport and dispersal of skeletal elements can be caused by animals, gravity, or water and fluvial processes (Marshall, 1989). Regardless of the taphonomic agent responsible, this dispersion of the remains tends to be associated with incomplete recoveries.

Through the act of scavenging, carnivores and rodents often disturb the remains by altering the position of the body or dragging entire limbs from the deposition area. Carnivores often drag limbs away from a body, resulting in significant scattering (Haglund, 1997a). In addition, rodents may disturb remains by transporting bones into burrows or nests. Remains can also become dispersed due to gravity. Remains on a relatively steep grade, for example, will tend to move downhill. Crania, due to their roughly spherical morphology, are especially susceptible to gravitational movement.

In aquatic environments, remains are subject to a number of different factors that affect movement and dispersion. Most bodies will sink when first deposited in water. This can be influenced by a number of factors including: body weight and density, temperature, horizontal velocity of the water, and pressure and volume of gases in the tissues (Dilen, 1984). Once on the bottom, the body can be moved due to drag forces from wave or current action. The movement of bodies or skeletal remains in aquatic environments is referred to as **fluvial transport**. Unless heavily weighted down or firmly caught on underwater debris, gases produced by putrefaction will increase buoyancy, and the remains will rise to the surface of the water and float. Once floating on the surface, body movement can be affected by factors such as surface currents, eddies, and winds.

The remains will float until they lose buoyancy through the release of decompositional gases, and will then typically sink again. Disarticulation in water is influenced primarily by the nature and relative anatomical position of the joint – more flexible joints (which are more affected by wave and current action) disarticulate more quickly than less flexible joints. The first to become disarticulated are usually the hands, followed by the mandible, cranium, and limbs, with the pelvic girdle disarticulating last. Other factors affecting disarticulation include whether remains are floating versus submerged, whether there is trauma present, scavengers, wave action, and the presence of clothing.

5.6 **Estimating time since death**

The estimation of time since death or the postmortem interval (PMI) is important because it can narrow the pool of potential decedents thus facilitating identification, confirm or refute reports from potential perpetrators, and in some cases can shed light on the circumstances of death. Estimating time since death generally involves determining the probable rate of postmortem changes to the body and working backward. In cases with a short postmortem interval (i.e., hours or days), methods used for estimating time since death (such as algor mortis, rigor mortis, and livor mortis) are typically more accurate because early postmortem changes show less variation. As the postmortem interval becomes longer (i.e., weeks, months, years, etc.), the primary methods used for estimating PMI are the decomposition of soft tissues and the modification of skeletal tissues. The potential for variation in the numerous contributing factors results in a decrease in the accuracy of time since death estimates. In such cases, estimates may be very broad or perhaps impossible to establish.

The primary determinant of soft tissue decomposition rate is temperature, which has been noted to account for more than 80% of the variation in the rate of soft tissue decomposition (Nawrocki, 2013; Megyesi et al., 2005). This is due to the fact that decomposition depends largely on bacterial proliferation and insect development, which are both highly dependent on temperature. For example, bacteria from the colon are most active between 60–95°F, so temperatures outside of this range will slow the progression of decomposition (Micozzi, 1997).

Other factors that affect the rate of decomposition include humidity, moisture, pH, the presence of clothing, the depositional environment (e.g., burial vs. surface), the presence and extent of animal modification, the presence and extent of perimortem trauma, body weight, and the presence and extent of chemicals including those involved in funerary practices. Although temperature should be given primary consideration, these factors should also be considered when estimating the PMI. It is therefore very important to have a thorough understanding of as much of the scene and context as possible.

Early studies to develop anthropological PMI estimation methods attempted to establish qualitative "stages" of decomposition based on broad observations of the level of (primarily soft tissue) decomposition (see Table 5.3). Although useful for general descriptive purposes, these approaches are over-simplified, highly subjective, do not account for regional variation, and offer little utility in estimating PMI.

Table 5.3 Generalized stages of decomposition

Stage	Features
Fresh	Flies are attracted to the body. Egg masses appear in orifices and in open wounds. The skin may show a marbled appearance. Fluids may be present around the nose and mouth.
Bloat	Maggots hatch and skin around the eyes and the nose may be missing. Slippage of skin and scalp hair may occur. Abdominal area appears bloated due to decompositional gases. Unusual coloration pattern and extensive marbling may be present. Significant bodily fluids appear from all orifices, often killing surrounding vegetation and leaving a decomposition stain. Carrion beetles and mammalian scavengers may be attracted to corpse. Odor is very pronounced.
Active decay	Bloating has subsided and remains are beginning to show signs of desiccation. Beetles replace maggots as dominate insect scavengers. Skin may appear mummified, and bones begin to be exposed through holes in desiccated tissue. Mold or adipocere may be present on the remains if the remains are in a humid or wet environment. Mammalian scavengers may remove skeletal elements away from the location of initial decomposition. Birds may remove scalp hair to use in nests.
Advanced decay	The remains may become completely skeletonized with little odor or grease present. Skeleton may shows early signs of sun bleaching or weathering. There may be signs of carnivore scavenging or rodent gnawing. Mice or wasps may utilize the skull as a nest.
Dry/Skeleton	Bone surfaces break down and have an exfoliated appearance. Longitudinal cracks occur, and external cortex may flake away. Bone will appear significantly weathered and will continue to show evidence of fragmentation over time.

(Adapted from Bass, 1997)

Recent approaches utilizing scoring systems that assess and quantify the progression of decomposition (e.g., Bass, 1997; Megyesi et al., 2005) have been shown to be more reliable and accurate for estimating the postmortem interval. These studies have resulted in formulae that can be used to calculate an estimate of PMI, which depend primarily on the temperature of the depositional environment (e.g., Megyesi et al, 2005; Vass, 2011). Because of the variation in decomposition rates between regions, methods specific to a particular area or similar physical or depositional environment should be utilized when available.

Because temperature is the primary factor influencing the rate of decomposition, the level of decomposition should be calculated with reference to the **accumulated degree days** (or ADD). The ADD represents the sum of the average daily temperatures for a given number of days, typically with reference to a particular temperature threshold. In the case of decomposing remains, the temperature below which decomposition processes cease is not actually known, but 0°C has been utilized as a threshold in decomposition studies because freezing temperatures are known to severely inhibit bacterial growth (Megyesi et al., 2005). In these calculations of ADD and estimation of PMI, any temperature below the 0°C threshold would be treated as 0. Because temperature is the most important factor influencing the level of insect activity (i.e., warmer temperatures tend to result in more rapid insect development), entomologists also commonly use accumulated degree days to estimate the postmortem interval (Haskell et al., 1997), using minimum temperatures associated with insect activity as a threshold.

In many recent methods for estimating the PMI from the condition of the remains themselves, the degree of decomposition is quantified by scoring features such as discoloration, bloating, purging, and the amount of soft tissue remaining (Tables 5.4–5.6). In some approaches (e.g., Megyesi et al., 2005), different scoring systems are applied to different areas of the body (for example: the trunk, head, and limbs), resulting in a summed score called a Total Body Score (TBS). This score is then used to estimate the accumulated degree days using the following formula (including the standard error of the regression):

$$ADD = 10^{(0.002 * TBS * TBS + 1.81)} \pm 388.16$$

For example, a set of remains with a TBS of *15* would be calculated as:

$$ADD = 10^{(0.002 * 15 * 15 + 1.81)} \pm 388.16$$

$$ADD = 181.97 \pm 388.16$$

The resulting number represents the accumulated degree days that would be required for the individual to reach the stage of decomposition represented by the TBS. To estimate the time since death, this result needs to be compared to local average daily temperatures where the individual was discovered (i.e., the closest weather station data). Working backward from the day that the remains were scored, the daily

Table 5.4 Scores for decomposition of the trunk	
Score	**Description**
1	Fresh, no discoloration
2	Pink-white appearance with skin slippage and marbling present
3	Gray to green discoloration, some flesh relatively fresh
4	Bloating with green discoloration and purging of fluids
5	Release of gases, discoloration changing from green to black
6	Decomposition of tissue producing sagging of flesh
7	Moist tissue with bone exposure over less than one half of the area being scored
8	Dry tissue with bone exposure over less than one half of the area being scored
9	Bones with decomposed tissue, fluids and grease still present
10	Dry tissue, bone exposure over more than one half of the area being scored
11	Bones largely dry, but retaining some grease
12	Dry bone
(Modified from Megyesi et al., 2005)	

Table 5.5 Scores for decomposition of the head and neck

Score	Description
1	Fresh, no discoloration
2	Pink-white appearance with skin slippage and some hair loss
3	Gray to green discoloration, some flesh relatively fresh
4	Brown discoloration, drying of nose, ears, lips
5	Purging of fluids via orifices, some bloating may be present
6	Brown to black discoloration
7	Caving in of flesh and tissues of eyes and throat
8	Moist tissue with bone exposure over less than one half of the area being scored
9	Dry tissue with bone exposure over less than one half of the area being scored
10	Greasy tissue with bone exposure over more than one half of the area being scored
11	Dry tissue and bone exposure over more than one half of the area being scored
12	Bones largely dry, but retaining some grease
13	Dry bone

(Modified from Megyesi et al., 2005)

Table 5.6 Scores for decomposition of the limbs

Score	Description
1	Fresh, no discoloration
2	Pink-white appearance with skin slippage of hands and/or feet
3	Gray to green discoloration, marbling, some flesh relatively fresh
4	Brown discoloration, drying of fingers, toes, projecting extremities
5	Brown to black discoloration, skin having leathery appearance
6	Moist tissue with bone exposure over less than one half of the area being scored
7	Dry tissue with bone exposure over less than one half of the area being scored
8	Remaining tissue and fluid, bone exposure over one half of the area being scored
9	Bones largely dry, but retaining some grease
10	Dry bone

(Modified from Megyesi et al., 2005)

average temperatures are summed until the calculated ADD is reached. The number of days required to reach the ADD represents the interval since death in days.

Botanical methods can also be used to estimate time since death. Examples include the analysis of plant debris found within burials, which may indicate when that area of soil was disturbed, accumulation of floral debris within parts of the skeleton such as the cranium (Figure 5.11), or the association of plants in a particular configuration with surface skeletal remains. The age of plants that have grown through foramina on skeletal elements, for example, may provide clues to the time since skeletonization, since the soft tissue would had to have already been absent for the plant to grow there (Figure 5.12). In cases where possible botanical evidence is associated with skeletal material, the expertise of a forensic botanist should be sought.

Decomposition in aquatic environments occurs through the same chemical processes as remains on land (autolysis and putrefaction), but typically at a somewhat different rate and with different affecting factors. Due primarily to the cooler temperatures associated with water compared to land, decomposition normally occurs at about half the rate in water as it would on land. Certain aspects of the water

FIGURE 5.11 Layered leaf litter recovered from cranium

FIGURE 5.12 Root growing through vertebral canal

(Photo courtesy of Melanie Beasley)

chemistry will affect the decomposition rate similarly to those on land. For example, stagnant water (which is typically associated with a higher bacterial content) will tend to accelerate decomposition. Salinity and pH of the water will also affect the decomposition rate (Christensen and Myers, 2011). Decomposition tends to occur more quickly in fresh water than in salt water due to the lower bacterial content in salt water. Factors affecting decomposition rate that tend to differ from terrestrial depositional environments include body movement due to wave and current action, buoyancy and sink/float cycle, and different local flora and fauna. For bodies that have resurfaced, developing terrestrial flies can be useful in estimating time since resurfacing.

Algal growth rates are strongly correlated with time since submersion. Nutrients released during decomposition affect algal growth, providing a substrate upon which algae can colonize and grow. The presence of barnacles may also provide evidence of time since skeletonization, because the size and morphology of a barnacle is correlated with its age. Adult barnacles generally remain attached to the same substrate throughout their lifetime (usually 3–5 years).

Estimating the postmortem interval can be challenging due to the large number of associated factors that need to be considered, as well as the complexity of most recovery scenes. Although formulae have been proposed for calculating PMI, it is difficult for any formula to account for all of the factors that contribute to variation in postmortem changes. Many methods for estimating the PMI are available in other scientific disciplines such as forensic entomology, forensic geology, and forensic botany. A multidisciplinary approach is usually most likely to result in the most accurate estimate of the PMI.

5.7 Additional considerations in forensic taphonomy

Although not yet widely utilized techniques, soil chemistry and certain biomarkers may be related to the postmortem interval and therefore have utility in estimating time since death and other forensic questions. For example, the appearance of certain acids that are theorized to be components of decomposition byproducts may indicate the presence of decomposing tissue in an area, and may indicate whether a body had decomposed in a particular area (Vass et al., 2000), even if it has since been moved from that location. The presence of certain biomarkers found in decomposing tissues such as the liver, kidney, brain, heart, and muscle tissue have been shown to have a relationship with time since death (Vass et al., 2002). These approaches, however, require fairly sophisticated sample preparation and analytical instrumentation and more rigorous validation, and are therefore not currently widely used.

Although **microbes** are known to be significant players in decomposition and postmortem change, the various roles of specific microbial organisms are just beginning to be understood. Recent studies have succeeded in characterizing human microbial communities, and suggest that individual microbial communities are highly variable and may contribute to some of the variation seen in decomposition (Costello et al.,

2009; Damann and Carter, 2013). Bacterial organisms noted to be present in bone during late-stage decomposition may also be involved in bioerosion of the skeleton (Damann and Carter, 2013). Much more research in this area is needed, but initial studies suggest that there is much that can be understood about decomposition by examining the microbes involved in this process.

In addition to the various other factors affecting postmortem change discussed in this chapter, humans may also play significant roles as taphonomic agents. Perpetrators of a crime, for example, may alter remains in order to avoid detection or inhibit identification of the remains. This may involve dismemberment, the application of chemicals, or burning the remains. Postmortem changes may be related to funerary practices, such as embalming or cremation, which can act to either preserve or significantly alter or reduce remains. The recovery process (see Chapter 6) can result in damage or modification to remains. For example, the use of construction equipment to locate remains, or careless probing or excavation practices can result in skeletal damage. Humans also sometimes modify and utilize bones for cultural or religious practices and rituals (Box 5.4).

BOX 5.4 PALO MAYOMBE, SANTERIA, AND TAPHONOMY

Palo Mayombe and Santeria are religious traditions of Afro-Caribbean origin (Gill et al., 2009). Both are practiced in areas of the United States, particularly Florida and New York, where large populations of these cultural groups have immigrated. The practice of Santeria often involves ritual activity using animal and artifact offerings, while the practice of Palo Mayombe often involves the use of human remains in altars or receptacles. In many cases, the human remains used in these rituals are of historic origin and were acquired by grave looting (rather than foul play). Taphonomic indicators suggesting historic origin for the remains typically involved in these cases are: the presence of soil staining, cortical exfoliation, anatomical hardware, sediment found in cranial foramina, and minor postmortem damage on the cranial base or dentition.

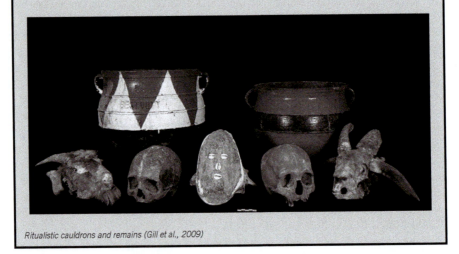

Ritualistic cauldrons and remains (Gill et al., 2009)

5.8 Case study – forensic taphonomy

In 2007, human remains were recovered from a shallow hillside grave in northern California. The skeleton was incomplete, primarily because large-bodied carnivores had scavenged the remains after removing them from a shallow burial. The decedent was estimated to be between 14 and 17 years of age, and most likely of European (white) ancestry. The decedent was later identified as a 16-year-old white male. Multiple skeletal elements showed evidence of taphonomic damage consistent with scavenging by canids. Alterations included missing bone, punctures, and grooves affecting the left radius, the left femur, the left and right tibiae and fibulae, several ribs, and several hand and foot elements (Figure 5.13). In addition, the enamel of several teeth was fractured (Figure 5.14). This can occur as a result of the drying out of the pulp chamber and tooth dentin, causing a separation at the dentino-enamel junction.

The tooth fractures later became important in the trial of the person accused of the decedent's murder. The prosecution's forensic dental expert witness testified that the teeth were fractured prior to or near the time of death, presumably caused by the accused. The forensic anthropology expert witnesses for both the prosecution and the defense, however, testified that the teeth were fractured after death (i.e., as a result of a taphonomic process) based on the fact that the fractures propagated from inside the tooth to the external surface. This finding was important, because evidence

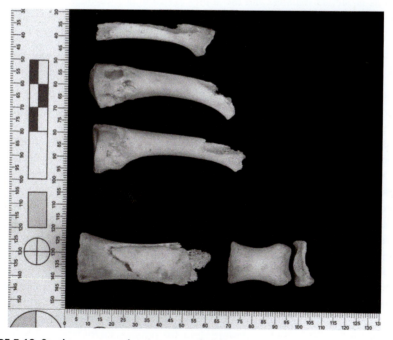

FIGURE 5.13 Carnivore scavenging damage on foot bones

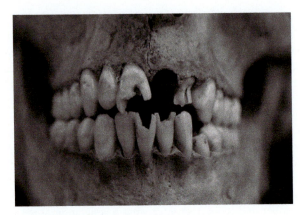

FIGURE 5.14 Tooth fractures resulting from taphonomic processes

of dental fractures near the time of death would have suggested trauma inflicted by the accused and supported a first degree murder conviction. The jury accepted the anthropological testimony that the dental fractures most likely were taphonomic in origin, and the case resulted in a second degree murder conviction. This case study points to the importance of having a thorough understanding of taphonomic modifications of human remains, and the ability to distinguish taphonomic change from trauma that may have been related to the death event.

5.9 Summary

- Forensic taphonomy is the study of postmortem processes which affect the preservation and recovery of human remains and that help reconstruct the circumstances surrounding the death event.
- Many taphonomic processes affect the state of preservation of remains, including decomposition, diagenesis, scavenging, movement, and the actions of other humans. Environmental factors such as temperature, humidity, and pH also influence the state of preservation.
- Forensic anthropologists study human decomposition to understand which taphonomic agents affected human remains, to aid in reconstructing the death event at a scene, and for estimating the time since death or postmortem interval.
- Decomposition occurs through autolysis and putrefaction. The soft tissues are modified first, and observable changes include algor mortis (body cooling), livor mortis (blood pooling), and rigor mortis (muscle stiffening).
- Human remains go through a series of decompositional stages that are somewhat predictable, with temperature being the primary factor responsible for the decomposition rate. Other factors in the local environment may also contribute to variation in decomposition rates.

- Because temperature is the primary factor responsible for variation in postmortem change, forensic scientists typically estimate time since death using accumulated degree days (ADD), which is used to count backward from the date of discovery to a likely time of death.
- A comprehensive understanding of taphonomy is essential for differentiating postmortem changes on remains from causes such as trauma.

5.10 Test yourself

- Police request your presence at a recovery scene for a set of skeletal remains which they believe were partially dismembered by the perpetrator of a homicide. The left arm and right lower leg are absent, and there are small punctures and grooves on some ribs and right arm bones. What alternate theories might you suggest to account for the missing skeletal elements?
- What are the means by which human agents modify human remains? Can you think of others that are not mentioned here?
- Why is taphonomy important for skeletal trauma analysis? What are the potential legal consequences of mistaking skeletal trauma for taphonomic changes (and vice versa)?
- How might you design a study to determine the effects of different types of clothing (or other body covering) on the rate of decomposition?
- In what ways do aquatic depositional environments differ from terrestrial ones? How do these differences affect the rate of decomposition? The dispersal of remains? Modification of the bones?
- Using Tables 5.4–5.6, calculate the Total Body Score for the following descriptions of remains:
  a. no discoloration of the head, torso or limbs;
  b. bloating and purging of the trunk, black discoloration of the head, and marbling of the limbs;
  c. dry tissue with bone exposed over more than half of the trunk, a dry skull retaining some grease, and dry bones of the limbs.

Using the composite score, calculate the ADD and then estimate the time since death based on an average daily temperature of 25°C (and assuming the same average for all days in the PMI). Note: you will need a scientific calculator for this exercise.

Definitions

Abiotic Non-biological; not from a living organism
Accumulated degree days (or ADD) The sum of the average daily temperatures for a given number of days, typically with reference to a particular temperature threshold
Adipocere A whitish, waxy substance produced during saponification

Algor mortis The cooling of the body after death

Artifactual preservation The preservation of a body or tissues by chemical substances, or by the destruction of decompositional bacteria

Autolysis The destruction of cells through the action of their own enzymes

Biotic Biological; derived from or relating to a living organism

Carnassials Modified last upper premolars and first lower molar teeth found in carnivores that are used for shearing

Decomposition The process by which organic material is broken down into simpler forms

Diagenesis Any chemical, physical, or biological change undergone by bone after its initial deposition

Differential decomposition The premature, irregular, or disproportional decomposition in an area or areas of the body

Fluvial transport The movement of bodies or skeletal remains in aquatic environments due to current or wave action

Forensic entomology The sub-field of entomology which studies those arthropods related to decomposition and the colonization of corpses for medicolegal purposes

Forensic taphonomy The study of postmortem processes which affect (1) the preservation, observation, or recovery of dead organisms, (2) the reconstruction of their biology or ecology, or (3) the reconstruction of the circumstances of their death

Intravascular hemolysis The darkening of vessels as a result of increased bacteria throughout the circulatory system during the decomposition process

Larviposit The deposition of maggot larvae

Livor mortis The pooling of blood after death

Marbling A pattern of discoloration created as a result of decomposition processes in the circulatory system

Microbe A micro-organism, usually a bacterium, that is responsible for disease or decomposition

Mummification To preserve a body by drying out or through the use of chemicals or wrappings

Necrophagous Feeding on dead or decaying corpses

Oviposit The deposition of egg masses

Postmortem interval (or PMI) The amount of time between death and discovery, usually in the context of forensic human remains; also called time since death

Putrefaction The microbial deterioration of tissues caused by the proliferation of bacteria associated with the digestive system

Rigor mortis The stiffening of muscles after death

Saponification A chemical process involving the hydrolysis of fatty acids; in decomposing remains, the resulting material is adipocere

Scavenging The consumption and modification of remains by other animals

Skeletonization The completion of soft tissue decomposition, leaving only the hard tissues of the skeleton

Skin slippage The shedding of the epidermis from the body caused by the deterioration of the junction between the dermis and epidermis

Succession The order in which different arthropods arrive at a corpse

Taphonomy The laws of burial, from the Greek *taphos* meaning burial and *onomy* meaning law

Taxon A taxonomic category of an organism such as genus or species

Weathering A postmortem modification process for hard tissues as a response to nature agents in their immediate environment over time

References

Anderson, G.S., 2010. Decomposition and invertebrate colonization of cadavers in coastal marine environments. In: Amendt, J., Campobasso, C.P., Grassberger, M., Goff, M.L. (Eds.), Current Concepts in Forensic Entomology. Springer, New York, pp. 223–272.

Bass, W.M., 1997. Outdoor decomposition rates in Tennessee. In: Haglund, W.D., Sorg, M.H. (Eds.), Forensic Taphonomy: The Postmortem Fate of Human Remains. CRC Press, Boca Raton, pp. 181–186.

Beary, M.O., Lyman, R.E., 2012. The use of taphonomy in forensic anthropology: Past trends and future prospects. In: Dirkmaat, D.C. (Ed.), A Companion to Forensic Anthropology. Blackwell Publishing, Oxford, pp. 499–527.

Behrensmeyer, A.K., 1978. Taphonomic and ecological information from bone weathering. Paleobiology 4, 150–162.

Berryman, H.E., 2002. Disarticulation pattern and tooth mark artifacts associated with pig scavenging of human remains: A case study. In: Haglund, W.D., Sorg, M.H. (Eds.), Advances in Forensic Taphonomy: Method, Theory, and Archaeological Perspectives. CRC Press, Boca Raton, pp. 487–496.

Brothwell, D., Gill-Robinson, H., 2002. Taphonomic and forensic aspects of bog bodies. In: Haglund, W.D., Sorg, M.H. (Eds.), Advances in Forensic Taphonomy: Method, Theory, and Archaeological Perspectives. CRC Press, Boca Raton, pp. 119–132.

Carson, E.A., Stefan, V.H., Powell, J.F., 2000. Skeletal manifestations of bear scavenging. J. Forensic Sci. 45 (3), 515–526.

Catts, E.P., Haskell, N.H., 1990. Entomology and death: a procedural guide. Joyce's Print Shop, Inc., Clemson.

Christensen, A.M., Myers, S.W., 2011. Macroscopic observations of the effects of varying fresh water pH on bone. J. Forensic Sci. 56 (2), 475–479.

Clark, M.A., Worrell, M.B., Pless, J.E., 1997. Postmortem changes in soft tissues. In: Haglund, W.D., Sorg, M.H. (Eds.), Forensic Taphonomy: The Postmortem Fate of Human Remains. CRC Press, Boca Raton, pp. 151–164.

Costello, E.K., Lauber, C.L., Hamaday, M., Fierer, N., Gordon, J.I., Knight, R., 2009. Bacterial community variation in human body habitats across space and time. Science 326, 1694–1697.

Dabbs, G.R., Martin, D.C., 2013. Geographic variation in the taphonomic effect of vulture scavenging: the case of Southern Illinois. J. Forensic Sci. 58, S20–S25.

Damann, F.E., Cartre, D.O., 2013. Human decomposition ecology and postmortem microbiology. In: Pokines, J., Symes, S. (Eds.), Manual of Forensic Taphonomy. CRC Press, Boca Raton, pp. 37–51.

Dilen, D.R., 1984. The motion of floating and submerged objects in the Chattahoochee River, Atlanta, GA. J. Forensic Sci. 29, 1027–1037.

Dirkmaat, D.C., Passalacqua, N.V., 2012. Introduction to Part VI: Forensic taphonomy. In: Dirkmaat, D.C. (Ed.), A Companion to Forensic Anthropology. Blackwell Publishing, Oxford, pp. 473–476.

Efremov, I.A., 1940. Taphonomy: New branch of paleontology. Pan-American Geologist 74, 81–93.

Fischer, C., 1998. Bog bodies of Denmark and northwest Europe. In: Cockburn, T.A., Cockburn, A., Reyman, T.A. (Eds.), Mummies, Disease and Ancient Cultures, second ed. Cambridge University Press, Cambridge, pp. 237–262.

Galloway, A., 1997. The process of decomposition: a model from the Arizona-Sonoran desert. In: Haglund, W.D., Sorg, M.H. (Eds.), Forensic Taphonomy: The Postmortem Fate of Human Remains. CRC Press, Boca Raton, pp. 139–150.

Gill, J.R., Rainwater, C.W., Adams, B.J., 2009. Santeria and Palo Mayombe: Skulls, Mercury and Artifacts. J. Forensic Sci. 54 (6), 1458–1462.

Gill-King, H., 1997. Chemical and ultrastructural aspects of decomposition. In: Haglund, W.D., Sorg, M.H. (Eds.), Forensic Taphonomy: The Postmortem Fate of Human Remains. CRC Press, Boca Raton, pp. 93–108.

Haglund, W.D., 1997a. Dogs and coyotes: Postmortem involvement with human remains. In: Haglund, W.D., Sorg, M.H. (Eds.), Forensic Taphonomy: The Postmortem Fate of Human Remains. CRC Press, Boca Raton, pp. 367–382.

Haglund, W.D., 1997b. Rodents and human remains. In: Haglund, W.D., Sorg, M.H. (Eds.), Forensic Taphonomy: The Postmortem Fate of Human Remains. CRC Press, Boca Raton, pp. 405–414.

Haglund, W.D., Sorg, M.H. (Eds.), 1997. Forensic Taphonomy: The Postmortem Fate of Human Remains. CRC Press, Boca Raton.

Haglund, W.D., Sorg, M.H. (Eds.), 2002. Advances in Forensic Taphonomy: Method, Theory, and Archaeological Perspectives. CRC Press, Boca Raton.

Haskell, N.H., Hall, R.D., Cervenka, V.J., Clark, Michael A., 1997. On the body: insect's life stage presence and their postmortem artifacts. In: Haglund, W.D., Sorg, M.H. (Eds.), Forensic Taphonomy: The Postmortem Fate of Human Remains. CRC Press, Boca Raton, pp. 415–448.

Haynes, G., 1980. Prey bones and predators: Potential ecologic information from analysis of bone sites. Ossa 7, 75–97.

Houck, M.M., Siegel, J.A., 2010. Fundamentals of forensic science, second ed. Elsevier, Amsterdam.

Klippel, W.E., Synstelien, J.A., 2007. Rodents as taphonomic agents: Bone gnawing by brown rats and gray squirrels. J. Forensic Sci. 52 (4), 765–773.

Knight, B. (Ed.), 2002. The Estimation of the Time since Death in the Early Postmortem Period. Edward Arnold, London.

Lyman, R.L., 1994. Vertebrate Taphonomy. Cambridge University Press, Cambridge.

Lyman, R.L., Fox, G.L., 1997. A critical review of bone weathering as an indication of bone assemblage formation. In: Haglund, W.D., Sorg, M.H. (Eds.), Forensic Taphonomy: The Postmortem Fate of Human Remains. CRC Press, Boca Raton, pp. 223–247.

Marks, M.M., Love, J.C., Dadour, I.R., 2009. Taphonomy and time: estimating the postmortem interval. In: Steadman, D.W. (Ed.), Hard Evidence: Case Studies in Forensic Anthropology, second ed. Pearson Education, Inc., Upper Saddle River, pp. 165–178.

Marshall, L.G., 1989. Bone modification and the laws of burial. In: Bonnichsen, R., Sorg, M.H., Modification, Bone (Eds.), Center for the Study of the First Americans, Orono, pp. 7–24.

Megyesi, M.S., Nawrocki, S.P., Haskell, N.H., 2005. Using accumulated degree-days to estimate the postmortem interval from decomposed human remains. J. Forensic Sci. 50 (3), 1–9.

Micozzi, M.S., 1997. Frozen environments and soft tissue preservation. In: Haglund, W.D., Sorg, M.H. (Eds.), Forensic Taphonomy: The Postmortem Fate of Human Remains. CRC Press, Boca Raton, pp. 171–180.

Moore, W.J., 1981. The Mammalian Skull. Cambridge University Press, New York.

Nawrocki, S.P., 2013. Modeling core and peripheral processes in human decomposition: A conceptual framework. Proceedings of the 65th annual meeting of the American Academy of Forensic Sciences, Washington, DC.

Nielsen-Marsh, C.M., Hedges, R.E.M., 2000. Patterns of diagenesis in Bone I: The effects of site environments. J. Archaeol. Sci. 27, 1139–1150.

Reeves, N.M., 2009. Taphonomic effects of vulture scavenging. J. Forensic Sci. 54 (2), 523–528.

Rippley, A., Larison, N.C., Moss, K.E., Kelley, J.D., Bytheway, J.A., 2012. Scavenging behavior of Lynx rufus on human remains during the winter months of Southeast Texas. J. Forensic Sci. 57 (3), 699–705.

Sorg, M.A., Dearborn, J.H., Mohanan, E.I., Ryan, H.F., Sweeney, K.G., David, E., 1997. Forensic Taphonomy in Marine Contexts. In: Haglund, W.D., Sorg, M.H. (Eds.), Forensic Taphonomy: The Postmortem Fate of Human Remains. CRC Press, Boca Raton, pp. 567–604.

Ubelaker, D.H., 1997. Taphonomic applications in forensic anthropology. In: Haglund, W.D., Sorg, M.H. (Eds.), Forensic Taphonomy: The Postmortem Fate of Human Remains. CRC Press, Boca Raton, pp. 77–90.

Ubelaker, D.H., Zarenko, K.M., 2011. Adipocere: what is known after two centuries of research. Forensic Sci. Int. 208, 167–172.

Vass, A.A., 2011. The elusive universal post-mortem interval formula. Forensic Sci. Int. 204, 34–40.

Victoria Experimental Network Under the Sea (VENUS). Venus.uvic.ca (accessed 05.14.13).

Forensic Archaeology and Scene Processing Methods

6

6.1 Principles of forensic archaeology

Forensic archaeology is the application of archaeological theory and methods to the resolution of medicolegal and humanitarian issues (Scientific Working Group for Forensic Anthropology [SWGANTH], 2013). It may include methods involved in searching for, locating, surveying, sampling, recording, and interpreting evidence, as well as the recovery and documentation of human remains and associated evidence (SWGANTH, 2013). Forensic anthropologists and archaeologists are therefore often requested to assist investigators and law enforcement in assessing the applicability of remote sensing techniques, developing recovery strategies, mapping recovery scenes, dating evidence, and reconstructing events. Proper implementation of forensic archaeological techniques provides a scientific basis for interpreting the context in which remains and associated evidence are found.

The origins of forensic archaeology lie in the fact that traditional crime scene processing methods were often abandoned when scenes occurred outdoors. It was long believed that outdoor contexts too quickly degraded evidence, and were not easily sketched or mapped because there were often no good points of reference. Instead, any obvious evidence was quickly photographed and collected for lab processing. It has recently become more standard practice to use forensic anthropologists with archaeological training to assist in crime scene recovery and evidence collection.

In the United States, archaeology and physical anthropology are considered subfields of anthropology. Thus, forensic anthropologists are typically educated and trained in both skeletal analysis and archaeological methods as part of their advanced studies. In other areas of the world, however, such as the United Kingdom, forensic archaeology is considered a separate discipline from forensic anthropology.

It is recognized that traditional archaeological methods can be very tedious and time-consuming, and that not all forensic archaeological investigations can be carried out in exactly the same fashion. Unlike many archaeological field projects, time is often more limited in forensic contexts because investigators may be trying to develop leads quickly, collect evidence before it is lost or destroyed, or identify a suspect. There may also be additional safety concerns for forensic searches in conflict situations, in remote locations, or under hazardous conditions. It is therefore important to maintain good communication with the investigating agency, and to balance

Forensic Anthropology. http://dx.doi.org/10.1016/B978-0-12-418671-2.00006-9

factors such as safety, scene security, resources (including personnel and equipment), evidence quality, and time.

The purpose of forensic archaeology is to properly investigate a recovery scene from the beginning of a search to the removal and transport of the evidence from the scene, and to maintain context and the chain of custody for all evidentiary materials recovered (Morse et al., 1983; Cox et al., 2008). Specific goals and objectives of forensic archaeological operations are summarized in Table 6.1. The rest of this chapter will provide an overview of the principles, recommended approaches, and challenges of forensic archaeological methods in locating and recovering human remains.

6.2 Recovery scenes

Human remains can be discovered in and recovered from a wide variety of scene types, including indoor and outdoor, confined, or dispersed. The location where human remains are found is often called a **scene** or **recovery scene** (the term *crime scene*, though often applied to recovery scenes, may not always be appropriate). Outdoor scenes may involve remains that are on the surface, buried, submerged, or involved in fires (which are technically specialized surface scenes, having factors that make recovery approaches somewhat more challenging). Large scale mass disasters typically involve more complex scene processing methods and multiple investigating agencies, and are addressed in more detail in Chapter 15.

Surface scenes occur when remains are deposited on the surface of the ground (i.e., are not deliberately buried or submerged). Sometimes the remains will be in a very similar location and position to that where they were deposited. More often, however, especially for remains that have decomposed to the point of skeletonization,

---

Table 6.1 Objectives of a forensic archaeological operation

1. To select a detection or recovery strategy that maximizes data recorded and physical evidence recovered from a scene while minimizing scene and evidence alteration.
2. To establish and fully document the context in which all evidence is found. The recording of all spatial and contextual associations should be such that any subsequent identification process will not be hindered or compromised.
3. To recover all evidence that may be relevant to identifying the remains, determining the cause and manner of death, reconstructing the scene, determining how the remains were deposited, estimating time since deposition, and identifying post depositional taphonomic processes should be recorded.
4. To ensure safe and secure collection, storage, and transportation of human remains and associated materials from the point of recovery to accession by the appropriate agency.
5. To maintain a chain of custody through documentary and photographic records that link the recovered evidence to the scene.
6. To ensure safe and secure transport of evidence to the responsible agency.

(From Scientific Working Group for Forensic Anthropology [SWGANTH], 2013)

scavenging and other natural and physical forces (e.g., water, wind, gravity) contribute to the scattering of remains from their initial deposition site. Remains that have been redistributed in this manner are referred to as a **surface scatter**.

Burial scenes involve remains that are **interred**, or deliberately buried underground in a grave. Because these remains are not usually visible on the surface, burial scenes are often more difficult to locate, sometimes requiring specialized search techniques and technologies. While in many cases, remains are intentionally buried by a perpetrator in a clandestine grave, remains may also become buried naturally by movement of water, soil, or debris, or transported underground into burrows by animals. Some burial scenes may also involve remains that were interred in cemeteries as part of funerary practices.

Submerged scenes are those involving remains that are in aquatic environments. These may be large bodies of water such as oceans, lakes, and large rivers, but may also be swamps, small or shallow ponds, or streams. Remains in these cases may be floating on the surface of the water, resting on the substrate at the bottom, or possibly suspended in between.

Fire scenes are those involving thermally altered remains, which are often intermixed with other burned debris such as building materials or plant debris (e.g., trees and leaves). While such remains may be found in buried or submerged scenes, they are most commonly surface scenes. Fire scenes are often very complex, requiring different methods of documentation and collection because they are often associated with a high degree of fragmentation as well as other scene considerations such as access and safety hazards.

6.3 Archaeological methods and theory

Forensic archaeological methods are typically applied to the outdoor location and recovery of remains including surface remains and burials, usually when substantial decomposition or fragmentation has occurred (Cox et al., 2008). Forensic archaeological principles, however, can also be applied to indoor scenes as well as underwater and fire scenes. One important feature of archaeological methods is that the processes are inherently and unavoidably destructive. When remains and evidence are collected and removed from the scene, the context is permanently altered and the actual spatial relationships are lost. Thorough documentation and careful preservation of the material and contextual information are therefore very important.

Archaeological methods have a long history of testing and application in a wide variety of complex environments. Given the success of these approaches in investigating and interpreting past events from the archaeological record, it makes sense that they can also be successfully applied to forensic casework, particularly for locating and processing scenes. In fact, most modern crime scene processing approaches (for both indoor and outdoor scenes) are now based largely on principles developed in the field of archaeology (Hunter and Cox, 2005). The main principles of archaeology are the understanding of temporal and spatial relationships which are exemplified in **Steno's Laws**, and which form the basis of the interpretation of context though the understanding of **stratigraphy** and relative positioning (Box 6.1).

BOX 6.1 NICOLAS STENO (1638–1686) AND STENO'S LAWS

Nicolas Steno was a Danish anatomist who spent much of his professional time working for the Medici family in Florence, Italy (Cutler, 2004). During his time in Florence, Steno dissected the head of a large shark caught by local fishermen and noted that the teeth of the shark were very similar to certain stones found throughout the countryside referred to as *glossoperae* ("stone tongues"). In reality these *glossoperae* were fossilized shark teeth, but fossils were not well understood at this time and most scholars believed that fossil shells and other forms naturally grew in the stone in which they were found. Based on his comparison of the shark teeth to the *glossoperae*, Steno began to look more closely at the geologic formations and processes around him. These observations culminated in the publication of his *dissertationis prodromus*: "*Prodromus to a dissertation on solids naturally enclosed in solids*" in 1669 (Steno, 1916). In this work, Steno defined the science of stratigraphy and developed Steno's four laws (below). Steno's laws form the basis of the interpretation of context though the understanding of relative positioning as well as **relative dating**, which is a system for sequencing artifacts or other materials and is commonly performed in archaeological investigations. Because stratigraphy relates specifically to geologic sedimentary layers, the term **soil horizon** is typically used in archaeology. The difference is that soil horizons (layers) may be formed from other natural processes than geologic phenomena; one may have multiple soil horizons in a single **stratum** (Holliday, 2004).

1. *Law of Superimposition*: Lower strata must have formed before upper strata
2. *Law of Original Horizontality*: Strata which are not horizontal formed horizontally and were later shifted out of their original position
3. *Law of Cross-Cutting*: If a burial pit is found in strata, the strata must have formed prior to the burial disturbance.
4. *Law of Lateral Continuity*: The size and shape of each stratum is determined by the natural boundaries it formed in.

There are four generally recognized phases of archaeological investigation, which can also be applied to forensic contexts (Dirkmaat and Adovasio, 1997).

Phase I – Systematic search: The search phase involves locating areas that may warrant further investigation. In archaeological investigations, this phase primarily involves surface survey, often by walking transects and noting archaeological features; remote survey using maps and aerial photography is also common. In a forensic context, Phase I involves a search for human remains, usually a burial feature or surface remains.

Phase II – Evaluation of an area for significance: Once a potential area of interest is located or identified, the area is evaluated to determine whether additional investigation is required. In archaeological investigations, this phase involves subsurface survey in order to determine site boundaries and focal areas. In certain applications of archaeology, particularly **Cultural Resource Management** (or CRM), Phase II is performed in order to evaluate whether an area of interest warrants full scale excavation, such as if a construction project during which ancient human remains were uncovered needs to be halted to permit a large scale archaeological excavation. The evaluation phase is typically brief and straightforward in forensic scenarios such as an isolated burial or surface scatter because the area of interest is rather small and can be investigated relatively quickly without significantly disturbing the scene. Phase

II evaluations may be more involved in large scale scenes such as a plane crash or conflict region, because these scenes can be quite large and often require complex investigative work prior to a full excavation.

Phase III – Recovery: Phase III encompasses the systematic recovery and preservation of the material of interest from the scene. In an archaeological context, this phase involves the excavation of an archaeological site, feature, or structure and collection of associated artifacts and ecofacts in order to gain information about a culture through the materials they left behind. In a forensic context, this phase involves the recovery and preservation of context and evidentiary materials in order to reconstruct the death event, deposition of the body, and taphonomic modifications that have occurred since deposition.

Phase IV – Interpretation and reporting: Phase IV involves the generation of a report and interpretations based on the activities and products of the previous three phases. Phase IV reporting should be accompanied by a map of the project area as well as interpretations and conclusions. In an archaeological context where sites may be investigated slowly over the course of many years, Phase IV reports are often completed annually, providing a summary of past work, detailing the current progress, discussing all findings to date, and making justifications and recommendations for the next year's work. In a forensic context, this report is submitted to the investigating agency, and provides a summary of the approaches used and the interpretation of the evidence that was located and collected. Even if a search did not result in the location of remains, the report should document the procedures used as well as the area that was searched. These details may help the investigating agency determine the next step of the investigation.

6.4 **Detection methods**

The detection of a scene involves the search for and location of remains. The selection of the methods used in the detection or identification of a recovery scene and its boundaries is dependent on the type and scale of the case as well as aspects of the terrain itself. Methods differ, for example, when searching for surface remains versus buried or submerged remains, and different approaches may be required in steep, dense terrain versus an open field. In many cases, the type of scene may not yet be known when the search begins, and detection methods may need to be modified depending on initial findings.

The most common search technique for outdoor scenes of virtually any type is the pedestrian survey or **line search** (see Figure 6.1). A line search is performed by having a number of search personnel form a straight line at one end of the search area. This often includes a forensic anthropologist or archaeologist as well as a team of law enforcement personnel and other specialists at the scene (e.g., search and rescue, cadaver dogs, forensic geologists). Each member of the line search stands approximately an arm's length apart so that their fields of vision overlap. Each person should also carry pin flags to mark areas of interest (including potential evidence such as

FIGURE 6.1 Standing line search

(Photo courtesy of Melanie Beasley)

FIGURE 6.2 Hands and knees line search

(Image courtesy of Dennis Dirkmaat)

bones or other features that may indicate a burial or other activity) as they are encountered in the search. The line search then progresses by walking on foot and closely observing the ground and surroundings at a slow, steady pace marking evidence as it is encountered (depending on the size of the area). Additional searches are often conducted after the first search; for example, a walking line search may be conducted to locate the remains, followed by a similar search on hands and knees in order to allow the searchers a better view of small details on the ground (Figure 6.2). If the area to be

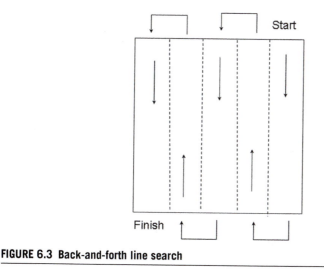

Start

Finish

FIGURE 6.3 Back-and-forth line search

covered exceeds the length of the personnel on the line search, a back-and-forth pattern approach can be used (Figure 6.3).

Care should be taken to avoid disturbing any possible evidence during the search. A line search should have a "line leader" who keeps the pace and direction of the line as it progresses through an area of interest, ensuring that the search occurs systematically. Often, the forensic anthropologist will follow behind the search, evaluating flagged items for forensic significance (e.g., whether flagged items are human bones or possible indicators of a burial). When remains are initially discovered, knowledge of potential scavengers in a particular geographic area as well as their feeding behavior may assist in further search strategies. In addition to the remains themselves, other relevant evidence may also be discovered that is associated with the scene, such as animal dragging trails or maggot trails, rodent burrows/nests, and artifacts such as clothing or jewelry. It is also important to visually scan the rest of the search area above ground, including up in trees. Birds will often take hair from remains to be incorporated into their nests.

Burial scenes can also be discovered by examining the surface in a line search. Buried bodies will often be associated with a soil depression, differential vegetation growth due to the disturbance of living plants when digging or changing of the soil from body decomposition, or abnormal accumulation of tree branches or other forest debris from perpetrators attempting to cover the disturbed area. Other soil disturbances associated with burials may include variation in soil color, cracks, soil mixing, and leftover dirt (**back-dirt**) (Figure 6.4). When a grave is dug, the horizons are disturbed, and the soils from the different horizons are mixed together. The new soil mixture that is placed back into the grave (called **infill**) will typically differ in color and quality from the individual undisturbed soil horizons, which may appear visibly different on the surface. Once a body is placed into the grave, all of the soil will not

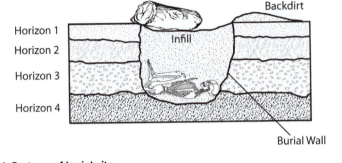

FIGURE 6.4 Features of burial site

fit back into the hole. This will result in left over dirt that can usually be found in a mound over the grave, or as a back-dirt pile near the grave. As the body decomposes and the infill settles and becomes more compact, a depression will usually form over the grave site. This settling may also result in cracks in the surface of the infill. Aerial surveys (photographs taken from airplanes) of the search area taken at different times can also be compared to look for possible surface disturbances.

Another method of burial scene detection is **subsurface probing**, which is useful for locating burial features or other soil disturbances. The utility of probing is based on the principle of relative soil compaction. The disturbed infill that is placed back into the grave will be less compact than the surrounding undisturbed soil. The probe will therefore insert more easily and to a greater depth in areas where the soil is disturbed (i.e., less compact). Soil probes are typically made of fiberglass or metal and are pushed into the ground surface at regular intervals (Figure 6.5). Subsurface probing should be performed in a systematic (usually linear) fashion, probing every 6–12 inches throughout an area of interest. Although the ends of probes are typically blunt, care should be taken to avoid potential damage to skeletal remains with the probe. Similar to subsurface probing, soil cores or small test pits can assist in the determination of whether the natural soil horizons have been disturbed.

Other methods of searching for buried remains involve the use of geophysical or remote sensing devices which detect anomalies in subsurface soil. Approaches include resistivity techniques which detect disturbances using electrical current and measuring resistance, ground penetrating radar (GPR) which detects soil disturbances using electromagnetic pulses, and magnetometry which detects minor magnetic changes in disturbed soil. These approaches are typically best in very specific terrains and soil types, and often require specialized training to operate and interpret. They are not considered standard forensic archaeological approaches, and are associated with a high degree of error (both false positives and false negatives). When geophysical and remote sensing approaches yield negative results, it should not be considered an indication that remains are not present.

Cadaver dogs can assist in locating decomposing human remains using their well-developed sense of smell which can detect the odor emitted by decomposing

FIGURE 6.5 Subsurface probing

tissue. Cadaver dogs are trained to systematically progress though a search area, honing in on the source of the odor, and to then alert (usually by sitting or barking) at the odor's strongest location. Cadaver dogs are typically only able to locate more recent remains which emit a stronger odor, and most are less successful in cases involving skeletonized or buried remains. In cases of buried bodies, probing the soil may release the odors of decomposition to the surface and allow the cadaver dog to detect the odor more easily. Various factors can affect the reliability and effectiveness of cadaver dogs in remains searches. For example, weather conditions may affect the ability of a cadaver dog to locate the source of the odor, or a large number of people at a scene may distract the animal. Moreover, cadaver dogs are frequently the pets of their handlers which can create emotional bonds that could affect performance. The effectiveness of cadaver dogs, as with other forensic tools, also relies heavily on the quality and integrity of the user (see Box 6.2).

Although minimally destructive search techniques using small or remote tools is the ideal approach, in certain circumstances, such as when a very large or deep area needs to be searched, it may be necessary to employ more extensive (and potentially destructive) methods to locate a burial site. These methods often involve the use of heavy construction equipment to remove large volumes of soil in a relatively

---

BOX 6.2 SANDRA ANDERSON

Sandra Anderson was once considered one of the best cadaver dog trainers and handlers in the United States. She claimed to have conducted ~200 cadaver dog searches per year for 17 years. In 2002, while working with her dog Eagle, the FBI discovered Anderson planting evidence (including bone fragments and carpet fibers) around a tree stump. Numerous other cases were later confirmed in which Anderson had planted evidence. In one case, Eagle alerted to a human toe found in a search area, but the missing man's body was later found with his boots on and his feet intact. In other searches in Michigan and Ohio, Anderson is said to have planted human bones in search areas and even used her own blood to stain a saw blade, coins, and a piece of cloth. Anderson was eventually convicted, sentenced to 21 months of jail time, and ordered to pay more than $14,500 in restitution for falsifying a material fact, making false representations, one count of obstruction of justice, and two counts of making false statements and representations.

---

short period of time. A backhoe is often the machine of choice because it can remove soil with its blade without having to drive over the search area, but bulldozers can also be utilized in a minimally invasive way (Christensen et al., 2009). Such machines should only be used as a last resort due to their potential to damage remains as well as destroy contextual information, and a smooth-edged bucket is preferred over a toothed bucket. If heavy equipment is employed, it should only be used until remains are discovered, and it is highly advisable that an anthropologist be present to assist in searching the excavated soil for skeletal remains. Once the scene is located, the excavation should proceed by more careful archaeological methods.

Detection methods for submerged remains usually involve specialists such as public safety divers or forensic divers who may perform an underwater dive search. They may also use sonar, remotely operated vehicles (ROVs), or other remote sensing techniques to potentially detect anomalies that may be human remains prior to entering the water. Underwater, divers use many of the same approaches as on land to locate evidence including the use of systematic linear searches and devices such as screens, metal detectors, and specialized light sources (Christensen et al., 2014). Ideally, a forensic anthropologist should be present during the search, and evaluate any potential human remains that are collected and brought to the surface to help determine whether a scene has been located.

6.5 Recovery methods

In any search that is successful, the medicolegal authority must be contacted immediately and prior to recovery. This is typically the responsibility of the investigating agency (such as a police department), but anthropologists involved in the recovery of remains should ensure that proper notifications and approvals have taken place prior to disturbing or removing any human remains from the scene. Recovery methods are aimed at removing the evidence from the scene in a systematic manner while maintaining context, which will allow reconstruction of the events that resulted in the creation of the recovery scene (Dirkmaat and Adovasio, 1997). Recovery operations should therefore include detailed field notes taken during the recovery which document scene processing procedures. These notes should eventually be accompanied by a scaled map documenting the locations of all evidentiary materials and other landmarks significant to maintaining context.

The first step in the recovery process is **denuding** the scene, or carefully clearing the **overburden** so that all evidentiary material is exposed but not disturbed. This allows for the general distribution of evidence as well as the scene perimeter to be visualized, photographed, and mapped. After the scene has been cleared, a **datum** should be established. The datum is the primary reference point used for mapping and should be placed in a location from which the evidence can be accurately mapped. In cases where there may be multiple layers of evidentiary material (e.g., a fire scene), the datum may need to be established prior to denuding so that evidence can be mapped, recorded, and moved to access the next layer beneath.

The recovery of surface remains is usually as simple as retrieving the items identified and flagged during the search process. Any overburden such as leaf litter or loose topsoil should be screened for small bones or other evidence items that may not have been detected in the initial search. Screens are typically constructed of wire mesh (commonly ¼ inch, but smaller sizes may be needed) attached to a wooden or metal frame, and often suspended by moveable legs so that the screen can be shaken (Figure 6.6). This configuration facilitates the movement of material through the screen, so that skeletal elements or evidence items can be located and removed. Depending on factors such as soil quality and available resources, material may be screened dry or wet screened.

With submerged remains, collection receptacles or lift bags may be used to remove the remains from water. Very few anthropologists are trained divers with

FIGURE 6.6 Screening

experience in underwater recovery procedures. There is a specialized area known as **underwater archaeology**, which employs all of the same principles and approaches as terrestrial archaeology, but is performed underwater. While the physical collection of submerged remains should be left to these trained specialists, an anthropologist should at least be on scene to address any questions of forensic significance and evidence handling.

The recovery of buried remains typically involves **excavation**, or the exposure and recovery of the remains through a slow and careful digging process. This usually involves small hand tools including trowels and brushes (Figure 6.7). When recovering buried remains, it is important to not only excavate and recover details of the

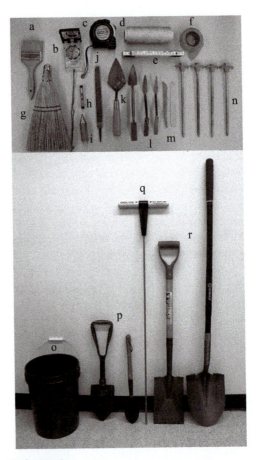

FIGURE 6.7 Archaeological tools

(a) Small brush, (b) sighting compass, (c) metric tape measure, (d) string, (e) folding tape measure, (f) flagging tape, (g) whisk broom, (h) line-level, (i) plumb-bob, (j) file (for trowel sharpening), (k) trowel, (l) small leaf trowels, (m) wooden carving tool, (n) stakes, (o) bucket, (p) small shovels, (q) probe, and (r) large shovels

remains themselves, but also those of the burial feature in which they are interred. The burial feature may contain evidence such as tool marks from the burial implement (such as a shovel) which may be present along the walls of the pit, shoe prints which may be found in the back-dirtpile or in the bottom of the burial, or disturbed vegetation may be mixed with the infill which could be examined by a forensic botanist to determine when the pit was dug.

Once the outline of the burial feature has been identified and defined, string held by stakes or chaining pins can be used to bisect the feature. Excavation of the infill of one half of the burial feature should then proceed slowly from the bisection line toward the grave wall using hand trowels. This approach allows for the preservation of possible tool marks in the walls of the burial. Exposing half of the remains also allows for documentation of the position of the body and the body's relationship to evidentiary material encountered and the burial feature itself. The interpretation of soil horizons and stratigraphy is also important in an excavation, because it can help to differentiate between undisturbed (sterile) soil and disturbed soil. After excavating one half of the grave feature, the exposed wall should be mapped, and the other half of the burial can then be excavated. In archaeology, it is common to **pedestal** artifacts and remains encountered during excavation. When potential evidence is encountered during a forensic excavation, it should be carefully exposed, photographed, mapped, and then removed. This will prevent it from becoming accidently disturbed and losing its context before it can be recorded, and will preserve the grave cut.

The excavation of a burial feature should result in an open grave resembling the feature as it was originally dug. Once the remains have been removed from the grave, a metal detector should be used on the grave floor to search for additional evidence such as bullets, coins, or jewelry still obscured by soil (Figure 6.8). Careful excavation of the bottom of a grave may also reveal shoe or tool impressions (Figure 6.9).

During excavation, all osseous and other evidentiary materials should ideally be recovered *in situ*. In some cases, however, bone fragments or other pieces of evidence (e.g., clothing items, bullets) may be small or difficult to see due to their small size or adhering soil, and may accidentally be excavated along with the soil and removed from the grave. Excavated soil should therefore always be screened

FIGURE 6.8 Metal detector used on the bottom of a burial

FIGURE 6.9 Tool impressions in a grave wall

for small bones and teeth or other associated evidence. If something of evidentiary value is recovered in a screen, it is helpful to document where in the feature or scene the soil came from (such as a grid quadrant) in order to maintain as much context as possible.

Fire scenes with burned remains are often complex recoveries because the remains may be very fragile and obscured by other burned materials. The removal of fallen burned debris covering human remains should be conducted carefully and systematically, layer by layer, and be accompanied by comprehensive documentation of the process. This allows investigators to observe, identify, and uncover patterns based on the relationships between the items recovered (Dirkmaat, 2002; King and King, 1989). In fatal fire scenes, documentation of the position of the body and its relationship to other features is important in the interpretation of the thermal alteration pattern of the remains during later lab analysis. In any of the scene types, after collection of the visible remains, the recovery area should be excavated somewhat below the surface (usually at least 10 cm) to look for remains or other evidence that may have settled into the soil or foundation material.

6.6 Scene documentation

Scene documentation should include detailed written notes and ample photographs of the overall scene, midrange views, and close-ups of the material recovered. Videography or laser scanning (e.g., Lidar) may also provide good overviews of the scene and the approaches used. It is most important to document the context and provenience of the evidentiary material recovered for later interpretation. The best way to accomplish this is by generating a map, which should document the spatial distribution of all remains and associated materials recovered. Mapping is best conducted after performing a thorough search, denuding the area, and exposing the remains and any associated evidence. Different types of recovery scenes are better documented using certain methods, and several approaches are discussed below.

Maps can be created in two or three dimensions depending on type and scale of the scene, and may range from hand-drawn sketches (for example, see case study and Figure 6.20) to electronic maps generated by mapping instruments (for example, see Figure 6.17). Maps should be as accurate as possible and at a minimum should include a north (N) arrow, indicate scale (or "not to scale"), and include the author's name, date, and the location of the datum. Mapping a scene can be accomplished using various methods including triangulation, trilateration, baseline, azimuth, or grid methods. The selection of the mapping approach to be used depends on the extent and terrain of the scene, as well as the proficiencies or preferences of the recovery personnel. Surface remains, for example, are typically better mapped using a baseline or trilateration, while burials are usually better mapped using a grid.

For any of these approaches it is important to keep the measurement tapes level to avoid adding measurement error. It is also strongly recommended to use a **plumb-bob** to keep vertical measurements straight (Figure 6.10). As a rule, measurements should be taken using metric units, which can later be converted to other units if necessary.

Triangulation is the process of determining the location of a point (here, the piece of evidence such as a bone) by measuring the angles to that point from a line between two known points (Figure 6.11). A similar process, **trilateration**, involves determining the location of a point by measuring the distance to that point from two known points (Figure 6.12). In either case, the approach essentially

FIGURE 6.10 Plumb-bob used to take a vertical measurement

(Image courtesy of Dennis Dirkmaat)

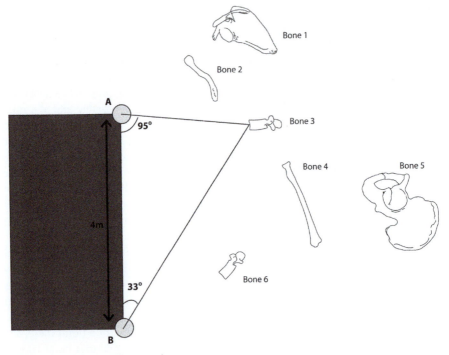

FIGURE 6.11 Triangulation mapping

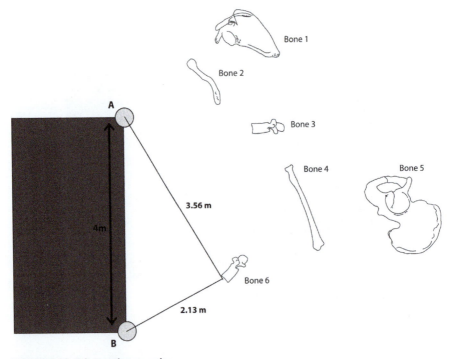

FIGURE 6.12 Trilateration mapping

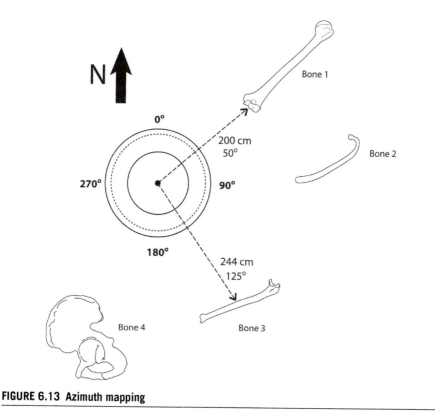

FIGURE 6.13 Azimuth mapping

involves forming a triangle where the locations of two of the points are known, and the third can then be derived from those two known points. The known points in these methods are typically fixed objects that can be easily located such as two corners of a building, one of which is usually the datum. The data collected in the field can be easily documented in a table that records the angles or distances between the points. It is important to also record the distance between the two known points.

Another approach is the use of an **azimuth**. This mapping technique involves the measurement of the distance and angle (from north) of an evidence item from a single, fixed point using an *azimuth board* (or *azimuth wheel*). The azimuth board is placed at a point of origin (typically the datum), aligned with 0/360 to north, and anchored. The zero end of the tape is also anchored at the center of the azimuth board, and evidence items are mapped using the distance along the tape and the angle of the azimuth (Figure 6.13). This method allows for very rapid measurements, and can be especially useful in scenes that are widely dispersed or involve uneven terrain.

A common mapping approach is the use of a **baseline**, which is a line that cuts through the scene transversely, from which the evidence items are measured. For

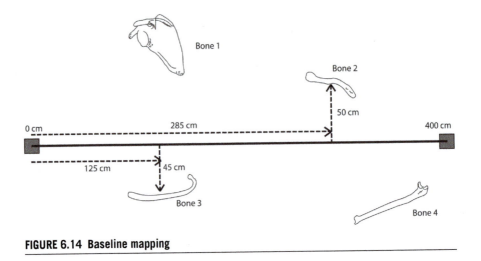

FIGURE 6.14 Baseline mapping

the baseline method, a tape measure is placed in a straight line between two points (one of which is often the datum), roughly bisecting the main concentration of evidence. A string tied between two stakes along with a line-level can help keep the tape measure level. Next, the distance of the evidence items are measured at right angles to the baseline, noting the distance on the tape from one of the ends of the baseline (Figure 6.14 and Box 6.3). It is also important to note from which side of the baseline the measurement was taken, which can be accomplished using positive and negative measurements (positive for one side of the baseline and negative for the other). Baseline mapping allows for quick measurements to be taken with little measurement error because of the relatively small distance from the baseline measuring tape and most of the evidence. While baseline approaches are most commonly used for horizontally mapping items resting on the ground surface, they can also be used to plot vertical distances by measuring above or below the baseline.

Another mapping approach is the use of a **grid** which uses quadrants based on two fixed axes. While grid systems can also be used to map surface remains, they are most commonly used to map burial scenes (Figure 6.15). Grid mapping allows for good control of small spaces and makes subsurface measurements somewhat easier and with less measurement error compared to other hand mapping methods. To set up a grid, the x- and y-axes are first established, usually using the datum as the point of origin (Figure 6.16a). The axes must meet at right angles (Box 6.4). Along the axes, stakes can be placed at intervals depending on the size of the area to be mapped, often at 1 m apart, with the total number of stakes depending on how many units or quadrants the excavation requires. Stakes can then be placed within the grid, making sure that the grids are accurate squares (Figure 6.16b and c). The rest of the grid stakes can then be placed as necessary (Figure 6.16d).

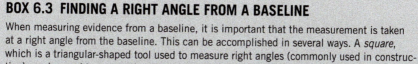

BOX 6.3 FINDING A RIGHT ANGLE FROM A BASELINE

When measuring evidence from a baseline, it is important that the measurement is taken at a right angle from the baseline. This can be accomplished in several ways. A *square*, which is a triangular-shaped tool used to measure right angles (commonly used in construction) can be used to ensure that the tapes are placed at right angles. Another approach that is useful in the field can be applied quickly and accurately to find a right angle to the baseline:

Place the end (the "zero") of the tape measure at the evidence item. Next, move/swing the free end of the tape along the baseline. Wherever the free end of the tape makes the *shortest* distance to the baseline is a right angle.

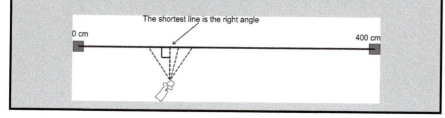

A number of more advanced technological mapping tools are also available. With proper training and use, these tools can facilitate very rapid and accurate scene documentation. A **total station** is a digital laser **theodolite** (or *transit*) used for three dimensional mapping (Figure 6.17). Total stations are commonly used in archaeology, surveying, and crime scene reconstruction. The benefits of using a total station include the rapid collection of three dimensional points over large areas, the instant creation of simple digital maps, and the ability to process the data later using computer software to make complex maps and analyze spatial patterns. Total stations, however, can be rather expensive and require specialized training, both in operating the total station itself and also in using the associated computer software.

Global Positioning Systems (GPS) measure the time it takes radio signals from GPS satellites to reach a GPS receiver from different angles to determine their position (Figure 6.18). The accuracy of a GPS location is determined by the number of satellites available, the number of points taken at one location, multipath interference, and atmospheric conditions. It is recommended that at least one GPS location is documented at every recovery scene; this will allow investigators to return to the exact area later if necessary. GPS data are especially useful for documenting the position of the site datum, the corners of a grid, and other landmarks at the scene. If a GPS is used, documentation of the data should include the number of satellites, the accuracy (e.g., ± 3 meters), the GPS grid system (e.g., MGRS), and the GPS datum (e.g., WGS-84). Most GPS receivers are fairly inexpensive and simple to use. The primary drawback of GPS is that it is not typically accurate enough to piece-plot multiple items at the scene. Most smart phones, for example, have GPS capabilities, but they also have very large associated error. GPS locations are typically only recorded on a limited number of features while still relying on detailed maps made using hand measuring tapes or total stations.

FIGURE 6.15 Grave with grid

(Image courtesy of Dennis Dirkmaat)

BOX 6.4 FINDING A RIGHT ANGLE FOR A GRID

When establishing a grid, there are a several approaches that can be used to determine a right angle for the axes and the smaller grids within them. One way is to use a construction square. If not readily available, however, other field methods can be used to quickly and accurately find a right angle. These approaches use the **Pythagorean Theorem** which describes the relationship between the lengths of the sides of any right-angled triangle. For lengths a, b, and c, the theorem states that: $a^2 + b^2 = c^2$ where c is the hypotenuse, and a and b are the other two sides.

One approach is to make a 3-4-5 triangle (see below). For a triangle that has sides of length 3, 4, and 5 in any units (or multiples of 3, 4, and 5 such as 6, 8, and 10), the angle between the 3- and 4-unit sides will form a right angle ($3^2 + 4^2 = 5^2$). From the datum point, simply measure 3 and 4 units away at approximate right angles using two tape measures. Using a third tape measure (which forms the hypotenuse), bring the two ends of the 3 and 4 unit tapes together until they measure 5 units apart. This approach can be used to establish the right angle, regardless of the units that will be used to map the site.

Another approach is to use standard unit sizes with known hypotenuse values (see below), and using these measures to find a right angle in the same manner as the 3-4-5 triangle. Finally, another approach is to calculate what the hypotenuse should be based on the lengths of the two sides of the grid using the derivative of the Pythagorean Theorem: $c = \sqrt{(a^2 + b^2)}$.

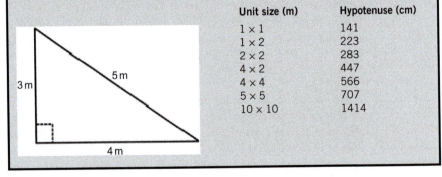

Unit size (m)	Hypotenuse (cm)
1 × 1	141
1 × 2	223
2 × 2	283
4 × 2	447
4 × 4	566
5 × 5	707
10 × 10	1414

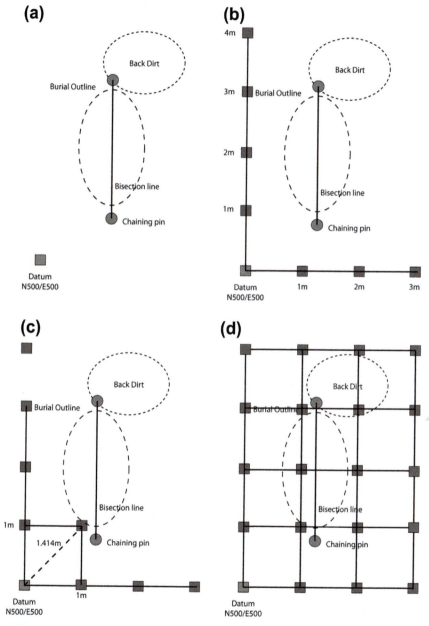

FIGURE 6.16 Grid mapping

Steps to setting up a burial feature excavation: (a) Establish datum and bisection line of the burial feature; (b) set up major grid axes; (c) triangulate hypotenuse to make sure grid stakes are placed correctly; (d) emplace additional grid stakes as needed

FIGURE 6.17 Total station (left) and map generated by total station (right)

(Images courtesy of Roland Wessling)

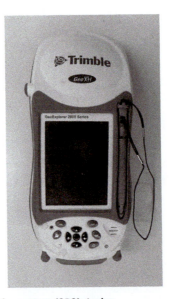

FIGURE 6.18 Global positioning system (GPS) device

6.7 Evidence collection and packaging

After the scene has been processed, human remains and associated evidence should be collected and packaged in a manner that preserves the integrity of the evidence and as much pertinent contextual information as possible. An inventory should be maintained of all items collected. Skeletal remains should generally be packaged in paper bags or other breathable material. This will prevent the growth of mold, which can occur if damp skeletal remains are packaged in materials such as sealed plastic bags. Mold on skeletal remains can obscure and stain surface features used in anthropological analyses, and can also complicate DNA analyses. If bones are wet, they should be allowed to dry prior to packaging. Plastic or other non-permeable packaging may be appropriate for skeletal material with a significant amount of adhering soft tissue, but they should be unpackaged and processed once they arrive at the medicolegal authority's office or forensic laboratory. Paper packaging will also offer some protection to the skeletal material during transport, preventing breakage or fracture from bones contacting one another.

Additional packaging and protection measures may need to be considered in certain circumstances, such as if the materials will be transported a long distance or mailed, or if the remains are thermally altered. Burned bones are often very fragile and the slightest movement may cause additional fragmentation. One approach is to carefully wrap foil around individual bones which can keep any subsequently formed bone fragments in relative anatomical position. Cotton, gauze, or other soft packaging may also help prevent further damage.

The packaging should be marked with the date and location of the recovery (including the name of site, grid position, etc.), the person who packaged or recovered the evidence, and a case identification number. In many instances, law enforcement officials and/or medical examiner personnel will be on the scene and take custody of the remains and associated evidence as it is collected. If skeletal remains are to be examined in a forensic anthropology laboratory, custody may be transferred to the anthropologist while still on scene, or the remains may be delivered to the laboratory at a later time (e.g., after autopsy).

6.8 Case study – burial recovery

In 2008, a sheriff-coroner's office in Northern California requested the services of a forensic anthropology team to aid in the excavation of a clandestine grave. Acting on information from an associate of an already convicted suspect, the sheriff's office identified what they believed to be a grave site. Each forensic anthropology team member was assigned a specific role, such as photography, excavating, mapping, screening, documentation, evidence collection, and metal detection. The suspect had already been convicted and sentenced for homicide in the absence of the victim's body, but the case was under appeal and it became essential to locate the victim's remains and reconstruct the circumstances surrounding death.

The grave outline was located by using trowels to scrape the surface and identify differences in soil color and texture. The excavation proceeded by excavating in approximately 5 cm levels using small hand tools such as trowels and small brushes. A datum was established near the southeast corner of the grave with a metal stake, and a baseline was established to map evidence and the position of the body within the grave. All soil removed from the gravesite was screened using 1/8 inch mesh. A metal detector was used over the grave multiple times during the course of the excavation, and indicated the presence of metallic objects near or within the skull. The decedent was discovered in a supine position within the grave, along with clothing and other material (Figure 6.19). The skeleton and associated evidence items were photographed, mapped (Figure 6.20), and placed into paper evidence bags. The remaining fill was carefully removed from below and near the body to completely empty the grave (Figure 6.21). Probable shovel tool marks were identified within the grave walls, but no tool marks or footprints were identified within the grave itself. A final metal detector search of the grave floor failed to locate any additional metallic objects. The laboratory analysis revealed evidence of multiple gunshot wounds to the skull, and the bullet remnants were linked to a firearm that had been in the possession of the suspect following the homicide. The evidence collected from the scene and in the subsequent analysis was instrumental in resolving the case.

FIGURE 6.19 Remains and other evidence within grave

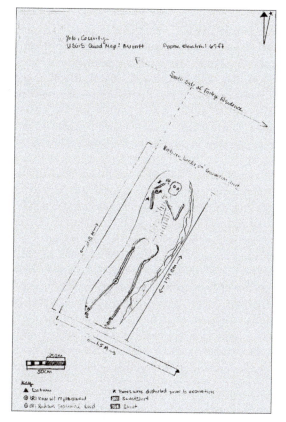

FIGURE 6.20 Sketched map of recovery scene

FIGURE 6.21 Grave after remains and evidence have been removed

6.9 Case study – fatal fire scene

In September of 2010, a natural gas pipeline exploded in a residential neighborhood of the San Francisco Bay Area. The explosion resulted in a massive crater that was 40 feet deep, 167 feet long, and 26 feet wide, and nearly 40 homes were destroyed. Fire suppression efforts continued into the following day, and law enforcement and search and rescue began an initial recovery effort for fire victims. Three days following the explosion, forensic anthropologists were requested at the scene to search for additional human remains at one of the residences affected by the explosion and resulting fire.

After conducting an initial site and risk assessment of the scene, the team consisting of 19 anthropologists began a systematic recovery operation (Figure 6.22). Each room in the residence was hand excavated, and debris was placed into buckets to be screened in an area outside the foundation of the residence (Figure 6.23). Using this approach, specific rooms could be excluded as containing human remains. One location eventually yielded the remains of multiple fire victims. Careful assessment, excavation, and screening were conducted at this location to maximize the recovery of highly fragmented, calcined remains. The team successfully recovered the remains of three fire victims, which was consistent with the number of individuals believed to be in the residence at the time of the explosion. In total, there were eight fatal fire victims within the vicinity of the explosion. Neighborhood-scale disasters such as this one often exceed a local jurisdiction's capabilities, and the coordination of multiple agencies in the recovery effort usually leads to a more successful outcome.

FIGURE 6.22 Fire scene recovery

FIGURE 6.23 Screening debris from fire scene

6.10 **Summary**

- Forensic archaeology is the application of archaeological theory and methods to medicolegal cases, including searching for, locating, surveying, sampling, recording, and interpreting evidence, as well as the recovery and documentation of human remains and associated evidence.
- A location where remains are found is called a scene or recovery scene. Common scene types include surface, burial, submerged, fire, and mass fatality.
- Similarly to excavating an archaeological site, processing a scene is inherently destructive, permanently altering the context. Documentation and preservation of contextual information is therefore critically important.
- Methods of locating a scene may include line searches, subsurface probing, thermal imaging, geophysical techniques, or cadaver dogs. Each has limitations, and certain approaches may only be appropriate in certain situations.
- The recovery process typically involves denuding the scene, establishing a datum, screening, excavation, and collection.
- Scenes can be mapped using a variety of approaches including triangulation, trilateration, azimuth, baseline, and grid. Specialized mapping approaches such as a total station and GPS may also be employed.
- After collection, remains should be packaged in a way that preserves the quality of the evidence. Skeletal remains should generally be packaged in paper bags or other breathable material that is marked with the date and location of the recovery, the person who packaged or recovered the evidence, and a case identification number.

6.11 Test yourself

- What are the goals of forensic archaeology? How can the methods used in the detection and recovery of human remains affect laboratory analyses?
- In addition to the scene types mentioned here (surface, burial, submerged, fire), can you think of any other scenes that might be encountered by a forensic anthropologist? What methods of detection, recovery, and documentation would you use and why?
- Forensic divers are utilizing sonar equipment to look for anomalies that may be consistent with a drowning victim in a lake. Which of the four phases of an investigation would you consider this?
- You are excavating a shallow burial feature, and within the soil horizon directly below the body is a coin dated to 2010. Based on principles of relative positioning, how would you interpret this?
- Identify some of the issues you should consider when attempting a search for remains that are suspected to be buried. What search techniques might you use? How would you document the remains?
- You have determined that a baseline will be the most appropriate method to document a surface scatter, but you have forgotten your construction square back at the office. Describe how you would determine whether you are measuring the evidence at a right angle from the baseline.
- Describe some of the complexities of recovery in a fire scene. Why might some of the methods described in this chapter be inappropriate for a fire scene?

Definitions

Azimuth A mapping approach that involves documenting the location of a point by measuring the distance to that point from a single known point, and the angle of the item from north using an azimuth wheel

Back-dirt Leftover soil that does not fit back into a grave after it is removed

Baseline A mapping approach that involves the use of a line that roughly bisects the scene transversely, from which the evidence items are measured at right angles

Cultural Resource Management (CRM) The process of protecting and managing cultural heritage as dictated by legislation

Datum A reference point at a scene from which measurements are taken

Denude To strip something of its covering

Excavation The exposure and recovery of material (including remains) through a slow and careful digging process

Forensic archaeology The application of archaeological theory and methods to the resolution of medicolegal and humanitarian issues

Grid A mapping approach involving the use of quadrants based on two fixed axes

In situ In its original position or place

Infill Soil used to fill in a hole or other feature such as a grave

Inter To bury a body in a grave

Line search A method of scene detection where pedestrians systematically walk over an area looking for and flagging possible evidence and other potentially significant items or features

Overburden The material that is covering an area or item of interest

Pedestal An excavation technique in which items are left *in situ* on columns of soil until the entire unit/feature is excavated

Plumb-bob A weight suspended from a string that is used to form a vertical reference line

Pythagorean Theorem The geometric relationship between the sides of any right-angled triangle; for a triangle with sides of lengths a, b, and c, the theorem states that $a^2 + b^2 = c^2$ where c is the hypotenuse, and a and b are the other two sides

Relative dating Determination of the relative order of past events (as opposed to *absolute dating* such as radiocarbon dating, which determines a numerical date and range)

Scene A location from which evidence is recovered; in forensic archaeological contexts, typically human remains and associated evidence; may be surface, burial, or submerged; also called a *recovery scene*

Soil horizon A layer in a soil profile that has different characteristics (mainly color and texture) than the surrounding layers

Steno's Laws Four laws developed by Nicolaus Steno which deal with properties of stratigraphic layers and their relative associations to other features and objects

Stratigraphy The study of the geological layers (strata) of the earth

Stratum One layer in a stratigraphic sequence (plural, *strata*)

Subsurface probing The technique of systematically inserting a thin blunt probe into the ground to assess relative soil compaction which can be an indicator of disturbed soil and a possible grave; also called probing

Surface scatter Scene type in which surface remains have been redistributed from the initial deposition site

Theodolite An instrument that is used for measuring horizontal and vertical angles and distances (also called a *transit*)

Total station A digital laser theolodite

Triangulation A mapping approach that involves documenting the location of a point by measuring the angles to that point from a line between two known points

Trilateration A mapping approach that involves documenting the location of a point by measuring the distance to that point from two known points

Underwater archaeology Archaeology performed underwater

References

Christensen, A.M., Horn, K.J., Smith, V.A., 2014. The use of an alternate light source for detecting bones underwater. J. Forensic Sci. In press.

Christensen, A.M., Lowe, W.M., Reinecke, G.W., 2009. The forensic bulldozer as a clandestine grave search tool. Forensic Sci. Commun. 11 (4).

Cox, M., Flavel, A., Hanson, I., Laver, J., Wessling, R., 2008. The Scientific Investigation of Mass Graves: Towards Protocols and Standard Operating Procedures. Cambridge University Press, Cambridge.

Cutler, A., 2004. The seashell on the mountaintop: How Nicolaus Steno solved an ancient mystery and created a science of the earth. Plume, New York.

Dirkmaat, D.C., 2002. Recovery and interpretation of the fatal fire victim: The role of forensic anthropology. In: Sorg, M.H., Haglund, W.D. (Eds.), Advances in Forensic Taphonomy: Method, Theory, and Archaeological Perspectives. CRC Press, Boca Raton, pp. 451–472.

Dirkmaat, D.C., Adovasio, J.M., 1997. The role of archaeology in the recovery and interpretation of human remains from an outdoor forensic setting. In: Haglund, W.D., Sorg, M.H. (Eds.), Forensic Taphonomy: The Postmortem Fate of Human Remains. CRC Press, Boca Raton, pp. 39–64.

Holliday, V.T., 2004. Soils in Archaeological Research. Oxford University Press, Oxford.

Hunter, J., Cox, M., 2005. Forensic Archaeology: Advances in Theory and Practice. Routledge, London and New York.

King, C.G., King, S., 1989. The archaeology of fire investigation. Fire Eng. 142 (6), 70–74.

Morse, D., Duncan, J., Stoutamire, J., 1983. Handbook of Forensic Archaeology and Anthropology. Rose Printing Co., Tallahassee.

Scientific Working Group for Forensic Anthropology, 2013. Scene Detection and Processing Revision 0.

Steno, N., 1916 (Original work published in 1669). The prodromus of Nicolaus Steno's dissertation concerning a solid body enclosed by process of nature within a solid (J. G. Winter, Trans). Macmillan Company, New York.

Processing and Preparing Remains

7.1 Principles of skeletal processing and preparation

Most forensic anthropological analyses involve the direct observation and analysis of the outer surfaces (and sometimes internal properties) of bones and teeth. Often skeletal material is delivered to the anthropologist dry and intact, making immediate observation of size and morphology fairly straightforward. It is not uncommon, however, for human remains to be presented to the forensic anthropologist for analysis with soft tissue or other adhering material (such as soil) obscuring the skeletal remains. Bones may also become damaged due to taphonomic processes or trauma before they are recovered and subjected to analysis. It is therefore fairly common for material to be fractured or fragmented, which can present certain challenges to anthropological analyses. Most often, skeletal remains brought to the forensic anthropologist are those of a single person, but sometimes the remains may represent more than one individual.

In those instances where skeletal remains require cleaning and reconstruction, several steps are usually taken prior to, or in conjunction with, the assessment of the bones for biological indicators, trauma, and features that may be useful for identification. Adhering material such as soft tissue can be removed and the bone surfaces cleaned using a combination of approaches called **processing**, allowing for gross visual analysis of the surface. In cases where bones are fractured or fragmented, the careful **reconstruction** of fragments can help clarify trauma patterns and restore original bone dimensions for metric analyses. If the remains could represent more than one individual, they should be assessed to resolve **commingling** and the number of individuals represented by the skeletal material should be determined. **Sampling** of skeletal material for DNA may be necessary, and anthropologists may be responsible for selecting an appropriate tissue sample (e.g., bone, tooth, soft tissue) for analysis as well as taking precautions to either acquire a DNA sample before processing or to avoid using processing methods which will degrade DNA. Finally, consideration should be given to the duration and conditions under which the skeletal material will be retained. In some cases, skeletal material may be sent directly back to investigators, while in other cases the remains may need to be **curated** in the forensic anthropology laboratory or medical examiner's office for relatively long periods of time (or indefinitely). The following sections describe how skeletal material can be processed and prepared for subsequent analyses and long-term storage.

Forensic Anthropology. http://dx.doi.org/10.1016/B978-0-12-418671-2.00007-0

7.2 Processing methods

Forensic anthropologists encounter skeletal remains with adhering material frequently during their careers (Figure 7.1). Very few will ever only examine dry, clean bones. Most often this adhering material will be associated soft tissue that is decomposed, mummified, saponified, or "fixed" through intentional preservation processes such as the use of formalin by medical examiners or embalming chemicals by morticians. Forensic anthropologists working in medical examiners' offices routinely encounter remains with adhering soft tissue, and are likely to have well-developed procedures for tissue removal or for removing only the requisite skeletal elements from a fleshed body for analysis. Other adhering material may include thick sediment, concrete, plant debris, or other materials either from the depositional environment or intentionally placed by perpetrators of a crime.

Adhering materials may obstruct skeletal features that are critical to observations and assessments, especially those relating to identification and trauma analysis. While soft tissues will eventually decompose on their own leaving dry bones, forensic cases normally require relatively expeditious examination and results, thus requiring the removal of these tissues by the forensic anthropologist before skeletal analysis. There are numerous approaches to processing, some of which are more appropriate than others in a forensic context, and consideration should be given to the condition of the skeletal material as well as evidence preservation before choosing a processing method. To preserve as much evidence and information as possible, remains should always be documented using both notes and photography in the condition in which they are first received and observed. Radiography can also be useful in visualizing and locating additional material evidence that may be associated with the remains but which may not be immediately visible. If clothing, personal effects, or evidence (e.g., a ligature around the neck or a projectile within the cranium) are present, these

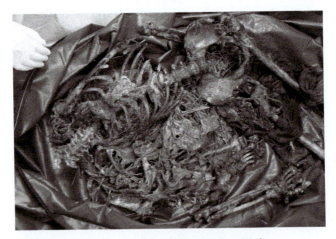

FIGURE 7.1 Skeletal material with adhering tissue and other debris

should be carefully documented prior to removal, and they should always be retained for analysis by other forensic specialists.

It is very important to perform an initial assessment, or in some cases a more in-depth examination, of the remains prior to skeletal processing. In some instances, processing procedures can destroy skeletal (or other) evidence, so this evidence must be documented and/or recovered prior to processing. Such cases may include those in which a trauma analysis may be performed. For example, early evidence of bone healing and other indicators of fracture timing such as differential staining (see Chapter 13) may be removed or destroyed by skeletal processing. In addition, decomposed and mummified skin may retain evidence of tattoos or prior surgery, and this should be documented and retained if present (Starkie et al., 2011; Haglund and Sperry, 1993) (Figure 7.2).

Following initial documentation and analysis, the remains can be processed using methods that preserve the evidentiary nature of the skeletal material (Fenton et al., 2003). There are three generally recognized methods of skeletal processing: maceration, carrion insects, and chemical approaches. The selection of a processing method may depend on the type of analysis being conducted as well as any long-term storage or curation plans. In any case, material that is removed during processing which may benefit from further analysis by another specialist (e.g., soft tissue, hairs, soil, insect larvae) should be carefully removed and preserved for further examination. In addition, any alterations caused by the processing approach including the methods and/or instruments used should be documented. Processing approaches should involve consideration for avoiding or minimizing alterations to bone dimensions, deterioration, production of postmortem damage of the bone, changes in bone structure, and commingling (Scientific Working Group for Forensic Anthropology [SWGANTH], 2011).

FIGURE 7.2 Tattoo on mummified skin

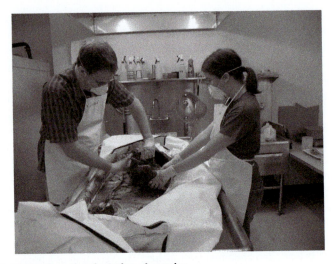

FIGURE 7.3 Mechanical disarticulation of remains

If a significant amount of soft tissue or other material is adhering to the skeletal remains, this may need to be removed by mechanical methods (Figure 7.3). As much of the adhering material as possible should be removed without the use of any tools or chemicals. In some cases, bones may be attached by tough connective tissue, and sharp tools such as scalpels and knives may be required to separate or **disarticulate** them. If tools must be used, it is preferable to use those that are less likely to damage or leave marks on the bone, such as those made of wood or plastic (versus metal). If any metal tools are used, care should be taken to avoid making any marks on the bones, and any incidental alterations should be noted in the case documentation. If it has not already been done (by a medical examiner, for example), a sample of the soft tissue should be removed and preserved for possible DNA analysis. In cases where the remains are nearly complete, approaches similar to anatomical dissection may be used, performed carefully with a scalpel. Scalpel nicks can usually be distinguished from other cut marks on the basis of their narrow dimensions and consistent and uniform pattern (Bartelink et al., 2001).

One of the most common methods used to remove any remaining tissue, soil, or other debris is **maceration**, or softening of the soft tissues by soaking the remains in water. Various approaches have been recommended involving different temperatures, times, and the addition of enzymatic detergents and ammonia. Cold (or room temperature) maceration involves simply placing the material into a sealed container with water and allowing the soft tissues to decompose slowly through bacterial action. This method is time-consuming (typically on the order of weeks or months) and has a strong associated odor. Cold water maceration does have the advantages of producing excellent preservation of skeletal details and being safe for the material and practitioner (because it involves no heat or chemicals). It is recommended when processing fetal and infant remains or otherwise very small or fragile remains. Note,

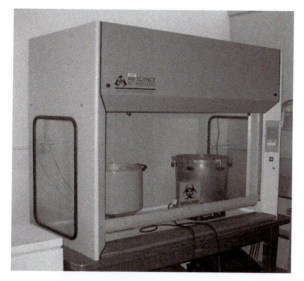

FIGURE 7.4 Warm water maceration equipment

however, that lengthy processing in water has been associated with a loss in DNA yield (Steadman et al., 2006).

Warm water maceration is the most common approach used by forensic anthropologists (Figure 7.4 and Box 7.1). For best results, the water temperature should be maintained near, yet below, a rolling boil, which can be accomplished through the use of pots and hot plates, incubators, crock-pots, or microwave ovens. These temperatures promote rapid breakdown of the tissues without bacterial action. As the remains are processed in this way, the tissues soften, degrade, and separate from the bone (imagine for example, boiling a chicken carcass to prepare stock – eventually the meat and other tissues "fall off the bone"). Depending on the amount of remaining soft tissue, this procedure may be repeated several times, changing the water solution to dispose of the excess tissues and fats. At this time, rinsing and some manual removal of remaining tissue (using, for example, tweezers or nylon brushes) may further facilitate processing.

Another approach to soft tissue removal involves the use of carrion insects that consume soft tissue, particularly mealworms and dermestid beetles (see Figure 7.5). The dermestid beetle colony is an efficient and non-destructive method for processing remains (Bemis et al., 2004; Sommer and Anderson, 1974). Dermestid beetle larvae will consume soft tissue in any stage of decay (although they tend to prefer soft tissue that is at least somewhat desiccated), but do not consume or damage the bones. Processing human remains using dermestid beetles can take up to several weeks, depending on the size of the colony, the amount of soft tissue present, and the condition of the remains. For remains that have only a small amount of soft tissue, processing can be complete in as little as a week. Beetle colonies can be maintained expressly for this purpose, kept in a sealed container such as an aquarium or metal box with a fastened lid. The creation and maintenance of beetle colonies, however,

BOX 7.1 PROCESSING AT THE HARRIS COUNTY INSTITUTE OF FORENSIC SCIENCES

The Harris County Institute of Forensic Sciences – Forensic Anthropology Division (FAD) handles an average of 175 cases per year which require some level of maceration. Approximately 90% of the cases consist of single or multiple bones or bone segments removed from decedents during the autopsy, and approximately 15% of the annual caseload consists of pediatric specimens. As a result, the FAD staff must be able to remove soft tissue from bone in an efficient and delicate manner. The technique employed by the staff is a warm water maceration approach. Full skeletons with adhering tissue are disarticulated into smaller segments in order to fit into the processing pans. A degreasing soap is often used, and the optimal concentration is dependent on the type of bone and amount of adherent soft tissue (for example, lower concentrations are used for pediatric specimens while more robust specimens often require higher concentrations). Large capacity incubators are utilized to elevate the water temperature in a controlled manner and protect against localized hotspots. Labels with the case identification number accompany specimens throughout the process. The processing time is dependent on the amount of adherent soft tissue and the fragility of the bone; pediatric specimens are often fully processed after 24 hours while full skeletons may take much longer. Once processed, the specimens are placed onto trays to dry.

Dr. Jennifer Love of the Harris County Institute of Forensic Sciences (HCIFS) placing specimens into an incubator for processing. Photo by Desmond Bostick

is often time-consuming, and the colony needs to be kept approximately at room temperature and in darkness. Dermestid colonies can be more effectively maintained if non-human animal carcasses are available to process in between partially fleshed cases, as dermestids require a continuous food supply to maintain a healthy colony. Occasionally, invasive insects (e.g., fly larvae, red-legged ham beetles) are inadvertently introduced, which can affect the overall health and productivity of the colony.

Chemical processing and preparation methods can be employed, including those involving bleaching agents (such as bleach, hydrogen peroxide, or commercial chemicals), antiformin, sodium hypochlorite, and papain. While chemical processing

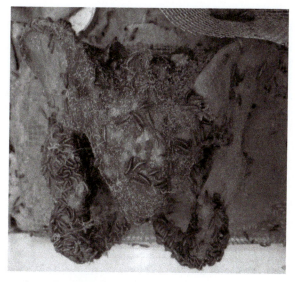

FIGURE 7.5 Dermestid beetle processing

can be quick (sometimes rendering remains in just a few hours), these approaches can degrade the bone, are hazardous to practitioners, are more expensive, and require special handling and storage of the chemicals (Fenton, 2003). Moreover, methods that involve bleach and acids have been shown to reduce DNA yield (Steadman et al., 2006). These methods are therefore not recommended in most cases. In rare cases, however, the use of chemicals may be required to remove adhering tissue. This may include cases where the remains have been preserved using chemicals, such as formalin used by forensic pathologists or embalming chemicals used by morticians. When chemical processing is performed, the material must be carefully monitored to prevent over-processing and disintegration of the bone.

In some cases, especially if the remains are to be curated for long periods of time, it may be helpful to degrease the bones following tissue removal. This can be accomplished by soaking the remains in a water and ammonia solution (Fenton, 2003). Again, other chemical methods have been employed (including bleach and acetone), but these can have deleterious effects on the bone.

Once the bones have been cleaned by one of the above processing methods, the remains can be carefully rinsed and cleaned using water and a soft nylon brush such as a toothbrush. Screens or cheesecloth can be used during the cleaning process to prevent the loss of small bone fragments or teeth down a drain, and to ensure that fractured bone pieces remain together. The disposal of soft tissue removed should follow appropriate protocols regarding biohazard waste (following universal precautions). The skeletal material can then be allowed to air-dry on wire racks or towels prior to analysis. The use of moving air will facilitate faster drying, but may also lead to a greater probability of drying artifacts such as linear cracks along the grain of the remains, particularly the long bones. Heat should not be applied to speed up drying.

7.3 Skeletal reconstruction

If skeletal remains are fractured due to trauma or postmortem damage, it is usually informative to reassemble them into their original anatomical locations to the extent possible (Figure 7.6). This can be useful for restoring the bones to their original dimensions to allow for metric analyses. It can also help to visualize and clarify fractures and trauma patterns to facilitate interpretation of their cause.

It may not always be necessary to physically affix or adhere fragments together, and as a rule, fragments should only be affixed when additional information may be gained. In some cases, it may only be necessary to hold fragments in place temporarily using tape, wax, or clay. If fragments need to be more permanently reconstructed, this is typically accomplished using glue or adhesive. Reconstruction should only be performed once the bones are clean and completely dry, and the reconstruction methods should be reversible (e.g., adhesives such as Paraloid B-72®, an acrylic resin; not Cellulose nitrate-based adhesives such as Duco® cement). It may be necessary to separate fragments after reconstruction for subsequent examination, or due to unintentional errors in reconstruction. By using reversible methods, the fragments can be separated without damaging the remains. Certain adhesives, for example, can be dissolved using water or acetone.

Fragments should only be affixed when the anthropologist is certain that there is a physical match (Christensen and Sylvester, 2008), and the same is true for affixing

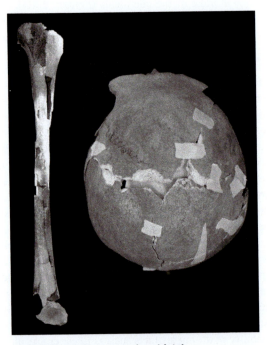

FIGURE 7.6 Reconstructed tibia (left) and cranium (right)

teeth into alveolar sockets. Care should be taken in the search for matching frag-ments, since excessive attempts to refit two fragments can damage the fractured edges to the point that they no longer fit together. The use of a microscope may be useful in confirming a match of small fragments or in cases where the surface area of the join is very small. In confirming a match, the anatomical and physical properties of the match should be given greater consideration than other factors such as color or condition, since such differences may be the result of taphonomic processes or may represent evidence of trauma or other alterations.

In cases where there is significant missing bone or where contact points are very small, the application of wooden struts may help stabilize and place bone fragments. This approach can be especially helpful when reconstructing highly fragmented facial bones. If adhesives are used, it is helpful to stabilize the bones during the dry-ing process, which can be accomplished with the use of a small sandbox. Bear in mind that complete reconstruction may not always be possible. Fragments that would join two additional portions may be missing due to taphonomic or intentional events. Warping of bone due to taphonomy or trauma may also prevent complete reconstruc-tion, causing fragments that would normally conjoin to fail to do so. This can be especially apparent on the skull. Matches should never be forced in order to correct for warping of the bone since this can lead to further damage. Also be aware that skeletal reconstruction requires patience. Depending on the condition of the remains and the level of fragmentation, the process of locating matches, affixing struts, and allowing adhesives to dry can be a repetitive, tedious, and time-consuming process.

7.4 Commingling

Commingle means to mix or to blend; anthropologically, **commingling** refers to the presence of more than one body or skeleton, or the intermixing of body parts from more than one individual. Sometimes potential commingling is suggested by the context or investigative information. For example, commingling is common and usu-ally expected in certain situations such as mass graves or mass fatality incidents (see Chapter 15). Sometimes, however, there may be no suggestion of commingling and it may be discovered in the course of an anthropological examination.

The process of recognizing commingling, segregating the remains into individual sets, and estimating the number of individuals present is referred to as resolving commingling, and is a common aspect of a forensic anthropological examination (Figure 7.7). This process assists with the identification of decedents and can have a role in the overall success of an investigation or identification effort (Scientific Work-ing Group for Forensic Anthropology [SWGANTH], 2013). For example, in cases where commingling is detected where it was not previously suspected, this may significantly change the course of the investigation. Whenever possible, all remains should be segregated by individual.

During field recovery (as described in Chapter 6), documentation of the **prove-nience** or location of each set of remains or skeletal element is crucial in preventing

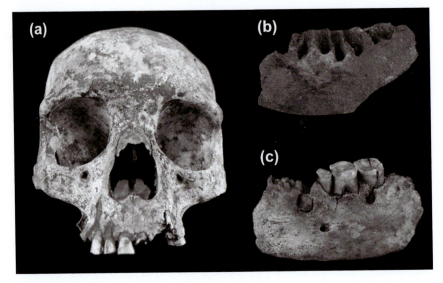

FIGURE 7.7 Commingled skeletal remains

The mandible fragments (b and c) are both lefts, and neither is associated with the cranium (a); the minimum number of individuals represented is therefore three (3).

or minimizing commingling as well as later interpretations from the recovered material. If elements were articulated when discovered, they should be recovered and maintained together, and their association can be later confirmed in the laboratory (Scientific Working Group for Forensic Anthropology [SWGANTH], 2013).

All anthropological examinations (whether commingling is suspected or not) should involve a thorough inventory of the remains present. This inventory is useful for documentation purposes, as well as for discovering or determining whether or not more than one individual may be represented. It is also very helpful to label skeletal specimens as early as possible in the examination process. The inventory alone may help to identify duplicate elements that can confirm that commingling has occurred. For example, a set of skeletal remains containing two right femora must be commingled (since an individual cannot have two of the same bone from the same side of the body). If commingling is suspected or confirmed, the skeletal elements should be sorted by element and side. It may sometimes be necessary to reconstruct fragments as described above in order to resolve commingling. For example, a distal left tibia and a proximal left tibia may be two fragments of the same bone from a single individual.

Other criteria such as biological parameters may also be used to sort potentially commingled remains. For example, the presence of bones from a skeletally mature adult along with bones from an infant represents commingling, even if individual skeletal elements are not duplicated. Similarly, size and sex indicators may be used to help sort commingled remains.

As additional segregating tools, bones representing the same individual may be associated using visual **pair-matching** (association of left and right elements based on similarities in morphology and size), **articulation** (association of congruent elements based on closeness of fit at the joint juncture with another bone), **osteometric sorting** (association of elements based on statistical evaluation of size and shape relationships), taphonomy (association of elements based on similarities in preservation such as color and condition), and DNA (association of elements based on shared mitochondrial or nuclear DNA sequences). Bear in mind that similarity in these aspects does not mean that it can be said with certainty that the elements originated from the same individual. Consideration should also be given to possible pathological conditions that may affect bone size, shape, and articulation. Greater confidence can be given to *exclusionary* conclusions (i.e., incompatibilities that indicate that two elements do *not* originate from the same individual) than those that suggest an association. Some joint articulations are easy to visualize, such as the hip joint, whereas others are harder to compare, such as a metacarpophalangeal joint.

Once all appropriate recovery and sorting methods have been employed, it may be possible to estimate the number of individuals present among the remains. There are several approaches to this which are dependent on the preservation of the material as well as the scale of the incident. The most common approach is to determine the **minimum number of individuals** present, or **MNI**. In its simplest form, MNI is calculated by counting the number of repeated elements (or portion thereof) after sorting by element, side, and developmental status (i.e., skeletal maturity), and then taking the highest number as the MNI estimate. For example, if an assemblage contains two left scapulae, one right humerus, two left humeri, three left ulnae, one right femur, and two left tibiae, the MNI would be three (due to the three left ulnae, which is the most repeated element).

When estimating MNI from fragmentary remains, every fragment used to calculate the MNI must share the same specific anatomical landmark to ensure that the portions do not represent the same bone. For example, the proximal and distal tibia portions referenced above should not be counted twice if they do not share an anatomical landmark, because they could be two portions of the same bone. Three proximal left tibiae that all have a tibial tuberosity present, however, would be counted as three different individuals.

Other approaches can be used to estimate the actual or likely number of individuals present (versus the minimum). The **Most Likely Number of Individuals** (**MLNI**) can be used if preservation is good and skeletal elements can be accurately pair-matched (Adams and Konigsberg, 2004). The formula for calculating MLNI is:

$$MLNI = [(L+1)(R+1)/(P+1)] - 1$$

where R = right, L = left, and P = pairs.

Resolving commingling becomes increasingly complicated with increasing number of individuals, as well as with increasing fragmentation of remains. Extremely fragmentary or poorly preserved remains may not be amenable to meaningful

FIGURE 7.8 Commingled remains recovered from the World Trade Center

Photo by Rich Press; used with permission of the Office of Chief Medical Examiner – New York City

osteological quantification techniques (Scientific Working Group for Forensic Anthropology [SWGANTH], 2013) (Figure 7.8). In some cases, DNA analysis may be useful in resolving commingled fragments (Budimlija et al., 2003).

7.5 Skeletal sampling

Although not necessarily the specific responsibility of the forensic anthropologist, skeletal material and/or associated soft tissue can be sampled (i.e., a small section removed) for DNA analysis. If soft tissue was present on the skeletal material, samples of various tissue types (such as muscle, brain, etc.) should be removed and preserved for possible DNA analysis prior to skeletal processing. Skeletal sampling for DNA analysis typically involves the removal of a small window of bone (see Figure 7.9) which is subsequently powdered. Due to this destructive process, it is very important that anthropological examination (including visual, radiographic, and microscopic analyses) be performed prior to DNA sampling. In addition, sections should not be sampled from areas that have trauma or pathological conditions.

Rather than actually cutting the sample, forensic anthropologists are often involved in the selection or recommendation of bones or bone portions for DNA sampling. This may involve assessment of the quality of bone preservation, or the recommendation of

FIGURE 7.9 Clavicle sampled for DNA analysis

bones or areas that lack other important skeletal evidence such as features that may be useful for identification, trauma, or disease. If the anthropologist is responsible for taking the sample, it is important to employ methods and instruments that reduce biological contamination, such as the use of new blades treated with bleach and/or UV light (Scientific Working Group for Forensic Anthropology [SWGANTH], 2011). In mass disaster and mass grave contexts where human remains have been subjected to various taphonomic processes, denser skeletal elements (i.e., those with more compact bone) may be more likely to yield suitable DNA (Mundorff et al., 2009; Miloš et al., 2007).

7.6 Skeletal preservation

Often, remains are returned directly to investigators or funeral homes following anthropological analyses and other forensic examinations. Sometimes, however, skeletons may be retained for longer periods of time, such as those still awaiting identification, those that have been donated and may be utilized for teaching or research purposes, or bone specimens retained as evidence. If remains are to be stored long term in the forensic anthropology laboratory or curated indefinitely (such as in skeletal study collections or museums), other considerations may apply in order to prevent the unintentional physical destruction or commingling of the skeletal material. There may also be ethical considerations regarding the long-term storage of human remains (Cassman et al., 2007).

In these cases, the storage medium should be considered. The remains may be given to the forensic anthropologist in paper bags or cardboard boxes, but for long-term storage, the use of archival storage media such as acid free storage boxes may be better for skeletal preservation and retention of evidence. Padding of storage containers can also help reduce bone destruction. In addition, remains should be stored under conditions that prevent access by insects or other animals such as rodents (which can find their way into even the most secure laboratories). Other storage conditions should include avoiding excessive temperature and humidity of the storage area. If remains are to be curated for teaching or research purposes (and will therefore be frequently

BOX 7.2 THE WILLIAM M. BASS DONATED SKELETAL COLLECTION

In the 1970s, Dr. William M. Bass helped develop the anthropology program at the University of Tennessee in Knoxville, TN, and was also instrumental in forming the Anthropology Research Facility (sometimes referred to as "The Body Farm"), which utilizes human donors to study decomposition in an outdoor laboratory setting (also see Box 4.4). Following decomposition, the skeletal remains are carefully excavated or collected from the research facility and processed using warm water maceration. The skeleton is inventoried, and each bone is labeled with that individual's unique identification number. The remains then become part of the skeletal collection named in Dr. Bass' honor, which now consists of more than one thousand sets of skeletal remains of known individuals. The skeletal remains are maintained at the Department of Anthropology and used for teaching and research.

The William M. Bass Donated Skeletal Collection
Image courtesy of the University of Tennessee Department of Anthropology

handled and removed from their storage containers), good organization and the use of careful handling procedures will help reduce damage and commingling (see Box 7.2).

In some cases, it may be beneficial to treat remains with chemical preservatives, such as a consolidant that provides protection against handling damage. These preservatives are chemical hardeners that penetrate through pore spaces on the bone and can offer some protection against breakage and discoloration. These approaches should only be considered for cases that have been resolved and adjudicated and will be

---

BOX 7.3 THREE-DIMENSIONAL PRINTING

Three-dimensional printing (also called additive manufacturing) is a process of making a solid object from a digital model whereby layers of material are deposited in successive (additive) layers (by contrast, most traditional machining techniques for making solid shapes rely on subtractive processes such as cutting or drilling). In much the same way that an ink-jet printer deposits ink on a page one line at a time, 3-D printers deposit material (often plastic, but also metal, ceramic, or other manufacturing material) onto a surface one layer at a time. This revolutionary process is now used in many industries, from toys to jewelry to machine part manufacturing. It is also finding applications in forensic anthropology. From digital data collected by Computed Tomography (CT) scan or laser scanner, 3-D printers can be used to make replicas of bones. These replicas can be used for sculpting a facial approximation (see Chapter 14), thereby eliminating the application of clay directly to a skull surface. They can be used as comparative reference materials similar to pubic symphyseal or sternal rib end casts (see Chapter 10). They can also be used for courtroom demonstration purposes in cases where the actual skeletal remains will not be available (such as if they will be interred or cremated between the analysis and the trial).

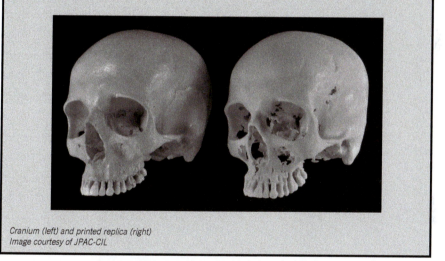

Cranium (left) and printed replica (right)
Image courtesy of JPAC-CIL

---

procured long term, for example in a museum. Preservation chemicals may be hazardous to the practitioner so should be used carefully and with appropriate safety considerations. Only soluble chemicals should be used in the event that the preservative needs to be removed. In most instances, however, the use of these chemicals is not advisable.

Another way to preserve the features of skeletal remains is through casting, molds, and other replicas. These methods result in the three-dimensional reproduction of the bone or certain features which can be preserved, examined, studied, or stored in place of the actual skeletal material. Casting methods include plasters, plastics, and epoxies. Latex and silicon can be used to make casts of impressions or tool marks for preservation and examination. Because the casting of remains creates such accurate replicas, this practice may replace the retention of bone as evidence. Laser scanning and three-dimensional printing, although more expensive, can also produce high-quality replicas (Box 7.3).

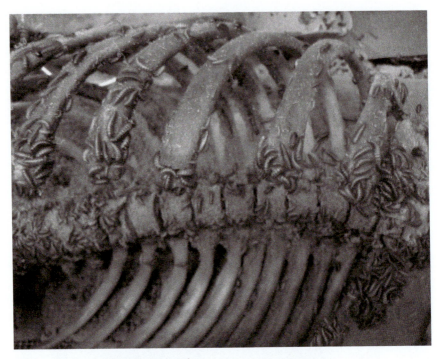

FIGURE 7.10 Dermestid beetle processing

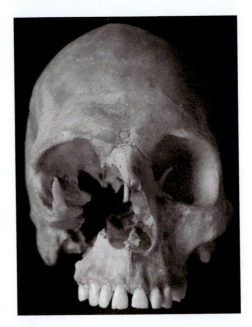

FIGURE 7.11 Facial trauma

7.7 Case study – processing

In 2006, human remains were recovered from a clandestine grave in northern California. The decedent, clothed in jeans and a T-shirt, was still fleshed, although a significant amount of decomposition and desiccation had taken place. Following a partial autopsy, the forensic pathologist and forensic anthropologist carefully removed bulk soft tissue using scalpels and hemostats. The remaining soft tissue and skeletal material was sealed for transport to the forensic anthropology laboratory for processing and analysis. Homicide was suspected, and investigators requested a rapid turnaround time (approximately two weeks) for the analysis. The remains were placed into a receptacle housing a dermestid beetle colony for processing (Figure 7.10). This processing method was selected because of the delicate nature of the facial area, which showed evidence of significant perimortem trauma (Figure 7.11). Although a significant amount of soft tissue was present, the dermestid beetles were able to remove all soft tissues within two weeks.

7.8 Summary

- When skeletal remains are presented with adhering substances such as soft tissue or soil, they can be removed through a number of approaches called skeletal processing. Processing techniques may include dissection, disarticulation, maceration, or the use of carrion insects or chemicals.
- In cases where skeletal remains are fragmented due to trauma or postmortem events, reconstruction of the fragments may be beneficial to anthropological assessments and interpretations. Fractured edges should only be affixed when necessary, and only when the anthropologist is confident of the match. Reversible methods such as soluble adhesives should be used.
- If remains are commingled, they can be segregated through inventory, sorting by side and biological indicators, pair-matching, articulation, osteometric sorting, and taphonomy. The minimum or likely number of individuals can then be estimated based on the number of duplicated bones and/or pair-matched bones.
- Bones are often sampled (i.e., a section removed) for DNA testing. Anthropologists may be responsible for selecting bones for sampling, which should only take place after anthropological assessments are complete, and should avoid areas that involve trauma or pathology.
- Remains are sometimes retained for long periods of time, either because they are awaiting identification or because they will be used for teaching or research. In these cases, consideration should be given to how the remains are handled and stored in order to avoid accidental damage or commingling.

7.9 Test yourself

- You are presented with a box full of bones and bone fragments, some of which still have decomposing soft tissue attached, that investigators recovered from a wooded area. In the absence of any additional contextual information, how would you begin your examination?
- Under what circumstances would you consider it appropriate to affix fractured bone fragments with adhesive? In which situations might you avoid it?
- Discuss the pros and cons of different processing methods. What considerations would you need to take into account for a case that might go to trial?
- Discuss four different criteria that could be useful for resolving commingling. Would they all be equally appropriate in all cases?
- If you were responsible for selecting and sampling an area of a bone for DNA analysis, what should you consider prior to and during the sampling process?
- Can you think of any other potential anthropological applications for 3-D printing?
- Determine the MNI from the following skeletal assemblage: one left proximal femur, one complete left radius, one complete right radius, one mandible, one distal right humerus, three distal left tibiae, one complete right tibia, and three complete left femora.
- How might storage considerations differ for evidentiary material at a medical examiner's office versus teaching specimens at a university?

Definitions

Articulation The association of congruent skeletal elements based on closeness of fit at the joint juncture with another bone

Commingling The mixing together of more than one individual or skeleton; resolving commingling refers to the process of segregating the remains back out by individual

Curation The practice of archiving and preserving

Disarticulate To remove from anatomical position

Macerate To soften by steeping in fluid

Minimum Number of Individuals (MNI) An estimate of the minimum number of individuals represented in a skeletal assemblage calculated by counting the greatest number of repeated elements (or portion thereof)

Most Likely Number of Individuals (MLNI) An estimate of the number of individuals represented in a skeletal assemblage calculated using a formula that depends on good preservation and accurate pair-matching

Osteometric sorting The association of skeletal elements based on statistical evaluation of size and shape relationships

Pair-matching The association of left and right skeletal elements based on similarities in morphology and size

Processing Any of a number of procedures used to remove soft tissue or other adhering materials from the surface of skeletal material

Provenience The original location or context of an item
Reconstruction The physical re-fitting of broken or fractured bone fragments
(DNA) Sampling The removal of a portion of a bone or tooth to be used for DNA testing

References

Adams, B.J., Konigsberg, L.W., 2004. Estimation of the most likely number of individuals from commingled human skeletal remains. Am. J. Phys. Anthropol. 125, 138–151.

Bartelink, E.J., Wiersema, J.M., Demaree, R.S., 2001. Quantitative analysis of sharp-force trauma: an application of scanning electron microscopy in forensic anthropology. J. Forensic Sci. 46, 1288–1293.

Bemis, W.E., Hilton, E.J., Brown, B., Arrindell, R., Richmond, A.M., Little, C.D., Grande, L., Forey, P.L., Nelson, G.J., Armbruster, J.W., 2004. Methods for preparing dry, partially articulated skeletons of osteichthyans, with notes on making ridewood dissections of the cranial skeleton. Copeia 3, 603–609.

Budimlija, Z.M., Prinz, M.K., Zelson Mundorff, A., Wiersema, J.M., Bartelink, E.J., MacKinnon, G., Nazzaruolo, B.L., Estacio, S.M., Hennessey, M.J., Shaler, R.C., 2003. World trade center human identification project: experiences with individual body identification cases. Croat. Med. J. 44, 259–263.

Cassman, V., Odegaard, N., Powell, J., 2007. Human Remains: Guide for Museums and Academic Institutions. Altamira Press, Lanham.

Christensen, A.M., Sylvester, A.D., 2008. Physical matches of bone, shell and tooth fragments: A validation study. J. Forensic Sci. 53 (3), 694–698.

Fenton, T.W., Birkby, W.H., Cornelison, J., 2003. A fast and safe non-bleaching method for forensic skeletal preparation. J. Forensic Sci. 48 (2), 274–276.

Haglund, W.D., Sperry, K., 1993. The use of hydrogen peroxide to visualize tattoos obscured by decomposition and mummification. J. Forensic Sci. 38 (1), 147–150.

Miloš, A., Selmanović, A., Smajlović, L., Huel, R., Katzmarzyk, C., Rizvić, A., Parsons, T.J., 2007. Success rates of nuclear short tandem repeat typing from different skeletal elements. Croat. Med. J. 48, 486–493.

Mundorff, A., Bartelink, E.J., Mar-Cash, E., 2009. DNA preservation in skeletal elements from the world trade center disaster: recommendations for mass fatality management. J. Forensic Sci. 54, 739–745.

Scientific Working Group on Forensic Anthropology, 2011. Skeletal Sampling and Preparation (Revision 1).

Scientific Working Group for Forensic Anthropology, 2013. Resolving Commingled Human Remains (Revision 2). Retrieved from http://www.swganth.org.

Sommer, H.G., Anderson, S., 1974. Cleaning skeletons with dermestids beetles: two refinements in the method. Curator: The Museum Journal 17 (4), 290–298.

Starkie, A., Birch, W., Ferllini, R., Thompson, T.J.U., 2011. Investigation into the merits of infrared imaging in the investigation of tattoos postmortem. J. Forensic Sci. 56 (6), 1569–1573.

Steadman, D.W., DiAntonio, L.L., Wilson, J.J., Sheridan, K.E., Tammariello, S.P., 2006. The effects of chemical and heat maceration techniques on the recovery of nuclear and mitochondrial DNA from bone. J. Forensic Sci. 51 (1), 11–17.

Sex Estimation

8.1 Principles of sex estimation

Estimating sex from skeletal remains involves the identification and evaluation of characteristics that tend to show differences between male and female skeletons, which are variably expressed throughout the skeleton. These differences are primarily related to size and architecture which result from different biomechanical functions of joints for efficiency in **locomotion** (movement, usually walking) and **parturition** (childbirth). In the analysis and identification of human skeletal remains, the correct determination of sex effectively eliminates approximately 50% of the population from further consideration, thus substantially assisting in the search of missing persons records and databases (see Chapter 14). In addition, many other analyses such as stature and age estimation are sex-specific, making sex estimation an important part of the biological profile, especially in the preliminary stages of an investigation.

The ability to differentiate between male and female skeletons is due to **sexual dimorphism**, or the expression of **phenotypic** differences between males and females of the same species. Sexual dimorphism usually relates primarily to differences in **morphology** (size and shape), but may also refer to differences in physiology and behavior. In forensic anthropology, morphological differences between males and females are the most useful for sex estimation.

In comparison to other animals, humans display relatively little sexual dimorphism (Figure 8.1). For example, many bird species differ significantly in color and ornamentation. Additionally, many male and female non-human primates including gorillas differ greatly in size. Humans, on the other hand, show only modest differences in size and certain body proportions. Human ancestors displayed a greater sexual dimorphism in size than modern humans, showing a reduction of dimorphism over the course of **hominin** evolution (Frayer and Wolpoff, 1985). Sexual dimorphism is also not uniform across all human populations, with some groups being more sexually dimorphic than others. It is therefore often advisable to consider ancestry when estimating sex from unknown remains.

On average, adult human males are larger and more robustly built than females, exceeding them in height, weight, and breadth (France, 1998). Their bones tend to be longer, thicker, and have more prominent muscle attachments (males tend to have

Forensic Anthropology. http://dx.doi.org/10.1016/B978-0-12-418671-2.00008-2

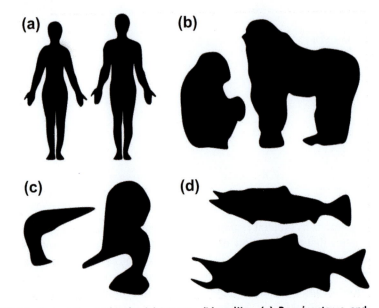

FIGURE 8.1 Sexual dimorphism in: (a) humans, (b) gorillas, (c) *Darwinopterus*, and (d) sockeye salmon

greater muscle mass, which requires greater surface area for attachment to the bone). Because human sexual dimorphism is not extreme, however, there tends to be considerable overlap; smaller males and larger females may be more difficult to differentiate (see Figure 8.2 for an example of male and female height). Many sexually dimorphic traits are secondary sexual characteristics that develop during puberty, largely due to the release of hormones that result in changes in the rate of bone growth and development (Bogin, 1999).

The terms **sex** and **gender** are often used interchangeably in both popular media and scientific (including anthropological) literature, but they do have distinct meanings which should be understood (Walker and Cook, 1998) (see Box 8.1). When referring to analyses and estimates performed by forensic anthropologists based on skeletal characteristics, "sex" is the appropriate term.

Various methods that generally fall into one of two categories have been developed for estimating sex from skeletal remains: non-metric (macroscopic, or visual) analysis and metric analysis. Each utilizes certain bones or overall patterns depending on the degree and quality of sexual dimorphism in that bone or anatomical region. As discussed in Chapter 3, metric methods are generally considered to be more objective, but in the case of sex estimation, visual assessment of the pelvis is the most accurate method. Methods involving dimensions of various long bones of the postcranial skeleton are typically the next most accurate, followed by methods involving the skull (Spradley and Jantz, 2011). Various issues associated

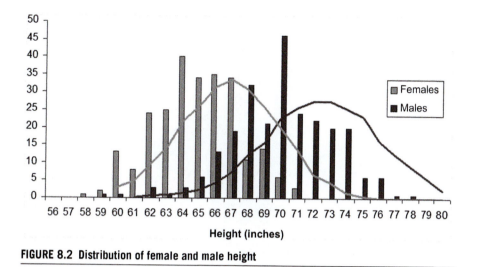

FIGURE 8.2 Distribution of female and male height

BOX 8.1 SEX VERSUS GENDER

Sex refers to the totality of characteristics of reproductive structure, functions, **phenotype**, and **genotype** which differentiate males from females. Such differences are the result of the inheritance and expression of sex chromosomes XX (female) or XY (male), and sex can therefore only be determined on the basis of anatomical or molecular evidence. Note that while sex is typically a binary dichotomy, a small number of individuals have an anatomy and/or biology that does not fit into the standard "male" or "female" classification. **Intersex** refers to individuals who display such characteristics, typically resulting from chromosomal or physical/genital anomalies.

Gender, on the other hand, refers to cultural expressions of feminine and masculine behaviors and attributes which are considered appropriate for men and women in a given society. Gender is culturally defined and context specific, and therefore does not necessarily correspond to traditions of masculine and feminine roles in any one particular culture. Some cultures, in fact, recognize multiple genders (often related to intersexuality or **androgeny**). Prior to the late 1960s, the term "gender" was only used to refer to feminine and masculine words in a language, but the feminist movement of the 1960s extended the meaning to refer to differences between men and women (Nicholson, 1994). The term "gender" was appropriated by scientists in the 1980s and 1990s as a politically correct way to refer to "sex" which was viewed as a loaded term, but disciplines such as anthropology, psychology, and physiology have been increasingly emphasizing the distinction between gender and sex in their discourse (Torgrimson and Minson, 2005).

While a person's sex is biologically fixed, their expression of the feminine-masculine continuum is more fluid, and gender therefore cannot be estimated from skeletal remains. Gender may be suggested by evidence associated with skeletal remains, however, and may be appropriate to note, especially for potential use in identification. For example, anatomically male skeletal remains found dressed in clothing typically associated with women should be noted since it may allow investigators to focus on certain social groups with which the individual may have associated during life.

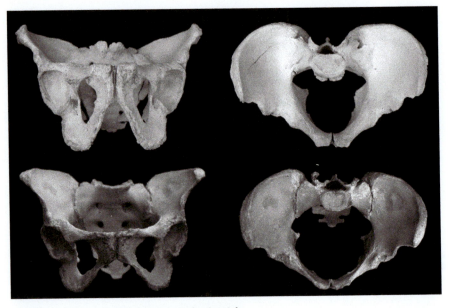

FIGURE 8.3 Female (bottom) and male (top) pelvis

with sex estimation such as estimation of sex from **juvenile** remains and molecular/genetic methods are addressed at the end of this chapter.

8.2 Morphoscopic (non-metric) analysis

Non-metric analysis in sex estimation involves a visual, qualitative assessment of skeletal features that tend to vary between males and females. These assessments involve observations of the degree of expression of certain traits, or a determination of the presence or absence of a particular feature.

Owing to the functions of childbirth, the pelvis is the most sexually dimorphic region of the human skeleton, displaying the most sexual variation in architecture, meaning that assessment of the pelvis is the most accurate method for estimating sex from skeletal material. In general, the different features reflect a wider female pelvis and pelvic inlet as a result of selective pressures to expand the birth canal. This expansion is necessary due to the large size of the human fetus (particularly the head) in relation to the size of the birth canal. There is, in fact, a direct relationship between a species' neonatal brain size relative to the birth canal and pelvic sexual dimorphism (Ridley, 1995). Other animals, including other primates, who have relatively small-brained infants show very little sexual dimorphism in the pelvis, other than overall size.

In general, the pelvis is shorter and broader in females than in males, with a more widely configured pelvic inlet and a wider sub-pubic angle (see Figure 8.3). On the ilium, a variably developed preauricular sulcus is often present in females but absent in males (Figure 8.4). The obturator foramen in females tends to be more triangular, while it is more oval in males. Some of the more varied morphological differences that are commonly utilized in sex estimation are described in Table 8.1.

The wider pelvis in females requires concomitant adaptations in other bones, notably, the angles of the knee and elbow (often called the "**Q-angle**" in the knee and the "**carrying angle**" in the elbow) (Figure 8.5). Due to having wider hips, the angle at which the femur meets the tibia at the knee is necessarily greater in females so that the knees are oriented under the trunk in a configuration efficient for locomotion (Livingston, 1998). Similarly, in order to clear the hips during arm swinging while walking, females have a greater carrying angle of the elbow (Potter, 1895; Atkinson and Elftman, 1945).

The Phenice (1969) method involves the evaluation of three traits of the *os pubis* and has a reported accuracy of around 96%. It is one of the most validated and commonly used methods of estimating sex from the pelvis when the pubic region is available for study. The three Phenice traits are:

(1) The *ventral arc* which is typically present in females and absent in males.
(2) The *sub-pubic concavity* of the ischiopubic ramus which is typically present in females and absent in males.
(3) The *medial aspect of the ischiopubic ramus* which is sharp and narrow in females and dull and wide in males (Figure 8.6).

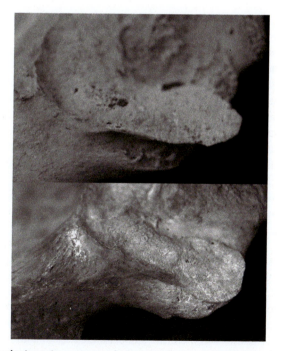

FIGURE 8.4 Preauricular sulcus, present in females (top) and absent in males (bottom)

Table 8.1 Traits of the female and male pelvis

Pelvic feature	Female pelvis	Male pelvis
Ilium	Low, wide, flared	High and vertical
Pelvic inlet	Oval	Heart-shaped
Ventral arc	Present	Absent
Sub-pubic concavity	Present	Absent
Medial ischiopubic ramus	Narrow and sharp	Wide and dull
Obturator foramen	Small and triangular	Large and ovoid
Sub-pubic angle	Larger	Smaller
Greater sciatic notch	Larger	Smaller
Preauricular sulcus	Present	Absent
Sacral shape	Short, wide, straight	Long, narrow, curved
Auricular surface (sacroiliac articulation)	Elevated	Flush with ilium
Pubic bone shape	Rectangular	Triangular
Acetabulum	Smaller	Larger
Sacral dimensions	Alae wider than promontory	Alae narrower than promontory

Some studies have reported very high accuracy (around 96%) based on the ventral arc alone (Sutherland and Suchey, 1991; Lovell, 1989; Ubelaker and Volk, 2002) and may even be useful in younger individuals as it is usually recognizable even in its "precursor" condition.

In addition to the Phenice traits, sexual dimorphism has been noted in the shape and width of the sciatic notch (Walker, 2005), with females having a wider notch and males having a narrower notch (Figures 8.7 and 8.8). Studies of documented collections have found that males sometimes have a wide notch, whereas females rarely show evidence of a narrow notch. Due to some overlap in the intermediate expressions of the sciatic notch, it is not recommended to estimate sex based solely on this feature.

Another source of sexual dimorphism is that human females tend to be more **neotenous** or **pedomorphic** than males, retaining more juvenile-like traits anatomically, including skeletally. Some pedomorphic traits include having less body hair, a higher voice, smaller teeth, larger eyes, and a more gracile skeleton. With age, however, skeletal remodeling may result in morphological changes in females that appear more masculine; thus, this should be taken into account during sex estimation of older individuals.

Sexual dimorphism may also develop as a function of different musculoskeletal activity (Buffa et al., 2001). In many cultures, males are more frequently involved in more laborious activities and therefore subject their skeletons to greater mechanical

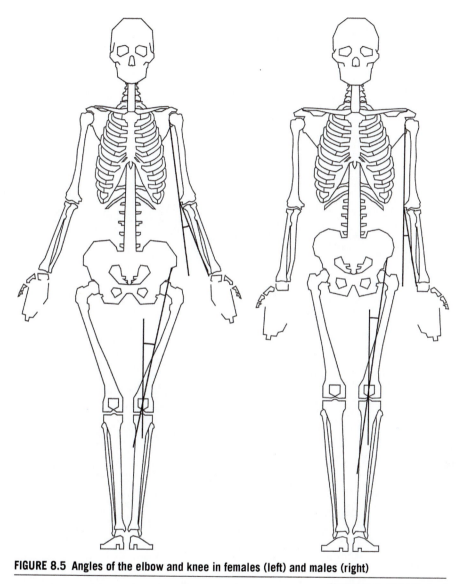

FIGURE 8.5 Angles of the elbow and knee in females (left) and males (right)

(Artwork by Craig Brodfuehrer)

loads. Bones that are subjected to greater mechanical loading and stress (especially the femur and tibia) tend to increase in cortical area (see Chapter 2). Where these loading and stress differences are greater between males and females, the bones may be more sexually dimorphic in terms of cortical area and/or the size of muscle attachments.

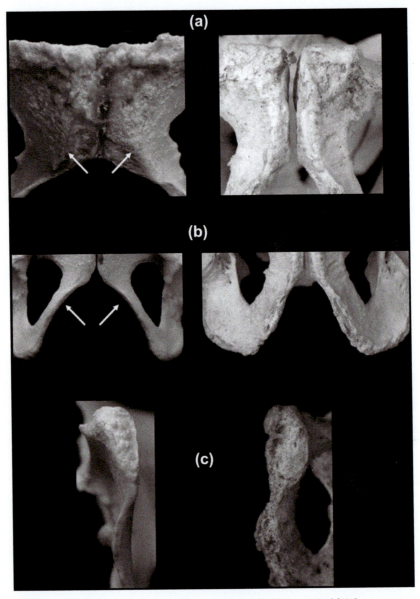

FIGURE 8.6 Phenice traits of the *os pubis* in the female (left) and male (right)

(a) Ventral arc – present in females, absent in males, (b) sub-pubic concavity – present in females, absent in males, and (c) medial ischiopubic ramus – sharp and narrow in females, wide and blunt in males

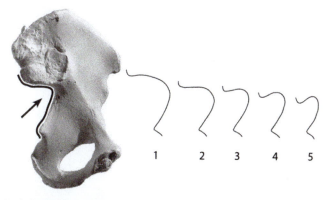

FIGURE 8.7 Variation in the sciatic notch

1 represents a more female configuration while 5 represents a more male configuration

(From Buikstra and Ubelaker, 1994)

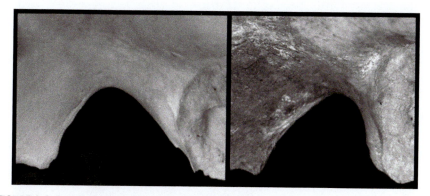

FIGURE 8.8 Female (left) and male (right) sciatic notch

Parturition and related events may leave various lesions on bones. Many of these have been the subject of anthropological study for the estimation of sex including the preauricular sulcus, separation of the pubic symphysis, osteitis condensans ilii, osteitis pubis, pubic pitting (Figure 8.9), bone density loss, and extension of the pubic tubercle. Many of these conditions, however, are not exclusively related to obstetrical events. Some may be found in nulliparous women and men, and may be absent in parous and multiparous women (Ubelaker and De La Paz, 2012).

Non-metric sex estimation based on the skull involves analysis of overall shape and relative size of certain cranial and mandibular features (see Figure 8.10, Figure 8.11, and Figure 8.12). In general, the skulls of males are larger and more rugged and robust than those of females which tend to be smaller and smoother (see Table 8.2). Although

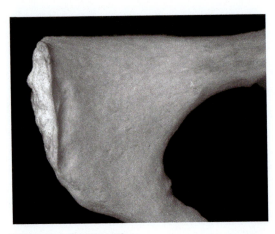

FIGURE 8.9 Dorsal pitting on a female pubis

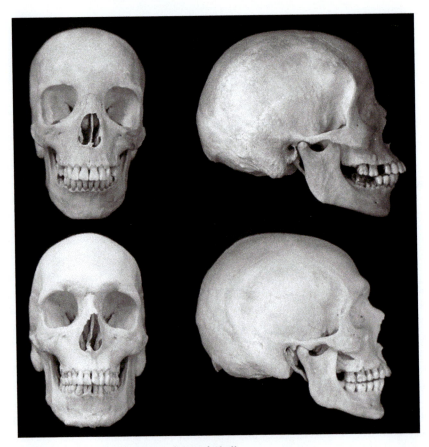

FIGURE 8.10 Female (top) and male (bottom) skull

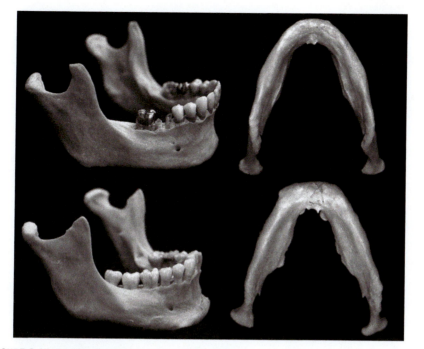

FIGURE 8.11 Female (top) and male (bottom) mandible

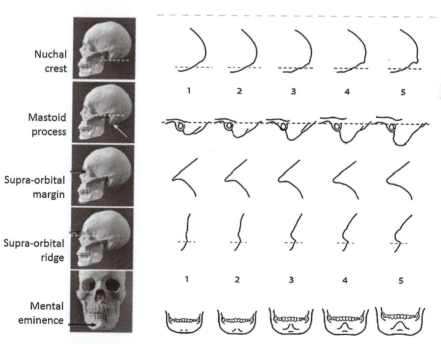

FIGURE 8.12 Differences in the male and female skull

1 represents a more female configuration while 5 represents a more male configuration

(From Buikstra and Ubelaker [1994], reprinted in White and Folkens [2005:390-391])

Table 8.2 Traits of the female and male skull

Skull feature	Female skull	Male skull
Nuchal crest	Small	Large
Mastoid process	Small	Large
Supraorbital margin	Sharp	Blunt
Superciliary arch/Glabella	Small/absent	Large
Chin shape	Round	Square
Mental eminence	Less pronounced	More pronounced
Frontals and parietals	More bossed	Less bossed
Gonial eversion	Less	Greater
Teeth	Smaller	Larger
Muscle attachments	Smaller	Larger
Palate depth	Shallow	Deep

relatively high accuracy can be achieved using certain features, inter-observer error rates for non-metric sex estimation from the skull have been shown to be relatively high (Konigsberg and Hens, 1998; Rogers, 2005; Williams and Rogers, 2006). The most reliable features tend to be mastoid size, supraorbital ridge size, general size and architecture, rugosity of the suprameatal and supramastoid crest, size and shape of the nasal aperture, and gonial angle. In some cases, it may even be possible to apply statistical tools such as regression models to these visual assessments (Konigsberg and Hens, 1998).

Various other bones and features have also been shown to display some degree of sexual dimorphism and to have some utility in sex estimation. The pattern of costal cartilage calcification (observed either directly or radiographically) shows sexual differences, with females showing a more central ossification pattern while the male pattern is more marginal (Navani et al., 1970; McCormick and Stewart, 1983; Stewart and McCormick, 1984; McCormick et al., 1985) (Figure 8.13). The accuracy of this method is age-dependent and may vary between populations.

Various other features show differences in their presence or expression between males and females. A suprascapular notch is often present in males and absent in females, and the presence of a septal aperture is more common in females than males (Finnegan, 1978) (Figure 8.14). The presence of a rhomboid fossa of the clavicle is more common in males (Rogers et al., 2000; Santos et al., 2008). Features of the posterior distal humerus have also been shown to be sexually dimorphic (Rogers, 1999) including trochlear constriction, trochlear symmetry, olecranon fossa shape, and the angle of medial epicondyle.

Certain diseases and skeletal conditions affect one sex more frequently than the other, and while there are few conditions that are reliably diagnostic as a sex estimation method, such assessments may suggest probabilities or corroborate other skeletal evidence of sex (Reichs, 1986). For example, groups from the genus *Streptococcus*

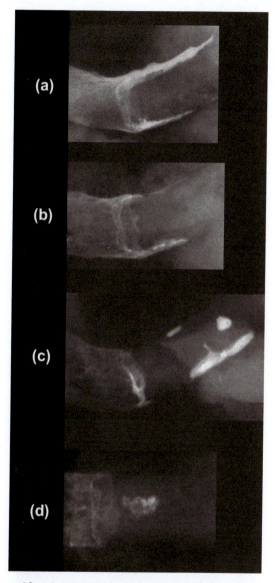

FIGURE 8.13 Male and female patterns of marginal costal cartilage ossification

Male pattern (a and b), and female pattern (c and d)

as well as avascular necrosis (tissue death from obstruction of arterial blood supply) are many times more common in males than females, many bone tumors and gout are more common in males, ankylosing spondylitis is 9–10 times more common in males, and rheumatoid arthritis and internal frontal hyperostosis (Figure 8.15) are more common in females (Reichs, 1986).

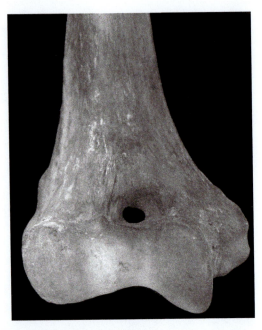

FIGURE 8.14 Septal aperture in a female humerus

(Image courtesy of Karen Gardner)

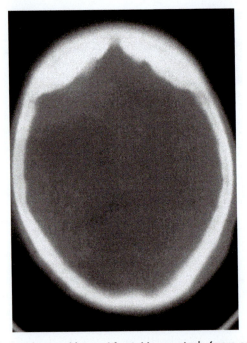

FIGURE 8.15 Radiological image of internal frontal hyperostosis (more common in females than males)

(From Brogdon, 2010)

8.3 **Metric analysis**

Metric analysis in sex estimation involves measuring maximum or minimum dimensions or taking measurements based on osteological landmarks to quantitatively evaluate size and shape differences between males and females. Some metric methods involve the evaluation of a single measurement or index of two measurements, while other more complex multivariate methods may combine numerous measurements into a single analysis (e.g., discriminant function analysis).

Among the most reliable metric methods for estimating sex are those involving dimensions of the long bones of the postcranial skeleton (Spradley and Jantz, 2011). Various approaches have been investigated involving measurements of postcranial bones, but most are based on the basic principle that males exceed females in size, especially in more weight-bearing joint areas. One recent comprehensive study (Spradley and Jantz, 2011) provides sectioning points and correct classification rates for sex estimation of American Whites and Blacks based on a series of standard postcranial measurements. Measurements with correct classification rates of 80% or greater are shown in Tables 8.3 and 8.4 for American Blacks and Whites, respectively. Examples of the more extensively studied and commonly employed long bone measurements for sex estimation include the maximum diameter of the femoral head (Stewart, 1979; Albanese, 2003) (Figure 8.16), femoral neck diameter (Seidemann et al., 1998), and vertical diameter of the humeral head (Stewart, 1979; France, 1998). Other postcranial bones including the scapula have also been studied for their utility in sex estimation (Stewart, 1979; Dabbs and Moore-Jansen, 2010).

Metric methods for sex estimation from the skull are generally considered less reliable than those based on the postcranial skeleton, but are still widely applied and useful in cases where no postcranial elements are available for analysis. Discriminant function analysis (see Chapter 3) was first applied to the estimation of sex from the skull in the 1960s (Giles and Elliot, 1963). Using measurements from more than 400 skulls, the method could correctly estimate sex at a rate of about 85%, which is considered to compare favorably to non-metric assessments (Meindl et al., 1985). A more widely used discriminant function tool for estimating sex currently is Fordisc (Ousley and Jantz, 2005).

Other metric assessments have also been investigated based on the skull including the lateral angle of the internal acoustic meatus which tends to be greater in females (Noren et al., 2005; Akansel et al., 2008; Lynnerup et al., 2006), and tooth size which tends to be larger in males.

Table 8.3 Univariate sectioning points and classification rates for American Blacks

Measurement (in mm)	Female			Male				
	N	Mean	SD	N	Mean	SD	SP	Class. Rate
Fem. Epicondylar Br. (62)[1]	33	72.88	3.86	65	83.35	3.97	78	0.89
Tib. Prox. Epiphyseal. Br. (70)	29	69.14	3.68	60	78.73	5.07	74	0.88
Scapula Height (38)	36	138.61	8.46	64	160.7	8.6	150	0.87
Fem. Max. Head Diam. (63)	39	41.33	2.18	69	47.22	2.47	44	0.86
Humerus Epicondylar Br. (41)	34	55.38	2.66	65	64.14	3.87	60	0.86
Humerus Head Diameter (42)	37	41.03	2.46	68	46.99	2.3	44	0.86
Scapula Breadth (39)	36	95.92	6.52	64	109.55	6.71	103	0.86
Radius Max. Length (45)	37	239.19	12.45	69	267.58	13.68	253	0.85
Clavicle Max. Length (35)	38	142.21	7.77	62	156.81	7.41	150	0.84
Calcaneus Max. Length (77)	20	76.45	4.62	50	85.38	4.74	81	0.83
Fem. AP Subtroch Diam. (64)	37	25.86	2.56	66	28.73	2.28	27	0.83
Ischium Length (59)	30	77.33	4.91	47	89.15	6.23	83	0.83
Ulna Max. Length (48)	33	256.42	15.01	63	285.56	13.89	271	0.83
Ulna Phys. Length (51)	25	226.48	13.38	53	254.51	13.94	240	0.83
Fibula Maximum Length (75)	32	367.09	22.11	65	400.55	22.05	384	0.82
Fem. Bicondylar Length (61)	36	444.94	25.63	65	484.32	25.9	465	0.81
Humerus Max. Length (40)	39	309.46	15.95	76	340.91	17.1	325	0.81
Os Coxa Height (56)	36	191.69	11.78	61	211.59	10.1	202	0.81
Tib. Diameter Nut. For. (72)	30	32.23	2.81	59	37.31	2.85	35	0.8

[1]Numbers correspond to measurements in Moore-Jansen et al., 1994
(From Spradley and Jantz, 2011)

Table 8.4 Univariate sectioning points and classification rates for American Whites

Measurement (in mm)	Female			Male				
	N	Mean	SD	N	Mean	SD	SP	Class. Rate
Tib. Prox. Epiphyseal. Br. (70)[1]	113	69.19	3.37	226	79.31	4.1	74	0.9
Scapula Height (38)	127	141.87	9.48	231	163.33	8.95	153	0.89
Fem. Epicondylar Br. (62)	129	74.53	3.8	248	85.27	4.38	80	0.88
Fem. Max. Head Diam. (63)	142	42.05	2.09	261	48.4	2.6	45	0.88
Humerus Epicondylar Br. (41)	136	54.9	3.8	258	64.38	3.64	60	0.87
Radius Max. Length (45)	130	228.22	11.21	251	253.41	12.95	241	0.86
Os Coxa Height (56)	124	201.06	13.71	235	222.94	10.8	212	0.85
Scapula Breadth (39)	127	95.48	5.07	237	108.15	6.33	102	0.84
Ulna Max. Length (48)	127	244.94	11.66	250	271.07	13.49	258	0.84
Humerus Head Diameter (42)	139	42.47	2.44	256	48.81	3.22	46	0.83
Clavicle Max. Length (35)	123	139.79	7.04	224	156.96	9.33	148	0.82
Humerus Max. Length (40)	144	305.75	14.43	263	333.99	17.03	320	0.82
Hum. Min. Diam. MS (44)	139	15.32	1.35	256	18.9	1.79	17	0.82
Ulna Phys. Length (51)	105	217.69	11.71	217	240.17	12.68	229	0.82
Fem. Bicondylar Length (61)	134	431.96	20.87	250	470.75	23.63	451	0.82
Tibia Circum. Nut. For. (74)	106	85.36	6.31	199	97.65	7.16	92	0.81
Fibula Maximum Length (75)	117	351.29	19.65	235	386.49	22.11	369	0.81
Femur Max. Length (60)	151	436.15	20.63	268	474.21	23.23	455	0.8

[1]Numbers correspond to measurements in Moore-Jansen et al., 1994
(From Spradley and Jantz, 2011)

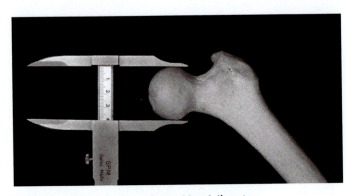

FIGURE 8.16 Measurement of maximum femoral head diameter

8.4 Other considerations in sex estimation

The review of various sex estimation methods above clearly demonstrates that sexual dimorphism is differentially expressed throughout the skeleton. Moreover, it can be influenced by genetic factors, nutrition, and health status. These factors should be considered when undertaking estimates of sex from skeletal remains.

There is no absolute cut-off for how valid or reliable a sex estimation method should be, but bear in mind that sex estimation is a binary (two-sided) decision, and a random guess will be correct 50% of the time. Sex estimation methods should therefore have significantly greater than 50% accuracy in order to be considered useful. Osteological sex estimation methods that are accurate less than 80% of the time are typically considered unreliable for most medicolegal cases.

Sex estimation methods from other bones may become available as shape differences are better understood, especially through the application of more robust analytical approaches. Geometric morphometric analysis, for example, examines the shapes of bones while controlling for size, and has been used to evaluate subtle shape differences between male and female skeletal elements (Passalacqua et al., 2010). These methods may reveal quantifiable differences between male and female skeletons that were previously not recognized or poorly understood (Figure 8.17).

Estimating sex in **subadults** is generally considered unadvisable because widely validated methods are currently unavailable (Scientific Working Group for Forensic Anthropology [SWGANTH], 2010). This is due to the fact that most sexual differences in the skeleton do not appear until the increase in sex hormones which stimulate the development of secondary sexual characteristics during puberty. Estimates of sex from the skeleton are therefore not considered reliable prior to around age 14. Another factor affecting the accuracy of subadult sex estimation is the limited availability of juvenile skeletal material of known sex to study.

Sexual differentiation has been noted to begin as early as the 10th fetal week (Weaver, 1986), and numerous studies have attempted to derive methods for estimating the sex of juveniles. For example, differences have been noted in the elevation of the auricular surface, with females generally exhibiting an auricular surface that is raised entirely above the plane of the ilium, while the male auricular surface is in

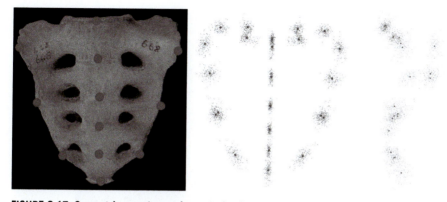

FIGURE 8.17 Geometric morphometric analysis of the sacrum in males and females

(From Passalacqua et al., 2010)

line with the ilium (Weaver, 1980; Mittler and Sheridan, 1992). Sex differences have also been reported in the fetal sciatic notch and sub-pubic angle (Boucher, 1955, 1957; Schutowski, 1993), as well as the mandibular arcade shape (Schutowski, 1993; Sutter, 2003). In general, however, accuracies of these methods are low and inter-observer error is high (Cardoso and Saunders, 2008).

Although not typically within the purview of forensic anthropologists, it is sometimes possible to determine the sex of skeletal remains based on molecular methods (DNA) (Stone et al., 1996). The amelogenin gene is found on the X and Y chromosomes, and differences in base pair number (from specific primers) between males and females can aid in sex determination (Stone et al., 1996). This method requires the amplification of DNA by Polymerase Chain Reaction (PCR). In rare cases, mutations can produce a false result, although this was found to occur less than 1% of the time in a sample of 1,224 individuals (Francès et al., 2007). Anthropologists may facilitate this process by selecting skeletal samples that are likely to yield DNA.

8.5 Case study – sex estimation

In 2006, human remains were recovered from a shallow grave in northern California. The skeleton was nearly complete, allowing for an in-depth assessment of the biological profile. The decedent expressed a number of characteristically male pelvic traits, including: a blunt expression of the ischiopubic ramus ridge, a narrow sub-pubic angle, lack of a sub-pubic concavity, absence of a ventral arc, and a narrow sciatic notch (Figure 8.18). In addition, the degree of robusticity of cranial features, such as the supraorbital region, supraorbital margins, external occipital protuberance, mastoid processes, temporal lines, and nuchal lines were consistent with male sex (Figure 8.19). Statistical comparisons of the postcranial measurements with samples from the Forensic Anthropology Databank (Fordisc 3.0, University of Tennessee) also strongly suggested the individual was male. The decedent was later identified as a 26-year-old white male with a living stature of 5 feet, 8 inches.

FIGURE 8.18 Case study innominates

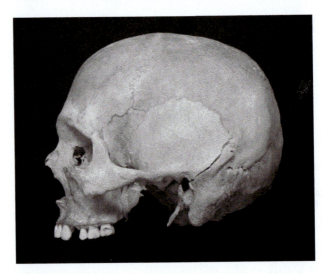

FIGURE 8.19 Case study cranium

8.6 Summary

- It is possible for forensic anthropologists to differentiate between male and female skeletons because humans are sexually dimorphic, that is, they differ in size and shape.
- Sex differences in the skeleton are related primarily to the functions of parturition and locomotion. Females must have a wide pelvis and birth canal due to the large size of human infant heads, while maintaining efficient locomotion.
- "Sex" refers to biological differences between males and females of an organism while "gender" refers to cultural expressions of femininity and masculinity.
- The pelvis is the most sexually dimorphic region of the human skeleton, and visual assessment of the pelvis is the most accurate method for estimating sex.

The Phenice method using the *os pubis* is one of the most validated, accurate, and widely used methods of estimating sex.

- Metric assessment of postcranial limb bones (based on the fact that males are larger on average than females, especially in weight-bearing joints) is the second most reliable method for sex estimation.
- Sex differences in the skull are less reliable than those of the pelvis and limb bones but still have utility in sex estimation; male skulls tend to be larger, rugged, and more robust than female skulls, which tend to be smaller, smoother, and more gracile.
- Since most sex differences in skeletal structure do not appear until puberty, estimating sex in subadults is unreliable and generally considered unadvisable.
- Sex can sometimes be determined from skeletal remains using DNA. While anthropologists typically do not perform DNA analysis themselves, they may be responsible for selecting skeletal specimens for DNA sampling.

8.7 Test yourself

- What is sexual dimorphism? How does human sexual dimorphism differ from that of other animals?
- A decomposed body is discovered in a forest. There is extensive scavenging of the pelvis. What areas of the skeleton might you use for estimating sex? What methods would you employ?
- What are carrying and Q-angles, and what is their significance in sex estimation from the skeleton?
- Using Table 8.4 for sex estimation from measurements of postcranial bones, what would you conclude about the sex of an American White individual with a maximum femoral head diameter of 47 mm?
- You are asked to help estimate a biological profile for an unidentified individual for whom only numerous radiographs (and no skeletal remains) are currently available. What methods might you be able to use to estimate sex?
- Why should parturition lesions or pathological conditions alone not be used to estimate sex?
- Why is sex estimation in subadults problematic? What methods *could* be employed to estimate sex of an individual who was 16 years old?
- What is the difference between gender and sex? Why is this distinction important? How would you report sex estimation findings on a case where clothing found at the scene pointed to the opposite sex as your skeletal findings?

Definitions

Androgeny Physical or psychological sexual ambiguity

Carrying angle The angle at which the upper and lower portions of the arm articulate; osteologically in humans, the angle at which the humerus articulates with the radius and ulna

Gender Socially constructed roles, behaviors, activities, and attributes considered appropriate for men and women

Genotype The genetic make up of an organism

Hominin Of the tribe Hominini (order Primates, family Hominidae, sub-family Homininae) which includes humans and their ancestors after the split from the tribe Panini

Intersex The condition of having anomalous or intermediate features that typically distinguish males and females in a species

Locomotion The act of or the ability to move from place to place; in humans, usually walking

Morphology The structure, size, and form of an organism or its parts

Neotenous/Pedomorphic Retaining juvenile characteristics into adulthood

Parturition Childbirth; the process of giving birth to offspring

Phenotype/Phenotypic Observable physical characteristics of an organism as determined by both genetics and environmental influences

Q-angle Quadriceps angle; the angle at which the upper and lower portions of the leg articulate; osteologically in humans, the angle at which the femur articulates with the tibia

Sex The classification of an organism as male or female based on reproductive organs and functions

Sexual dimorphism Phenotypic differences between males and females of the same species

Subadult An individual who has not reached physiological adulthood or has not yet attained adult characteristics; osteologically, an individual who has not reached skeletal maturity; juvenile

References

Akansel, G., Inan, N., Kurtas, O., Sarisoy, H.T., Arslan, A., Demirci, A., 2008. Gender and the lateral angle of the internal acoustic canal meatus as measured on computerized tomography of the temporal bone. Forensic Sci. Int. 178, 93–95.

Albanese, J., 2003. A metric method for sex determination using the hip bone and the femur. J. Forensic Sci. 48 (2), 263–273.

Atkinson, W.B., Elftman, H., 1945. The carrying angle of the human arm as a secondary sex character. Anat. Rec. 91, 49–52.

Bogin, B., 1999. Patterns of human growth, second ed. Cambridge University Press, Cambridge.

Boucher, B.J., 1955. Sex differences in the foetal sciatic notch. J. Forensic Med. 2, 51–54.

Boucher, B.J., 1957. Sex differences in the foetal pelvis. Am. J. Phys. Anthropol. 155, 81–600.

Brogdon, G.B., 2010. Radiological identification: Anthropological Parameters. In: Thali, M.J., Viner, M.D., Brogdon, B.G. (Eds.), Brogdon's Forensic Radiology, second ed. CRC Press, Boca Raton, pp 85–106.

Buffa, R., Marini, E., Giovanni, F., 2001. Variation in sexual dimorphism in relation to physical activity. Am. J. Human. Biol. 13 (3), 341–348.

Buikstra, J.E., Ubelaker, D.H., 1994. Standards for data collection from Human Skeletal Remains. Archaeological. Surv. Res. Semin Ser. 44 Fayetteville.

Cardoso, F.V., Saunders, S.R., 2008. Two arch criteria of the ilium for sex determination of immature skeletal remains: A test of their accuracy and an assessment of intra- and inter-observer error. Forensic Sci. Int. 178, 24–29.

Dabbs, G.R., Moore-Jansen, P.H., 2010. A method for estimating sex using metric analysis of the scapula. J. Forensic Sci. 55 (1), 149–152.

Finnegan, M.J., 1978. Non-metric variation of the infra-cranial skeleton. J. Anat. 125, 23–37.

France, D.L., 1998. Observational and metric analysis of sex in the skeleton. In: Reichs, K.J. (Ed.), Forensic Osteology: Advances in the Identification of Human Remains, second ed. Charles C. Thomas Press, Springfield, pp. 441–458.

Francès, F., Portolés, O., González, J.I., Coltell, O., Verdú, F., Castelló, A., Corella, D., 2007. Amelogenin test: from forensics to quality control in clinical and biochemical genomics. Clin. Chim. Acta. 386 (1–2), 53–56.

Frayer, D.W., Wolpoff, M.H., 1985. Sexual dimorphism. Annu. Rev. Anthropol. 14, 429–473.

Giles, E., Elliot, O., 1963. Sex determination by discriminant function analysis of crania. Am. J. Phys. Anthropol. 21 (1), 53–68.

Konigsberg, L.W., Hens, S.M., 1998. Use of ordinal categorical variables in skeletal assessment of sex from the cranium. Am. J. Phys. Anthropol. 107 (1), 97–112.

Livingston, L.A., 1998. The quadriceps angle: A review of the literature. J. Orthop & Sports Phys. Ther. 28 (2), 105–109.

Lovell, N.C, 1989. Test of Phenice's technique for determining sex from the os pubis. Am. J. Phys. Anthropol. 79, 117–120.

Lynnerup, N., Schultz, M., Madelung, A., Graw, M., 2006. Diameter of the human internal acoustic meatus and sex determination. Int. J. Osteoarchaeology 16 (2), 118–123.

Moore-Jansen, P.M., Ousley, S.D., Jantz, R.L., 1994. Data Collection Procedures for Forensic Skeletal Material. Report of Investigations No. 48, Department of Anthropology, University of Tennessee, Knoxville.

McCormick, W.F., Stewart, J.H., 1983. Ossification patterns of costal cartilages as an indicator of sex. Arch. Pathol. Lab. Med. 107 (4), 206–210.

McCormick, W.F., Stewart, J.H., Langford, L.A., 1985. Sex determination from chest plate roentgenograms. Am. J. Phys. Anthropol. 68 (2), 173–195.

Meindl, R.S., Lovejoy, C., Mensforth, R.P., Don Carlos, L., 1985. Accuracy and direction of error in sexing of the skeleton: Implications for paleodemography. Am. J. Phys. Anthropol. 68, 79–85.

Mittler, D.M., Sheridan, S.G., 1992. Sex determination in subadults using auricular surface morphology: A forensic science perspective. J. Forensic Sci. 37, 1068–1075.

Navani, S., Shah, J.R., Levy, P.S., 1970. Determination of sex by costal cartilage calcification. Am. J. Roentgenol. Radiogr. 108 (4), 771–774.

Nicholson, L., 1994. Interpreting gender. Signs: J. Women in Cul. and Society 20, 79–105.

Noren, A., Lynnerup, N., Czarnetzki, A., Graw, M., 2005. Lateral angle: A method for sexing using the petrous bone. Am. J. Phys. Anthropol. 128 (2), 318–323.

Ousley, S.D., Jantz, R.L., 2005. FORDISC 3.0: Personal computer forensic discriminant functions. The University of Tennessee, Knoxville.

Passalacqua, N.V., Vollner, J.M., Rainwater, C.W., 2010. Geometric morphometric analysis of the human sacrum and its utility in sex estimation. Poster presented at the American Association of Physical Anthropology 79th annual meeting, Albuquerque, NM.

Phenice, T.W., 1969. A newly developed visual method of sexing the Os pubis. Am. J. Phys. Anthropol. 30, 297–302.

Potter, H.P., 1895. The obliquity of the arm of the female in extension. The relation of the forearm with the upper arm in flexion. J. Anat. London 29, 488–493.

Reichs, K.J., 1986. Forensic implications of skeletal pathologies: Sex. In: Reichs, K.J. (Ed.), Forensic Osteology: Advances in the Identification of Human Remains. Charles C. Thomas, Springfield, pp. 196–217.

Ridley, M., 1995. Pelvic sexual dimorphism and relative neonatal brain size really are related. Am. J. Phys. Anthropol. 97 (2), 197–200.

Rogers, T.L., 1999. A visual method of determining the sex of skeletal remains using the distal humerus. J. Forensic Sci. 44 (1), 57–60.

Rogers, T.L., 2005. Determining the sex of human remains through cranial morphology. J. Forensic Sci. 50 (3), 493–500.

Rogers, T.L., Flournoy, L.E., McCormick, W.F., 2000. The rhomboid fossa of the clavicle as a sex and age estimator. J. Forensic Sci. 39, 1047–1056.

Santos, L.S.M., Berzin, F., Prado, F.B., Preza, A.D.G., Daruge, E., 2008. Gender determination using rhomboid fossa from the clavicle. Brazilian Journal of Morphological Sciences 25 (1–4), 157–214.

Schutowski, H., 1993. Sex determination of infant and juvenile skeletons: I. morphognostic features. Am. J. Phys. Anthropol. 90, 199–205.

Scientific Working Group for Forensic Anthropology, 2010. Sex Assessment Revision 0. Accessed from www.swganth.org.

Seidemann, R.W., Stajanowski, C.M., Doran, G.H., 1998. The use of the supero-inferior femoral neck diameter as a sex assessor. Am. J. Phys. Anthropol. 107 (3), 305–313.

Spradley, M.K., Jantz, R.L., 2011. Sex estimation in forensic anthropology: Skull versus postcranial elements. J. Forensic Sci. 56 (2), 289–296.

Stewart, J.H., McCormick, W.F., 1984. A sex- and age-limited ossification pattern in human costal cartilages. Am. J. Clin. Pathol. 81 (6), 765–769.

Stewart, T.D., 1979. Essentials of Forensic Anthropology. Charles C. Thomas, Springfield.

Stone, A.C., Milner, G.R., Pääbo, S., Stoneking, M., 1996. Sex determination of ancient human skeletons using DNA. Am. J. Phys. Anthropol. 99, 231–238.

Sutherland, L.D., Suchey, J.M., 1991. Use of the ventral arc in pubic sex determination. J. Forensic Sci. 36 (2), 501–511.

Sutter, R.C., 2003. Nonmetric subadult skeletal sexing traits: I. A blind test of the accuracy of eight previously proposed methods using prehistoric known-sex mummies from northern Chile. J. Forensic Sci. 48 (5), 927–935.

Torgrimson, B.N., Minson, C.T., 2005. Sex and gender: what is the difference? J. Appl. Phys. 99 (3), 785–787.

Ubelaker, D.H., De La Paz, J.S., 2012. Skeletal indicators of pregnancy and parturition: A historical review. J. Forensic Sci. 57 (4), 866–872.

Ubelaker, D.H., Volk, C., 2002. A test of the Phenice method for the estimation of sex. J. Forensic Sci. 47 (1), 19–24.

Walker, P.L., 2005. Greater sciatic notch morphology: sex, age, and population differences. Am. J. Phys. Anthropol. 127, 385–391.

Walker, P.L., Cook, D.C., 1998. Gender and sex: Vive la difference. Am. J. Phys. Anthropol. 106, 255–259.

Weaver, D.S., 1980. Sex differences in the ilia of a known sex and age sample of fetal and infant skeletons. Am. J. Phys. Anthropol. 52, 191–195.

Weaver, D.S., 1986. Forensic aspects of fetal and neonatal skeletons. In: Reichs, K.J. (Ed.), Forensic Osteology: Advances in the Identification of Human Remains. Charles C. Thomas, Springfield, pp. 90–100.

Williams, B.A., Rogers, T.L., 2006. Evaluating accuracy and precision of cranial morphological traits for sex determination. J. Forensic Sci. 51 (4), 729–735.

Ancestry Estimation

9.1 Principles of ancestry estimation

Ancestry refers to an individual's ancestral geographic region of origin (Scientific Working Group for Forensic Anthropology [SWGANTH], 2013). The estimation of ancestry from human skeletal remains is possible due to geographically-patterned human variation. Human populations differ in various ways as a function of evolutionary processes such as natural selection, genetic drift, mutation, and gene flow, which collectively shape phenotypic variation, including variation in the skeleton. Ancestry estimations are based on observation and measurement of these skeletal variations. Moreover, because ancestry has both biological and social aspects (particularly in terms of how individuals self-identify and how they are identified by others), the estimation of ancestry also often involves interpreting skeletal variation within the context of social labels.

Ancestry, like the other components of the biological profile, is estimated in order to facilitate the identification of an unknown individual by helping to narrow the pool of possible matches with missing persons. In addition, other aspects of the biological profile may depend on the correct estimation of ancestry, because sexual dimorphism, limb proportions, and growth rates tend to vary between different ancestral groups.

Ancestry estimation in forensic anthropology involves the study of morphoscopic traits and skeletal measurements that correspond to geographically-patterned genetic variation (Figure 9.1). Because of the range of variation in modern humans, however, the estimation of ancestry is not always straightforward. Different populations express phenotypic traits differentially. Typically, ancestry is estimated for large geographic regions (often at the continental level, and most frequently as European, African, or Asian). In some cases, however, it may be more appropriate to distinguish an individual as being more similar to, for example, Southeast Asian groups than Hispanic groups, or 20th-century White males than 19th-century White males. In all cases, these choices depend upon the methods available, the extent and condition of the remains, the reporting requirements of the forensic anthropology laboratory, the availability of appropriate reference samples for comparison, and the background and training of the analyst.

A number of human classification systems have been utilized throughout history (especially by early anthropologists), such as **race** and **subspecies**, and the classification of humans into discrete groups has a rather controversial history

Forensic Anthropology. http://dx.doi.org/10.1016/B978-0-12-418671-2.00009-4

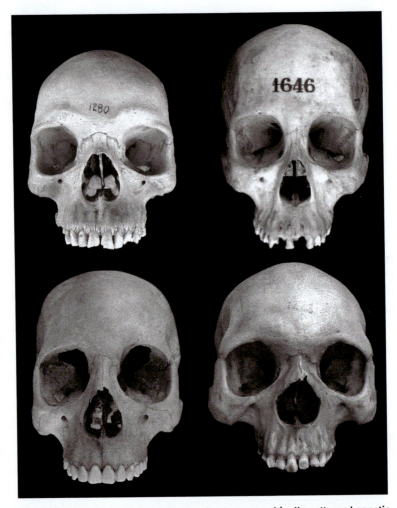

FIGURE 9.1 Differences in cranial morphology due to geographically-patterned genetic variation

(Armelagos and Goodman, 1998; Spradley and Weisensee, 2013; Steadman, 2013) (Box 9.1). While some argue that the race concept is strictly a social construct with no biological basis (Armelagos and van Gerven, 2003; Littlefield et al., 1982; Montagu, 1972; Mukhopadhyay and Moses, 1997), recent analyses have demonstrated significant and meaningful differences between populations due to the heritability of skeletal morphology (Sparks and Jantz, 2002). Forensic anthropologists recognize that differences can be identified between groups by focusing on the morphoscopic and metric traits that show a moderate to high level of heritability (Hefner et al., 2012; Spradley and Weisensee, 2013).

Skeletal differences exist between human populations which reflect geographically-patterned variation, but forensic anthropologists must be cautious in how that

---

BOX 9.1 THE RACE CONCEPT IN ANTHROPOLOGY

Interest in human classification peaked as Europeans increasingly came into contact with different cultures through the age of exploration and colonialism (Brues, 1977; Gates, 1997). Carolus Linnaeus was the first to scientifically classify the human species into discrete groups, identifying four subspecies designations (i.e., races) for humans: *Homo sapiens americanus, asiaticus, africanus, and europaeus,* representing Native Americans, Asians, Africans, and Europeans, respectively (Wolf, 1994). Earnest Hooton (1887–1954), a Harvard University professor, later created a comprehensive trait list for classifying skulls into three major racial groups: Negroid, Mongoloid, and Caucasoid. The idea of discrete biological human groups paved the way for theories of the origins of humanity as well as beliefs in racial differences in intelligence and morality. In many instances, physical and cultural attributes assigned to a particular group were used to justify racism and discrimination, and often influenced public policy.

Since the 1970s, major advancements in human genetics have changed the way anthropologists view human variation and the race concept. For example, one study compared genetic variation between major racial groups and found that approximately 85% of human genetic variation occurs *within* populations, with only a small percentage contributing to genetic differences *between* populations (Lewontin, 1972). Subsequent genetic studies continue to demonstrate that biological race is not a meaningful construct since the human species shows much greater within-group variation than between-group variation (Templeton, 1998).

The most important revelation in the examination of biological race is that the general differences, once believed to be co-patterned racial features (such as skin color, eye shape, hair color, etc.), are actually independently varying traits. These traits vary along **clines**, or gradients based on geography and environment, and indicate that the human species does not meet the biological criteria for race. For a more thorough discussion of the race concept, readers are referred to: *"Race" is a four-letter word: The genesis of the concept,* by C. Loring Brace (Brace, 2005).

---

variation is interpreted. For example, population differences in the shape of the nasal aperture may reflect evolutionary adaptations to a particular climate – shorter and wider noses are more efficient at cooling air in hot and humid climates, contrasting with tall and narrow noses which are more efficient at warming air in cool and dry climates. These differences, however, are not directly associated with skin pigmentation, hair color, or eye color.

When estimating ancestry from skeletal remains, it is important to understand how certain phenotypic traits are distributed within and between populations. The gradient or continuum of a given trait across geographic space or environment is known as a *cline* or a *clinal distribution*. Examination of the distribution of numerous genetic traits suggests that they often follow a clinal distribution. For example, human skin color tends to be darkest nearer the equator and lighter nearer the poles, reflecting geographic origin and exposure to UV radiation rather than membership in a particular race (Figure 9.2). In other words, no single trait or suite of traits accurately defines a population, including a particular ancestral category.

Even within the forensic anthropological community there is disagreement on the usage of terminology and appropriate application of reference populations. For example, at present in the United States, the largest minority group is Hispanic

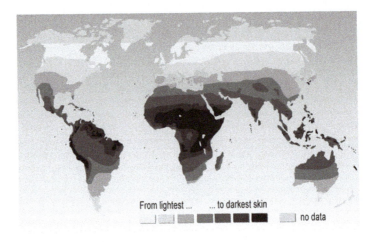

FIGURE 9.2 Clinal distribution of human skin color

(From Chaplin, 2004)

(Spradley et al., 2008). The term "Hispanic" is complex because, like other ethnic terms, it is socially constructed, and is often generically applied to any Spanish-speaking individuals regardless of geographic origin (e.g., Mexico, Chile, Cuba, Puerto Rico, Spain). The Spanish language, however, is a poor indicator of genetic history and phenotypic expression. Depending on what traits are being compared, people in present-day Mexico may be very different from individuals in Spain, or relatively similar to individuals in Brazil. Until recently, it was common to use reference data from prehistoric or historic Native American groups in order to classify Asian or Hispanic individuals due to similarities in cranial morphology, based largely on a shared, though distant, genetic relationship from the Asian colonization of the New World. Today, data from known individuals is being collected for many different Asian, Central, and South American populations (such as Thailand, Mexico, and Chile) and will serve as more appropriate reference samples for modern Asian and Asian-descended New World populations.

Forensic anthropologists continue to grapple with the distinctions between the biological and social race construct, and have at times experienced significant criticism for including ancestry estimates as part of the biological profile (Armelagos and Goodman, 1998; Sauer, 1992; Kennedy, 1995). For forensic anthropologists, the ability to translate skeletal assessments of ancestry to a social race category is a central issue in ancestry estimation due to police procedure and reporting (Ousley et al., 2009). For law enforcement, information on ancestry helps to narrow down a pool of missing persons, providing a useful preliminary line of investigation to facilitate identification of unidentified skeletal remains. Databases utilized by many law enforcement organizations, however, typically allow only a limited number of coded entries. Options in the National Crime Information Center (NCIC) Unidentified Person File, for example, are: White,

---

BOX 9.2 RACE AND CENSUS DATA

The US Census is mandated by the Constitution to be conducted once every ten years, and is used to track demographic trends and reveal changes in the ethnic make up within the United States. The census includes socially identified racial categories such as Black or African-American, White, American Indian, Native Alaskan, Asian, Native Hawaiian, or other Pacific Islander, as outlined by the Office of Management and Budget (United States Census, n.d.). Individuals who self-identify as Latino, Hispanic, or Spanish, however, are treated as an ethnic category and could be a member of any racial group. These categories are not meant to reflect biological heritage, and respondents can select more than one category.

The way census data is collected is very different in other countries. For example, in Mexico and Australia, individuals are asked to identify whether they are of indigenous or aboriginal origin, with this being the primary census data collected. The English census, similarly to the US, offers a wide variety of choices including a number of admixed options not included in the US census, although it does not allow more than one selection.

Black, Asian or Pacific Islander, American Indian/Alaskan Native, or Unknown. Censuses similarly offer few selections for ancestry, which are often a poor representation of the ancestries of a country's citizens (Box 9.2).

Positive assortative mating practices (i.e., mating between individuals of similar groups) maintains an identifiable degree of concordance between an individual's social race and his or her skeletal biology (Ousley et al., 2009; Spradley and Weisensee, 2013), but it is widely recognized that individuals do not always mate with individuals of the same ancestry. An individual who is a product of parents from two different ancestral backgrounds is an example of gene flow, and is considered to be "**admixed**," although these individuals may more strongly identify or be associated with one particular group socially (see Box 9.3). Morphological traits more frequently found in a particular population may be expressed differently in admixed individuals due to differential gene expression, environmental factors, and other factors that contribute to human variation. Since the frequency distributions of particular **character states** in admixed groups are not well understood, it is generally not advisable to automatically conclude that an individual is of mixed ancestry; it is better to simply identify the ancestry group that the remains most closely resemble, and include other possibilities (Hefner, 2009; Hefner et al., 2012; Hughes et al., 2011). Despite the known biological basis for many geographically-varying morphological traits, ancestry estimation remains one of the most challenging assessments for most modern forensic anthropology practitioners.

9.2 Morphoscopic (non-metric) analysis

Morphoscopic traits are quasi-continuous morphological features that show varying forms, degrees of expression, or frequencies in presence or absence. There are a number of morphoscopic traits that show variation associated with ancestry, and these traits can be utilized to estimate ancestry from unidentified skeletal remains.

BOX 9.3 PRESIDENT BARACK OBAMA – RACE AND ANCESTRY

Race is a social construct that tells us little about the underlying genetic variation in the human species. In the United States, certain geographically-varying traits are weighed much more heavily than others in racial grouping. For example, on January 20th, 2009, Barack Hussein Obama was elected the 44th President of the United States of America, and is acknowledged as being the first elected African-American US president. A closer look at President Obama's ancestry, however, reveals a more complex genetic heritage. Born to a mother of European ancestry and a father of Kenyan ancestry, he shares genes that derive from two different continents. Regardless of his admixed biological heritage, people commonly perceive President Obama as being of African ancestry, largely based on the color of his skin.

(From Wikipedia)

The methods used to assess morphoscopic traits in the estimation of ancestry have changed significantly over time. Historically, forensic anthropologists relied upon lists of character states of certain traits (known as "trait lists") that were generally thought to correspond to particular ancestral groups, and which were developed largely based on practitioners' experience (e.g., Gill, 1998; Rhine, 1990; Gill and Rhine, 1990; Birkby et al., 2008). For example, a trait such as *orbit shape* may have been described as having a character state of round or rectangular, each corresponding to a different ancestral group.

This "trait list" approach lead to significant interpretive problems because the ancestry groups were described by simple lists of trait-states with no associated methods for actually estimating ancestry, and they lacked a scientific approach for weighing the different states of individual traits (Figure 9.3). Moreover, many of the sample sizes upon which these trait lists were based were too small to be statistically meaningful, and some of the character states did not correspond to the

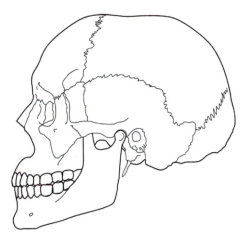

Cranial Vault Traits	Maxillary/Mandibular traits	Facial Traits
Post-bregmatic depression present	Marked prognathism	Rectangular orbit shape
Long cranial base chord	Crenulated molars	Flared nasal opening
Low cranial base angle	Hyperbolic dental arcade	Slight nasal depression
Simple cranial sutures	Bulging palatine suture	Small nasal spine
Rounded external auditory meatus	Slanted ascending ramus	Guttered lower nasal border

FIGURE 9.3 Example of the "trait list" approach to ancestry assessment ("American Black" skull and traits listed)

group thought to most commonly exhibit that state (see discussion in Hefner, 2009 and Hefner et al., 2012). Despite the major limitations and lack of scientific rigor of the trait list approach, many forensic anthropologists continue to rely upon it exclusively for ancestry estimation (Hefner et al., 2012), and several popular texts still provide ancestry trait lists or unrealistic skull shape stereotypes (e.g., Bass, 2005; Burns, 2013; Gill and Rhine, 1990; Klepinger, 2006; Byers, 2011; Birkby et al., 2008).

More recently, scientifically and statistically-valid methods for identifying and scoring morphoscopic traits to estimate ancestry have been presented (see Hefner, 2007, 2009; Hefner and Ousley, in press; Hefner et al., 2012; and references therein). Rather than subjectively assessing the similarity of a skull to character state trait lists, morphoscopic features have been demonstrated to vary between groups in predictable ways which can be assessed and meaningfully scored to assess ancestry. Scoring morphoscopic traits allows the application of statistical procedures to assess ancestry of an unknown individual. Many of the morphoscopic traits used in these approaches resemble previous trait lists, but have now been evaluated in a scientifically meaningful way. Two of the more recent examples of morphoscopic ancestry estimation methods are **Optimized Summed Scoring Attributes** (OSSA), and **Decision Tree Modeling** (Hefner and Ousley, in press).

OSSA uses the frequency of morphoscopic traits and their character states to estimate ancestry as either American White or American Black (Hefner and Ousley,

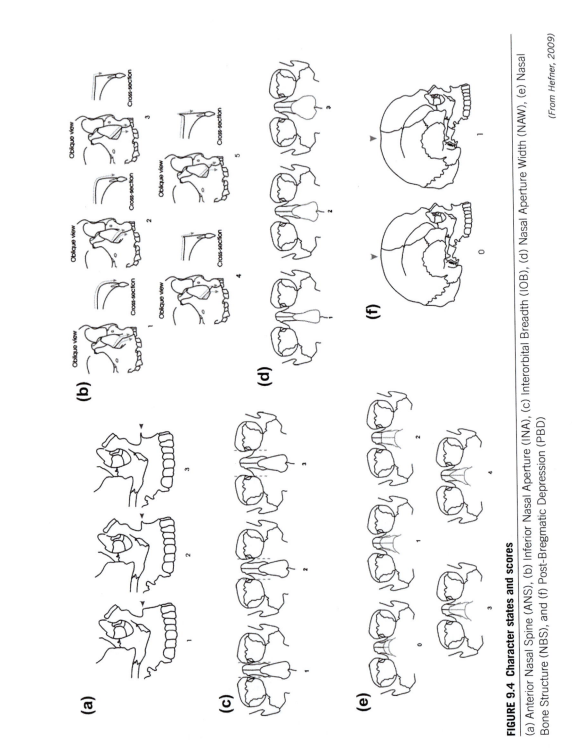

FIGURE 9.4 Character states and scores

(a) Anterior Nasal Spine (ANS), (b) Inferior Nasal Aperture (INA), (c) Interorbital Breadth (IOB), (d) Nasal Aperture Width (NAW), (e) Nasal Bone Structure (NBS), and (f) Post-Bregmatic Depression (PBD)

(From Hefner, 2009)

in press). The traits assessed in the OSSA method include: Anterior Nasal Spine (ANS), Inferior Nasal Aperture (INA), Interorbital Breadth (IOB), Nasal Aperture Width (NAW), Nasal Bone Structure (NBS), and Post-Bregmatic Depression (PBD). Each character state is scored on the basis of shape, presence or absence, or degree of expression (Figure 9.4). Scores are then transformed into binary (0,1) variables (Figure 9.5). Scores more common in American Blacks are optimized to a score of 0, while those more common in American Whites are optimized to a

Trait Anterior Nasal Spine (ANS)	Expression				
	Slight	Intermediate	Marked		
Character State Score	1	2	3		
OSSA Score	0	1	1		
Inferior Nasal Aperture (INA)					
	Pronounced Slope	Moderate Slope	Straight	Partial Sill	Sill
Character State Score	1	2	3	4	5
OSSA Score	0	0	0	1	1
Interorbital Breadth (IOB)					
	Narrow	Intermediate	Wide		
Character State Score	1	2	3		
OSSA Score	1	1	0		
Nasal Aperture Width (NAW)					
	Narrow	Medium	Broad		
Character State Score	1	2	3		
OSSA Score	1	1	0		
Nasal Bone Structure (NBS)					
	Low/Round	Oval	Marked Plateau	Narrow Plateau	Triangular
Character State Score	0	1	2	3	4
OSSA Score	0	0	1	1	1
Post-Bregmatic Depression (PBD)					
	Absent	Present			
Character State Score	0	1			
OSSA Score	1	0			

FIGURE 9.5 Binary transformation of OSSA scores

(modified from Hefner and Ousley, in press)

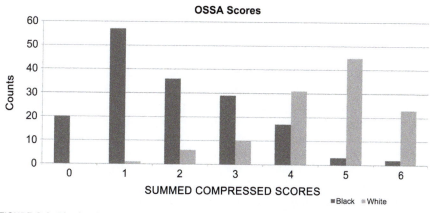

FIGURE 9.6 Distribution of American Black and White individuals based on OSSA score

(Hefner and Ousley, in press)

score of 1. For a detailed discussion on OSSA, the reader is referred to Hefner and Ousley (in press).

Once all traits have been transformed to their binary scores, the character state scores are summed. Summed scores of 0–3 are classified as American Black while scores of 4 or greater are classified as American White (Figure 9.6). OSSA estimates ancestry correctly at a rate of ~86% (Hefner and Ousley, in press). OSSA does make the assumption that the individual is of either European or African ancestry, and will always classify an individual into one of these two groups (even if they are actually from a different group). Moreover, all traits must be present and scoreable in order to use the OSSA method.

Another more robust statistic is a decision tree, or classification tree (Hefner and Ousley, in press). Decision trees are regression-based models that use sequential rules to determine group membership through a series of nodes. These nodes separate the group into two or more subgroups in order to achieve the most accurate classification possible for each individual based on known group memberships (Sherrod, 2006). Morphoscopic traits are scored and used to classify an unknown individual into one of three groups: White, Black, or Hispanic (Hefner and Ousley, in press). Following this approach, morphoscopic traits, ANS, INA, IOB NAW, and NBS (several of the same traits used in the OSSA method) are scored. Beginning at the top of the decision tree, the splitting nodes are followed using the character state score for each trait until the final (terminal) node is reached (see Figure 3 in Hefner and Ousley, in press). Classification of an unknown individual to an ancestry is based on the ancestry group in the terminal node that has the greatest amount of individuals present in that node. This decision tree approach has been shown to correctly classify individuals into the appropriate ancestry group ~80% of the time (Hefner and Ousley, in press).

9.3 Craniometric analysis

Craniometric analysis involves measuring the dimensions of the skull, such as the maximum and minimum length or width, or measurements between anatomically defined landmarks such as those described in Chapter 3. Craniometric analyses are often used in the estimation of ancestry because geographic variation in cranial size and shape is known to exist, but is difficult to assess with the naked eye. Metric analysis therefore helps identify patterns in skull shape that may not be appreciated visually. In some cases, analyses may involve one or two measurements or a ratio of two measurements, but the most accepted approach is the use of the discriminant functions, first developed in the 1960s (Giles and Elliot, 1962). A popular method used in modern forensic anthropology is the program Fordisc (Jantz and Ousley, 2005, 2012). As discussed in Chapter 3, Fordisc classifies the measurements of unknown skeletons on the basis of their similarity with measurements of known individuals in the reference database. It can be used for estimating sex and stature, but ancestry estimation is the application for which Fordisc is most widely utilized.

Fordisc can be used to simultaneously classify sex and ancestry, and when using it in ambiguous cases or those in which only a skull is available, all measurements and all groups can be selected for inclusion in the analysis. Ancestry estimation is often more accurate and straightforward, however, when sex can be assessed by other methods (and recall from Chapter 8 that postcranial methods such as pelvic morphology and postcranial metrics are better for estimating sex than cranial features). Once sex has been estimated, analyses in Fordisc can then be limited to include only the groups of that sex, providing a more accurate estimate of ancestry and eliminating the effects of size differences associated with sex.

The use of Fordisc for the estimation of ancestry begins by taking the relevant and available skeletal measurements, inserting them into the electronic data forms, and selecting the appropriate groups for comparison. Two examples of Fordisc results and interpretations of likely ancestry classification are shown in Figures 9.7 and 9.8.

9.4 Postcranial methods

Compared to the skull, the postcranial skeleton has received relatively little attention for ancestry estimation (Spradley and Weisensee, 2013). This in part reflects a historic emphasis on the skull for ancestry assessment, but also the fact that ancestry variation in the postcranial skeleton is poorly understood. It is also possible that geographic adaptations are simply less strongly correlated with postcranial morphology. Recent approaches, however, have identified evidence of ancestry-associated shape variation in postcranial elements, suggesting that more research in the area is needed.

Ancestry-based variation has been reported for numerous single postcranial skeletal elements, including the tibia, talus, and humerus, but the femur is by far the most extensively studied (Gill, 2001). For example, anterior femoral curvature has been cited as being less expressed in Blacks, with other groups having more anteriorly

```
           Multigroup Classification of Current Case
-----------------------------------------------------------------------------
   Group     Classified    Distance    Probabilities
               into          from     Posterior  Typ F   Typ Chi   Typ R
-----------------------------------------------------------------------------
    HF        **HF**          5.1        0.791    0.723    0.651    0.702 (15/47)
    AF                        9.2        0.099    0.419    0.236    0.207 (24/29)
    BF                        9.3        0.097    0.300    0.234    0.268 (53/71)
    WF                       13.4        0.013    0.078    0.064    0.077 (168/181)
    JF                       31.2        0.000    0.001    0.000    0.017 (59/59)
-----------------------------------------------------------------------------
  Current Case is closest to HFs
-----------------------------------------------------------------------------
```

FIGURE 9.7 Fordisc example 1

The associated postcranial remains in this case were estimated to be female using morphological indicators of the pelvis, thus only females were included in the analysis of cranial measurements. The measurements of the unknown individual are most similar to the Hispanic females in the reference database. In this case, an ancestry estimate of *Hispanic* is most appropriate.

Group	Classified into	Distance from	Probabilities			
			Posterior	Typ F	Typ Chi	Typ R
CHM	**CHM**	11.2	0.337	0.866	0.742	0.586 (30/70)
VM		12.2	0.202	0.872	0.665	0.510 (25/49)
GTM		12.3	0.192	0.815	0.658	0.600 (29/70)
JM		12.6	0.160	0.770	0.630	0.624 (33/85)
HM		14.5	0.064	0.567	0.490	0.503 (97/193)
AM		16.4	0.024	0.669	0.353	0.481 (28/52)
HF		18.7	0.008	0.597	0.228	0.298 (34/47)
JF		19.2	0.006	0.490	0.205	0.169 (50/59)
BM		20.0	0.004	0.318	0.173	0.291 (74/103)
AF		20.8	0.003	0.767	0.144	0.138 (26/29)

FIGURE 9.8 Fordisc example 2

In this case, the results for a cranium where the groups with typicality levels below .05 have already been removed. The measurements of the unknown cranium are most similar to those of Chinese males (CHM), but the Mahalanobis distances to Vietnamese males (VM), Guatemalan males (GTM), and Japanese males (JM), are all very similar. In this case, an ancestry estimate of *Asian* is most appropriate.

curved femora (Stewart, 1962; Gilbert, 1976; Ballard, 1999), and the intercondylar shelf angle has been shown to distinguish American Whites and Blacks, with Blacks having a more acute angle (Craig, 1995). Subtrochanteric shape has been shown to distinguish Native American femora from those of American Blacks and Whites, being more **platymeric** (flat in the anterior-posterior direction) than the other groups (Wescott, 2005). A discriminant function analysis using seven postcranial measurements was able to classify ancestry between African and European Americans with relatively high accuracy (Holliday and Falsetti, 1999). Analyses, however, are often limited to a small number of populations, and some methods have shown high levels of intra- and inter-observer error (Berg et al., 2007), or show poorer performance when tested on independent samples.

Fordisc can also be utilized to estimate ancestry based on postcranial measurements, although reference samples are currently limited to Black and White male and female groups. Assuming that the individual is from one of these groups, however, Fordisc likely represents the greatest potential for accurate ancestry estimation from postcranial material. Applying Fordisc to postcranial measurements is the same process as for cranial analyses, but the measurements are entered onto the "Postcranial Measurements" form. When estimating ancestry from postcranial remains using Fordisc, particular caution must be taken with individuals who may possibly be Hispanic (Spradley et al., 2008) as well as other groups due to population differences in sexual dimorphism.

9.5 Other considerations in ancestry estimation

Various other methods can be utilized in the estimation of ancestry including dental methods, three-dimensional (3D) morphometric approaches, and other complex statistical analyses. Several dental characteristics show variation with ancestral groups. For example, shovel-shaped incisors, which are incisors with raised ridges on the lingual side of the teeth (Figure 9.9), are noted to be more common in Asian (and Asian-descended) ancestral groups. Carabelli's cusp, a small additional cusp of the maxillary first molar, is a heritable trait that is observed most frequently in those of European ancestry (Figure 9.10). One scoring approach (Edgar, 2013) uses morphology of the dentition in order to classify individuals as either African-American, European-American, or Hispanic using discriminant functions. Because the upper first molar is included in all of the discriminant functions, it must be present in order to use this method. These dental approaches, while suggesting possible ancestral groups, are not themselves considered sufficient for the estimation of ancestry.

Although not considered reliable methods of estimating ancestry, there are certain diseases that are more commonly associated with certain ancestral groups. For example, thalassemia is more commonly found in Mediterranean populations, Paget's disease is more common in those of European ancestry and rare in Asians, and rickets is more common in African ancestry individuals living in temperate climates (Reichs, 1986). In addition, certain cranial suture variants tend to show different frequencies by ancestry. For example, extrasutural bones tend to be more common in those of Asian ancestry (Hanihara and Ishida, 2001), and metopism tends to occur more commonly in those of European ancestry (Gill and Rhine, 1990).

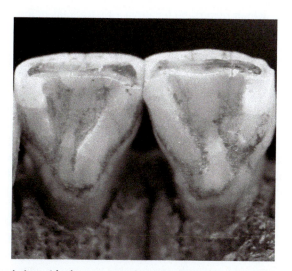

FIGURE 9.9 Shovel-shaped incisors, suggesting Asian ancestry; the degree of wear on the occlusal surface suggests likely Native American ancestry

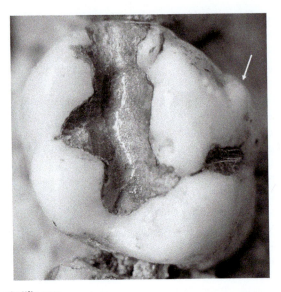

FIGURE 9.10 Carabelli's cusp

Three-dimensional morphometric approaches control for the variable of size, singling out shape differences for analysis. These approaches are now being utilized more frequently, including in the estimation of ancestry, as 3D data are becoming increasingly easier to obtain and analyze. Most 3D data are collected using digitizers, which record the locations of particular points (such as skeletal landmarks) in three dimensions (see the figure in Box 1.5 in which Dr. Kate Spradley is utilizing a 3D digitizer). Software programs such as ThreeSkull (Ousley, 2010) have been developed to transfer 3D landmark data into databases which can then be extracted into other statistical programs for analysis to estimate ancestry.

Ancestry can also be estimated by using other complex multivariate statistical approaches, such as frequency distributions, *k*-nearest neighbor analysis, logistic regression, or other Bayesian approaches (Hefner, 2009). These analyses are conducted using statistical software packages that can assist in ancestry estimation and include classification accuracy statistics, but require significant training and experience in statistics and computer programming to use properly.

Many of the skeletal dimensions and characteristics associated with ancestry are underdeveloped until around puberty. While a few methods have been proposed, based largely on features of the skull (Wilson, 1994; Buck and Vidarsdottir, 2004), it is difficult and generally unadvisable to estimate ancestry from subadult skeletons.

An analysis of secular trends in the skulls of American Blacks and Whites born between 1850 and 1975 found significant temporal change within each ancestral group (Jantz, 2001). For example, cranial vaults have become significantly taller and faces have become narrower over time, and these trends are correlated with birth year. These changes may reflect improvement in nutrition and better access to health care. Evidence of this secular trend in craniofacial dimensions indicates that temporally appropriate (modern) reference samples are important for ancestry estimation of recent forensic cases (Jantz, 2001; Jantz and Meadows Jantz, 2000; Wescott and Jantz, 2005).

9.6 Case study – ancestry estimation

In 2012, a surface scatter of human remains was discovered along a wooded hillside in northern California. The skeleton was incomplete and highly fragmentary, but an intact skull was located, permitting the estimation of ancestry. Although most pelvic features could not be assessed due to carnivore scavenging, the morphological assessment of the skull and postcranial osteometrics was consistent with male. Age assessment was also severely hindered by the extent of scavenging, although examination of cranial sutures and extensive osteophytic lipping on the vertebral column suggested the decedent was at least middle-aged (40+ years). Stature was estimated as 6 feet ± 4.5 inches based on the maximum length of the ulna. The law enforcement agency was especially interested in the ancestry of the decedent, as it would help them narrow the search to a smaller pool of missing persons from the local area.

Based on a comparison of 16 measurements of the decedent's cranium with each male sample group, Fordisc 3.0 classified the measurements of the decedent's skull as being closest to those of other White males (i.e., had the smallest Mahalanobis D^2 to the White male centroid) (Figures 9.11 and 9.12). The high posterior probability value ($p = .984$) indicates a strong similarity to the White male reference sample relative to Hispanic males. The high typicality value ($p = .366$) indicates the skull as typical of White males in the reference sample, though it is not atypical of Hispanic males. Overall, these results suggest the decedent is of European (White) ancestry. The decedent

```
Two Group Discriminant Function Results
---------------------------------------------------------------------------
  Group     Classified   Distance    Probabilities
            into         from        Posterior  Typ F   Typ Chi   Typ R
---------------------------------------------------------------------------
   WM       **WM**       27.4        0.984      0.366   0.239    0.322 (159/233)
   HM                    35.6        0.016      0.164   0.045    0.101 (134/148)
---------------------------------------------------------------------------
```

FIGURE 9.11 Fordisc classification results for unknown male skull

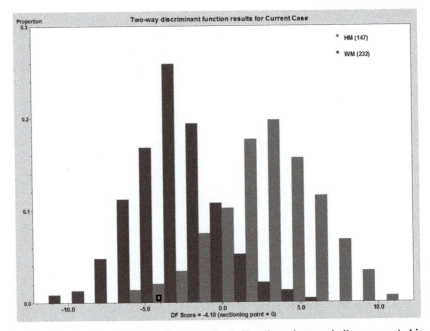

FIGURE 9.12 Plot comparing the unknown male skull to the unknown skulls represented in Fordisc 3.0. The "X" represents the unknown skull, which is close to the group centroid for white males

was ultimately identified through DNA analysis, and was a 54-year-old White male who was 6 feet, 3 inches in height, consistent with the biological profile assessment.

9.7 Summary
- Ancestry refers to an individual's geographic region of ancestral origin. Ancestry, however, has both biological and social aspects, so the estimation of ancestry by forensic anthropologists often involves interpreting skeletal variation within the context of social labels.
- Ancestry differences in the skeleton relate to genetic differences between human populations, which result from evolutionary processes.
- In many cases, it is possible for forensic anthropologists to identify the most likely ancestry of an individual based on craniometric and morphoscopic characteristics because these measures are associated with genetic heritage.
- The classification of humans into subgroups has a long and at times controversial history. The divisions of "race" and "subspecies" have been shown to be poor categorizations of ancestral variation.

- The skull is the most useful area of the skeleton for assessing ancestry, and is typically assessed using either morphoscopic or metric approaches.
- Morphoscopic approaches for estimating ancestry include OSSA and Decision Tree Modeling, which apply statistical analyses to character states assessed from the cranium.
- Craniometric approaches are often more objective and less subject to observer error. Craniometric programs such as Fordisc provide statistically-based estimates for assigning group membership.
- Metric and non-metric approaches for ancestry estimation from the postcranial skeleton have had limited success. This may be because geographic adaptations are less strongly correlated with postcranial morphology.
- New approaches using 3D morphometrics may provide an additional tool for ancestry estimation.
- Since many ancestry characteristics are underdeveloped until around puberty, it is difficult to assess ancestry in subadult skeletons.

9.8 Test yourself

- Why is the concept of racial types invalid from a biological perspective? Compare and contrast "social race" from the historical view of race as a biologically meaningful construct. How is ancestry estimation in forensic anthropology different from a racial typology approach?
- Why is the "trait list" approach problematic for ancestry estimation? How is this different from statistically-based predictions of ancestry using morphoscopic traits and metric analysis?
- Interpret the following Fordisc 3.0 results. Define what the "Distance from," "Posterior Probabilities," and "Typicality Probabilities" columns represent and then interpret the results for this particular skull. How comfortable are you with this classification? How likely are the 2nd, 3rd, and 4th choices? What would you tell the law enforcement agency regarding the ancestry of the individual?

```
          Multigroup Classification of Current Case
    ---------------------------------------------------------
      Group      Classified     Distance     Probabilities
                   into           from      Posterior   Typ F
    ---------------------------------------------------------
       JF         **JF**          18.1        0.924     0.516
       BF                         24.2        0.043     0.482
       WF                         25.0        0.030     0.207
       AF                         30.2        0.002     0.795
    ---------------------------------------------------------
```

- What are some of the limitations when attempting to estimate ancestry from the postcranial skeleton? From children?

Definitions

Admixed A product of parents from two different ancestral groups

Ancestry An individual's geographic region or ancestral origin

Character state The form, degree of expression, or presence/absence of a morphoscopic trait

Cline A gradient (often of phenotypic form) based on geography and environment

Decision tree modeling A regression-based model that uses sequential rules to determine group membership through a series of nodes; also called classification tree modeling

Morphoscopic traits Quasi-continuous morphological features that show varying forms, degrees of expression, or frequencies in presence or absence

Optimized Summed Scoring Attributes (OSSA) A method of ancestry estimation that uses statistical analysis of morphoscopic traits and their character states

Overfitting A statistical problem encountered when the sample size of a group or groups in an analysis is too small relative to the number of variables being analyzed

Platymeric Flat in the anterior-posterior direction

Positive assortative mating Mating between individuals of like groups

Race A population with a common history or origin, as opposed to one with a fixed biological character

Subspecies A geographically isolated subdivision of a species

References

Armelagos, G.J., Goodman, A.H., 1998. Race, racism, and anthropology. In: Goodman, A.H., Leatherman, T.L. (Eds.), Building a New Biocultural Synthesis: Political-Economic Perspectives on Human Biology. University of Michigan Press, Ann Arbor, pp. 359–378.

Armelagos, G.J., Van Gerven, D.P., 2003. A century of skeletal biology and paleopathology: contrasts, contradictions, and conflicts. Am. Anthropol. 105, 53–64.

Ballard, T.M., 1999. Anterior femoral curvature revisited: Race assessment from the femur. J. Forensic Sci. 44, 700–707.

Bass, W.M., 2005. Human Osteology: A Laboratory and Field Manual, fifth ed. Missouri Archaeological Society, Columbia.

Berg, G.E., Ta'Ala, S.C., Kontanis, E.J., Leney, S.S., 2007. Measuring the intercondylar shelf angle using radiographs: intra- and inter-observer error tests of reliability. J. Forensic Sci. 52, 1020–1024.

Birkby, W.H., Fenton, T.W., Anderson, B.E., 2008. Identifying Southwest Hispanics using nonmetric traits and the cultural profile. J. Forensic Sci. 53, 29–33.

Brace, C.L., 2005. "Race" is a four-letter word: The genesis of the concept. Oxford University Press, New York.

Brues, A.M., 1977. People and Races. Macmillan Publishing, New York.

Buck, T.J., Vidarsdottir, U.S., 2004. A proposed method for the identification of race in sub-adult skeletons: A geometric morphometric analysis of mandibular morphology. J. Forensic Sci. 49 (6), 1159–1164.

Burns, K.R., 2013. Forensic Anthropology Training Manual, third ed. Prentice Hall, Boston.

Byers, S.N., 2011. Introduction to Forensic Anthropology, fourth ed. Pearson, Boston.

Chaplin, G., 2004. Geographic distribution of environmental factors influencing human skin coloration. Am. J. Phys. Anthropol. 125, 292–302.

Craig, E.A., 1995. Intercondylar shelf angle: a new method to determine race from the distal femur. J. Forensic Sci. 40, 777–782.

Edgar, H.J., 2013. Estimation of ancestry using dental morphology characteristics. J. Forensic Sci. 58 (S1), S3–S8.

Gates, N., 1997. Critical Race Theory: Essays on the Social Construction and Reproduction of "Race". Routledge, New York.

Gilbert, B.M., 1976. Anterior femoral curvature: Its probable basis and utility as a criterion of racial assessment. Am. J. Phys. Anthropol. 45, 601–604.

Giles, E., Elliot, O., 1962. Race identification from cranial measurements. J. Forensic Sci. 7, 147–157.

Gill, G.W., 1998. Craniofacial criteria in the skeletal attribution of race. In: Reichs, K.J. (Ed.), Forensic Osteology: Advances in the Identification of Human Remains, second ed. Charles C. Thomas, Springfield, pp. 293–318.

Gill, G.W., 2001. Racial variation in the proximal and distal femur: heritability and forensic utility. J. Forensic Sci. 46, 791–799.

Gill, G.W., Rhine, S. (Eds.), 1990. Skeletal Attribution of Race: Methods for Forensic Anthropology. Maxwell Museum of Anthropological Papers No. 4. University of New Mexico, Albuquerque.

Hanihara, T., Ishida, H., 2001. Os icae: Variation in frequency in major human population groups. J. Anat. 198, 137–152.

Hefner, J.T., 2007. The statistical determination of ancestry using cranial nonmetric traits. Doctoral Dissertation, University of Florida, Gainesville, FL.

Hefner, J.T., 2009. Cranial nonmetric variation and estimating ancestry. J. Forensic Sci. 54, 985–995.

Hefner, J.T, Ousley, S.D., (in press). Statistical classification methods for estimating ancestry using morphoscopic traits. J. Forensic Sci.

Hefner, J.T., Ousley, S.D., Dirkmaat, D.C., 2012. Morphoscopic traits and the assessment of ancestry. In: Dirkmaat, D.C. (Ed.), A Companion to Forensic Anthropology. Wiley-Blackwell Publishing, Oxford, pp. 287–310.

Holliday, T.W., Falsetti, A.B., 1999. A new method for discriminating African-American from European-American skeletons using postcranial osteometrics reflective of body shape. J. Forensic Sci. 44, 926–930.

Hughes, C.E., Juarez, C.A., Hughes, T.L., Galloway, A., Fowler, G., Chacon, S., 2011. A simulation for exploring the effects of the "trait list" method's subjectivity on consistency and accuracy of ancestry estimations. J. Forensic Sci. 56, 1094–1106.

Jantz, R.L., 2001. Cranial change in Americans: 1850–1975. J. Forensic Sci. 46, 784–787.

Jantz, R.L., Jantz, L.M., 2000. Secular change in craniofacial morphology. Am. J. Phys. Anthropol. 12, 327–338.

Jantz, R.L., Ousley, S.D., 2005. FORDISC 3.0: Personal computer forensic discriminant functions. The University of Tennessee, Knoxville.

Kennedy, K.A.R., 1995. But professor, why teach race identification if races don't exist? J. Forensic Sci. 40, 797–800.

Klepinger, L.L., 2006. Fundamentals of Forensic Anthropology. John Wiley & Sons, Hoboken.

Lewontin, R.C., 1972. The apportionment of human diversity. Evol. Biol. 6, 381–398.

Littlefield, A., Lieberman, L., Reynolds, L.T., 1982. Redefining race: the potential demise of a concept in physical anthropology. Curr. Anthropol. 23, 641–647.

Montagu, A., 1972. Statement on Race. Oxford University Press, London.

Mukhopadhyay, C., Moses, Y., 1997. Re-establishing race in anthropological discourse. Am. Anthropol. 99, 517–533.

Ousley, S.D., 2010. Threeskull. Version 2.0.

Ousley, S.D., Jantz, R.L., 2012. Fordisc 3 and statistical methods for estimating sex and ancestry. In: Dirkmaat, D.C. (Ed.), A Companion to Forensic Anthropology. Wiley-Blackwell Publishing, Oxford, pp. 400–412.

Ousley, S.D., Jantz, R.L., Freid, D., 2009. Understanding race and human variation: why forensic anthropologists are good at identifying race. Am. J. Phys. Anthropol. 139, 68–76.

Reichs, K.J., 1986. Forensic implications of skeletal pathology: Ancestry. In: Reichs, K.J. (Ed.), Forensic Osteology: Advances in the Identification of Human Remains. Charles C Thomas, Springfield, pp. 196–217.

Rhine, S., 1990. Nonmetric skull racing. In: Gill, G.W., Rhine, S. (Eds.), Skeletal Attribution of Race: Methods for Forensic Anthropology. Maxwell museum of Anthropological Papers No. 4. University of New Mexico, Albuquerque, pp. 9–20.

Sauer, N.J., 1992. Forensic anthropology and the concept of race: if races don't exist, why are forensic anthropologists so good at identifying them? Soci. Sci. Med. 34, 107–111.

Scientific Working Group on Forensic Anthropology, 2013. Ancestry Assessment Revision 0.

Sherrod, P.H., 2006. DTREG: Classification and Regression Trees and Support Vector Machines for Predictive Modeling and Forecasting. Retrieved from http://www.dtreg .com/DTREG.pdf. Retrieved July 2013.

Sparks, C.S., Jantz, R.L., 2002. A reassessment of human cranial plasticity: Boas revisited. Proc Natl. Acad Sci 99 (23), 14636–14639.

Spradley, M.K., Weisensee, K., 2013. Why do forensic anthropologists estimate ancestry, and why is it so controversial? In: Tersigni-Tarrant, M.T., Shirley, N.R. (Eds.), Forensic Anthropology: An Introduction. Charles C. Thomas, Boca Raton, pp. 231–243.

Spradley, M.K., Jantz, R.L., Robinson, Al, Peccerelli, F., 2008. Demographic change and forensic identification: Problems in metric identification of Hispanic skeletons. J. Forensic Sci. 53 (1), 21–28.

Steadman, D.W., 2013. The places we will go: paths forward in forensic anthropology. In: Ubelaker, D.H. (Ed.), Forensic Science: Current Issues, Future Directions. John Wiley & Sons, Boca Raton, pp. 131–159.

Stewart, T.D., 1962. Anterior femoral curvature: Its utility for race identification. Hum. Biol. 34, 49–62.

Templeton, A.R., 1998. Human races: a genetic and evolutionary perspective. Am. Anthropol. 100, 632–650.

United States Census. http://www.census.gov/population/race/. Retrieved May 14, 2013.

Wescott, D.J., 2005. Population variation in femur subtrochanteric shape. J. Forensic Sci. 50 (2), 286–293.

Wescott, D.J., Jantz, R.L., 2005. Assessing craniofacial secular change in American blacks and whites using geometric morphometry. In: Slice, D.E. (Ed.), Modern Morphometrics in Physical Anthropology. Kluwer Academic/Plenum Publishers, New York, pp. 231–245.

Wikipedia, n.d. http://en.wikipedia.org/wiki/Barack_Obama. Retrieved July 24, 2013.

Wilson, J.L., 1994. Estimation of Race from Subadult Crania. The University of Tennessee, Knoxville.

Wolf, E.R., 1994. Perilous ideas: race, culture, people. Curr. Anthropol. 35, 1–12.

Age Estimation

10

10.1 Principles of age estimation

Age estimation from the skeleton is of interest to forensic anthropologists for several reasons. In the case of unidentified skeletal remains, estimation of age-at-death is part of the biological profile used to narrow the list of potential missing persons. For presumptive identifications, age estimation may be used to determine whether that individual should be included or excluded from further consideration on the basis of the consistency between the reported age and estimated age. Additionally, forensic anthropologists are sometimes asked to apply age estimation methods to living individuals (typically using radiography), to determine whether someone has reached the **age of majority** (or the age to be legally considered an adult), which may be a factor in determining whether an individual is prosecuted as a juvenile or an adult (Black et al., 2010).

Estimation of age from the skeleton is possible through a comprehensive understanding of the nature, sequence, and timing of skeletal changes across the lifespan, and understanding the relationship between these processes and chronological measures. Skeletal age estimation therefore involves correlating **biological age** (or physiological age) with **chronological age** (the length of time a person has been alive). Traits or processes useful as age indicators should change unidirectionally with age, correlate with chronological age, and change consistently across individuals (Scientific Working Group for Forensic Anthropology [SWGANTH], 2010).

It is important to note that chronological age and biological age are not perfectly correlated because the skeletal aging process is variable between individuals (Nawrocki, 2010). This discrepancy arises because biological age varies as a function of genetics, nutrition, environmental factors, and activity level, among other factors, while chronological age is measured by time (e.g., days, months, or years) (Nawrocki, 2010; Garvin et al., 2012). The discrepancy between biological age and chronological age widens as people get older, and is known as the **trajectory effect** (Nawrocki, 2010) (Figure 10.1).

Skeletal age estimation can be described as a transformative process, where the anthropologist must translate the descriptive skeletal age indicator into a chronological age. Unfortunately, this process introduces error due to the steps involved in quantifying skeletal morphology and transforming these data into a chronological age (Nawrocki, 2010). In many cases, this may result in having a wide age interval that can be considered accurate but not very precise. Reported age intervals often

Forensic Anthropology. http://dx.doi.org/10.1016/B978-0-12-418671-2.00010-0

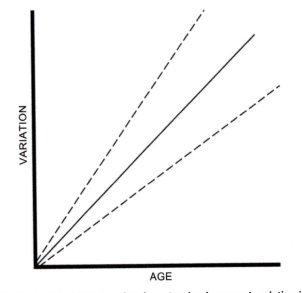

FIGURE 10.1 Trajectory effect in age estimation, showing increased variation in skeletal age indicators with advancing age

(Adapted from Nawrocki, 2010)

encompass decades for adults; an estimated age interval should be as narrow as possible but should take into account all possible variation in biological age.

In some cases, age estimation may be facilitated by knowledge of other biological parameters first. For example, development in females occurs earlier than in males, and growth trajectories show variation between populations. Any evidence for sex or ancestry should therefore be considered when estimating age, and when possible, standards for age estimation should be used that are based on the population of the skeletal material examined. When population-specific standards are not available, standards that are more inclusive and which have wider age intervals should be used (SWGANTH, 2010).

10.2 Age categories

In childhood, the skeleton changes as a function of growth and development – structures mineralize, increase in size, and model their shape to achieve their mature adult form. These changes are influenced largely by genetic and other **intrinsic** factors. In adulthood, the skeleton begins to show degenerative changes as the body attempts to maintain **homeostasis**. These changes are influenced largely by **extrinsic** factors such as biomechanical loading, diet, and health status. This pattern has evolutionary underpinnings; theoretically, selective pressures only affect growth and development processes until sexual maturity has been reached. Once individuals reach adulthood, selective forces are no longer acting to control biological maintenance rates and thus rates of degenerative changes can vary widely both between different anatomical structures of a single individual and between individuals from the same population (Partridge and Barton, 1996; Crews, 1993).

Because age estimation approaches are fundamentally different for the growth and development and degenerative phases of the lifespan, skeletal age can be considered to be in one of two broad categories: **juvenile** (also called **subadult**) – those ages during the growth and development process including the embryonic, fetal, infant, child, and adolescent periods; and **adult** – those ages occurring during the mature, degenerative stage of skeletal change (see Table 10.1). The growth and development of the skeleton is considered complete when all permanent teeth have erupted and all epiphyses have fused. For interested readers, there are several texts on skeletal aging that cover different periods of the human lifespan (Black et al., 2010; Fazekas and Kosa, 1978; Iscan, 1989; Latham and Finnegan, 2010; Scheuer and Black, 2000).

The skeletal age category (juvenile or adult) should be assessed early in the examination process because the ability to estimate other biological parameters such as sex, ancestry, and stature may depend on whether an individual is a juvenile or adult. For example, stature increases during growth and development (until around age 18), but typically decreases with advanced adult age due to degenerative changes in the vertebral column. Stature estimates therefore need to take into account the decedent's age (Smith, 2007). Skeletal indicators used to estimate the sex of an unidentified individual are generally absent or underdeveloped until after puberty, so it is not advisable to estimate sex from juvenile skeletal material (see Chapter 8). Among adult females, certain skeletal characteristics such as muscle attachment sites may become more robust with advancing age, which should be taken into account when assessing the skeletal remains of older adult individuals. Craniofacial characteristics related to ancestry are also often absent or are less pronounced in subadults compared to adults.

Table 10.1 Growth and development stages

Stage	Time period
Embryo	First 8 weeks of intra-uterine life
Fetus	From 8 intra-uterine weeks to birth
Infant	Birth to 1 year
Child	1 to 15 years
Adolescent	15 to 17 years
Adult	17 years and older
(Modified from Lewis, 2009)	

10.3 Juvenile (subadult) age estimation

Age estimation of subadults relies on the fairly predictable processes of growth and development of the bones and teeth. The growth and development process proceeds at a very rapid pace from birth to the first year of life, and then rapidly declines from infancy through childhood. For teeth, the processes most relevant to age estimation are formation, mineralization, and eruption of the deciduous (primary) and permanent (secondary) dentition. For bones, ossification, long bone growth, and epiphyseal union are most relevant. The appropriate methods to apply depend on the age category of the juvenile individual (e.g., fetal, infant, child) as well as the material available for analysis. In general, dental development is more highly correlated with chronological age than is bone development, and therefore dental methods are typically most accurate and are preferable when possible. The reason for this higher correlation is that dental development appears to be under stronger genetic control (i.e., is more strongly **canalized**), while bone development is more susceptible to environmental influences such as physical loading, nutrition, and health status (Liversidge, 1998). Large discrepancies between dental and skeletal development, in fact, may result from illness or malnutrition affecting bone growth, although in severe cases, dental development and eruption sequences may be affected as well (Scheuer and Black, 2000; Ulijaszek, 1996).

Dental methods

As discussed in Chapter 2, dental development begins around the sixth fetal week and does not reach completion until early adulthood, making it a very useful means of estimating age during virtually the entire juvenile period. At or soon after birth, a neonatal line is formed in all deciduous teeth and often on the first permanent molar, which is evident as a dark line in histological sections of teeth (Rushton, 1933; Schour, 1936) (Figure 10.2). This feature, likely caused by the stresses of the birthing process, may have medicolegal significance as it indicates that an infant was born alive versus stillborn (Whittaker and MacDonald, 1989). However, more research is needed to validate the accuracy of the neonatal line as an indicator of live birth.

At the time of birth, all deciduous teeth and the first permanent molar have begun to mineralize (Scheuer and Black, 2000) (Figure 10.3). By age 3, all deciduous teeth have erupted with completion of root formation. The permanent anterior teeth (incisors and canines) and first molars begin to mineralize during the first year of life, followed by the premolars and second molars from ages 2 to 4. Finally, the third molar crowns form between ages 6 and 12 (Scheuer and Black, 2000). The permanent incisors, canines, premolars, and first two molars erupt during two major intervals (ages 6–8 and ages 10–12), followed by the third molars, which usually do not erupt until the late teens to early twenties. Because dental enamel is the hardest and most radiopaque substance in the body, radiographic examination of the developing dentition is very easy and often necessary, allowing visualization of root apices and unerupted teeth not visible to the naked eye (Figure 10.4).

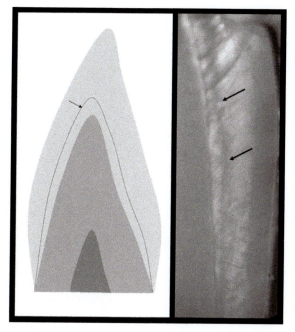

FIGURE 10.2 Neonatal line

(Right image courtesy of Nicole Burt)

One of the most commonly used juvenile aging methods is the assessment of dental development stages (e.g., Moorrees et al., 1963a, b; Demirjian et al., 1973). The method proceeds by determining the developmental stage of each available tooth, including the development of the crown and root, by reference to illustrated developmental stages. Although development follows the same sequence for each tooth (progressing from the crown cusp(s) to the root apex), the timing is different for each tooth position. Once the degree of development is assessed, skeletal age is estimated by referencing calculated mean ages for achieving that developmental stage for each tooth (see Figure 10.5 and Tables 10.2 and 10.3). Absolute accuracy (the maximum amount of error) of dental age estimation is between six months and one year (Liversidge, 2008).

There are some variations that need to be considered when applying dental age estimation methods. For example, females tend to be more advanced in their dental development compared to males during most of the growth and development period. Tooth calcification rates also vary between populations. Because sex and ancestry are often not known for juvenile skeletal remains, these issues can pose some limitations. When sex is unknown, however, a revised method can be used that combines the male and female reference samples (Smith, 1991). Certain methods (e.g., Moorrees et al., 1963a, b; Demirjian et al., 1973) are only based on the mandibular dentition, and are therefore not applicable to maxillary teeth.

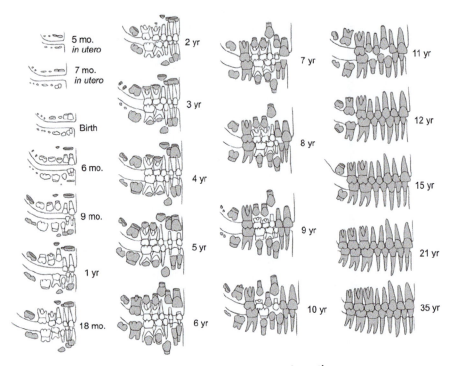

FIGURE 10.3 Primary and secondary dental development and eruption

(From Ubelaker, 1989)

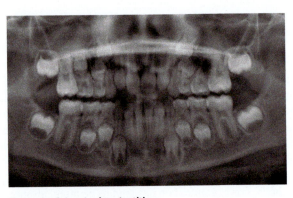

FIGURE 10.4 Radiograph of developing dentition

(Image courtesy of Mikylee Vaughan)

Tooth eruption is the process whereby a tooth advances from the alveolar crypt where it develops to its functional occlusal position (i.e., the occlusal plane) in the oral cavity (Schour and Massler, 1944; Massler et al., 1941; Scheuer and Black, 2000). The sequence of tooth eruption follows a particular pattern that is correlated with age. The eruption sequences for the teeth shown in Figure 10.3 are based on Native

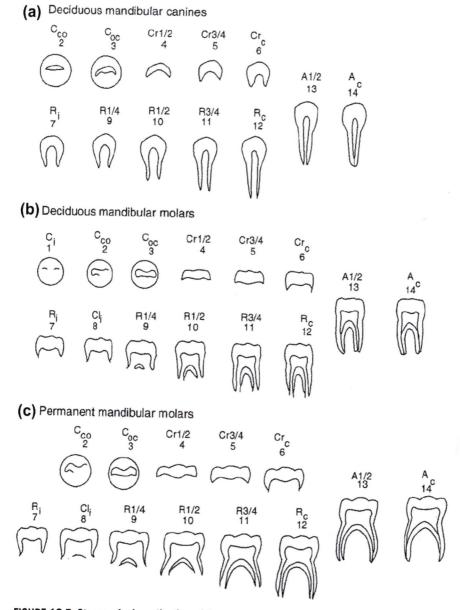

(a) Deciduous mandibular canines

(b) Deciduous mandibular molars

(c) Permanent mandibular molars

FIGURE 10.5 Stages of mineralization of the crown, root, and apex of canine and molar teeth

(From Moorrees et al., 1963a, b, modified by Buikstra and Ubelaker, 1994)

Americans, and although there is some variation between sexes and different populations, the overall pattern and timing are very similar for all children. To estimate age based on dental eruption, dentition is compared to the developmental sequence shown in Figure 10.3 to determine which pattern most closely resembles the unknown

Table 10.2 Abbreviations of tooth formation stages

C_i	Initial cusp formation
C_{co}	Coalescence of cusps
C_{oc}	Cusp outline complete
$Cr_{1/2}$	Crown half complete
$Cr_{3/4}$	Crown three-quarters complete
Cr_c	Crown complete
R	Initial root formation
Cl_i	Initial cleft formation
$R_{1/4}$	Root length quarter
$R_{1/2}$	Root length half
$R_{3/4}$	Root length three-quarters
R_c	Root length complete
$A_{1/2}$	Apex half closed
A_c	Apical closure complete

(From Moorees et al., 1963b)

Table 10.3 Estimation of age (in years) from permanent mandibular dentition

Stage	I1	I2	C	PM1	PM2	M1	M2	M3
Female								
C_i	–	–	0.6	2.0	3.3	0.2	3.6	9.9
C_{co}	–	–	1.0	2.5	3.9	0.5	4.0	10.4
C_{oc}	–	–	1.6	3.2	4.5	0.9	4.5	11.0
$Cr_{1/2}$	–	–	3.5	4.0	5.1	1.3	5.1	11.5
$Cr_{3/4}$	–	–	4.3	4.7	5.8	1.8	5.8	12.0
Cr_c	–	–	4.4	5.4	6.5	2.4	6.6	12.6
R	–	–	5.0	6.1	7.2	3.1	7.3	13.2
Cl_i	–	–	–	–	–	4.0	8.4	14.1
$R_{1/4}$	4.8	5.0	6.2	7.4	8.2	4.8	9.5	15.2
$R_{1/2}$	5.4	5.6	6.2	7.4	8.2	4.8	9.5	15.2
$R_{3/4}$	6.4	7.0	8.6	9.6	10.3	5.8	11.0	16.9
R_c	7.0	7.9	9.4	10.5	11.3	6.5	11.8	17.7
$A_{1/2}$	7.5	8.3	10.6	11.6	12.8	7.9	13.5	19.5
A_c	–	–	–	–	–	–	–	–
Male								
C_i	–	–	0.6	2.1	3.2	0.1	3.8	9.5
C_{co}	–	–	1.0	2.6	3.9	0.4	4.3	10.0
C_{oc}	–	–	1.7	3.3	4.5	0.8	4.9	10.6
$Cr_{1/2}$	–	–	2.5	4.1	5.0	1.3	5.4	11.3

Table 10.3 Estimation of age (in years) from permanent mandibular dentition—cont'd

Stage	I1	I2	C	PM1	PM2	M1	M2	M3
$Cr_{3/4}$	–	–	3.4	4.9	5.8	1.9	6.1	22.8
Cr_c	–	–	4.4	5.6	6.6	2.5	6.8	12.4
R	–	–	5.2	6.4	7.3	3.2	7.6	13.2
Cl_i	–	–	–	–	–	4.1	8.7	14.1
$R_{1/4}$	–	5.8	6.9	7.8	8.6	4.9	9.8	14.8
$R_{1/2}$	5.6	6.6	8.8	9.3	10.1	5.5	10.6	15.6
$R_{3/4}$	6.7	7.7	9.9	10.2	11.2	6.1	11.4	16.4
R_c	7.3	8.3	11.0	11.2	12.2	7.0	12.3	17.5
$A_{1/2}$	7.9	8.9	12.4	12.7	13.5	8.5	13.9	19.1
A_c	–	–	–	–	–	–	–	–

(From Moorees et al., 1963b, modified by Smith, 1991)

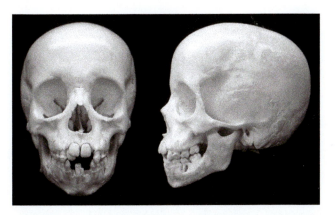

FIGURE 10.6 Juvenile skull (~7 years old) showing mixed dentition in various stages of eruption

dentition. For example, a dentition that has recently erupted the first adult molars would be aged at age 6 ± 2 years. In some cases, developing and erupting dentition can only be assessed radiographically, but in other cases, especially those involving mixed adult and deciduous dentition, eruption stages can be viewed visually (Figure 10.6).

Osteological methods

As discussed in Chapter 2, postcranial long bone growth proceeds longitudinally and appositionally, accounting for increased length and diameter, respectively. One method of assessing age is by diaphyseal growth (e.g., see Tables 10.4–10.6). There is a strong linear relationship between diaphyseal length and age, especially during fetal development (Fazekas and Kosa, 1978; Hoffman, 1979), and there is little

Table 10.4 Age and length (in mm) of fetal long bone diaphyses

Age (weeks)	12	14	16	18	20	22	24	26	28	30	32	34	36	38	40
Humerus	8.8	12.4	19.5	25.8	31.8	34.5	37.6	39.9	44.2	45.8	50.4	53.1	55.5	61.3	64.9
Radius	6.7	10.1	17.2	21.5	26.2	28.9	31.6	33.4	35.6	38.1	40.8	43.3	45.7	48.8	51.8
Ulna	7.2	11.2	19.0	23.9	29.4	31.6	35.1	37.1	40.2	42.8	46.7	49.1	51.0	55.9	59.3
Femur	8.5	12.4	20.7	26.4	32.6	35.7	40.3	41.9	47.1	48.7	55.5	59.8	62.5	69.0	74.4
Tibia	6.0	10.2	17.4	23.4	28.5	32.6	35.8	38.0	42.0	43.9	48.6	52.7	54.7	60.1	65.2
Fibula	6.0	9.9	16.7	22.6	27.8	31.1	34.3	36.5	40.0	42.8	46.8	50.5	51.6	57.6	62.0

(Adapted from Fazekas and Kosa, 1978)

Table 10.5 Mean lengths of diaphyses of major long bones at ten lunar fetal months

Bone	Length (mm)
Humerus	64.9
Radius	51.8
Ulna	59.3
Femur	74.3
Tibia	65.1
Fibula	62.3

(From Fazekas and Kosa, 1978)

Table 10.6 Diaphyseal lengths of the humerus and femur (in mm) from 2 months to 12 years (without epiphyses)

Age (years)	Males			Females		
	n	Mean	SD	*n*	Mean	SD
Humerus						
0.125	59	72.4	4.5	69	71.8	3.6
0.25	59	80.6	4.8	65	80.2	3.8
0.5	67	88.4	5	78	86.8	4.6
1	72	105.5	5.2	81	103.6	4.8
1.5	68	118.8	5.4	84	117.0	5.1
2	68	130	5.5	84	127.7	5.8
2.5	72	139	5.9	82	136.9	6.1
3	71	147.5	6.7	79	145.3	6.7
3.5	73	155	7.8	78	153.4	7.1
4	72	162.7	6.9	80	160.9	7.7
4.5	71	169.8	7.4	78	169.1	8.3
5	77	177.4	8.2	80	176.3	8.7
5.5	73	184.6	8.1	74	182.6	9
6	71	190.9	7.6	75	190.0	9.6
6.5	72	197.3	8.1	81	196.7	9.7
7	71	203.6	8.7	86	202.6	10
7.5	76	210.4	8.9	83	209.3	10.5
8	70	217.3	9.8	85	216.3	10.4
8.5	72	222.5	9.2	82	221.3	11.2
9	76	228.7	9.6	83	228	11.8
9.5	78	235.1	10.7	83	234.2	12.9
10	77	241	10.3	84	239.8	13.2
10.5	76	245.8	11	75	245.9	14.6
11	75	251.7	10.7	76	251.9	14.7
11.5	76	257.4	11.9	75	259.1	15.3
12	73	263	12.8	71	265.6	15.6

Continued

Table 10.6 Diaphyseal lengths of the humerus and femur (in mm) from 2 months to 12 years (without epiphyses)—cont'd

Age (years)	Males			Females		
	n	Mean	SD	*n*	Mean	SD
Femur						
0.125	59	86	5.4	68	71.8	4.3
0.25	59	100.7	4.8	65	80.2	3.6
0.5	67	112.2	5	78	86.8	4.6
1	72	136.6	5.8	81	103.6	4.9
1.5	68	155.4	6.8	84	117	6.4
2	68	172.4	7.3	84	127.7	7.1
2.5	72	187.2	7.8	82	136.9	7.7
3	71	200.3	8.5	79	145.3	8.7
3.5	73	212.1	11.4	78	153.4	10
4	72	224.1	9.9	80	160.9	10.1
4.5	71	235.7	10.5	78	169.1	11.4
5	77	247.5	11.1	80	176.3	11.5
5.5	73	258.2	11.7	74	182.6	12.2
6	71	269.7	12	75	190	13.5
6.5	72	280.3	12.6	81	196.7	13.8
7	71	291.1	13.3	86	202.6	13.6
7.5	76	301.2	13.5	83	209.3	15.2
8	70	312.1	14.6	85	216.3	15.6
8.5	72	321	14.6	82	221.3	15.8
9	76	330.4	14.6	83	228	16.8
9.5	78	340	15.8	83	234.2	18.6
10	77	349.3	15.7	84	239.8	19.1
10.5	76	357.4	16.2	75	245.9	21.4
11	75	367	16.5	76	251.9	22.4
11.5	76	375.8	18.1	75	259.1	23.4
12	74	386.1	19	71	265.6	22.9

(Adapted from Scheuer and Black, 2000)

variation between the sexes or different populations. This method is useful until the epiphyses begin to fuse with the diaphysis, typically at around age ten (Hoffman, 1979). The method is not only more accurate but is particularly useful for aging fetal skeletal material because dental development may be minimal. Forensic anthropologists are sometimes involved in estimating fetal age in cases where the **viability** of the infant is in question, which may be relevant to the manner of death. Measurement of the lengths of the major limb bone diaphyses (Tables 10.4–10.5) may assist in this determination.

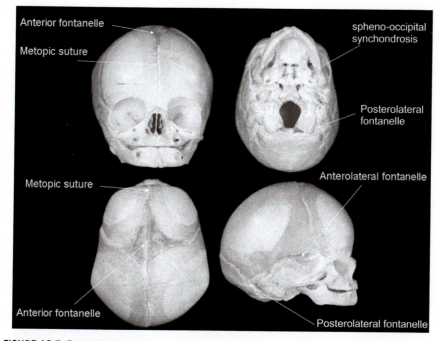

FIGURE 10.7 Fetal skull, showing open fontanelles (unfused primary ossification centers) and open (unfused) metopic suture

Table 10.7 Fusion of primary ossification centers of the skull

Bone/Feature	Age of closure
Sphenoid and mastoid fontanelle	Soon after birth
Occipital fontanelle	During first year
Frontal fontanelle	During second year
Left and right mandible halves	Completed by second year
Left and right frontal halves (metopic suture)	During second year
Occipital squamous and lateral portions	During fifth year
Occipital lateral and basilar portions	During sixth year
(Modified from Stewart, 1979)	

The appearance and fusion of certain primary ossification centers can also be useful in the estimation of juvenile age because of the correlation with age. Among these are the bones of the cranium, whose union results in the closure of the fontanelles and metopic sutures (see Figure 10.7 and Table 10.7).

Many bones, including the long bones of the limbs, hands and feet, ribs, vertebrae, clavicle, and scapula form from a primary ossification center (Figure 10.8), and several (usually at least two) secondary ossification centers (see Figures 10.9–10.12

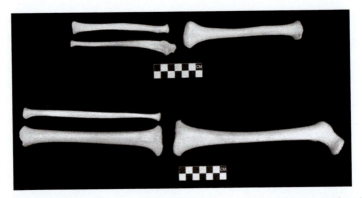

FIGURE 10.8 Long bone diaphyses (primary ossification centers) of the arm (top) and leg (bottom) in a juvenile (~7 years of age)

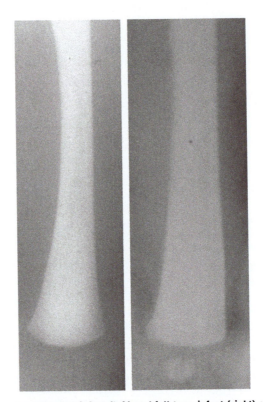

FIGURE 10.9 Knee of a premature infant (left) and full-term infant (right) showing the appearance of a secondary ossification center of the distal femur

(Modified from Brogdon, 2010)

FIGURE 10.10 Primary and secondary ossification centers

Tibial shaft and unfused proximal epiphysis (left), sternal end of clavicle with developing epiphysis (middle), and iliac crest in the process of fusing (right)

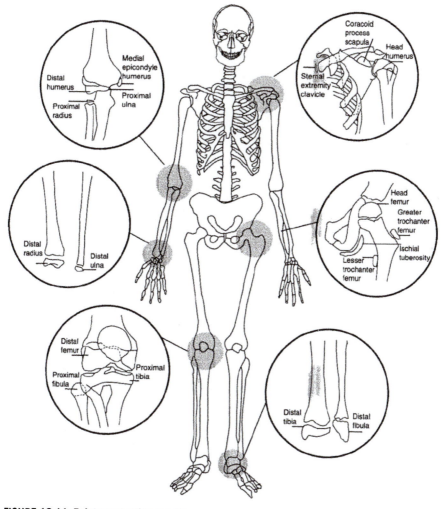

FIGURE 10.11 Epiphyseal union locations

(Buikstra and Ubelaker, 1994)

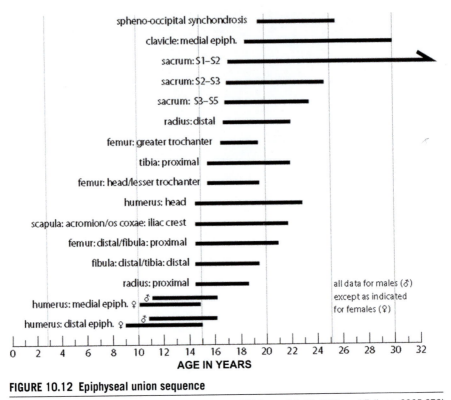

FIGURE 10.12 Epiphyseal union sequence

(From Buikstra and Ubelaker, 1994 – reprinted in White and Folkens, 2005:373)

and Tables 10.8–10.9). The primary and secondary ossification centers unite in a process referred to as epiphyseal union. The sequence of epiphyseal union is consistent and is correlated with chronological age. Most epiphyses unite between the ages of 10 and 25, making epiphyseal union a reliable method for estimating age from adolescent and young adult remains. Because epiphyseal union occurs as a process rather than an event, it is often necessary to assess the degree of union on a scale from commencement to completion (Scheuer and Black, 2000). Early in union, a distinct line is visible between the two components which tends to obliterate through remodeling with age. The process of initial union to final epiphyseal closure may take several years. The iliac crest of the innominate and the sternal end of the clavicle (Figure 10.9) are the last epiphyses to fuse, which can occur as late as the mid-twenties to early thirties (Webb and Suchey, 1985; Langley-Shirley and Jantz, 2010).

For intact bodies or living individuals, assessment of the appearance and union of the ossification centers is accomplished using radiography. The appearance of ossification centers and stages of epiphyseal union, however, can appear somewhat differently in visual assessments as compared to assessments of radiographs. These differences should be taken into consideration when the assessment approach varies from that described in the method.

Table 10.8 Ossification and epiphyseal union in males

Adolescent and post adolescent aging (years) – Males				
Epiphyseal	**Union in males**	**Open**	**Partial**	**Complete**
Humerus	Proximal	<20	16–21	>18
	Medial	<18	16–18	>16
	Distal	<15	14–18	>15
Radius	Proximal	<18	14–18	>16
	Distal	<19	16–20	>17
Ulna	Proximal	<16	14–18	>15
	Distal	<20	17–20	>17
Hand	MCs & Phalanges	<17	14–18	>15
Femur	Proximal	<18	16–19	>16
	Greater Trochanter	<18	16–19	>16
	Lesser Trochanter	<18	16–19	>16
	Distal	<19	16–20	>17
Tibia	Proximal	<18	16–20	>17
	Distal	<18	16–18	>16
Fibula	Proximal	<19	16–20	>17
	Distal	<18	15–20	>17
Foot	Calcaneus	<16	14–20	>16
	MTs & Phalanges	<17	14–16	>15
Scapula	Coraco-Glenoid*	<16	15–18	>16
	Acromion	<20	17–20	>17
	Inferior Angle	<21	17–22	>17
	Medial Border	<21	18–22	>18
Pelvis	Tri-radiate Complex**	<16	14–18	>15
	Ant Inf Iliac Spine	<18	16–18	>16
	Ischial Tuberosity	<18	16–20	>17
	Iliac Crest	<20	17–22	>18
Sacrum	Auricular Surface	<21	17–21	>18
	S1-S2 Bodies	<27	19–30+	>25
	S1-S2 Alae	<20	16–27	>19
	S2-S5 Bodies	<20	16–28	>20
	S2-S5 Alae	<16	16–21	>16
Vertebrae***	Annular Rings	<21	14–23	>18
Ribs***	Heads	<21	17–22	>19
Clavicle	Medial	<23	17–30	>21
Manubrium	1st Costal Notch	<23	18–25	>21

*Includes union of coracoid process, and the subcoracoid and glenoid epiphyses.
**Includes union of primary elements on both pelvic and acetabular surfaces and the acetabular epiphyses.
***At least one vertebra or one rib displays this type of activity.
(From Schaefer et al., 2009)

Table 10.9 Ossification and epiphyseal union in females

Adolescent and post adolescent aging (years) – Females				
Epiphyseal	**Union in females**	**Open**	**Partial**	**Complete**
Humerus	Proximal	<17	14–19	>16
	Medial	<15	13–15	>13
	Distal	<15	11–15	>12
Radius	Proximal	<15	12–16	>13
	Distal	<18	14–19	>15
Ulna	Proximal	<15	12–15	>12
	Distal	<18	15–19	>15
Hand	MCs & Phalanges	<15	11–16	>12
Femur	Proximal	<15	14–17	>14
	Greater Trochanter	<15	14–17	>14
	Lesser Trochanter	<15	14–17	>14
	Distal	<16	14–19	>17
Tibia	Proximal	<17	14–18	>18
	Distal	<17	14–17	>15
Fibula	Proximal	<17	14–17	>15
	Distal	<17	14–17	>15
Foot	Calcaneus	<12	10–17	>14
	MTs & Phalanges	<13	11–13	>11
Scapula	Coraco-Glenoid*	<16	14–18	>16
	Acromion	<18	15–17	>15
	Inferior Angle	<21	17–22	>17
	Medial Border	<21	18–22	>18
Pelvis	Tri-radiate Complex**	<14	11–16	>14
	Ant Inf Iliac Spine	<14	14–18	>15
	Ischial Tuberosity	<15	14–19	>16
	Iliac Crest	<16	14–21	>18
Sacrum	Auricular Surface	<20	15–21	>17
	S1-S2 Bodies	<27	14–30+	>21
	S1-S2 Alae	<19	11–26	>14
	S2-S5 Bodies	<20	12–26	>19
	S2-S5 Alae	<14	10–19	>13
Vertebrae***	Annular Rings	<21	14–23	>18
Ribs***	Heads	<21	17–22	>19
Clavicle	Medial	<23	17–30	>21
Manubrium	1st Costal Notch	<23	18–25	>21

*Includes union of coracoid process, and the subcoracoid and glenoid epipyses.
**Includes union of primary elements on both pelvic and acetabular surfaces and the acetabular epiphyses.
***At least one vertebra or one rib displays this type of activity.
(From Schaefer et al., 2009)

There is also a strong correlation between chronological age and the morphology of ossification centers, but assessment of epiphyseal union is more practical than assessment of epiphyseal morphology (Scheuer and Black, 2000). Epiphyses are often poorly preserved due to their fragility and can be difficult to identify as specific bones.

10.4 **Adult age estimation**

The adult aging process occurs as a consequence of our evolutionary history and as a result of maintenance of bodily homeostasis (Partridge and Barton, 1996; Crews, 1993; Nawrocki, 2010). After growth and development is complete, the skeleton continues to maintain its functions, but begins the slow process of degeneration over time. Many skeletal degeneration processes have been described, though many aspects are not well understood.

Pubic symphysis

The pubic symphysis is the best documented area of the skeleton for adult age estimation, with a long history of study beginning in the 1920s (Todd, 1920). Several modifications to the original method gained in popularity and were commonly employed into the early 1990s (e.g., McKern and Stewart, 1957; Gilbert and McKern, 1973). Today, the most commonly used method for estimating age from the pubic symphysis is the Suchey-Brooks method (Brooks and Suchey, 1990; Katz and Suchey, 1986), which is a six-phase system with detailed morphological descriptions of the pubic symphysis corresponding to each phase (see Figure 10.13 and Table 10.10). Casts representing the six phases have also been made to facilitate the use of this method (Figure 10.14). Recent studies have added a seventh phase to represent more advanced stages of degeneration, especially for females (Berg, 2008; Hartnett 2010a). Figure 10.15 shows the anatomical location of key features of the pubic symphysis.

The Suchey-Brooks method focuses on the changing features found on and surrounding the face of the pubic symphysis. In young individuals, the pubic symphyseal face is characterized by a series of horizontally-oriented ridges and furrows (also referred to as billowing) (Figure 10.16a). In younger individuals, the symphyseal face lacks a distinctive border, meaning there is no defined edge where the symphyseal face separates from the ischial and pubic rami. With increasing age, the billows disappear as new bone is deposited on the symphyseal face (Figure 10.16b). An ossific nodule fuses to the upper portion of the symphyseal surface, and the face becomes smooth and defined with a distinct rim. In the last stages of aging, the symphyseal surface becomes roughened in appearance and the symphyseal rim shows evidence of osteophytic lipping (bony projections extending from the joint margin) (Figure 10.16c).

Auricular surface

The auricular surface of the ilium also goes through age-related changes, characterized by remodeling of the joint surface, the development of a rim around the

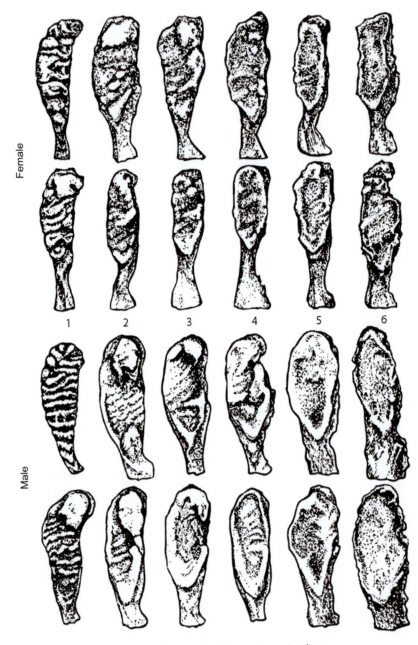

FIGURE 10.13 Six Suchey-Brooks phases of pubic symphyseal aging

(From White and Folkens, 2005)

Table 10.10 Description of Suchey-Brooks pubic symphyseal aging phases

Phase 1   Symphyseal face has a billowing surface (ridges and furrows), which usually extends to include the pubic tubercle. The horizontal ridges are well-marked, and ventral beveling may be commencing. Although ossific nodules may occur on the upper extremity, a key to the recognition of this phase is the lack of delimitation of either extremity (upper or lower).

Phase 2   The symphyseal face may still show ridge development. The face has commencing delimitation of lower and/or upper extremities occurring with or without ossific nodules. The ventral rampart may be in beginning phases as an extension of the bony activity at either or both extremities.

Phase 3   Symphyseal face shows lower extremity and ventral rampart in process of completion. There can be a continuation of fusing ossific nodules forming the upper extremity and along the ventral border. Symphyseal face is smooth or can continue to show distinct ridges. Dorsal plateau is complete. Absence of lipping of symphyseal dorsal margin; no bony ligamentous outgrowths.

Phase 4   Symphyseal face is generally fine-grained, although remnants of the old ridge and furrow system may still remain. Usually the oval outline is complete at this stage, but a hiatus can occur in upper ventral rim. Pubic tubercle is fully separated from the symphyseal face by definition of upper extremity. The symphyseal face may have a distinct rim. Ventrally, bony ligamentous outgrowths may occur on the inferior portion of the pubic bone adjacent to symphyseal face. If any lipping occurs, it will be slight and located on the dorsal border.

Phase 5   Symphyseal face is completely rimmed with some slight depression of the face itself, relative to the rim. Moderate lipping is usually found on the dorsal border with more prominent ligamentous outgrowths on the ventral border. There is little or no rim erosion. Breakdown may occur on superior ventral border.

Phase 6   Symphyseal face shows ongoing depression as rim erodes. Ventral ligamentous attachments are marked. In many individuals the pubic tubercle appears as a separate bony knob. The face may be pitted or porous, giving an appearance of disfigurement with the ongoing process of erratic ossification. Crenulations may occur. The shape of the face is often irregular at this stage.

Descriptive statistics						
	Females (n = 273)			Males (n = 739)		
Phase	Mean	S.D.	95% range	Mean	S.D.	95% range
1	19.4	2.6	15–24	18.5	2.1	15–23
2	25.0	4.9	19–40	23.4	3.6	19–34
3	30.7	8.1	21–53	28.7	6.5	21–46
4	38.2	10.9	26–70	35.2	9.4	23–57
5	48.1	14.6	25–83	45.6	10.4	27–66
6	60.0	12.4	42–87	61.2	12.2	34–86

(From Brooks and Suchey, 1990)

FIGURE 10.14 Pubic symphyseal aging casts

(Casts by Diane France Casting ©)

FIGURE 10.15 Anatomical regions of the pubic symphysis assessed for age estimation

Pubic symphysis: (1) ventral margin, (2) dorsal margin, (3) superior demiface, and (4) inferior demiface

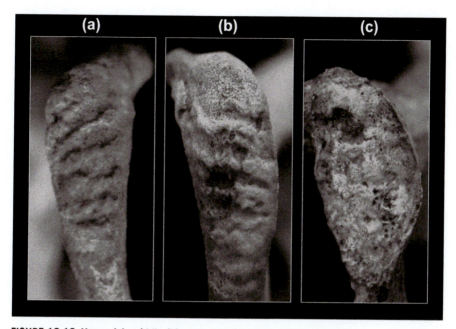

FIGURE 10.16 Young (a), middle (b), and older (c) adult pubic symphysis

surface, an increase in cortical bone porosity, and the growth of bony spicules in the retroauricular area (Lovejoy et al., 1985) (Figure 10.17). Like the pubic symphysis, the young auricular surface initially has horizontally distributed billows which are reduced to faint striae over time. With increasing age, the striae become finer until the surface eventually becomes smooth. The texture of the bone changes from finely grained to coarsely grained (having a sandpaper-like texture) to smooth, dense (remodeled) bone. The apex, located at the intersection of the arcuate line and auricular surface, undergoes degenerative changes with age. Typically, the surface is smooth and rounded, and becomes progressively irregular with age, often showing osteophytic lipping among older individuals. Also associated with increasing age is the appearance and proliferation of porosity of the auricular surface, which can be characterized as microporosity (very small holes) or macroporosity (larger-sized holes). Osteophytic lipping of the rim occurs with advancing age, and is most obvious on the inferior margin of the auricular surface, often projecting inferiorly. The retroauricular area is located on the ilium posterior to the auricular surface. As a muscle attachment site, changes that occur are related to the ossification of ligaments, resulting in increasing rugosity and the formation of bony spicules. These stages are outlined in Table 10.11 and Figure 10.18. Summary statistics for each phase are provided in Table 10.12.

One advantage of auricular surface aging is that due to its more protected location and greater bone density this area is often better preserved than other adult aging features such as the pubic symphysis or sternal rib ends. The morphological changes

FIGURE 10.17 Pelvic features assessed for age estimation

Auricular surface: (1) apex, (2) superior demiface, (3) inferior demiface, and
(4) retroauricular area

Table 10.11 Auricular surface phase descriptions	
Phase 1	Transverse billowing and very fine granularity. Articular surface displays fine granular texture and marked transverse organization. There is no porosity, retroauricular, or apical activity. The surface appears youthful because of broad and well-organized billows, which impart the definitive transverse organization. Raised transverse billows are well-defined and cover most of the surface. Any subchondral defects are smooth-edged and rounded (Age: 20–24).
Phase 2	Reduction of billowing but retention of youthful appearance. Changes from the previous phase are not marked and are mostly reflected in slight to moderate loss of billowing, with replacement by striae. There is no apical activity, porosity, or retroauricular activity. The surface still appears youthful owing to marked transverse organization. Granulation is slightly more coarse (Age: 25–29).
Phase 3	General loss of billowing, replacement by striae, and distinct coarsening of granularity. Both demifaces are largely quiescent with some loss of transverse organization. Billowing is much reduced and replaced by striae. The surface is more coarsely and recognizably granular than in the previous phase, with no significant changes at apex. Small areas of microporosity may appear. Slight retroauricular activity may occasionally be present. In general, coarse granulation supersedes and replaces billowing. Note smoothing of surface by replacement of billows with fine striae, but distinct retention of slight billowing. Loss of transverse organization and coarsening of granularity is evident (Age: 30–34).

Table 10.11 Auricular surface phase descriptions—cont'd

Phase 4	Uniform, coarse granularity. Both faces are coarsely and uniformly granulated, with marked reduction of both billowing and striae, but striae may still be present. Transverse organization is present but poorly defined. There is some activity in the retroauricular area, but this is usually slight. Minimal changes are seen at the apex, microporosity is slight, and there is no macroporosity (Age: 35–39).
Phase 5	Transition from coarse granularity to dense surface. No billowing is seen. Striae may be present but are very vague. The face is still partially (coarsely) granular and there is a marked loss of transverse organization. Partial densification of the surface with commensurate loss of granularity. Slight to moderate activity in the retroauricular area. Occasional macroporosity is seen, but this is not typical. Slight changes are usually present at the apex. Some increase in macroporosity, depending on degree of densification (Age: 40–44).
Phase 6	Completion of densification with complete loss of granularity. Significant loss of granulation is seen in most specimens, with replacement by dense bone. No billows or striae are present. Changes at apex are slight to moderate, but are almost always present. There is a distinct tendency for the surface to become dense. No transverse organization is evident. Most or all of the microporosity is lost to densification. There is increased irregularity of margins with moderate retroauricular activity and little or no macroporosity (Age: 45–49).
Phase 7	Dense irregular surface of rugged topography and moderate to marked activity in periauricular areas. This is a further elaboration of the previous morphology, in which marked surface irregularity becomes the paramount feature. Topography, however, shows no transverse or other form of organization. Moderate granulation is only occasionally retained. The inferior face is generally lipped at the inferior terminus. Apical changes are almost invariable and may be marked. Increasing irregularity of margins is seen. Macroporosity is present in some cases. Retroauricular activity is moderate to marked in most cases (Age: 50–59).
Phase 8	Breakdown with marginal lipping, macroporosity, increased irregularity, and marked activity in periauricular areas. The paramount feature is a nongranular, irregular surface, with distinct signs of subchondral destruction. No transverse organization is seen and there is a distinct absence of any youthful criteria. Macroporosity is present in about one-third of all cases. Apical activity is usually marked, but is not requisite. Margins become dramatically irregular and lipped, with typical degenerative joint change. Retroauricular area becomes well defined with profuse osteophytes of low to moderate relief. There is clear destruction of subchondral bone, absence of transverse organization, and increased irregularity (Age: 60+).

(From Lovejoy et al., 1985)

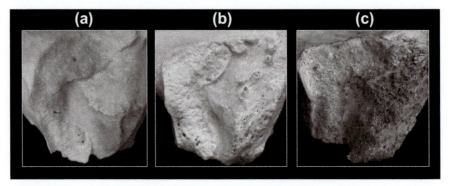

(a) **(b)** **(c)**

FIGURE 10.18 Young (a), middle (b), and older (c) adult auricular surface

Table 10.12 Mean ages and 95% prediction intervals by phase for the auricular surface

Phase	n	Mean	S.D.	95% range
1	5	18.2	4.09	5.8–30.6
2	10	20.5	3.10	13.1–27.8
3	13	29.2	7.91	11.3–47.1
4	37	42.4	13.67	14.4–70.4
5	52	47.3	14.20	18.6–76.0
6	30	48.7	13.70	20.1–77.3
7	17	53.1	11.14	22.3–83.9
8	102	59.9	15.24	28.4–89.4

(Adapted from Osborne et al., 2004)

to this area, however, are much more subtle and thus auricular surface methods can be more difficult to apply. Methods typically involve phase analysis similar to those applied to the pubic symphysis, and have become increasingly refined through simplification of phasing criteria, more refined statistics, and larger, more diverse samples (Lovejoy et al., 1985; Iscan and Loth, 1986; Osborne et al., 2004).

Other auricular surface age estimation techniques have included "component system" methods (e.g., Buckberry and Chamberlain, 2002). These methods generally use the same basic traits as phase methods, but rather than assessing the entire gestalt (the overall appearance) of the feature, component system methods examine each characteristic separately (e.g., microporosity), and categorize them (e.g., 1 = no microporosity present, 2 = microporosity present on one demiface, 3 = microporosity present on both demifaces). These methods have shown varied success, with some suggesting that they produce reasonably accurate age estimates for some age categories (Mulhern and Jones, 2005), while others suggest that the methods perform poorly (Falys et al., 2006).

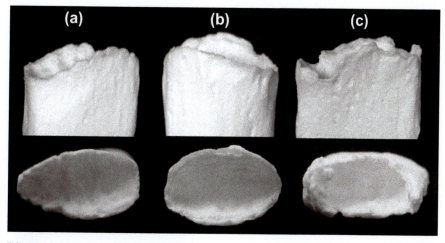

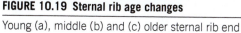

FIGURE 10.19 Sternal rib age changes

Young (a), middle (b) and (c) older sternal rib end

(Casts by Diane France Casting ©)

Sternal rib ends

The sternal ends of the ribs (where the bone connects to the costal cartilage) also undergo systematic, age-related changes. Much work has focused on the fourth rib (İşcan et al., 1984; 1985) because it is easily accessible at autopsy, but it has been shown that most ribs undergo similar changes at slightly different rates (Yoder at al., 2001; DiGangi et al., 2009). The estimation of age from this region focuses on changes in the shape of the rib as well as the overall quality of the bone. Generally, the sternal ends of the ribs go from a billowy, flat appearance when young, to a cupped, flared shape when middle aged, to a wide shape with irregular sharp margins in advanced age. Along with these changes in shape, the overall quality of the rib tends to decrease with age, becoming lighter, more fragile, and more porous. Figure 10.19 and Table 10.13 show age-related morphological changes of the right fourth sternal rib. Casts representing the different stages have been made available to facilitate the use of this method (Figure 10.20). In a recent assessment of rib age estimation methods, updated phase descriptions and confidence intervals which are most appropriate for modern forensic cases were reported (Hartnett, 2010b).

Histological aging methods

Anthropologists are increasingly employing bone **histomorphometry** to estimate skeletal age (Stout and Crowder, 2012; Streeter, 2012). Histomorphometric age estimation methods were first developed in the 1960s (Kerley, 1965), although modifications (such as Kerley and Ubelaker, 1978) and paradigm shifts in skeletal physiology (Frost, 1998) have lead to significant improvements. As discussed in Chapter 3, bone histology involves making very thin sections of bone that are examined using

Table 10.13 Descriptions of sternal rib changes

Phase 1	The pit is shallow and flat, and there are billows in the pit. The pit is shallow and U-shaped in cross-section. The bone is very firm and solid, smooth to the touch, dense, and of good quality. The walls of the rim are thick. The rim may show the beginnings of scalloping.
Phase 2	There is an indentation to the pit. The pit is V-shaped in cross-section, and the rim is well defined with round edges. The rim is regular with some scalloping. The bone is firm and solid, smooth to the touch, dense, and of good quality. There is no flare to the rim edges; they are parallel to each other. The pit is still smooth inside, with little to no porosity. In females, the central arc, which manifests on the anterior and posterior walls as a semicircular curve, is visible.
Phase 3	The pit is V-shaped, and there is a slight flare to the rim edges. The rim edges are becoming undulating and slightly irregular, and there may be remnants of scallops, but they look worn down. There are no bony projections from the rim. There is porosity inside the pit. The bone quality is good; it is firm, solid, and smooth to the touch. The rim edges are rounded, but sharp. In many females, there is a build-up of bony plaque, either in the bottom of the pit or lining the interior of the pit, creating the appearance of a two-layer rim. An irregular central arc may be apparent.
Phase 4	The pit is deep and U-shaped. The edges of the pit flare outwards, expanding the oval area inside the pit. The rim edges are not undulating or scalloped but are irregular. There are no long bony projections from the rim, and the rim edges are thin, but firm. The bone quality is good but does not feel dense or heavy. There is porosity inside the pit. In some males, two distinct depressions are visible in the pit. In females, the central arc may be present and irregular; however, the superior and inferior edges of the rim have developed, decreasing the prominence of the central arc.
Phase 5	There are frequently small bony projections along the rim edges, especially at the superior and inferior edges of the rim. The pit is deep and U-shaped. The rim edges are irregular, flared, sharp, and thin. There is porosity inside the pit. The bone quality is fair; the bone is coarse to the touch and feels lighter than it looks.
Phase 6	The bone quality is fair to poor, light in weight, and the surfaces of the bone feel coarse and brittle. There are bony projections along the rim edges, especially at the superior and inferior edges, some of which may be over 1 cm long. The pit is deep and U-shaped. The rim is very irregular, thin, and fragile. There is porosity inside the pit. In some cases, there may be small bony extrusions inside the pit. In females, the central arc is not prominent.
Phase 7	The bone is very poor quality, and in many cases, translucent. The bone is very light, sometimes feeling like paper, and feels coarse and brittle to the touch. The pit is deep and U-shaped. There may be long bony growths inside the pit. The rim is very irregular with long bony projections. In some cases, much of the cartilage has ossified and window formation occurs. In some females, much of the cartilage in the interior of the pit has ossified into a bony projection extending more than 1 cm in length.

Table 10.13 Descriptions of sternal rib changes—cont'd

Variant	In some males, the cartilage has completely or almost completely ossified. The ossification tends to be a solid extension of bone, rather than a thin projection. All of the bone is of very good quality, including the ossification. It is dense, heavy, and smooth. In these instances, bone quality should be the determining factor. There are probably other factors, such as disease, trauma, or substance abuse that caused premature ossification of the cartilage. When the individual is truly very old, the bone quality will be very poor. Be aware of these instances where a rib end may appear very old because of ossification of the cartilage but is actually a young individual, which can be ascertained by bone quality. In these cases, consult other age indicators in conjunction with the rib end.

(From Hartnett, 2010b)

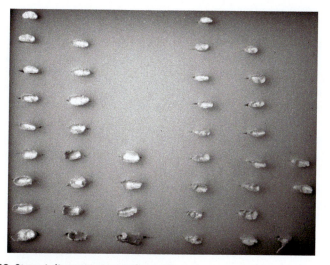

FIGURE 10.20 Sternal rib morphology aging casts

(Casts by Diane France Casting ©)

a microscope. The basis of bone histomorphometric methods of age estimation is bone remodeling; bone is continually remodeling through osteoclastic and osteoblastic activity. Primary lamellar bone is eventually replaced by primary osteons, and primary osteons are replaced by secondary osteons as a result of the remodeling process.

Most histomorphometric approaches involve determining the osteon population density (OPD), which is a function of the number of complete intact osteons and the number of osteon fragments (portions of older osteons that were resorbed as newer ones were created) (see Figure 10.21). Other structures and features are also considered in some methods, including the amount of remaining primary lamellar bone

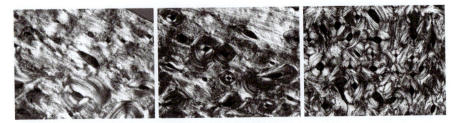

FIGURE 10.21 Histological changes in bone with age

Left: Young adult anterior femur showing unremodeled bone, primary osteons, and low secondary osteon population density. Middle: Middle aged adult anterior femur showing increase in secondary osteon population density and remaining areas of unremodeled bone. Right: Old aged adult anterior femur showing high secondary osteon population density and no areas of unremodeled bone.

(100x, polarized light, images courtesy of Christian Crowder and Amy Beresheim)

and the number of primary vascular canals. With enough remodeling over time, a maximum OPD is eventually reached, such that the OPD no longer increases with increasing age (Crowder, 2012). After this OPD has been reached, estimations can only indicate that the individual is older than a certain age. This maximum OPD is attained at different times for different bones. Because remodeling rates vary by element, most methods are bone-specific (separate methods have been developed for the femur, tibia, humerus, fibula, ulna, metacarpals, ribs, and clavicle [Streeter, 2012]), and it is important to adhere to the method in terms of skeletal element, population demographics, magnification, sampling area, and definitions of features.

Histomorphometry may be useful in very fragmentary skeletons where other morphological methods cannot be reliably applied. In addition to varying by element, remodeling rates are also affected by age, sex, ancestry, physical activity, and nutritional/health status, so these should be considered when interpreting histomorphometric results. Most approaches are also invasive and destructive, requiring a complete cross-section of bone (though core removal methods such as Thompson, 1979 have been proposed), so histomorphometric approaches should be considered after less destructive methods. Although they are becoming more frequently used and provide fairly accurate age estimates, the major deterrents to their use are the necessary equipment and training involved.

Dentition

With advancing age, teeth undergo microscopic changes that can be detected histologically. In one method (Gustafson, 1950; Maples and Burns, 1976), six criteria of single-rooted teeth are examined: attrition (occlusal surface wear); secondary dentin deposition (dentin deposited in the pulp chamber); root transparency (the ability of light to pass through tooth roots); root resorption (loss of root tips); degree of irregularity of the paradentium (area of tooth root that connects to the periodontal ligament); and cementum apposition (the incremental addition of cementum to the tooth root). The characteristics are scored using a four-point scale (0 to 3), and a regression formula is applied to the summed score to predict age. Although this method provides accurate age estimates, it is destructive and requires sophisticated equipment, proper training, and experience. Additional studies have focused on particular characteristics, such as root transparency, and have shown a reasonable degree of success (Lamendin et al., 1992; Prince and Ubelaker, 2002).

General indicators of advanced age

In addition to adult age estimates using specific changes in features or traits, there are other methods that generally reflect advanced age with little correlation to a particular age. These methods are typically used when other areas like the pubic symphysis and sternal rib ends are unavailable or unsuitable for examination, and provide only a general estimate of adult skeletal age such as younger or older adult.

There is a general trend for the sutures of the cranium and palate to close and obliterate with age. Although some methods gained popularity among forensic anthropologists (e.g., Meindl and Lovejoy, 1985) and subsequent studies have tried to refine the method for forensic applications (Nawrocki, 1998), specific cranial suture closure patterns have been shown to correlate rather poorly with chronological age. Cranial suture closure appears to be more closely related to individual brain and connective tissue (dura) development and somatic dysfunction rather than advancing chronological age (Smith and Tondury, 1978). Complete suture closure and obliteration, however, are generally indicative of more advanced age.

Cranial suture closure studies typically focus on the ectocranial and/or endocranial surfaces (Masset, 1989). In applying these methods, the sutures are usually scored as:

(1) Open, with no evidence of bony bridging across the suture.
(2) Minimal closure, indicated by any evidence of bony bridging up to 50% closure.
(3) Significant closure, indicated by evidence of bony bridging of greater than 50%.
(4) Obliteration, with no trace remaining of the suture margins (Buikstra and Ubelaker, 1994) (Figure 10.22).

Depending on the method used, various suture areas (usually within a 1 cm area) of the cranial vault or palate are scored, and the sum of the scores (i.e., the composite score) corresponds to a very broad age range (Buikstra and Ubelaker, 1994; Meindl and Lovejoy, 1985). A separate composite score is provided for the vault sutures (mid-coronal, bregma, anterior sagittal, obelion, lambda, and mid-lambdoid) and lateral-anterior sutures (sphenofrontal, pterion, mid-coronal, inferior sphenotemporal, and superior sphenotemporal). For the endocranial surface, the sagittal suture and the left coronal and lambdoidal sutures are scored. Evaluation of different vault regions indicates that the lateral-anterior sutures performed better than the vault sutures and especially sutures on the endocranial surface.

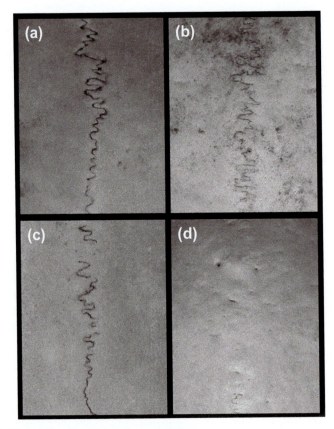

FIGURE 10.22 Progression of cranial suture closure

(a) Open suture, (b) minimal closure, (c) significant closure, and (d) obliteration of suture

The palatal sutures have also been examined as a possible age indicator. This method involves assessing the incisive suture, the anterior and posterior median palatine sutures, and the transverse suture (Mann et al., 1987; Gruspier and Mullen, 1991; Mann et al., 1991; Ginter, 2005). Unlike cranial suture closure scoring systems, obliteration for the maxillary suture is scored as the presence of any closure (bony bridging) along the suture line (Mann et al., 1987; Mann et al., 1991). Much more research is needed on diverse samples to evaluate the accuracy and reliability of suture closure methods in forensic anthropology.

Osteoarthritis is more common with advanced age and may result in osteophytic lipping in conjunction with destruction of articular cartilage, the latter resulting in mechanical polishing of the joint surface (i.e., **eburnation**) (Figure 10.23). Osteophytic lipping on synovial joint margins and on vertebral centra (vertebral osteophytosis) are more prevalent with advancing age (Stewart, 1979), likely due to a combination of factors, such as functional stress, cumulative injury, occupation, diet, and genetics (Figure 10.23).

Advanced age is often associated with **osteoporosis**, or an increase in bone porosity (or decrease in bone density). It typically results as a consequence of the

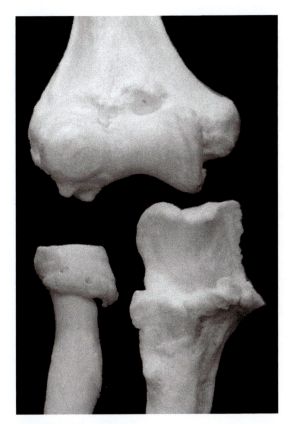

FIGURE 10.23 Osteoarthritis of the elbow

imbalance between bone resorption and bone formation, with resorption outpacing formation resulting in a net loss of bone. While both men and women may experience osteoporosis with age, women are typically affected to a greater degree and at a younger age due to the relationship between hormones and bone remodeling, which particularly impacts postmenopausal women (Agarwal, 2008; Agarwal and Stout, 2003; Golden, 1998).

When examining the skeleton for specific or general age-related changes, it is important to be attentive to pathological conditions that might have an effect on traits used for aging, especially degenerative changes.

10.5 **Other considerations in age estimation**

Traditional age estimation methods are being enhanced through a more thorough understanding of physiological skeletal changes (including microstructural and biochemical), as well as through the application of more robust statistical approaches such as multifactorial age estimation and transition analysis. Multifactorial age estimation is the use of multiple individual age indicators which are statistically combined to produce a single age estimate (Lovejoy et al., 1985; Uhl and Nawrocki 2010). One multifactorial aging method involved developing a new way to score traits, combining estimates from cranial sutures, the pubic symphysis, and the auricular surface, and applying Bayesian statistics (e.g., a maximum likelihood ratio) though a computer program called ADBOU (Boldsen et al., 2002). Although statistically robust, several tests of multifactorial methods have found them to work about as well as single age estimates (Bethard, 2005; Saunders et al., 1992; Martrille et al., 2007; Passalacqua and Cabo, 2007). It would appear that regression approaches generate the most accurate and precise age estimates (Uhl and Nawrocki, 2010).

One recent multifactorial aging method combines the Suchey-Brooks pubic symphysis and Lovejoy et al.'s auricular surface methods, and this was found to be more successful than most attempts at multifactorial aging (Samworth and Gowland, 2007; Passalacqua, 2010). The Samworth and Gowland method uses "look-up" tables which were developed from updated skeletal samples and provide more accurate age-at-death estimates than the original Suchey-Brooks pubic symphysis or Lovejoy auricular surface methods.

Transition analysis is a relatively recent development in age estimation methods (Boldsen et al., 2002; Konigsberg et al., 2002). This generally involves estimating the mean age of the transition from one phase or state to the next. For example, with the Suchey-Brooks method, a transition analysis would estimate the mean age of transitioning from a Phase III to a Phase IV. While very complicated statistically, when properly applied, this method relies on statistical probability functions to estimate the age of an individual. ADBOU is an example of a multifactorial aging method which uses transition analysis statistics to generate age estimates.

10.6 Case study: juvenile age estimation

In 2008, human remains from an unsolved homicide case were exhumed from a cemetery in northern California. Although buried for over 30 years, the body was in a surprisingly good state of preservation, with the skeletal elements still fully encased in flesh. The skeletal remains represented a complete subadult individual, which was determined based on observations of several growth and development indicators. The decedent's biological age was estimated using dental eruption, dental development, and epiphyseal union as being 6.0 ± 2 years. For example, the maxillary and mandibular first molars were almost completely erupted, but not yet in the occlusal plane, and the permanent central incisors were about to erupt and replace the deciduous ones (see Figure 10.24). The degree of fusion of the vertebrae, lack of union of all epiphyses, early state of development of several epiphyses, and diaphyseal lengths of several limb bones also indicated an age of approximately 6–8 years (Figure 10.25). The individual was identified as a six-year-old child of Native American ancestry.

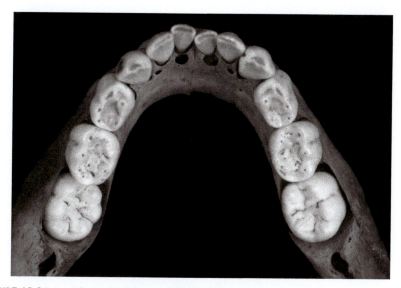

FIGURE 10.24 Juvenile case study – mandible

10.7 Case study: adult age estimation

In 2006, human remains were recovered from an outdoor scene in northern California. The skeleton was nearly complete, allowing for an in-depth assessment of age. The analysis suggested the individual was a white male. All epiphyses were fused with the exception of the sternal end of the clavicle which was in the final stage of union, suggesting an age of 25–30 years (Figure 10.26). The pubic symphyseal surfaces were a Phase II for males (based on Brooks and Suchey, 1990), suggesting an age of 23.4 ± 3.6 (1 SD) years. The auricular surface was assessed as being between Phase II and III (based on Lovejoy et al., 1985), suggesting an age of 25–34 years. The fourth sternal rib was aged as Phase IV (based on Iscan et al., 1984), suggesting an age of 28.2 ± 3.83 years. In this particular case, more weight was given to the nearly fused medial clavicle and to the somewhat youthful appearance of the pubic symphysis, which resulted in a final reported age estimate of approximately 23–35 years of age.

The decedent was later identified as a 26-year-old white male. This case study highlights the complexity surrounding adult age estimation, especially given the multiple methods available that vary in accuracy, precision, and quality of the reference samples upon which each method is based. Although much emphasis has been placed on statistically-based age estimates, a final age estimate using all skeletal features typically involves a degree of professional judgment, giving more consideration to those methods known to perform best for particular age groups.

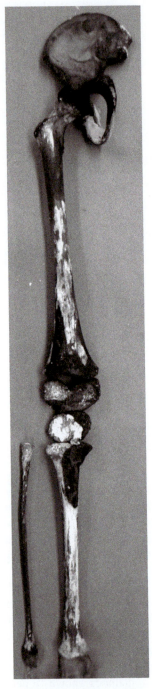

FIGURE 10.25 Juvenile case study: right innominate and leg

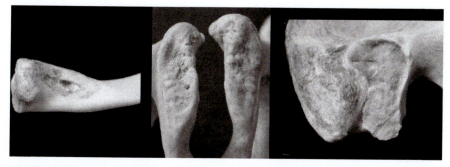

FIGURE 10.26 Adult case study: medial clavicle, pubic symphysis, and auricular surface

10.8 Summary

- It is possible to categorize an individual's age as *juvenile* or *adult* based on whether the skeleton is in the growth and development process or is mature and in the degeneration process.
- At birth, both the bones and teeth form at a rapid rate, and this process slows down considerably after infancy. The skeletal growth and development process is complete when all permanent teeth have erupted and all epiphyses have closed.
- The estimation of age from juvenile remains can be accomplished through the assessment of the degree of dental development, dental eruption, long bone growth, and epiphyseal union.
- Biological age and chronological age are not perfectly correlated, especially during late adulthood.
- Tooth development is more strongly correlated with chronological age than skeletal development because the latter is more susceptible to environmental factors such as poor nutrition or disease.
- Adult age indicators reflect degenerative changes that occur with advancing age. The pubic symphysis is one of the most reliable areas of the skeleton for adult age estimation. Other methods include changes in the morphology of the auricular surface and sternal rib end.
- Some age estimation methods, such as cranial suture closure, osteoarthritis, and osteoporosis only provide general age information (young versus older adult).
- Age estimation methods using bone or tooth histological analysis require advanced training and more sophisticated instrumentation. These methods may be useful when macroscopic age indicators are absent.
- Many aging standards are sex and/or population-specific. This should be considered when selecting the appropriate method to apply, and also taken into account when the sex and ancestry are unknown.
- It is best to use all available indicators when estimating age from the skeleton, giving appropriate weight to the methods that have been shown to be most accurate and reliable.

10.9 Test yourself

- What are some of the challenges of age estimation of juvenile individuals? What are some of the challenges of age estimation of adult individuals? Why is adult age estimation less precise than age estimation of juvenile remains?
- What age would you estimate for a fetus with a maximum femoral length of 49 mm? For a child whose first premolar crown is half complete?
- Under what circumstances might you rely on cranial suture closure as an age indicator? What caveats would you provide to investigators regarding the age estimate?
- An intact skeleton of a juvenile is recovered from a shallow grave. The coroner has requested an estimate of age to compare with missing person files, indicating that there are only three missing children from the region: ages 4, 8, and 12. What methods would you use to estimate age? Could you confidently narrow down which of the three missing children are most likely consistent with the remains?
- What are some of the advantages to using the pubic symphysis aging method over the auricular surface?
- You are presented a pelvis and have decided to estimate age using the Suchey-Brooks method based on pubic symphysis morphology. You look at the phase descriptions and casts, and note that the symphyseal face is very flat (no billowing), and has a well-defined rim. You observe osteophytic (bony) lipping of the dorsal margin, and note the surface has lost its oval appearance. Which phase is most consistent with this pattern?
- You are examining highly fragmentary human remains from a building collapse. You note that the iliac crest is in the early stages of fusion, the clavicle is unfused, and pubic symphysis shows signs of advanced degenerative changes. What would be your preliminary thoughts regarding these discrepancies in age indicators? How would you proceed?
- What is the significance of the neonatal line found in teeth? Under what circumstances would this have potential forensic implications?
- When would an anthropologist be consulted to provide an age estimate of a living person? What limitations would there be based on assessments of radiographs of the dentition and the skeleton?

Definitions

Adult Those ages occurring during the mature, degenerative stage of skeletal change

Age of Majority An age threshold at which an individual is legally considered to be an adult; in most countries, this is 18 years of age

Biological Age Age as determined physiologically, including physical changes in body structure and functional ability

Canalized (or canalization) Development along a predictable growth channel or pathway, despite external factors

Chronological Age The amount of time an individual has been in existence (typically the number of years since birth, but may also be used to describe fetal age chronology)

Eburnation Mechanical joint polishing, often observed in connection with osteoarthritis

Extrinsic External factors, such as biomechanical loading, diet, and health status

Histomorphometry Quantitative study of the microscopic structure of tissue

Homeostasis Maintaining internal equilibrium through physiological processes

Intrinsic Internal factors, such as sex and genetic variation

Juvenile (or subadult) Those ages during the skeletal growth and development process including the embryonic, fetal, infant, child, and adolescent periods

Osteoarthritis Mechanical degradation of joints

Osteoporosis An increase in bone porosity, or decrease in bone mineral density, often associated with advanced age

Trajectory Effect The increasing discrepancy between biological age and chronological age as one gets older

Viability The ability of an organism to maintain itself, or the ability of a fetus to survive outside the womb

References

Agarwal, S.C., 2008. Light and broken bones: examining and interpreting bone loss and osteoporosis in past populations. In: Katzenberg, A.M., Saunders, S.R. (Eds.), Biological Anthropology of the Human Skeleton, second ed. Wiley-Liss, New York, pp. 387–410.

Agarwal, S.C., Stout, S. (Eds.), 2003. Bone loss and osteoporosis: an anthropological perspective. Kluwer Academic/Plenum Publishers, New York.

Berg, G.E., 2008. Pubic bone age estimation in adult women. J. Forensic Sci. 53, 569–577.

Bethard, J.D., 2005. A Test of the Transition Analysis Method for Estimation of Age-at-Death in Adult Human Skeletal Remains. MA Thesis. The University of Tennessee, Knoxville.

Black, S., Agarwal, A., Payne-James, J. (Eds.), 2010. Age Estimation in the Living: The Practitioner's Guide. John Wiley & Sons, Ltd, Winchester.

Boldsen, J.L., Milner, O.R., Konigsberg, L.K., Wood, J.W., 2002. Transition analysis: a new method for estimating age from skeletons. In: Hoppa, R.D., Vaupel, J. (Eds.), Paleodemography: age distributions from skeletal samples. Cambridge University Press, Cambridge, pp. 73–106.

Brooks, S., Suchey, J.M., 1990. Skeletal age determination based on the os pubis: A comparison of the Acsadi-Nemeskeri and Suchey-Brooks methods. Hum. Evol. 5, 227–238.

Buckberry, J.L., Chamberlain, A.T., 2002. Age estimation from the auricular surface of the ilium: A revised method. Am. J. Phys. Anthropol. 119 (3), 213–239.

Buikstra, J.E., Ubelaker, D.H., 1994. Standards for data collection from human skeletal remains. Arkansas Archeological Survey Research Series, 44. Arkansas Archeological Survey, Fayetteville.

Crews, D.E., 1993. Biological anthropology and human aging: Some current directions in aging research. Ann. Rev. Anthropol. 22, 395–423.

Demirjian, A., Goldstein, H., Tanner, J.M., 1973. A new system of dental age assessment. Hum. Biol. 45, 211–227.

Digangi, E.A., Bethard, J.D., Kimmerle, E.H., Konigsberg, L.W., 2009. A new method for estimating age-at-death from the first rib. Am. J. Phys. Anthropol. 138 (2), 164–176.

Falys, C.G., Schutkowski, H., Weston, D.A., 2006. Auricular surface aging: worse than expected? A test of the revised method on a documented historic skeletal assemblage. Am. J. Phys. Anthropol. 130, 508–513.

Fazekas, I.Gy, Kosa, F., 1978. Forensic Fetal Osteology. Akademiai Kaido, Budapest.

Frost, H.M., 1998. Changing concepts in skeletal physiology: Wolff's law, the mechanostat, and the "Utah paradigm." Am. J. Hum. Biol. 10, 599–605.

Garvin, H.M., Passalacqua, N.V., Uhl, N.M., Gipson, D.R., Overbury, R.S., Cabo, L.L., 2012. Developments in forensic anthropology: Age-at-death estimation. In: Dirkmaat, D.C., (Ed.), A companion to forensic anthropology and archaeology. Blackwell Publishing, Chichester, pp. 202–223.

Gilbert, B.M., McKern, T.W., 1973. A method for aging the female os pubis. Am. J. Phys. Anthropol. 38, 31–38.

Ginter, J.K., 2005. A test of the effectiveness of the revised maxillary suture obliteration method in estimating adult age at death. J. Forensic Sci. 50, 1303–1309.

Golden, B., 1998. The prevention and treatment of osteoporosis. Arthritis Care Res. 11, 124–134.

Gruspier, K.L., Mullen, G.J., 1991. Maxillary suture obliteration: a test of the Mann method. J. Forensic Sci. 36, 512–519.

Gustafson, G., 1950. Age determination of teeth. J. Am. Dental Assoc. 41, 45–54.

Hartnett, K.M., 2010a. Analysis of age-at-death estimation using data from a new, modern autopsy sample – part I: pubic bone. J. Forensic Sci. 55, 1145–1151.

Hartnett, K.M., 2010b. Analysis of age-at-death estimation using data from a new, modern autopsy sample – part 2: sternal end of first rib. J. Forensic Sci. 55, 1152–1156.

Hoffman, J.M., 1979. Age estimations from diaphyseal lengths: two months to twelve years. J. Forensic Sci. 24, 461–469.

Iscan, M.Y., 1989. Age Markers in the Human Skeleton. Charles C. Thomas, Springfield, IL.

Iscan, M.Y., Loth, S.R., Wright, R.K., 1984. Age estimation from the rib by phase analysis: White males. J. Forensic Sci. 29, 1094–1104.

Iscan, M.Y., Loth, S.R., Wright, R.K., 1985. Age estimation from the rib by phase analysis: White females. J. Forensic Sci. 30, 853–863.

Katz, D., Suchey, J.M., 1986. Age determination of the male os pubis. Am. J. Phys. Anthropol. 69 (4), 427–435.

Kerley, E.R., 1965. The microscopic determination of age in human bone. Am. J. Phys. Anthropol. 23, 149–164.

Kerley, E.R., Ubelaker, D.H., 1978. Revision in the microscopic method of estimating age at death in human cortical bone. Am. J. Phys. Anthropol. 49, 545–546.

Lamendin, H., Baccino, E., Humbert, J.F., Tavernier, J.C., Nossintchouk, R.M., Zerilli, A., 1992. A simple technique for age estimation in adult corpses: the two criteria dental method. J. Forensic Sci. 37, 1373–1379.

Langley-Shirley, N., Jantz, R.L., 2010. A Bayesian approach to age estimation in modern Americans from the clavicle. J. Forensic Sci. 55, 571–583.

Latham, K.E., Finnegan, M. (Eds.), 2010. Age estimation of the human skeleton. CC Thomas, Springfield.

Lewis, M.E., 2009. The Bioarchaeology of Children: Perspectives from Biological and Forensic Anthropology. Cambridge University Press, Cambridge.

Liversidge, H., 2008. Dental age revisited. In: Irish, J.D., Nelson, G.C. (Eds.), Technique and Application in Dental Anthropology. Cambridge University Press, Cambridge, pp. 234–252.

Lovejoy, C.O., Meindl, R.S., Mensforth, R., Barton, T.J., 1985. Chronological metamorphosis of the auricular surface of the ilium: A new method for the determination of adult skeletal age at death. Am. J. Phys. Anthropol. 68, 15–28.

Mann, R.W., Symes, S.A., Bass, W.M., 1987. Maxillary suture obliteration: aging the human skeleton based on intact or fragmentary maxilla. J. Forensic Sci. 32, 148–157.

Mann, R.W., Jantz, R.L., Bass, W.M., Willey, P.S., 1991. Maxillary suture obliteration: a visual method for estimating skeletal age. J. Forensic Sci. 36, 781–791.

Maples, W.R., Burns, K.R., 1976. Estimation of age from individual teeth. J. Forensic Sci. 21, 343–356.

Martrille, L., Ubelaker, D.H., Cattaneo, C., Seguret, F., Tremblay, M., Baccino, E., 2007. Comparison of four skeletal methods for the estimation of age at death on White and Black adults. J. Forensic Sci. 52 (2), 1–6.

Masset, C., 1989. Age estimation on the basis of cranial sutures. In: Iscan, M.Y. (Ed.), Age Markers in the Human. Charles C. Thomas, Springfield, pp. 71–103.

Massler, M., Shour, I., Poncher, H.G., 1941. Developmental pattern of child as reflected in the calcification pattern of teeth. Am. J. Dis. Children 62, 33–67.

McKern, T.W., Stewart, T.D., 1957. Skeletal age changes in young American males. Headquarters Quartermaster Research and Development Command Technical Report EP-45, Natick, Massachusetts.

Meindl, R.S., Lovejoy, C.O., 1985. Ectocranial suture closure: a revised method for the determination of skeletal age at death based on the lateral-anterior Sutures. Am. J. Phys. Anthropol. 68, 57–66.

Moorrees, C.F.A., Fanning, E.A., Hunt Jr., E.E., 1963a. Formation and resorption of three deciduous teeth in children. Am. J. Phys. Anthropol. 21, 205–213.

Moorrees, C.F.A., Fanning, E.A., Hunt Jr., E.E., 1963b. Age variation of formation stages for ten permanent teeth. J. Dental Res. 42, 1490–1502.

Mulhern, D.M., Jones, E.B., 2005. Test of revised method of age estimation from the auricular surface of the ilium. Am. J. Phys. Anthropol. 126 (1), 61–65.

Nawrocki, S.P., 1998. Regression formulae for the estimation of age from cranial suture closure. In: Reichs, K.J. (Ed.), Forensic Osteology: Advances in the identification of human remains. CC Thomas, Springfield, pp. 276–292.

Nawrocki, S.P., 2010. The nature and sources of error in the estimation of age at death from the human skeleton. In: Latham, K.E., Finnegan, M. (Eds.), Age estimation of the human skeleton. CC Thomas, Springfield, pp. 79–101.

Osborne, D.L., Simmons, T.L., Nawrocki, S.P., 2004. Reconsidering the auricular surface as an indicator of age at death. J. Forensic Sci. 49 (5), 768–773.

Partridge, L., Barton, N.H., 1996. On measuring the rate of ageing. Proc. Biol. Sci. 263 (1375), 1365–1371.

Passalacqua, N.V., Cabo, L.L., 2007. Forensic Age-at-death Assessment: Multiple Methodologies Based on Four Techniques. Am. J. Phys. Anthropol. 132 (S44), 184.

Passalacqua, N.V., 2010. The utility of the Samworth and Gowland age-at-death "look-up" tables in forensic anthropology. J. Forensic Sci. 55 (2), 482–487.

Prince, D.A., Ubelaker, D.H., 2002. Application of Lamendin's adult dental aging technique to a diverse skeletal sample. J. Forensic Sci. 47, 107–116.

Rushton, M.A., 1933. On the fine contour lines of the enamel of milk teeth. Dental Record 53, 170–171.

Samworth, R., Gowland, R., 2007. Estimation of adult skeletal age-at-death: Statistical assumptions and applications. Int. J. Osteoarchaeol. 17, 174–188.

Saunders, S.R., Fitzgerald, C., Rogers, T., Dudar, C., McKillop, H., 1992. A test of several methods of skeletal age estimation using a documented archaeological sample. Can. Soc. Forensic Sci. J. 25 (2), 97–118.

Schaefer, M., Black, S., Scheuer, L., 2009. Juvenile osteology: a laboratory and field manual. Academic Press, San Diego.

Scheuer, L., Black, S., 2000. Developmental Juvenile Osteology. Academic Press, San Diego.

Schour, I., 1936. The neonatal line in the enamel and dentin of the human deciduous teeth and first permanent molar. J. Am. Dental Assoc. 23, 1946–1955.

Schour, I., Massler, M., 1944. Development of the human dentition. J. Am. Dental Assoc. 28, 1153–1160.

Scientific Working Group for Forensic Anthropology, 2010. Age Estimation Revision 0.

Smith, B.H., 1991. Standards of human tooth formation and dental age assessment. In: Kelly, M.A., Larsen, C.S. (Eds.), Advances in Dental Anthropology. Wiley-Liss, New York, pp. 143–168.

Smith, S.L., 2007. Stature estimation of 3–10-year-old children from long bone lengths. J. Forensic Sci. 52 (3), 538–546.

Smith, D.W., Töndury, G., 1978. Origin of the calvaria and its sutures. Am. J. Dis. Children 132, 662–666.

Stewart, T.D., 1979. Essentials of Forensic Anthropology. Charles C. Thomas, Springfield.

Stout, S., Crowder, C.M., 2012. Bone remodeling, histomorphology, and histomorphometry. In: Crowder, C., Stout, S. (Eds.), Bone Histology: An Anthropological Perspective. CRC Press, Boca Raton, pp. 1–22.

Streeter, M., 2012. Histological age-at-death estimation. In: Crowder, C., Stout, S. (Eds.), Bone Histology: An Anthropological Perspective. CRC Press, Boca Raton, pp. 135–152.

Thompson, D.D., 1979. The core technique in the determination of age at death in skeletons. J. Forensic Sci. 24 (4), 902–915.

Todd, T.W., 1920. Age changes in the pubic bone I: The male white os pubis. Am. J. Phys. Anthropol. 3 (3), 285–334.

Ubelaker, D.H., 1989. Human Skeletal Remains: Excavation, Analysis, Interpretation, second ed. Taraxacum, Washington, DC.

Uhl, N.M., Nawrocki, S.P., 2010. Multifactorial estimation of age at death from the human skeleton. In: Latham, K.E., Finnegan, M. (Eds.), Age Estimation of the Human Skeleton. CC Thomas, Springfield, pp. 243–26.

Ulijaszek, S.J., 1996. Age of eruption of deciduous dentition of Anga children, Papua New Guinea. Annal. Hum. Biol. 23, 495–499.

Webb, P.A., Suchey, J.M., 1985. Epiphyseal union of the anterior iliac crest and medial clavicle in a modern multiracial sample of American males and females. Am. J. Phys. Anthropol. 68, 457–466.

White, T.D., Folkens, P.A., 2005. The Human Bone Manual. Academic Press, San Diego.

Whittaker, D., MacDonald, D., 1989. A Color Atlas of Forensic Dentistry. Wolfe Medical Publications, London.

Yoder, C., Ubelaker, D.H., Powell, J.F., 2001. Examination of variation in sternal rib end morphology relevant to age assessment. J. Forensic Sci. 46, 223–227.

Stature Estimation

11.1 Principles of stature estimation

The estimation of living **stature** from the skeleton is possible because there is a relationship between an individual's skeletal dimensions and his or her height. Forensic anthropologists typically estimate stature as part of the biological profile in order to narrow the pool of potential missing persons to whom the remains might belong, although individuals are usually not excluded from further consideration based on differences in estimated and known stature unless the differences between the two are particularly extreme. Early stature estimation methods involved attempts to completely rearticulate the entire skeleton and measure it directly (Stewart, 1979). While these methods potentially have a high degree of accuracy, they are also considered quite impractical and are rarely if ever used today.

Most methods currently employed involve the metric analysis of skeletal elements, measuring certain bone dimensions and using these measurements to calculate a stature estimate. The resulting stature estimate attempts to take into account biological variation, error, and reporting biases such that the estimate has a high probability of including the individual's actual stature. The selected stature estimation method depends on the skeletal elements present as well as the condition of these elements, and stature estimates are most accurate when the majority of the skeletal material is present and in good condition. The most accurate methods are full skeleton methods. As the name suggests, however, a mostly complete skeleton is necessary and therefore these methods are not as frequently used. The most commonly utilized methods of estimating stature are regression methods, which are based on a mathematical relationship between bone dimensions and stature. Each of these methods is discussed in more detail below.

11.2 Full skeleton methods

Full skeleton methods, or anatomical methods, involve estimating stature based on the sum of the vertical measurements of all bones that contribute to stature along with a correction factor for soft tissue (Fully, 1956; Stewart, 1979; Lundy, 1988a)

(Table 11.1), or by applying a formula to the skeletal element sum (Raxter et al., 2006). Bones typically measured in these methods are the height of the skull, the heights of the vertebrae, the lengths of the femur and tibia, and the height of the ankle (Figure 11.1). To apply this method, it is therefore necessary that the skeleton is relatively complete, which is somewhat uncommon in forensic anthropological casework.

Table 11.1 Soft tissue corrections for full skeletal methods

Skeletal sum	Soft tissue addition
≤153.5 cm	10.0 cm
153.6–165.5 cm	10.5 cm
≥165.5 cm	11.5 cm

(From Fully and Pineau, 1960)

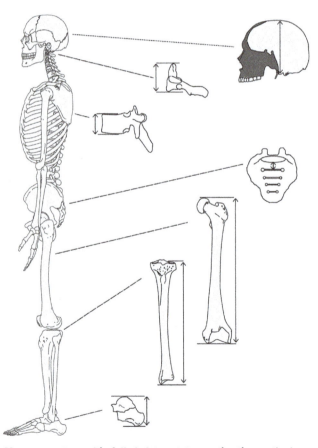

FIGURE 11.1 Measurements used in full skeleton stature estimation methods

(Adapted from Willey, 2009)

In the case of a missing vertebra, it may be possible to estimate the height by averaging the heights of the vertebra immediately above and below (Stewart, 1979; Willey, 2009).

An advantage of full skeleton methods is that they can be applied regardless of the sex or ancestry of the individual (this differs from regression methods discussed below, which ideally employ population-specific formulae). Moreover, full skeleton methods should result in the most accurate estimates of stature. One study found that a particular anatomical method estimated true stature within 4.5cm in 95% of individuals studied (Raxter et al., 2006). Improved accuracy with these methods versus regression methods is even greater in cases where, for example, the individual has an anomalous (e.g., extra or fewer) number of vertebrae (Lundy 1988b; Raxter and Ruff, 2010) or unusual proportions such as a short trunk and long limbs.

11.3 Regression methods

Regression methods, also known as mathematical methods, are the most commonly utilized methods for estimating stature. These methods are based on a mathematical relationship (**correlation**) between height and body segments (i.e., taller people tend to have longer body segments than shorter people). For skeletal remains, these segments are represented by the lengths of single or multiple long bones, typically the maximum length of long bones of the legs and arms (see Figure 11.2). Methods that use the dimensions of complete limb bones (versus incomplete bones or non-limb bones, each discussed further below) are the most accurate. In general, the femur is the most accurate because it contributes most to stature, followed by lower leg bones and arm bones. It should be noted that when allometric differences are more pronounced, stature estimates that combine multiple long bone measurements are typically more accurate than estimates based solely on a single skeletal element.

The correlation between stature and long bone length was first extensively studied by anthropologists in the 1950s (Trotter and Gleser, 1952; Trotter, 1970), and formed the basis for most stature estimation methods developed today. The equations resulting from these early studies should be employed with caution, however,

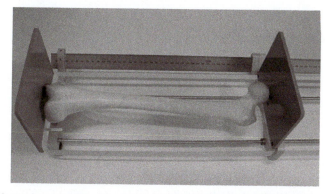

FIGURE 11.2 Maximum length of the femur measured using an osteometric board

since later studies have shown that methods used for taking certain measurements (specifically the tibia) were incorrectly reported (Jantz et al., 1995). Moreover, these studies were based on individuals born in the mid- to late-1800s and early 1900s; as discussed below, these may not be the most appropriate for modern forensic cases.

Regression analysis (as discussed in Chapter 3) is an approach used to examine the relationship between a dependent variable and one or more independent variables. Regression methods for stature estimation are typically developed by measuring bones from a population where the stature of the individuals is known, and mathematically determining how the known stature varies with different bone lengths. Note that in stature estimation approaches in the forensic anthropological literature, stature is typically considered the dependent variable (y), which is predicted by independent variables such as a bone length (x); in other literature, bone length is considered the dependent variable (Konigsberg et al., 1998). The result is a regression equation into which the forensic anthropologist can insert bone measurements to predict the individual's likely stature (see Figure 11.3). The correlation, however, is not perfect. If regression methods are employed, it is common to report a point estimate along with a 95% prediction interval (see Chapter 3). A 95% prediction interval indicates that 95% of individuals who have those same bone measurements will have a stature that falls within that interval. It also means that in 5% of cases where those bone measurements are found, the individual's stature would be expected to fall outside of this interval.

Because the relationship between stature and one or more bone lengths is not as strong as that between stature and *all* bones contributing to height, regression methods are typically less accurate than full skeleton methods and the standard errors are somewhat higher. Moreover, regression methods cannot adequately account for peculiarities in anatomy or proportions. Stature estimates based on lengths of the bones of the lower limb are more accurate than those based on bones of the upper limb, and those based

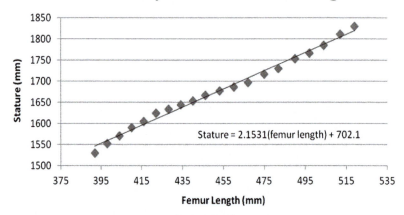

FIGURE 11.3 Example of a regression of femur length on stature in a population of European males and accompanying regression formula

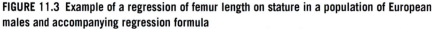

(Data from Hrdlicka, in Krogman, 1962)

on multiple bones are more accurate than those based on a single bone. This is usually seen in the standard errors of the estimates. Notice in Table 11.2, for example, that the standard error is always lowest for the femur and always greatest for the humerus.

Importantly, the relationship between stature and individual bones varies between different groups. In other words, these relationships are not the same in males and females, and also show variation between populations and through time. As discussed in Chapter 8, males and females vary in both size and shape, and also in their relationship between bone length and stature. As discussed in Chapter 9, different geographic and ancestral groups also vary in their body proportions. In addition, the relationship between bone length and stature has changed over time. US Americans, for example, are taller today than in the past, and these changes in height are not always directly proportional to changes in bone length. This change in growth pattern of a population over time is called **secular change**. Relationships between bone lengths and stature are different for contemporary populations as compared to individuals who were born even just a century ago (Meadows and Jantz, 1995; Ousley and Jantz, 1998). It is therefore important that regression approaches utilize formulae that are specific to the sex, ancestry, and **temporal cohort** of the unknown individual.

Stature estimation has been widely studied across groups and various regression formulae have been developed for different population groups (such as those shown in Table 11.2). When regression equations are not known for the population of interest, forensic anthropologists should use discretion in selecting the most appropriate reference sample and equations. It may be advisable in some cases to refrain from providing a stature estimate, but in most cases, a suitable (or at least defendable) reference population can be utilized.

Table 11.2 Regression formulae for different sex and ancestral groups for the femur, fibula, and humerus

	Stature equation	Standard error
European males	2.38 × (femur length) + 61.41	±3.27
	2.68 × (fibula length) + 71.78	±3.29
	2.89 × (humerus length) + 78.10	±4.57
African males	2.11 × (femur length) + 70.35	±3.94
	2.19 × (fibula length) + 85.65	±4.08
	2.88 × (humerus length) + 75.48	±4.23
European females	2.47 × (femur length) + 54.10	±3.72
	2.93 × (fibula length) + 59.61	±3.57
	3.36 × (humerus length) + 57.97	±4.45
African females	2.28 × (femur length) + 59.76	±3.41
	2.49 × (fibula length) + 70.90	±3.80
	3.08 × (humerus length) + 64.67	±4.25

All in cm
From Trotter and Gleser, 1952

Using the formula from Table 11.2 for calculation of stature of European males from the length of the femur:

$$2.38 \text{ (femur length)} + 61.41 \pm 3.27,$$

for a femur length of 500mm (50cm), the calculation would be carried out as follows:

$$(2.38) \times (50\text{cm}) + (61.41) \pm (3.27)$$

$$= 180.41 \pm 3.27\text{cm}$$

$$= 177.14\text{cm to } 183.68\text{cm}$$

$$= 69.74'' \text{ to } 72.31''$$

or about 5'10" to 6'2" tall

FIGURE 11.4 Manual calculation of stature from regression formulae

Stature estimates using regression formulae may be carried out manually (see Figure 11.4), or can be performed using software packages such as Fordisc (Jantz and Ousley, 2005). If using Fordisc, available skeletal measurement data (following measurement guidelines in Moore-Jansen et al. (1994) or as reprinted in Buikstra and Ubelaker, 1994) is entered, and the most appropriate reference sample can be selected by the user. Fordisc can then carry out an automated calculation of stature including selected prediction intervals (e.g., 90%, 95%, and 99%) and graphic representation of the results (see Table 11.3 and Figure 11.5). The stature equations based on the mis-measured tibiae from 19th-century individuals have also been corrected in the Fordisc database. For cases where ancestry cannot be estimated, there is an option to select formulae that will use the entire reference sample to derive the estimate; however, this will result in larger standard errors than population-specific formulae.

In some cases, bones may be incomplete due to traumatic or taphonomic causes and may therefore fail to maintain their maximum dimension. It is possible to use fragmentary limb bones to estimate stature, but the accuracy is reduced and the prediction interval becomes wider, giving it less probative value unless such tests reveal that the individual was extremely tall or extremely short. Nonetheless, it is often still considered desirable to provide a stature estimate based on the fragmentary bone(s), and several methods have been developed for doing so. These methods are based on the principle that there is a correlation between a bone's segment length and its total length. Some of these methods work by estimating stature from measurements of the fragmentary bone itself (Holland, 1992), but most involve first estimating the maximum length of the bone, and then using that estimated maximum length to estimate stature (Steele, 1970; Simmons et al., 1990; Wright and Vasquez, 2003). Because the segment is used to estimate the length which in turn is used to estimate stature, the error in these stature estimation methods is compounded, resulting in wider prediction intervals.

Table 11.3 Example stature results and equations from Fordisc with 95% prediction interval

Stature	SE	P.I.	Regression formulae
67.1″ +/−	4.0″	(prediction interval 63.2 to 71.1″);	formula is: 0.050* FEMXLN+TIBXLN (826 mm) + 26.11″
67.1″ +/−	4.0″	(prediction interval 63.2 to 71.1″);	formula is: 0.051* FEMXLN+FIBXLN (821 mm) + 25.63″
67.2″ +/−	4.0″	(prediction interval 63.2 to 71.1″);	formula is: 0.034* FEMXLN+FIBXLN+TIBXLN (1194 mm) + 26.79″
67.2″ +/−	4.0″	(prediction interval 63.2 to 71.2″);	formula is: 0.040* FEMXLN+FIBXLN+ULNXLN (1084 mm) + 23.50″
67.2″ +/−	4.0″	(prediction interval 63.2 to 71.2″);	formula is: 0.040* FEMXLN+RADXLN+TIBXLN (1072 mm) + 24.70″
67.2″ +/−	4.0″	(prediction interval 63.2 to 71.2″);	formula is: 0.040* FEMXLN+TIBXLN+ULNXLN (1089 mm) + 23.85″
67.2″ +/−	4.0″	(prediction interval 63.2 to 71.2″);	formula is: 0.040* FEMXLN+FIBXLN+RADXLN (1067 mm) + 24.52″
67.5″ +/−	4.0″	(prediction interval 63.5 to 71.5″);	formula is: 0.037* FEMXLN+HUMXLN+TIBXLN (1158 mm) + 24.63″
67.5″ +/−	4.0″	(prediction interval 63.5 to 71.5″);	formula is: 0.037* FEMXLN+FIBXLN+HUMXLN (1153 mm) + 24.42″
67.6″ +/−	4.0″	(prediction interval 63.5 to 71.6″);	formula is: 0.037* FIBXLN+HUMXLN+TIBXLN (1073 mm) + 27.68″

From Fordisc 3.1 (Jantz and Ousley, 2005)

Non-limb bones have also been used to estimate stature. In most cases, this relationship to stature is not as strong, resulting in estimates with greater error than those based on complete skeletons or limb bones. Elements studied have included the calcaneus and talus (Holland, 1995), metatarsals (Byers et al., 1989), metacarpals (Musgrave and Harneja, 1978; Meadows and Jantz, 1992), vertebral segments (Jason and Taylor, 1995), and sacral and coccygeal vertebrae (Pelin et al., 2005). Because of the higher error associated with these methods, it is generally not considered advisable to use them unless there are no limb bones available for measurement.

In some cases, non-skeletal material associated with forensic anthropological cases may also be used to estimate stature. Relationships have been noted, for example,

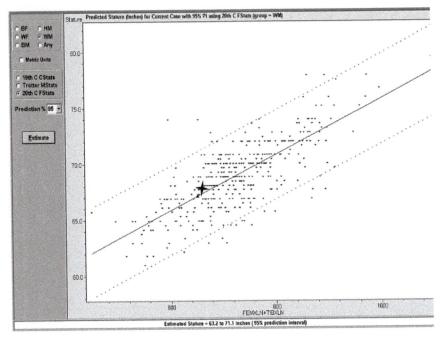

FIGURE 11.5 Graphic representation of Fordisc stature results

From Fordisc 3.1 (Jantz and Ousley, 2005)

Table 11.4 Stature estimation from foot length		
	Stature equation	**70% CI**
Males	3.447 × (foot length) + 82.206	±5.0
Females	3.614 × (foot length) + 75.065	±4.9
All in cm *Data from Giles and Vallandingham, 1991*		

between stature and fleshed body segments (Adams and Herrmann, 2009). Shoes associated with skeletal remains or intact feet or footprints may also be used to estimate stature (Giles and Vallandigham, 1991; Robbins, 1986; Bodziak, 2000) (see Table 11.4).

11.4 Other considerations in stature estimation

The estimation of stature of subadults is possible, though these estimations should be performed with caution. Stature estimation formulae for subadults have been developed (Feldesman, 1992; Ruff, 2007), but research in this area is not nearly as extensive as that relating to adult stature. Estimating stature of subadults is also usually of limited utility because children grow very quickly and therefore reported statures are quickly out of date. In addition, some subadult age estimation methods are based on long bone lengths, so estimating stature from these same lengths may not contribute additionally to limiting the pool of potential matches. If stature estimates are provided for children and compared to potential matches for identification, the fact that the reported stature may be significantly shorter than the estimated stature should not form the basis for exclusion without further consideration, and the elapsed time between when the reported stature was measured and when the individual went missing should be considered. Much more research is needed before accurate stature estimation methods are available for subadults of different ages.

Stature tends to decrease with advancing adult age, usually a result of loss or compression of cartilage (especially the intervertebral discs), or fractures of the vertebral centra, which may be influenced by **osteoporosis**. Loss of disc height due to compression of cartilage or fractures of vertebral centra may result in significant curvature of the upper back, known as **kyphosis** of the spine. Methods for adjusting stature estimates based on advanced adult age have been proposed (Trotter and Gleser, 1951; Trotter, 1970; Galloway, 1988; Giles, 1991), but their application is problematic for various reasons (Scientific Working Group for Forensic Anthropology [SWGANTH], 2012). The correlation between age and decreased stature is not linear and varies between individuals, and therefore considerable error is introduced when attempting to apply age-related corrections. Moreover, it usually is not known whether the individual's reported stature takes this reduction of height into account.

There are numerous issues involved with the concepts of "antemortem stature" and "known stature" since they can be derived in various ways which may or may not represent an individual's true height (or **biological stature**). Known statures may be based on cadaver length (**cadaveric stature**) which may have error associated with differing measurement techniques. Antemortem information is not always in the form of a recent, measured height. Often, the antemortem stature information is retrieved from a legal document such as a driver's license where the indicated stature is self-reported, or may be based on the remembrance of family members or friends (all referred to as **reported stature**). This stature *may* be based on a recent measured height, but may only approximate the individual's actual stature, especially due to biases in self-reported data. For example, both men and women tend to over-report their statures on driver's licenses, and taller individuals tend to report their stature with greater accuracy than shorter individuals (Ousley, 1995; Willey and Falsetti, 1991; Giles and Hutchinson, 1991). When stature estimation methods are based on the relationship between estimated stature and reported stature, it is referred to as **forensic stature**. Such estimates are often the most accurate, but prediction intervals are typically wider to account for biases in reported stature.

In addition, even when stature is accurately measured, there is variation within an individual's stature depending on how it is measured (with or without shoes, for example) and when (including different times of the day). **Circadian** or **diurnal** variation in stature (or change in stature throughout the day) has been widely noted. Stature tends to be greater in the morning, decreasing slightly in the first few upright hours of the day as a result of compression of intervertebral discs in the spinal column. The extent of this effect appears to be greater in children than adults (Krishan et al., 2009).

Pathological conditions and other skeletal anomalies (see Chapter 12) may also affect stature estimates, either by directly affecting the length of the bone(s) of interest, or by affecting the relationship between bones and total stature (such as those that might affect body proportions). In these cases, stature estimates should be reported with a caveat that the estimation is problematic, or perhaps avoided altogether.

Regardless of the stature estimation method employed, it should be used in accordance with the study in which it is described, or deviations should be appropriately explained. For example, the bones must be measured in exactly the same manner as described in the method used – there are not universally applied "standard" measurements, and not all researchers measure bones the same way in their studies. If the original study utilized dry bones, this should be taken into consideration if the case at hand involves fresh remains; the use of fresh/wet bones may affect the accuracy of that method since bones shrink somewhat when dry (see Chapter 7). The method by which the "known" height was determined should also be considered (for example, cadaveric or reported). Finally, each stature estimation method is based on a specific set of parameters and associated with a specific prediction interval. This means that it is inappropriate to average multiple stature estimates for a single individual using the results of different methods.

11.5 Case study – stature estimation

In the summer of 2008, human remains were discovered in a wooded area of northern California (see Figure 11.6). The estimated biological profile suggested that the decedent was an adult male of European ancestry, approximately 50 to 80 years of age. Although the remains were heavily scavenged by carnivores, several postcranial elements were complete and available for measurements that could be used in stature estimation. Osteometric data was collected on the left femur, tibia, fibula, humerus, radius, ulna, scapula, and clavicle. These measurements were entered into Fordisc and a stature estimate was computed using formulae derived for 20th-century White males. Using all available elements, several stature estimates were generated. The top five are shown in Table 11.5. In Fordisc, the user can rank the formulae based on the standard error (with the smallest SE ranked first). As is shown in Table 11.5, the best stature estimate is based on the maximum length of the clavicle, femur, and tibia. This combination of measurements used in the regression formula generated a stature estimate of 67 inches ± 3.3 inches. The standard error value (3.3 inches) encompasses uncertainty in the prediction at a 95% confidence level. In this particular case, the 95% interval encompasses a minimum stature of 63.7 inches and a maximum stature of 70.3 inches (or about 5 feet, 4 inches to 5 feet, 10 inches).

In this case, the biological profile closely matched an individual in the missing persons file, which helped to narrow down the pool of missing persons for making a personal identification. The decedent was identified as a 70-year-old White male with a living stature of 68 inches (5 feet, 8 inches).

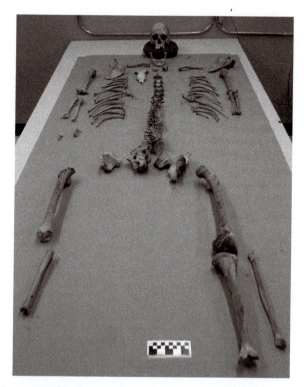

FIGURE 11.6 Human remains discovered in a wooded area of California

Table 11.5 The five stature estimates computed in Fordisc for this case with the smallest standard error

Stature	SE	P.I.	Regression formulae
67.0″ +/–	3.3″	(range 63.7 to 70.2″):	0.050 (CLAXLN+FEMXLN+TIBXLN(970 mm)) + 18.56″
67.1″ +/–	3.3″	(range 63.7 to 70.4″):	0.050 (CLAXLN+FEMBLN+TIBXLN(969 mm)) + 18.82″
66.7″ +/–	3.3″	(range 63.3 to 70.0″):	0.049 (FEMXLN+SCAPHT+TIBXLN(968 mm)) + 19.31″
67.1″ +/–	3.4″	(range 63.7 to 70.4″):	0.059 (FEMXLN+INNOHT+RADXLN(909 mm)) + 13.00″
66.9″ +/–	3.4″	(range 63.6 to 70.3″):	0.043 (FEMXLN+RADXLN+TIBXLN(1056 mm)) + 22.02″

11.6 **Summary**

- Stature estimations from skeletal remains are possible because there is a relationship between bone lengths and height.
- Stature is most accurately measured using full skeleton methods, which utilize measurements of all bones that contribute to stature. An advantage of these methods is that they can be applied to any skeleton, regardless of sex or ancestry. A disadvantage is that these methods require a mostly complete skeleton.
- Stature is most often estimated using regression methods, which utilize the mathematical relationship (correlation) between bone lengths and stature using regression formulae. An advantage of these methods is that a complete skeleton is not required. A disadvantage is that sex- and ancestry-specific formulae should be used, so these parameters are best known prior to stature estimation in order to reduce error.
- Stature may be estimated using incomplete bones and non-long bones, but these methods have considerably higher error than intact long bones.
- Stature estimations can be carried out manually or using software packages such as Fordisc.
- Estimating stature of juveniles from skeletal material is generally considered unadvisable. Known statures of juveniles are quickly out of date, and there are few studies on the estimation of stature from juvenile remains.
- "Known" stature can refer to many things which may not necessarily represent the true biological height.
- Self-reported statures may be subject to bias and should be taken into consideration when comparing indicated antemortem statures to forensic estimates.

11.7 **Test yourself**

- Assuming you have an incomplete skeleton, what is the most accurate method for estimating the individual's stature? What are some advantages and disadvantages of the method you selected?
- A European male adult skeleton is found at a construction site, associated with historic coffin hardware dating to the late 1800s. What considerations would you need to make in selecting the most appropriate stature estimation formula?
- Using the formulae provided in Table 11.2, calculate the stature of an African ancestry female with a maximum fibula length of 330 mm.
- Look at the height reported on your driver's license and then measure your current height and compare the two. What is the discrepancy (if any), and what might account for this difference?
- What does it mean if a stature estimate has a 90% prediction interval of 5 feet, 5 inches to 5 feet, 10 inches? How often would you expect the individual's actual stature **not** to fall within this prediction interval?
- List the following skeletal elements in order of most accurate to least accurate for estimating stature: complete left femur, complete right humerus, complete calcaneus, fragmentary right femur, and complete left innominate.

Definitions

Cadaveric stature Measured length of a cadaver

Circadian Relating to 24-hour periodicity; recurring on a 24-hour cycle

Correlation The relationship between two variables

Diurnal Of or relating to the daytime

Forensic stature Stature estimated from skeletal remains, specifically as it relates to reported stature

Full skeleton stature estimation methods (or anatomical methods) Methods of estimating stature that involve summing the heights of all bones that contribute to stature along with a correction factor for soft tissue

Kyphosis A condition of over-curvature of the thoracic vertebrae, sometimes associated with arthritis or osteoporosis in older adult individuals and may also result from trauma or developmental disorders

Osteoporosis A medical condition involving the net loss of bone density, often associated with advanced age

Regression stature estimation methods (or mathematical methods) Methods of estimating stature that involve taking bone measurements and inserting them into regression formulae that represent the mathematical relationship between that measurement and height for a given population

Reported stature A stature that is reported by the individual or a family member or friend and is not necessarily measured

Secular change A change in the average pattern of growth or development of a population over time

Stature (or biological stature) An individual's true natural (living) height in an upright position

Temporal cohort A group of people that were alive or existed during the same time period

References

Adams, B.J., Herrmann, N.P., 2009. Estimation of living stature from selected anthropomorphic (soft tissue) measurements: Applications for forensic anthropology. J. Forensic Sci. 54 (4), 753–760.

Bodziak, W.J., 2000. Footwear impression evidence: detection, recovery, and examination, second ed. CRC Press, Boca Raton.

Buikstra, J.E., Ubelaker, D.H., 1994. Standards for data collection from human skeletal remains. Archaeological Survey Research Seminar Series 44, Fayetteville.

Byers, S.N., Churchill, S., Curran, B., 1989. Determination of stature from metacarpals. Am. J. Phys. Anthropol. 79, 275–279.

Feldesman, M.R., 1992. Femur/stature ratio and estimates of stature in children. Am. J. Phys. Anthropol. 87 (4), 447–459.

Fully, G., 1956. Un Nouvelle Methode de determination de la taille. Annales de Medecine Legale 35, 266–273.

Fully, G., Pineau, H., 1960. Determination de la stature au moyen de squelette. Annales de Medecine Legale 40, 145–154.

Galloway, A., 1988. Estimating actual height in the older individual. J. Forensic Sci. 33, 126–136.

Giles, E., 1991. Corrections for age in estimating older adults' stature from long bones. J. Forensic Sci. 36, 898–901.

Giles, E., Hutchinson, D.L., 1991. Stature- and age-related bias in self-reported stature. J. Forensic Sci. 36, 765–780.

Giles, E., Vallandingham, P.H., 1991. Height estimation from foot and shoeprint length. J. Forensic Sci. 36 (4), 1134–1151.

Holland, T.D., 1992. Estimation of adult stature from fragmentary tibias. J. Forensic Sci. 37 (5), 1223–1229.

Holland, T.D., 1995. Estimation of adult stature from the calcaneus and talus. Am. J. Phys. Anthropol. 96 (3), 315–320.

Jantz, R.L., Ousley, S.D., 2005. Fordisc 3.0 Personal computer forensic discriminant functions. The University of Tennessee, Knoxville.

Jantz, R.L., Hunt, D.R., Meadows, L., 1995. The measure and mismeasure of the tibia: Implications for stature estimation. J. Forensic Sci. 40, 758–761.

Jason, D.R., Taylor, K., 1995. Estimation of stature from the length of the cervical, thoracic, and lumbar segments of the spine in American whites and blacks. J. Forensic Sci. 40 (1), 59–62.

Konigsberg, L.W., Hens, S.M., Jantz, L.M., Jungers, W.L., 1998. Stature estimation and calibration: Baysean and maximum likelihood perspectives in physical anthropology. Yrbk. Phys. Anthropol. (Suppl. 27), 65–92.

Krishan, K., Sidhu, M.C., Kanchan, T., Menezes, R.G., Sen, J., 2009. Diurnal variation in stature – is it more in children or adults? Biosci. Hypotheses 2 (3), 174–175.

Krogman, W.M., 1962. The Human Skeleton in Forensic Medicine. Charles C Thomas, Springfield.

Lundy, J.K., 1988a. A report on the use of Fully's anatomical method to estimate stature in military skeletal remains. J. Forensic Sci. 33 (2), 534–539.

Lundy, J.K., 1988b. Sacralization of a sixth lumbar vertebra and its effect upon the estimation of living stature. J. Forensic Sci. 33 (4), 1045–1049.

Meadows, L., Jantz, R.L., 1992. Estimation of stature from metacarpal lengths. J. Forensic Sci. 37 (1), 147–154.

Meadows, L., Jantz, R.L., 1995. Allometric secular change in the long bones from the 1800s to the present. J. Forensic Sci. 37, 147–154.

Moore-Jansen, P.M., Ousley, S.D., Jantz, R.L., 1994. Data collection procedures for forensic skeletal material. The University of Tennessee, Knoxville.

Musgrave, J.H., Harneja, N.K., 1978. The estimation of adult stature from metacarpal bone length. Am. J. Phys. Anthropol. 8 (1), 113–119.

Ousley, S., 1995. Should we estimate biological or forensic stature? J. Forensic. Sci. 40, 768–773.

Ousley, S.D., Jantz, R.L., 1998. The Forensic Data Bank: Documenting skeletal trends in the United States. In: Reichs, K.J. (Ed.), Forensic osteology: Advances in the identification of human remains, second ed. Charles C. Thomas, Springfield, pp. 441–458.

Pelin, C., Duyar, I., Kayahan, E.M., Zagyapan, R., Agildere, A.M., Erar, A., 2005. Body height estimation based on dimensions of sacral and coccygeal vertebrae. J. Forensic Sci. 50 (2), 294–297.

Raxter, M.H., Ruff, C.B., 2010. The effect of vertebral numerical variation on anatomical stature estimates. J. Forensic Sci. 55, 464–466.

Raxter, M.H., Auerbach, B.M., Ruff, C.B., 2006. Revision of the Fully technique for estimating statures. Am. J. Phys. Anthropol. 130, 374–384.

Robbins, L.M., 1986. Estimating height and weight from size of footprints. J. Forensic Sci. 31, 79–98.

Ruff, C., 2007. Body size prediction from juvenile skeletal remains. Am. J. Phys. Anthropol. 133 (1), 698–716.

Scientific Working Group for Forensic Anthropology, 2012. Stature Estimation (Revision 1). Retrieved from http://www.swganth.org.

Simmons, T., Jantz, R.L., Bass, W.M., 1990. Stature estimation from fragmentary femora: A revision of the Steele method. J. Forensic Sci. 35 (3), 628–636.

Steele, D.G., 1970. Estimation of stature from fragments of long limb bones. In: Stewart, T.D. (Ed.), Personal Identification in Mass Disasters. National Museum of Natural History. Smithsonian Institution, Washington, DC, pp. 85–97.

Stewart, T.D., 1979. Essentials of Forensic Anthropology. Charles C Thomas, Springfield.

Trotter, M., 1970. Estimation of stature from intact long bones. In: Stewart, T.D. (Ed.), Personal Identification in Mass Disasters. National Museum of Natural History. Smithsonian Institution, Washington, DC, pp. 71–83.

Trotter, M., Gleser, G.C., 1951. The effect of aging on stature. Am. J. Phys. Anthropol. 9, 311–324.

Trotter, M., Gleser, G.C., 1952. Estimation of stature from long bones of American Whites and Negroes. Am. J. Phys. Anthropol. 10, 463–514.

Willey, P., 2009. Stature estimation. In: Blau, S., Ubelaker, D.H. (Eds.), Handbook of Forensic Anthropology and Archaeology. Left Coast Press, Walnut Creek, pp. 236–245.

Willey, P., Falsetti, T., 1991. Inaccuracy of height information on driver's licenses. J. Forensic Sci. 36 (3), 813–819.

Wright, L.E., Vasquez, M.A., 2003. Estimating the length of incomplete long bones: forensic standards from Guatemala. Am. J. Phys. Anthropol. 120, 233–251.

Individual Skeletal Variation

12

12.1 Principles of skeletal variation

In Chapter 2, normal skeletal growth and development and normal anatomical features of bones and teeth were reviewed. Chapters 8–10 discussed how skeletal morphology can vary between the sexes, across geographic groups, and throughout an individual's life. Skeletal variation also exists at the individual level. As a result of different genetic and environmental influences, an individual's skeleton contains **idiosyncrasies** or individual morphological variations. These variants may be **congenital**, developmental, degenerative, or may result from disease processes or trauma. Variations in skeletal morphology can provide valuable information to forensic anthropologists, particularly for personal identification (Chapter 14). Individual variants can reveal features of an individual's health, lifestyle, or **life history,** thereby helping to further narrow the pool of potential matches. Moreover, individual variants may be rare enough to be useful for personal identification comparisons, and certain conditions (such as those requiring medical treatment) increase the chance that a record may be available that can be used for comparison. Certain skeletal variants or conditions, such as diseases or injuries that may have been fatal, may also provide information relevant to circumstances surrounding death.

It is also important for forensic anthropologists to be familiar with possible skeletal morphological variants so that they are not confused with trauma or taphonomic alterations (Chapter 13). All of the variants discussed in this chapter refer to those that result from *in vivo* processes, or those that occurred while an individual was living. Some conditions and skeletal alterations that were present during life could be mistaken for trauma, but traumas are typically associated with fractures and recently exposed internal bone surfaces, whereas individual variants reviewed in this chapter will typically have a different appearance and bone quality. A working knowledge of these individual variants combined with a conservative analytical approach should prevent or minimize any confusion of these conditions with trauma or taphonomic alterations.

Individual skeletal variations typically fall into one of four categories:

(1) Normal anatomical variation,
(2) Skeletal **anomalies**,
(3) Pathological conditions, and
(4) Skeletal changes related to repetitive activity.

Forensic Anthropology. http://dx.doi.org/10.1016/B978-0-12-418671-2.00012-4

The final conclusion as to which variant or condition is present on skeletal remains is ideally achieved through a process called **differential diagnosis**. Differential diagnosis is a deductive process of elimination used to narrow down and identify a likely condition or a small number of possibilities that cannot be excluded.

A differential diagnosis begins with a description of the variant including its location (i.e., the name of the bone or bones involved), and distribution (i.e., how much and which part or parts of the bone or bones is affected). The diagnosis then proceeds by ruling out conditions that are inconsistent with the observations, and may involve comparison with published clinical and research literature or exemplars (such as photographs, casts, or documented pathological specimens). If the condition is present on a paired bone or tooth, the suspected variant can also be compared to its normal **antimere** (the same bone or tooth from the other side) as a reference, which may help in confirming the presence or extent of the condition.

Differential diagnosis of a particular skeletal variant or condition is not always possible. In many cases, specialized methods such as radiography, microscopy, and histology may be useful. When a differential diagnosis cannot be made, a detailed description of the lesion or variant including its pattern and distribution is recommended (Scientific Working Group for Forensic Anthropology [SWGANTH], 2012). In any case, the analysis of skeletal variants should be amply supplemented with notes, diagrams, photos, etc., and all reasonable interpretations should be presented.

12.2 Normal skeletal variation

Normal skeletal variation refers to the range of morphological expression commonly observed in various skeletal regions. Examples of normal variation include differences in paranasal sinus shapes, cranial suture patterns, trabecular bone pattern, and external bone contours. These features and characteristics are all present in normal bone anatomy, but show small but significant differences between different people. Because these features are present in almost everyone and because they tend to show so much individual variation, they are often studied for their potential to facilitate personal identification (see Chapter 14).

Paranasal sinus shape is one example of a normal anatomical variant, with the frontal sinus being the most thoroughly studied in terms of its individual variation (e.g., Schuller, 1921; Asherson, 1965; Christensen, 2005a,b). To a lesser extent, the individual variation in maxillary sinuses has also been studied, particularly in relation to uses in personal identification (Soler, 2011). Because they are located within the cranial bones, the shapes of the sinuses are usually only visible radiographically. The examination of radiographs allows visualization of the dimensions, placement, and outline shape of the sinuses. Particularly in an anterior/posterior view, the variations in frontal sinus shape are quite apparent (Figure 12.1). Frontal sinuses usually appear as two irregularly shaped, asymmetric cavities that project a variable distance into the frontal bone. Although some changes in adulthood have been noted (due to, for example, trauma, disease, or bone thinning with age), they typically complete growth by around

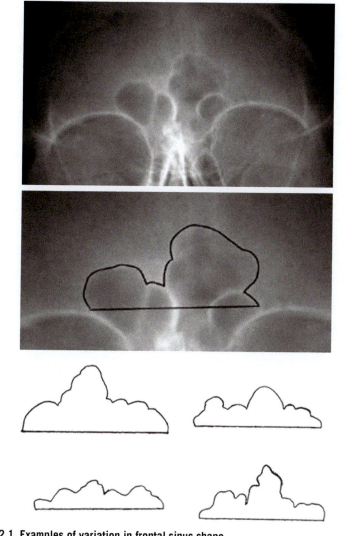

FIGURE 12.1 Examples of variation in frontal sinus shape

(From Christensen, 2003)

age 20, after which their shape is stable. The variation in frontal sinus shape has been attributed to various factors including craniofacial configuration, hormonal factors, biomechanical factors, genetics, ambient air pressure, or unknown factors. It has been hypothesized that each individual's frontal sinus shape is as unique as a fingerprint.

Recall that the bones of the cranium join together along cranial sutures. During the growth process, the margins of the bones of the cranium develop projections and recesses that eventually interlock with each other, resulting in suture lines that are

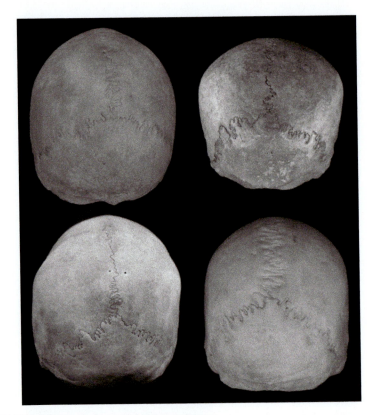

FIGURE 12.2 Differences in cranial suture patterns

jagged and seam-like on the ectocranial surface (remaining relatively straight and less remarkable on the endocranial surface). Because the growth of cranial bones is controlled largely by external stimuli (particularly neurocranial growth), cranial suture patterns are highly variable, and the inherent complexity of these projections and recesses (which are largely random) results in a nearly infinite number of possible patterns (Figure 12.2). The exact paths of the lines, therefore, vary from person to person and have been shown to be highly individualistic with no two crania having an identical pattern; in fact, bilateral suture patterns within the same individual are also different (Sekharan, 1985). It is also possible to quantify the variation in these patterns by examining the location, length, and slope of the lines of a suture's components (Rogers and Allard, 2004).

Bone's internal trabecular structure, which is visible radiographically, is also highly variable and said to be unique to each individual (Mann, 1998; Kahana et al., 1998). Normal internal bone structures have a nearly unlimited number of combinations of radiographically discernible features that show variability, including radiolucent vessel foramina and radiodense lines (Figure 12.3). Although there is a normal overall pattern to bone's external shape and contours, individual variation in these

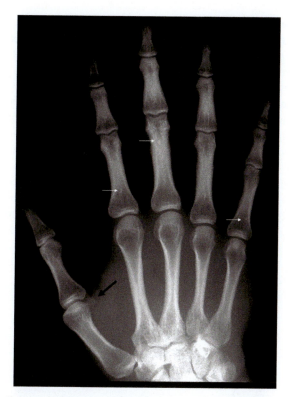

FIGURE 12.3 Individual variants of the hand bones (white arrows) and sesamoid bone (black arrow)

surfaces has also been demonstrated. Sites studied include the clavicle and cervical spine (Stephan et al., 2011), thoracic and lumbar vertebrae (Watamaniuk and Rogers, 2010; Valenzuela, 1997), and the hyoid (Cornelison et al., 2002). Some studies have involved the examination of individual variation in multiple features such as external morphology/contour as well as trabecular pattern (e.g., Koot et al., 2005).

12.3 Anomalies

Anomalies are characteristics that are considered deviations from normal skeletal anatomy, though they may not necessarily be rare or unique. Anomalies are a product of the interaction of genetic signals and **epigenetic** interference (non-genetic factors that affect gene expression) during specific developmental events, resulting in deviations from the normal outcome (Barnes, 2012). Anomalies may be caused by disturbances from genetic mutations, maternal conditions, exposure to detrimental environmental conditions, or nutritional disorders during a particular developmental event (Barnes, 2012). These variants are also sometimes called non-metric (i.e., qualitative) or epigenetic variants. Examples of skeletal anomalies include **accessory** or **supernumerary** (extra, or more than the normal number) bones or teeth, accessory foramina, and non-fusion anomalies. Note that many accessory foramina and some accessory bones are technically the result of non-fusion anomalies, but certain cases will be addressed here as separate types of anomalies. An accessory facet occurs when two bones articulate in a location in addition to their normal articulation.

Accessory bones can occur in many parts of the skeleton. Examples of more commonly encountered accessory bones include having extra vertebrae, ribs, sesamoid bones, and cranial vault bones. Other "extra" bones that are technically unfused portions of parent bones will be addressed with non-fusion anomalies. Supernumerary vertebrae typically appear as transitional vertebrae at the thoracicolumbar, lumbosacral, or sacrococcygeal borders, with extra vertebrae at the cervical-thoracic border being extremely rare (Barnes, 2012). When an extra vertebra is located in the thoracic region, it is typically also associated with extra ribs. In a forensic context, it may be difficult to detect the presence of a supernumerary vertebra or ribs unless the skeleton (or at least the thorax) is relatively complete. Rather than complete extra vertebrae, sometimes partial vertebrae, or **hemivertebrae,** are present, often resulting in misalignment of the spine (Figure 12.4). Sometimes a vertebra takes on characteristics of

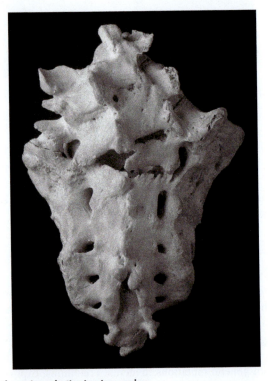

FIGURE 12.4 Hemivertebrae in the lumbar region

(Photo by Rebecca Meeusen; specimen courtesy of the National Museum of Natural History)

another segment of the spine, a phenomenon called a **vertebral shift**. For example, a 12th thoracic vertebrae may have lumbar-like characteristics (articular facets, body shape, etc.), sometimes even resulting in the fusion of the 12th rib pair, which often appear as rudimentary structures (Barnes, 1994) (Figure 12.5).

Sesamoid bones are bones that are located within tendons where they pass over joints. The patella and the pisiform are sesamoid bones which are part of normal skeletal anatomy, but sesamoid bones can also be commonly found in other parts of the hand (particularly around the distal first metacarpal) (Figure 12.3) and the foot (often at the junction of the first metatarsal and the first proximal pedal phalanx). The number of sesamoid bones in these regions typically varies between zero and two.

Extra bones also occur in cases of accessory appendages. **Polydactyly** (or polydactylism), for example, is a condition of having extra fingers or toes. It is considered the most common congenital digital anomaly of the hand and foot, and can occur either as part of a syndrome or in isolation (Mumoli et al., 2008). Although rarely a complete and functioning digit, accessory fingers and toes often do contain bones which may occur with or without joints. They most commonly occur on the ulnar (little finger) side of the hand, but can also occur on the radial (thumb) side. Like accessory vertebrae, the identification of polydactyly in skeletonized forensic cases may be difficult unless the remains are complete, although in some cases it can be recognized by the shape of the adjacent metacarpal or metatarsal which may be broadened or bifurcated.

Another common location for accessory bones is along cranial sutures, where they are called **extrasutural bones**. These tend to occur most often along the lambdoidal suture (where they are also called *Wormian bones*), but can be found along any suture of the cranium and are typically small and irregular in appearance (Figure 12.6). Certain configurations occur regularly and have been studied more often including Inca bones, or *os incae* (so named because they were first studied in Peruvian crania), defined as a division of the squamous portion of the occipital bone (Hanihara and Ishida, 2001). Inca bones typically appear as a single, large, triangular **ossicle**, but can vary in their divisions and number of extra ossicles.

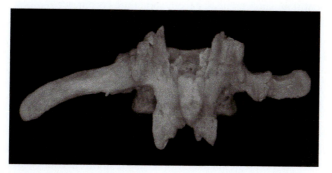

FIGURE 12.5 Vertebral shift – lumbar vertebra with fused rudimentary ribs

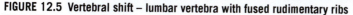

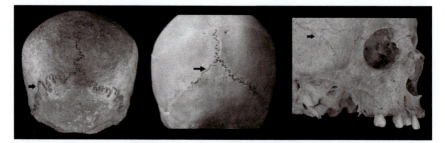

FIGURE 12.6 Extrasutural bones in the lambdoidal suture, also known as a Wormian bone (left), at lambda, or Inca bone (center), and at the landmark pterion, also known as an epipteric bone (right)

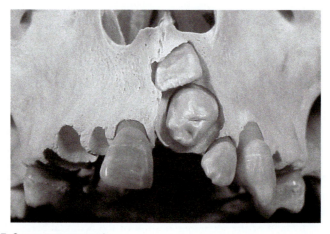

FIGURE 12.7 Supernumerary teeth

(From Christensen and Anderson, 2013)

In the dentition, supernumerary teeth sometimes occur, a condition referred to as **hyperdontia** (Figure 12.7). Extra teeth can occur anywhere within the oral cavity, but are most common in the anterior maxillary dentition, and more often found in permanent than primary dentition (Garvey et al., 1999). They typically result from anomalies in dental development and although they can be asymptomatic, they often lead to clinical problems such as failure of eruption, displacement, crowding, and pathology (Garvey et al., 1999).

Accessory foramina (or extra holes in bone cortices where they typically would not be found) are seen in a number of locations throughout the skeleton including the cranium, long bones, and sternum. They are commonly the result of non-fusion or incomplete fusion. Perforations in bone can also result from trauma (such as gunshot wounds) and taphonomic agents (such as carnivore scavenging or weathering). They

FIGURE 12.8 Septal aperture in a distal humerus

(Photo by Rebecca Meeusen; specimen courtesy of the National Museum of Natural History)

should therefore always be assessed carefully to differentiate skeletal anomalies or conditions from those that result from other events or processes.

When there is incomplete ossification of the bony septum that separates the olecranon fossa from the coranoid fossa of the distal humerus, a **septal aperture** (sometimes also called a *supratrochlear foramen*) may be present (Figure 12.8). This trait tends to occur more frequently in females, more often on the left side, and may be associated with joint hypermobility (Mays, 2008; Koyun, 2011; Ndou, 2012). Although a septal aperture is expressed as an *in vivo* condition, care should be exercised when examining dry bones to ensure that a perforation in this region of typically thin bone did not result from taphonomic damage (Finnegan, 1978).

Occasionally a hole is seen in the sternum, called a **sternal foramen** (Figure 12.9). The sternum ossifies from a number of ossification centers, and a sternal foramen can result from incomplete union of any number of the sternabrae segments. It is usually seen in the inferior sternal body, but can also occur in the xiphoid process.

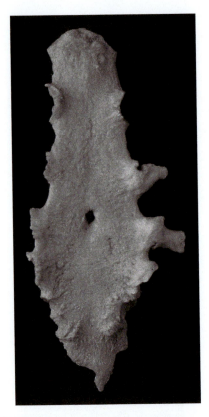

FIGURE 12.9 Sternal foramen

(Photo by Rebecca Meeusen; specimen courtesy of the National Museum of Natural History)

Although potentially mistaken for trauma (such as a gunshot wound) at first glance, careful inspection of a sternal aperture will reveal well-organized, mature bone and an absence of fractures around the margins.

Non-fusion anomalies result from a failure of union between two ossification centers, and can occur in virtually any part of the skeleton. The result can be a cleft or perforation in the bone, or accessory bone portions. They may simply be developmental anomalies, but may also be linked to pathological conditions including trauma. In cases where non-fusion may result in accessory bones, it is especially important that these regions are carefully assessed to differentiate them from traumas. In forensic contexts, the failure to recover these (typically small) unfused portions can make the diagnosis particularly challenging.

Cleft neural arch occurs when the two sides of the neural arch of the vertebra fail to unite (Figure 12.10). It typically affects only one or sometimes two presacral vertebrae, and can range in appearance from a slight bifurcation of the vertebral laminae to cleft laminae with or without the spinous process, and can even involve complete aplasia of one-half of the neural arch (Barnes, 2012). **Spina bifida**, a defect

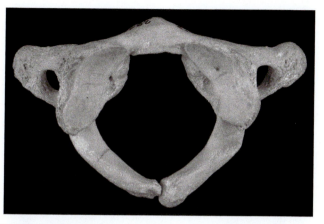

FIGURE 12.10 Cleft neural arch of C1

(Image courtesy of the National Museum of Health and Medicine)

FIGURE 12.11 Spina bifida occulta

(Photo by Rebecca Meeusen; specimen courtesy of the National Museum of Natural History)

of the developing spinal cord, also disrupts neural arch development, but can be distinguished from a cleft neural arch by its widened vertebral canal, distorted pedicles, and involvement of more than two presacral vertebrae (Barnes, 2012). *Spina bifida occulta* is a less severe, often asymptomatic, form of spina bifida (Figure 12.11).

The scapula has a number of secondary ossification centers which can fail to unite, resulting in additional ossicles. The distal end of the acromion process is a

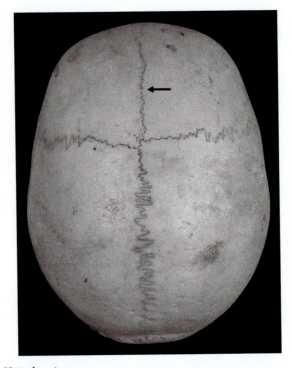

FIGURE 12.12 Metopic suture

(Image courtesy of the National Museum of Health and Medicine)

common location, resulting in a condition called **os acromiale**. A **bipartite patella**, or segmented patella, occurs when the ossification centers of the patella fail to coalesce. It usually appears as a notch in the superolateral border of the patella. The smaller, separated ossicle may eventually partially unite, may be connected only by fibrocartilage, or may fail to ossify at all.

Another type of non-fusion anomaly occurs in the cranium when parts of the cranial bones fail to coalesce prior to ossification, resulting in two ossification centers for the bone. While extra sutures can arise in the parietals or occipital, the most commonly observed location is the frontal bone. In normal growth and development, the frontal bone begins as two halves which unite along the midline. This union normally occurs by around age four (Scheuer and Black, 2000), but occasionally the two halves fail to unite, resulting in a condition called **metopism**, or the retention of a metopic suture (Figure 12.12). The suture typically has the appearance of the other normal sutures of the cranium. This feature also tends to show population differences, being more commonly seen in those of European ancestry. Facial clefts such as cleft palate are also non-fusion anomalies and tend to result in significant facial deformities.

Another type of non-union anomaly is a **pseudarthrosis**, or "false joint," which is created when two fractured portions of a bone fail to reunite. It can result from repeated disruption of the fracture callus which impedes mineralization (Ortner, 2003). When a fracture occurs in infancy and progresses to non-union, it is referred

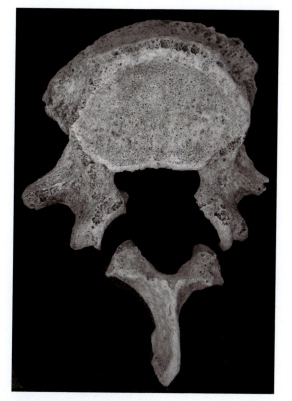

FIGURE 12.13 Spondylolysis of L5 with nonunion

to as a congenital or infantile pseudarthrosis. While congenital pseudarthrosis can occur in any long bone in the body, it is most frequently seen in the tibia, is typically unilateral, and will usually also involve the fibula of the same limb. It may be associated with disease, hereditary, or mechanical factors (Hefti et al., 2000).

Another example of a common non-union anomaly at a fracture site is **spondylolysis**, also known as *pars defect*. In this condition, the posterior portion of the neural arch is separated from the rest of the vertebra at the pars interarticularis (Figure 12.13). Although sometimes attributed to a congenital defect, it most often results from a fatigue fracture from low-grade stress in the lower back (Ortner, 2003). While it has been known to occur in any thoracic or lumbar vertebra, it is most common in the lower lumbar region, particularly at L5.

12.4 Pathological conditions

Pathology refers to the study of **disease**, and a **pathological condition** is the abnormal anatomy which is a manifestation of a disease process. These disease processes may be the result of infection, injury, or a disorder. Not all diseases affect the skeleton, of course, but when they do, they manifest as localized bony alterations that are

BOX 12.1 OSTEOGENESIS IMPERFECTA (OI)

Osteogenesis imperfecta (or OI) is the name for a group of pathological conditions, all of which result in osteoporosis and skeletal and dental fragility (Ortner, 2003; Waldron, 2009). The condition is uncommon, affecting approximately one in 35,000. Individuals with OI commonly suffer from skeletal fractures due to the fragile nature of their bones. Type I OI is the most common variant and predominately affects periosteal bone formation. Individuals with Type I OI often exhibit thin cancellous bone and delayed cortical remodeling. Type II OI is a more severe variant where the bones are so fragile that death often occurs during birth or childhood.

In some cases of alleged child abuse, defense attorneys have argued that the child's fractures were due to an undiagnosed form of OI rather than abuse. The simplest way to differentiate OI from trauma is through the examination of the bone histologically and evaluating the quality of the bone. The images shown below feature an infant skeleton recovered from a human rights context in Guatemala. Examination of the numerous healed long bone fractures is consistent with a diagnosis of OI.

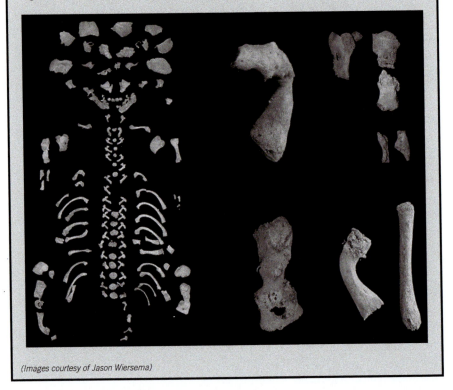

(Images courtesy of Jason Wiersema)

called **lesions**. Pathological lesions on bone may be proliferative, lytic, or deformative (Ortner, 2003). **Proliferative** (or osteoproliferative) **lesions** are those that are characterized by excess deposition of bone, while **lytic** (or osteolytic) **lesions** involve a loss of bone. **Deformative lesions** involve changes in overall bone shape.

As with other skeletal variants, pathological conditions and lesions must be examined carefully to distinguish them from other types of skeletal conditions that may be the result of traumatic or taphonomic processes (Box 12.1). Proliferative lesions

FIGURE 12.14 Proliferative lesion of the proximal tibia and fibula

(Photo by Rebecca Meeusen; specimen courtesy of the National Museum of Natural History)

are typically not confused with possible taphonomic alterations; naturally, in order to produce additional bone, the individual must have been alive. Lytic lesions, on the other hand, may require closer examination. Pathological processes and taphonomic processes can both result in destruction of bone, so caution should be exercised in distinguishing lytic lesions from taphonomic change. Likewise, bone deformation can be an *in vivo* process, but can also result from traumatic forces and taphonomic processes such as warping. **Pseudopathology** is the term used for a skeletal condition or alteration that can mimic a pathological condition. Certain pathological conditions, particularly some diseases, may provide information regarding medicolegal significance. For example, certain diseases were much more prevalent in ancient or historic contexts and are rarely seen in modern populations due to improved hygiene and healthcare.

Proliferative lesions result from increased osteoblastic activity as a reaction to a disease (Figure 12.14). They may involve a localized increase in bone density (**osteosclerosis**), or the projection of bony processes from the normal bone anatomy. Proliferative lesions that are commonly seen include those that are associated with infections of the bone, or **osteomyelitis**. Abnormal periosteal bone formation (i.e., on

FIGURE 12.15 Periostitis of the tibial shaft

(Photo by Rebecca Meeusen; specimen courtesy of the National Museum of Natural History)

the outer surface of the bone) is commonly referred to by the general term **periostitis**, meaning inflammation of the periosteum (Figure 12.15); the term *periostoses* may be more appropriate when lesions are traumatic in nature (Ortner, 2003). Inflammatory processes affecting the inner bone structures and the medullary cavity are called **osteitis**.

Some proliferative lesions are the result of ossification of other soft tissues such as cartilage and muscle. With increasing age, many cartilaginous regions have a tendency to become calcified. One such region is the costal cartilages (Figure 12.16), and as was discussed in Chapter 8, the pattern or progression of this ossification tends to vary between men and women. In some cases, especially in response to trauma, the attached connective tissue can become ossified in response to the trauma by producing bone directly in the tissue. Generally the condition is called **heterotopic**

FIGURE 12.16 Ossification of costal cartilage with fusion of first ribs to sternum

(Photo by Rebecca Meeusen; specimen courtesy of the National Museum of Natural History)

ossification (Figure 12.17), however specifically in muscle the condition is called **myositis ossificans**, and in tendons is called **ossific tendonitis**. This excess bone growth may be completely separated from the bone, or may become part of the bone, often appearing as a bony projection (Ortner, 2003).

Other proliferative lesions also take the form of bony projections. **Osteophytes** are bony projections that form at the margins of joints and signify joint damage. They are often associated with **osteoarthritis** and other degenerative joint conditions in older individuals. They are commonly found along the spine (Figure 12.18) but can be found in virtually any joint in the body (Figure 12.19). **Enthesophytes** are bony projections that form at the site of ligament or tendon attachments (Figure 12.20). Osteoarthritis can also be associated with the wearing away of joint cartilage, exposing subchondral bone and resulting in the **eburnation** of joint surfaces, a form of sclerosis that gives the bone a hard and dense quality and sometimes a shiny surface (as on the capitulum of the humerus in Figure 10.23).

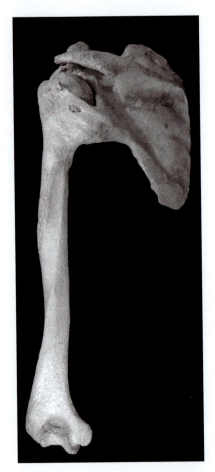

FIGURE 12.17 Heterotopic ossification of the tissues surrounding the shoulder

(Photo by Christopher Rainwater; specimen courtesy of the Cleveland Museum of Natural History)

Primary **neoplasms** (or tumors) of bones are those that arise primarily in bone, and can result in prominent proliferative lesions. Osteosarcoma, for example, can form prominent bone spicules or have the appearance of cauliflower. Button osteomas are typically small benign growths found on the cranial vault (Figure 12.21). If the nerve supply to bone is damaged (often due to an injury), the lack of pain in that site can lead to continued use of the broken bone and affect healing. The resulting exuberant bony response in these cases is called a **Charcot joint** (Ortner, 2003) (Figure 12.22).

Lytic lesions involve the destruction of bone. The speed of bone destruction can affect the appearance of the lesion (Ortner, 2003). Lytic lesions that form very slowly will typically have reactive, normal density bone at their margins which have a more smooth appearance. If the pathological process destroys the bone more quickly, less

FIGURE 12.18 Osteophytosis of vertebrae

reactive bone will form and the margins of the lesion will have more sharply defined borders. These sharper borders could potentially be confused with trauma and should therefore be carefully examined.

Necrosis is a general term that refers to the death of any tissue. In bone, necrosis (also called osteonecrosis) presents as a lytic lesion often resulting from a lack of blood supply to the bone. This disrupted blood supply can result from a fracture or dislocation, especially in locations such as the shoulder, hip, and knee. The resulting condition is called **avascular necrosis** which typically appears as a collapse or destruction of the joint surface.

Secondary neoplasms (also called metastatic tumors) of bone are those that arise in other parts of the body and metastasize (spread) to the bone, and are much more common than primary bone neoplasms. In contrast with primary neoplasms of bone which tend to produce proliferative lesions, many secondary neoplasms produce lytic lesions (Ortner, 2003). Examples include osteolytic sarcoma, metastatic carcinoma (Figure 12.23), and multiple myeloma.

FIGURE 12.19 Osteoarthritis of the knee

A number of infectious diseases result in lytic bone lesions. **Brucellosis** is an infectious disease that in humans presents as a chronic infection of the lungs and associated fever. The disease also produces cavitating lytic lesions of the spine or sacroiliac joint (Figure 12.24). It is rarely seen in modern populations, and its presence may suggest that the remains are historic rather than modern in origin. Other infectious diseases including tuberculosis (Figure 12.25), leprosy, and syphilis also produce osteolytic lesions.

Osteoporosis (and its less severe manifestation, **osteopenia**) is a condition of lower than normal bone density. Although these conditions also involve a loss of bone, they are not technically considered lesions since they are not localized. Bones with osteoporosis and osteopenia retain the basic gross morphology of the bone, but simply have a lower overall bone density and typically an associated loss in bone quality. Prolonged immobility is also associated with a loss of bone density, as well as prolonged periods in low-gravity conditions of outer space, a condition referred to as **spaceflight osteopenia** (Box 12.2).

BOX 12.2 SPACEFLIGHT OSTEOPENIA

Spaceflight osteopenia is the loss of bone mass associated with prolonged exposure to the low-gravity conditions of spaceflight. The skeletal system is adapted to mechanical loading regimes that oppose gravity during normal activities such as walking, and mechanical loads play a major role in the development and maintenance of bone. Spaceflight, due to the change in gravity and weight bearing, has been shown to result in altered calcium homeostasis and bone mineral density, with the greatest losses being observed in the pelvic bones, lumbar vertebrae, and femoral neck, and the magnitude of bone loss is likely related to the duration of the flight (Turner, 2000). The precise mechanism of this loss is not well-understood, but may result from increased bone remodeling, reduced bone remodeling, or an uncoupling between bone formation and resorption. It is unclear whether these changes can have long-term consequences for bone health. Astronaut Garrett Reismann reported a 3% loss in bone density after 95 days in orbit, but states that countermeasures such as resistive exercise (pictured below) help minimize bone loss.

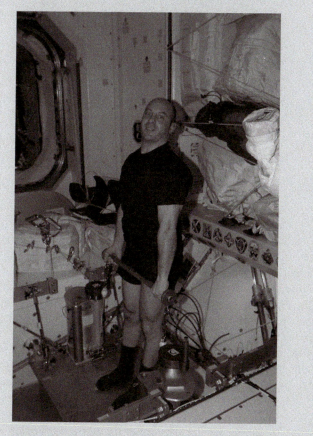

Astronaut Garrett Reismann engaged in resistive exercise which helps minimize bone loss in space (Image courtesy of Garrett Reismann)

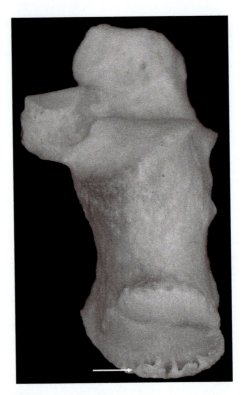

FIGURE 12.20 Enthesophyte

Some lesions involve both proliferative and lytic processes. These conditions, which normally result in proliferative periostitis, may also result in lytic necrosis if the bone in that area is deprived of blood supply and becomes necrotic. In these cases, the dead bone can become separated from the surrounding bone and is called a **sequestrum**. Hyper-developing reactive bone surrounding the sequestrum in the process of repair is called the **involucrum**. Often there is an opening in the involucrum called a **cloaca** that allows debris and pus to leave the sequestrum.

One of the more widely studied pathological conditions in skeletal remains that involves both proliferative and lytic processes is **porotic hyperostosis**, or the porous enlargement of the bone tissue, which is often associated with forms of anemia (Figure 12.26). It is commonly seen in the skull as an enlargement of the diploë, as the bone attempts to increase the available marrow space for increased red blood cell formation. Radiographically, this condition has a moth-eaten or hair-on-end appearance. When visible within the orbits, the condition is sometimes called **cribra orbitalia** (Figure 12.26).

Deformative lesions are those that involve pathologic changes in the overall bone contour or shape. Some skeletal deformations may be the result of intentional

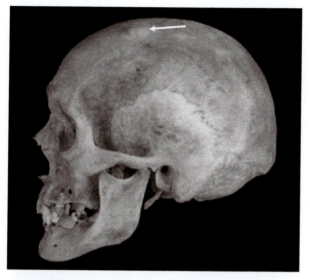

FIGURE 12.21 Button osteoma

FIGURE 12.22 Charcot joint affecting the knee

(Image courtesy of the National Museum of Health and Medicine)

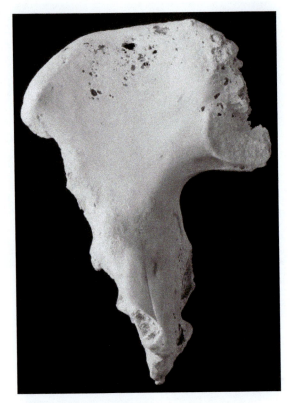

FIGURE 12.23 Metastatic carcinoma of the ilium

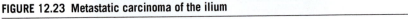

(Photo by Rebecca Meeusen; specimen courtesy of the National Museum of Natural History)

cultural practices and are not considered pathological. Examples include foot bind-ing and head binding (Box 12.3). Others may be the result of trauma such as plastic deformation, or taphonomic processes such as warping.

Several skeletal deformities are recognized in the spine. **Lordosis** refers to an abnormal degree of the inward curve of the lower spine resulting in a "saddleback" appearance. **Kyphosis** is a condition of too much concave curvature of the thoracic spine resulting in a "hunchback" appearance. **Scoliosis** refers to lateral deviations of the spinal column from the midsagittal plane (Ortner, 2003). The factors leading to these deformations are varied, including compression fractures of the vertebrae, growth disturbances, or congenital defects such as hemivertebrae, a condition in which only one portion of the vertebral body develops resulting in a wedge-shaped vertebra.

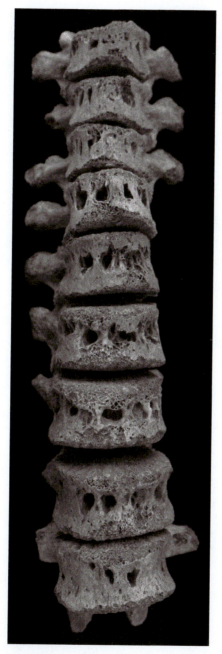

FIGURE 12.24 Brucellosis lesions of the spine

(Image courtesy of Todd Fenton)

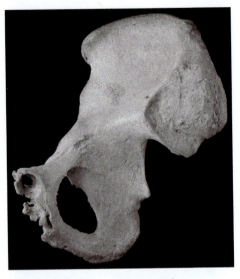

FIGURE 12.25 Tuberculosis lesions of the pubic symphysis

(Photo by Rebecca Meeusen; specimen courtesy of the National Museum of Natural History)

BOX 12.3 ARTIFICIAL CRANIAL DEFORMATION

Cranial deformation, or artificial cranial modification, is a cultural phenomenon which has been found to have been practiced on every continent except Australia (Ortner, 2003). Artificial cranial deformation is generated by applying pressure to certain areas of the cranium during the growth period, specifically the frontal, occipital, or temporoparietal. This pressure forces the bones of the vault to expand into a controlled shape. Cranial modification does not affect brain development, nor does it have any negative health consequences. Culturally, these practices were likely related to cosmetic or status ideologies.

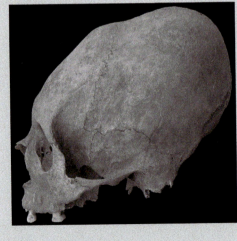

(Photo courtesy of Diana Messer and Valerie Andrushko)

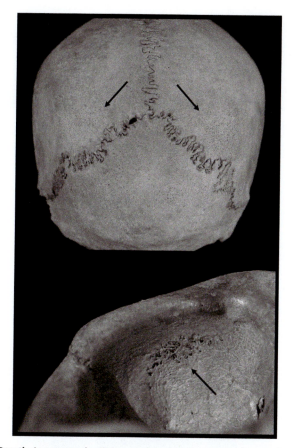
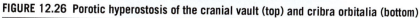

FIGURE 12.26 Porotic hyperostosis of the cranial vault (top) and cribra orbitalia (bottom)

Inadequate bone mineralization caused by insufficient calcium and phosphorus can result in a softening of the bones due to defective mineralization called **osteomalacia**. One common cause is a deficiency in vitamin D due to inadequate nutrition or any of a variety of disorders. In adults it may lead to an increase in fracture potential, deformities of the pelvis, or lordosis of the spine. In children (where the condition is called **rickets**) it can lead to significant bowing of the long bones (Figure 12.27). Poliomyelitis (polio) is a viral disease that can cause paralysis and bone deformities. Poliomyelitic paralysis affects bone growth and maintenance which can result in significant reduction in overall bone size (Figure 12.28).

Abnormalities of the development and fusion of the cranial sutures can result in the deformation of the cranium (Figure 12.29). **Craniostenosis** refers to premature fusion of the sutures of the cranium, resulting in significant cranial deformation because the normal growth of the head is altered. The alteration of cranial shape depends on which sutures are involved and the age of onset (Ortner, 2003), with the

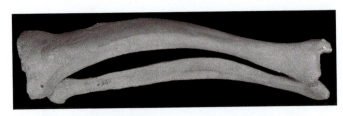

FIGURE 12.27 Rickets in a tibia and fibula

(Photo by Christopher Rainwater; specimen courtesy of the Cleveland Museum of Natural History)

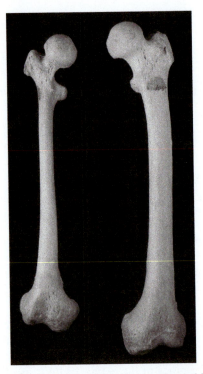

FIGURE 12.28 Reduction in the size of the femur due to poliomyelitis

(Photo by Rebecca Meeusen; specimen courtesy of the National Museum of Natural History)

head typically expanding in the direction parallel to the closed suture. The condition is also often associated with altered facial features. **Hydrocephaly** is a condition involving the accumulation of fluid in the ventricles of the brain, usually causing an enlargement of the skull and a small face (Figure 12.30), and typically associated with severe neurological symptoms.

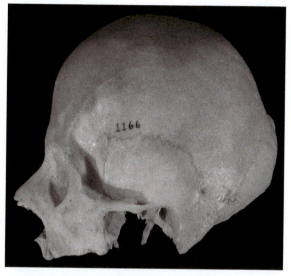

FIGURE 12.29 Craniostenosis

(Photo by Christopher Rainwater; specimen courtesy of the Cleveland Museum of Natural History)

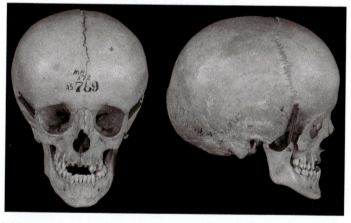

FIGURE 12.30 Hydrocephalic skull

(Image courtesy of the National Museum of Health and Medicine)

Another form of skeletal pathology is a fracture, which may result in proliferative lesions such as calluses associated with healed fractures (Figure 12.31), lytic lesions such as necrosis from traumatic interruption of blood supply, or deformation such as misalignment from improper fracture reduction. Many of these

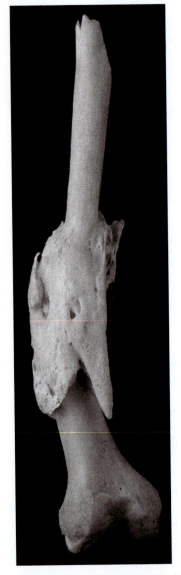

FIGURE 12.31 Proliferative bone and deformation associated with fracture

(Photo by Rebecca Meeusen; specimen courtesy of the National Museum of Natural History)

conditions have been addressed in previous sections of this chapter, and fracture mechanics and healing are addressed in more detail in the next chapter. In addition to lesions at a fracture site, proliferative bone often forms around the sites of surgical implants (Figure 12.32).

FIGURE 12.32 Proliferative bone growth around a surgical implant

(From Christensen and Anderson, 2013)

12.5 **Repetitive activity**

Repeated mechanical stresses on the skeleton can cause the bones to adapt their morphology in response to these stresses (recall Wolff's Law and the Utah Paradigm from Chapter 2). These adaptations are sometimes called "**markers of occupational stress**" or "occupational markers," in reference to their origins of often resulting from work-related physical activities. Any repetitive skeletal stresses, however, can produce changes in morphology, including those related to repetitive recreational activities or other frequent tasks or actions. Due to the many different types of activities that result in skeletal adaptations and modifications, it is not advisable to attribute any particular condition to a particular occupation in forensic anthropological casework.

One such adaptation is **hyper-development**, or the increase in size of muscle attachments or the bone's cortical area. Many studies have demonstrated an increase in the cortical area of bones that are loaded in particular ways, especially in relation to various recreational activities and sports (e.g., Bass et al., 2002; Sylvester et al., 2006). In addition, an increase in muscle size typically requires an increase in the size of the muscle attachment on the bone (larger muscles require greater surface area for attachment). For example, well-developed deltoid muscles are often associated with pronounced deltoid tuberosities of the humerus.

If an activity is performed more frequently or more intensely on one side of the body (such as with a dominant limb), asymmetry can sometimes be seen in the size or shape of paired bones, with the dominant side being larger and/or more robust. Various studies have examined the relationship between these asymmetries and handedness (for examples, see Ubelaker and Zarenko, 2012) but few have been successful

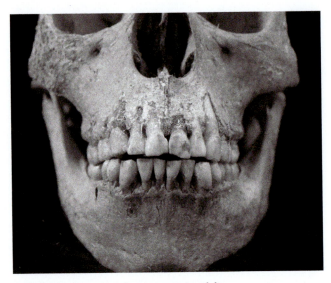

FIGURE 12.33 Central incisors worn from repeated activity

in demonstrating good predictive value for forensic casework. One reason for this is that the majority of people are right-handed, and handedness therefore has relatively little importance in forensic applications. Moreover, because of the prevalence of right-handedness, any method used to predict handedness must perform with a very high degree of accuracy and none have so far been achieved.

Teeth also show signs of repeated mechanical forces including facets, grooves, notches, and attrition. Occlusal attrition is typical with increasing age as the cusps become worn down over time from normal mastication forces. This attrition can be more pronounced if the diet contains higher grit (either from the nature of the food itself or from methods used to prepare it). Notches, grooves, and wear can occur from repeatedly holding things between the teeth. This is commonly seen in long-term pipe smokers who hold the pipe between the teeth, also known as pipe-mouth formation (Joe Hefner, personal communication, 2013), or seamstresses who hold needles between the teeth (Figure 12.33).

12.6 Case study – ankylosis

In 2012, partially mummified human remains were discovered along a river bank in northern California. The remains consisted of a complete skeleton of a White female, approximately 50–60 years of age. The skeleton exhibited a number of individual variants such as ossification of costal cartilage, and several degenerative changes of the spinal column including osteophytic lipping of vertebral centra, eburnation and osteophytic lipping of articular facets, and **ankylosis** (fusion) of two pairs of vertebrae. While the other variants of the vertebral column are

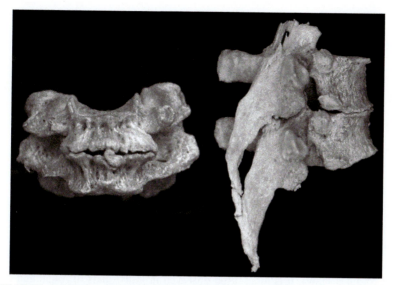

FIGURE 12.34 Ankylosis of C5 and C6 (left) and T5 and T6 (right)

relatively common among older individuals, ankylosis of vertebrae is somewhat rare. Ankylosis was identified on C5 and C6 of the cervical spine, and on T5 and T6 of the thoracic spine. Both fused pairs of vertebrae showed evidence of disc degeneration such as loss of disc height, bony bridging between vertebral bodies, and osteophyte projection beyond the normal anatomical margin (Figures 12.34). This can result from trauma such as compression fractures of the spine, which is a common finding among older females with advanced signs of osteoporosis (Ortner, 2003), or may also result from immune disorders which may be congenital. Given the decedent's age and the degenerative changes observed throughout the vertebral column, it is likely that the fused vertebrae are the result of disc collapse as opposed to a specific disease. Identification of the skeletal variants in this case was relatively straightforward, but a precise diagnosis was more complicated. In this case, the degenerative changes were an indication of relatively advanced age, and the ankylosis may be useful for identification if suitable medical records are available for comparison.

12.7 Case study – dental anomalies

In 2012, decomposed remains were recovered from along a recently flooded river bank in northern California. The remains consisted of a nearly intact skeleton of a Hispanic male, approximately 25–35 years of age. Dental anomalies were identified including "winged" incisors and a supernumerary tooth (Figure 12.35). Winged incisors are a dental feature involving a distinctive bilateral mesial rotation of the central maxillary incisors (making the incisor junction appear V-shaped

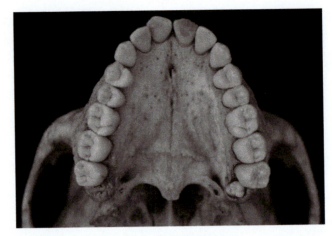

FIGURE 12.35 "Winged" incisors and supernumerary tooth

in the occlusal view). It is most often observed in individuals of Asian and Native American ancestry. The extra tooth represented a rudimentary, non-functional tooth located distolingual to the left maxillary third molar. Supernumerary teeth that form in this location are often impacted. In this case, the tooth would likely have been considered impacted or unerupted, and would have only been visible radiographically. Dental anomalies such as these are relatively rare, and can be useful in personal identification.

12.8 Summary

- In addition to differences between sexes, across geographic groups, and throughout an individual's lifetime, skeletal variation also exists on an individual level.
- Skeletal variation can be useful for personal identification, and it is important to be familiar with possible skeletal variants so that they are not confused with trauma or taphonomic damage.
- The main types of individual skeletal variants are those that represent variations in the shape of normal anatomy, those that are considered deviations from normal (anomalies), those that are the result of a disease process (pathological conditions), and those that result from repetitive activity.
- Variations in normal anatomy include differences in paranasal sinus shape, cranial suture pattern, trabecular pattern, and external bone contours.
- Anomalies consist of variations including supernumerary bones and teeth (such as extra vertebrae or extrasutural bones), accessory foramina (such as septal apertures or sternal apertures), and non-fusion anomalies (such as metopism or cleft neural arches).
- Pathological conditions result in localized lesions that may be proliferative (excess growth of bone), lytic (destruction of bone), or deformative (change in bone shape).

- Repetitive activities can lead to bone adaptations including increases in cortical area and density, increases in the size of muscle attachments, and the development of accessory facets.

12.9 Test yourself

- You are presented with skeletal remains that include a bone with a foramen in an unexpected (i.e., not "normal") location. Describe the differential diagnosis process you would use to determine the likely cause of this foramen.
- Identify three sources/causes (not conditions) of variation in bone morphology.
- Explain why the detection of accessory bones can sometimes be difficult in forensic contexts.
- Describe the difference between these three types of osteoproliferative bony projections: osteophyte, enthesophyte, and myositis ossificans.
- What is the principle behind variants that result from habitual activities? Why might it be inappropriate to call these variants "occupational markers"?
- How might you be able to differentiate a traumatic fracture, a taphonomic fracture, and a rapidly formed lytic lesion?
- Why can cranial suture and paranasal sinus shape be used to facilitate identifications?
- Describe the difference between normal variation (e.g., the presence of an "Inca bone") and pathological variation (e.g., premature cranial suture closure).

Definitions

Accessory bone An extra bone which does not occur normally

Ankylosis Fusion of two or more bones of the skeleton

Anomaly A deviation from the normal form

Antimere The opposite corresponding (left or right) part

Avascular necrosis Bone tissue death due to disruption of blood supply

Bipartite patella A condition where the ossification centers of the patella fail to coalesce; also called segmented patella

Brucellosis An infectious disease involving chronic infection of the lungs that produces cavitating lytic lesions of the spine or sacroiliac joint

Charcot joint A proliferative lesion resulting from continued use of a broken bone due to nerve supply damage and resulting lack of pain at that site

Cleft neural arch A condition where the two sides of the neural arch of the vertebra fail to unite

Cloaca An opening in an involucrum that allows debris and pus to leave a sequestrum

Congenital A defect that is present at birth, typically either arising during gestation or due to hereditary tendencies

Craniostenosis Premature fusion of the sutures of the cranium

Cribra orbitalia Porotic hyperostosis that is visible within the orbits

Deformative lesion A pathological lesion characterized by abnormal bone shape

Differential diagnosis A systematic method for narrowing down the identity of a condition

Disease An abnormal condition affecting the body including infections, injuries, and disorders

Eburnation A degenerative condition that results in the bone being hard and ivorylike; often associated with osteoarthritis

Enthesophyte A bony projection that forms at the site of ligament or tendon attachments

Epigenetic Non-genetic factors that cause genes to express themselves differently, resulting in different phenotypes or morphology

Extrasutural bone An accessory bone of a cranial suture; depending on the location and configuration, also called Wormian bone or Inca bone

Hemivertebrae A condition in which only one portion of the vertebral body develops resulting in a wedge-shaped vertebra and causing spinal deformity

Heterotopic ossification The presence of extra, irregularly shaped bony growths typically attached to long bones

Hydrocephaly A condition involving the accumulation of fluid in the ventricles of the brain

Hyper-development Development to a high or excessive degree

Hyperdontia A condition of having more than the normal number of teeth

Idiosyncrasy A structural characteristic of a particular individual

In vivo A process occurring in a living organism

Involucrum New bone that forms around a sequestrum

Kyphosis Abnormal concave curvature of the thoracic spine

Lesion A localized alteration of a tissue, usually resulting from disease or trauma

Life history The history of changes that an organism undergoes throughout its lifetime

Lordosis Abnormal inward curve of the lower spine

Lytic lesion A pathological lesion characterized by abnormal loss or destruction of bone; also called osteolytic lesion

Markers of occupational stress Modifications to bone as a result of repetitive, work-related activity

Metopism Retention of a metopic suture (between the two halves of the frontal bone)

Myositis ossificans A condition where muscle tissue produces bone, usually in response to trauma

Necrosis Tissue death

Neoplasm An abnormal new growth of tissue or tumor; *primary* neoplasms of bone are those that arise in bone, while *secondary* neoplasms (or metastatic tumors) are those that arise in other tissues and metastasize to bone

Os acromiale A condition where the lateral end of the acromion process of the scapula fails to unite

Ossicle A small bone

Ossific tendonitis Heterotropic ossification occurring in the tendons

Osteitis Inflammation involving the inner structures and medullary cavity of a bone

Osteoarthritis A disease of the joints characterized by degeneration of the cartilage and underlying bone, often associated with bony overgrowth; also called degenerative joint disease

Osteogenesis imperfecta (OI) The general name for a group of conditions which all result in pathological osteoporosis and abnormal fragility of the skeleton

Osteomalacia Softening of the bones due to defective mineralization, often caused by a lack of vitamin D

Osteomyelitis An infection of the bone or bone marrow

Osteopenia Low bone density that is less severe than osteoporosis

Osteophyte A bony projection that forms at the margins of joints

Osteoporosis Lower than normal bone density

Osteosclerosis A localized increase in bone density

Pathological condition Abnormal anatomy which is a manifestation of a disease process

Pathology The study of disease

Periostitis Inflammation involving the periosteal (outer) surface of a bone

Polydactyly A condition of having extra fingers or toes; also called polydactylism

Porotic hyperostosis A condition of porous enlargement of the bone tissue, often associated with anemia and commonly seen in the skull

Proliferative lesion A pathological lesion characterized by an abnormal excess of bone; also called osteoproliferative lesion

Pseudarthrosis A "false" joint that results from a failure of two fractured bone portions to reunite

Pseudopathology An condition or alteration that mimics a pathological condition

Rickets Osteomalacia in children

Scoliosis Lateral curvature of the spine

Septal aperture A foramen in the distal humerus superior to the trochlea; also called a supra-trochlear foramen

Sequestrum A piece of dead bone that becomes separated from the surrounding bone during the process of necrosis

Spaceflight osteopenia Decrease in bone density associated with prolonged exposure to low-gravity and non-weight-bearing conditions

Spina bifida A defect of the developing spinal cord which disrupts vertebral neural arch development, usually affecting the sacrum and numerous presacral vertebrae

Spondylolysis A non-union of a fracture at the pars interarticularis; also called pars defect

Sternal foramen A foramen occurring in either the sternal body or xyphoid process, usually a non-union anomaly

Supernumerary More than the normal number

Vertebral shift A condition where a vertebra takes on characteristics of another segment of the spine

References

Asherson, N., 1965. Identification by Frontal Sinus Prints: A Forensic Medical Pilot Survey. H.K. Lewis & Co. Lts, London.

Barnes, E., 1994. Developmental Defects of the Axial Skeleton in Paleopathology. University Press of Colorado, Niwot.

Barnes, E., 2012. Atlas of Developmental Field Anomalies of the Human Skeleton: A Paleopathology Perspective. Wiley-Blackwell, Hoboken.

Bass, S.L., Saxon, L., Daly, R.M., Turner, C.H., Robling, A.G., Seeman, E., Stucket, S., 2002. The effect of mechanical loading on the size and shape of bone in per-, peri-, and postpubertal girls: A study in tennis players. J. Bone. Miner. Res. 17, 2274–2280.

Christensen, A.M., 2003. An empirical examination of frontal sinus outline variability using elliptic Fourier analysis: Implications for identification, standardization, and legal admissibility [PhD dissertation]. The University of Tennessee, Knoxville.

Christensen, A.M., 2005a. Testing the reliability of frontal sinus outlines in personal identification. J. Forensic Sci. 50 (1), 18–22.

Christensen, A.M., 2005b. Assessing the variation in individual frontal sinus outlines. Am. J. Phys. Anthropol. 127 (3), 291–295.

Christensen, A.M., Anderson, B.E., 2013. Personal identification. In: Tersigni-Tarrant, M.T., Shirley, N. (Eds.), Forensic Anthropology: An Introduction. CRC Press, Boca Raton, pp. 397–420.

Cornelison, J.B., Fenton, T.W., Sauer, N.J., 2002. Comparative radiography of the lateral hyoid: A new method for human identification. Proceedings of the 54th Annual Meeting of the American Academy of Forensic Sciences, February 17–23, Atlanta, GA.

Finnegan, M., 1978. Non-metric variation of the infracranial skeleton. J. Anat. 125 (1), 23–37.

Garvey, M.T., Barry, H.J., Blake, M., 1999. Supernumerary teeth – an overview of classification, diagnosis and management. J. Can. Dent. Assoc. 65, 612–616.

Hanihara, T., Ishida, H., 2001. Os incae: Variation in frequency in major human population groups. J. Anat. 198 (2), 137–152.

Hefti, F., Bollini, G., Dungl, P., Fixsen, J., Grill, F., Ipoolito, E., Romanus, B., Tudisco, C., Wientraub, S., 2000. Congenital pseudarthrosis of the tibia: History, etiology, classification and epidemic data. J. Pediatr. Orthop. B. 9 (1), 1–2.

Kahana, T., Hiss, J., Smith, P., 1998. Quantitative assessment of trabecular bone pattern identification. J. Forensic Sci. 43 (6), 1144–1147.

Koot, M.G., Sauer, N.J., Fenton, T.W., 2005. Radiographic human identification using bones of the hand: A validation study. J. Forensic Sci. 50 (2), 263–268.

Koyun, N., Aydinlinglu, A., Gumrukcuoglu, F.N., 2011. Aperture in coronoid-olecranon septum: A radiologic evaluation. Indian J. Orthopaedics 45 (5), 392–395.

Mann, R.W., 1998. Use of trabeculae to establish positive identification. Forensic Sci. Int. 98, 91–99.

Mays, S., 2008. Septal aperture of the humerus in a mediaeval human skeletal population. Am. J. Phys. Anthropol. 136 (4), 432–440.

Mumoli, N., Gandini, D., Wamala, E.K., Cei, M., 2008. Left hand polydactyly: A case report. Cases Journal 1, 346.

Ndou, R., Smith, P., Gemell, R., Mohatla, O., 2012. The supratrochlear foramen of the humerus in a South African dry bone sample. Clin. Anat. http://dx.doi.org/10.1002/ca.22132 (published online, not yet in print).

Ortner, D.J., 2003. The Identification of Pathological Conditions in Human Skeletal Remains, second ed. Academic Press, San Diego.

Rogers, T.L., Allard, T.T., 2004. Expert Testimony and Positive Identification of Human Remains through Cranial Suture Patterns. J. Forensic Sci. 49 (2), 203–207.

Scheuer, L., Black, S., 2000. Developmental Juvenile Osteology. Academic Press, San Diego.

Schuller, A., 1921. Das Rontgenogram der Stirnhohle: ein Hilfsmitten fur die Identitasbestimmung von Schadeln. Monatsschrift feur Ohrenheikunde und Laryngo-Rhinologie 5, 1617–1620.

Scientific Working Group on Forensic Anthropology, 2012. Identifying and Describing Pathological Conditions, Lesions and Anomalies – Revision 0.

Sekharan, P.C., 1985. Identification of skull from its suture pattern. Forensic Sci. Int. 27, 205–214.

Soler, A., 2011. Positive identification through comparative panoramic radiography of the maxillary sinuses: A validation study. Proceedings of the 63rd Annual Meeting of the American Academy of Forensic Sciences, February 20–26, Chicago, IL.

Stephan, C.N., Winburn, A.P., Christensen, A.F., Tyrrell, A.J., 2011. Skeletal identification by radiographic comparison: Blind tests of a morphoscopic method using antemortem chest radiographs. J. Forensic Sci. 56 (2), 320–332.

Sylvester, A.D., Christensen, A.M., Kramer, P.A., 2006. Factors influencing osteological changes in the hands and fingers of rock climbers. J. Anat. 209 (5), 597–610.

Turner, R.T., 2000. Invited review: What do we know about the effects of spaceflight on bone? J. Appl. Phys. 89 (2), 840–847.

Ubelaker, D.H., Zarenko, K.M., 2012. Can handedness be determined from skeletal remains? A chronological review of the literature. J. Forensic Sci. 57 (6), 1421–1426.

Valenzuela, A., 1997. Radiographic comparison of the lumbar spine for positive identification of human remains. A case report. Am. J. Forensic Med. Pathol. 18 (2), 215–217.

Waldron, T., 2009. Paleopathology. Cambridge University Press, Cambridge.

Watamaniuk, L., Rogers, T., 2010. Positive personal identification of human remains based on thoracic vertebral margin morphology. J. Forensic Sci. 55 (5), 1162–1170.

Analysis of Skeletal Trauma

13.1 Principles of trauma analysis

The analysis of trauma and other alterations to the skeleton by forensic anthropologists can help answer important questions, including those that might be related to the circumstances of death or could facilitate personal identification. An **alteration** is any change to the physical properties of a bone, while **trauma** refers to the physical disruption of living tissues by outside forces. The conclusions reached from the analysis of skeletal trauma typically include the *timing* of the trauma relative to the death event, and the *mechanism* or type of force that caused the trauma. Trauma timing can be categorized as **antemortem** (occurring before death) or **perimortem** (occurring around the time of death). **Postmortem** alterations are not considered trauma (because by definition they no longer disrupt *living* tissue) but will also be addressed in this chapter. Trauma mechanism is usually categorized as blunt force, high velocity projectile, sharp force, thermal, or some combination of these categories.

Trauma analysis in forensic anthropology is a rather recent development. It was not until the 1980s that anthropologists began to routinely consult on skeletal trauma, but today it is a standard part of forensic anthropological examinations. Trauma analysis should involve careful observation, thorough documentation, and cautious interpretation. When analyzing trauma on skeletonized remains, definitive conclusions are not always possible, and in some cases it is best to simply describe the alterations that are observed. Interpreting traumatic alterations to bone requires knowledge and application of a variety of scientific principles, including those relating to physics, biomechanics, and engineering. While a thorough discussion of bone biomechanics is beyond the scope of this text, some basic principles will be presented in the following section. Readers interested in more technical aspects of bone biomechanics are directed to Cowin (2001) and Martin et al. (1998).

13.2 Forces, bone biomechanics, and fractures

Skeletal trauma often results from the application of **force**, or the action of one object on another. The science that deals with the effects of forces on objects is called **mechanics**, and bones are physical objects that obey mechanical laws (Cowin, 2001) (Box 13.1). This relationship between force and deformation is one of the primary

Forensic Anthropology. http://dx.doi.org/10.1016/B978-0-12-418671-2.00013-6

BOX 13.1 MECHANICAL LAWS

The primary laws that concern deformable objects such as bone are the laws of motion (Newton, 1687) and the law of elasticity of solid materials (Hooke, 1678). Three Newtonian laws form the basis of classical mechanics:

1) A body remains at rest or moves at a constant speed in a straight line unless acted upon by a force.
2) The force acting on a body is equal to the mass of the body multiplied by its acceleration (f = ma).
3) If a body exerts a force on a second body, the second body exerts a force on the first body that is equal in magnitude and opposite in direction to the first force.

Hooke's law states that there is a relationship between the force and deformation of a solid object.

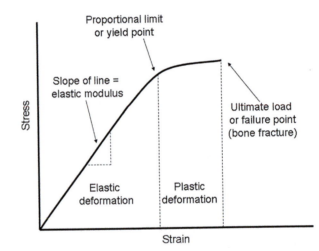

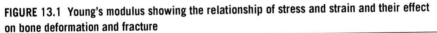

FIGURE 13.1 Young's modulus showing the relationship of stress and strain and their effect on bone deformation and fracture

---

principles in understanding bone fracture mechanics. For normal **loading** (the application of force to an object), a material's intrinsic **stiffness** (or the ability to resist deformation) is known as the **elastic modulus** or **Young's modulus**. Bone's reaction to loading can be visualized as a load-deformation curve, showing a material's response to force as a function of **stress** and **strain** (Figure 13.1), where stress is the load per unit area, strain is the change in dimension (relative deformation) of a loaded body (Martin et al., 1998), and the slope of the line represents the elastic modulus. Strain in bone has been reported to rarely exceed about 3% (Currey, 1970).

Load and deformation are linearly proportional until the proportional limit or **yield point** is reached, at which point the slope is reduced. When acted upon by a force less than the yield point, bone will react through **elastic deformation**. Elastic deformation is temporary because the bonds between atoms are not broken or irreversibly

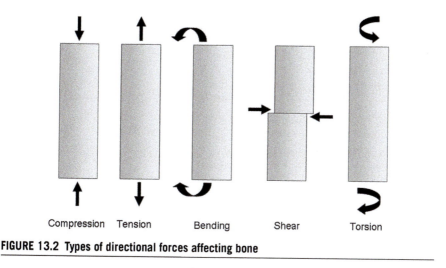

Compression   Tension   Bending   Shear   Torsion

FIGURE 13.2 Types of directional forces affecting bone

deformed, and when the force is no longer applied, the bone will go back to its original shape. With greater force (stress), the bone will reach the yield point after which it will respond through **plastic deformation**, which causes a permanent change to the bone structure. With increasing load, the ultimate load (**failure**) is eventually reached, and it is at this point that **fracture** occurs. The load at the failure point corresponds to a bone's **strength.** The area under the curve is a measure of the amount of total energy needed to cause a fracture, and corresponds to the material's energy absorption or **toughness.** Toughness is an important bone biomechanical property because a tough bone is more resistant to fracture even though it may be less resistant to yielding. Deformation and fracture in bone can be observed at both the microscopic and macroscopic levels (Berryman and Symes, 1998; Smith et al., 2003).

The effect of force on skeletal material is dependent upon both extrinsic and intrinsic factors. Extrinsic factors include the direction, magnitude, and the rate at which the force is applied (Berryman and Symes, 1998). The primary directional forces that affect bone are compression, tension, bending, shear, and torsion (Figure 13.2) (note that compression, tension, and shear are considered "pure" forces while the others are combinations of these forces). **Compression** is a force acting to decrease the dimension of the bone in the direction of the applied force (i.e., "squeeze" the bone). **Tension** is a force acting to increase the dimension of the bone in the direction of the force (i.e., "stretch" the bone). In **bending**, one side of the bone (the concave side) is subjected to a compressive force, while the other side (the convex side) is subjected to a tensile force (often creating shear force). **Shear** is a force that acts to slide portions of the bone relative to one another, parallel to the direction of force. **Torsion** is a force involving a combination of shear and rotation or twisting.

Understanding these forces is important because the strength of a material varies with the direction of force. For example, most materials are weaker in shear than in compression. Bone is stronger under compression than in tension, so fractures typically initiate on surfaces under tension. Even in the absence of external traumatic forces, bones in living vertebrates are continually subjected to a variety of forces arising from gravity, body movements, impacts, and other forces exerted on the skeleton by the viscera (Evans, 1973).

Magnitude refers to the amount of force applied. Typically, the greater the magnitude of force, the greater the severity of the fracture will be. The surface area over which the force is applied will also affect how bone responds to a certain magnitude of force. Bone will be better able to resist deformation in response to the same amount of force applied over a large surface area versus a small surface area because the greater the surface area, the less the force per unit area.

The rate at which force is applied, which relates to the rate of absorption of the force's energy, is also an important factor affecting how bone fractures (Evans, 1973). Force may be applied as either **dynamic** or **static** loading. Dynamic loading refers to a force that is applied suddenly and at relatively high speed. This type of loading is most often responsible for fractures seen in forensic contexts. Static loading is a low-speed force, applied slowly. Bone can support a greater load before failure if the load is applied slowly rather than rapidly (Evans, 1973).

Even stress applied at levels below the failure point can cause fractures due to either time-dependent or cycle-dependent loading (Caler and Carter, 1989; Evans, 1973). If a relatively low static force is applied over an extended period of time, the bone may continue to deform and fracture; such fractures are called **creep fractures** (Caler and Carter 1989; Galloway, 1999). Repetitive loading at pre-failure forces can eventually degrade the mechanical properties of bone by causing small cracks in the bone which will eventually grow and coalesce, causing failure; such fractures are called **fatigue fractures** (Turner and Burr, 1993), or "stress fractures." The fatigue strength of bone has been shown to be far less than its static strength (Agarwal and Broutman, 1980).

The effect that forces have on bone also depends on a number of intrinsic factors that affect the ability of bone to resist deformation and failure including its composition, cross-sectional area, and geometry. Many biological materials, including bone, have a "grain," or an internal organized structure that is not the same in all directions (recall from Chapter 2 that the general orientation of bone structure is in the longitudinal direction; wood is another example of a material with a grain). Because of this, bone does not have the same structural properties in all directions. Materials that have the same properties in all directions (such as steel) are called **isotropic**. Materials like bone that have different properties in different directions are called **anisotropic**. Human osteonal bone is actually considered transversely isotropic because it has the same properties in all transverse directions, but has different properties in the longitudinal direction (Reilly and Burstein, 1975).

Bone composition, area, and geometry vary between the sexes and across populations, and can also change over time or in association with certain pathological conditions. This means that there are often population-, age-, and pathology-related differences in bone strength and stiffness. Age-related decreases in bone density such as osteoporosis or osteomalacia can affect bone's mechanical properties, as can skeletal diseases such as osteogenesis imperfecta or rickets. Diet and mechanical loading also affect bone's biomechanical properties.

It is also important to note that these forces do not always occur in isolation, and traumatic events affecting bones may involve various types of force. Moreover, these principles apply primarily to cortical bone. Assessment of the mechanical properties of trabecular bone is much more difficult because individual trabeculae each have their own stiffness (material stiffness), and the structure they comprise together has its own stiffness (structural stiffness).

The failure (fracture) of bone under these different forces and loading regimes are varied, and fractures can be classified based on their degree and morphology. The broadest category of fracture is whether it is **incomplete** or **complete**, and fractures can be further categorized by type (Table 13.1). Incomplete fractures are those where some continuity is retained between the fractured bone portions, and these occur more commonly in children due to the greater elasticity of their bones

Table 13.1 Classification of bone fractures

Fracture types		Fracture characteristics
Incomplete fractures	Bow fracture	Fracture with exaggerated curvature along the length of the bone; more common in children
	Torus or buckle fracture	Fracture resulting from buckling of bone cortex due to compressive force; appears as a rounded expansion of the bone
	Greenstick fracture	Fracture resulting from bending or angulation forces on one side and compression on the other; appears as a transverse fracture with fractures deviating at right angles along the long axis of the bone
	Depressed fracture	Fracture resulting in a "caving in" of the bone; occurs primarily in the skull
Complete fractures	Transverse fracture	Fracture occurring at approximate right angles to the long axis of the bone; typically from blunt trauma directed perpendicular to the shaft
	Oblique fracture	Fracture running diagonally across the diaphysis; usually the result of a combination of angulation and compressive force
	Spiral fracture	Fracture that circles the shaft, usually from rotational forces
	Comminuted fracture	Fracture in which more than two fragments are generated; usually resulting from relatively high levels of force; butterfly and segmental are types of comminuted fracture
	Epiphyseal fracture	Fracture involving the growth plate; such fractures may be limited to the cartilage, but may also involve the surrounding bone

(Modified from Galloway, 1999 and Gozna, 1982)

(Rogers, 1978). Complete fractures are those in which there is discontinuity between two or more bone fragments. Whether a fracture is complete or incomplete is often dependent on the magnitude and direction of force. For example, comminuted fractures tend to be associated with greater magnitude forces, and butterfly fractures (Box 13.2) tend to result from bending. Categorization of

BOX 13.2 BUTTERFLY FRACTURES

Butterfly fractures are comminuted fractures that result from bending forces which create tension on one side of the bone and compression on the other. The bone fails first on the surface under tension (the convex side of the bend), and oblique transverse fractures (usually bilateral) due to shear forces then propagate toward the surface under compression (the concave side of the bend). The result is often a dissociated triangular "butterfly fragment." It is often possible to determine the direction of the force based on the directionality of this butterfly fragment. The impact is typically on the compression side, with the fracture initiating on the opposing tension side. Butterfly fragments were long thought to be produced by force applied to the tension side, resulting in the misinterpretation of the direction of the applied force. Butterfly fractures are commonly seen in motor vehicle-pedestrian victims where the bumper impacts the legs. The butterfly fragment can be useful in interpreting which direction the pedestrian was facing when struck.

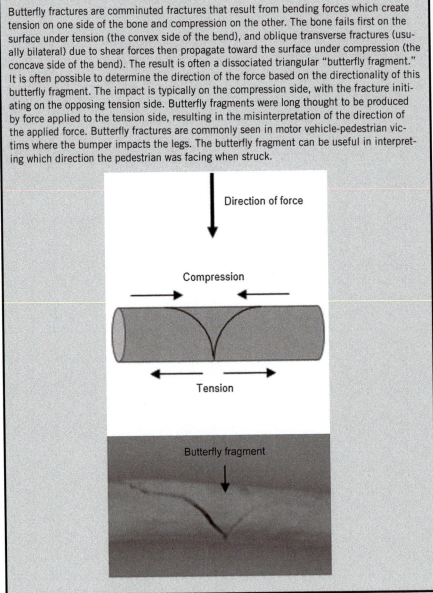

fracture type (which is common in biomechanics) may be part of a skeletal trauma analysis, but typological systems are usually too vague to account for all aspects of the trauma event. A thorough skeletal trauma analysis should also involve an interpretation the trauma event including the forces involved and directionality.

13.3 Trauma timing

Trauma timing can be categorized according to when it occurred relative to the death event. Antemortem trauma is an alteration produced before an individual's death. The primary evidence of antemortem trauma is **osteogenic reaction** (or the formation of new bone) since, naturally, such responses will only occur if an individual is still alive. Osteogenic reaction is usually in the form of fracture healing (Box 13.3) or infectious response. Fracture healing may be evidenced by rounded fracture edges or a fracture callus (Figure 13.3). Infectious response may be evidenced by proliferative or lytic lesions.

Although the identification of antemortem trauma typically eliminates that injury from being directly related to the death event, certain antemortem trauma patterns can indicate a particular injury history (such as a major accident, a history of abuse, or human rights violations) which may provide clues regarding possible causes of death, or may have indirectly contributed to the death. In addition, the presence of antemortem trauma in unidentified skeletal remains serves as information that can be useful in the identification process (see Chapter 14).

BOX 13.3 STAGES OF FRACTURE REPAIR

Fracture repair occurs in three primary stages. The first stage is the reactive or inflammation stage, which occurs during the first few days following a fracture. First, bleeding occurs due to the broken blood vessels near the fracture site. This blood often pools in the adjacent area, forming a **hematoma**. **Inflammation** also occurs as the body increases the amount of plasma and white blood cells in the injured area to facilitate healing. Osteoclasts work in fracture sites to resorb dead bone which may appear radiographically as a blurring of the fracture margin and widening of the fracture gap (Rogers, 1992). Fractures also stimulate osteoid formation within the first few days to begin to bridge the broken surfaces and repair the fracture. This osteoid formation may not be immediately obvious in an anthropological examination (Barbian and Sledzik, 2008). It may not be visible to the naked eye or radiographically, and may require microscopy or histology to detect. Histologically, new bone formation can be seen by approximately 5–7 days as spicules of woven bone, but these spicules are delicate and may be lost if the body is completely skeletonized.

The second stage of fracture healing is the reparative stage, which occurs over the following weeks and months. Within the first few weeks, a soft **fracture callus** of fibrous bone forms, building on the framework of the deposited osteoid. This becomes a hard callus by 6–12 weeks, and eventually clinical union of bone is reached. Calluses are typically quite visible during gross examination and radiographically due to their raised appearance and lower bone quality.

The third and final stage of fracture repair is the remodeling stage, which occurs months to years following the fracture, and involves remodeling of the quickly deposited bone at the fracture site. In the early remodeling stages, the fracture callus may still be visible, but after years of remodeling, the fracture site may become difficult to detect.

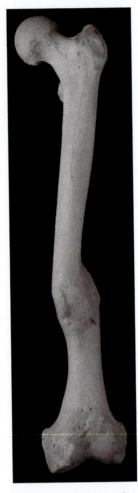

FIGURE 13.3 Healed fracture (antemortem trauma) on a femur

(Photo by Rebecca Meeusen; specimen courtesy of the National Museum of Natural History)

Other antemortem alterations in which bone remodeling processes are observed include healing from surgical procedures such as trephination (Figure 13.4) as well as the resorption or filling in of the vacant alveolar space when teeth are lost or extracted (Figure 13.5). This resorption usually takes several months following tooth loss. When all teeth have been lost with complete resorption of the alveolar space, the individual is considered **edentulous**.

Perimortem trauma refers to an injury that occurred relatively near the time of death. Because of the varying temporal specificity associated with this term when used by practitioners in different fields, it requires a more detailed explanation. When forensic pathologists, for example, use the term 'perimortem,' they typically mean within

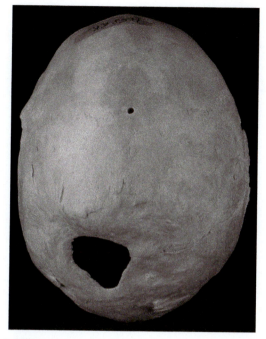

FIGURE 13.4 Trephination

(Photo by Rebecca Meeusen; specimen courtesy of the National Museum of Natural History)

a very short time period surrounding death (e.g., seconds or minutes) and directly related to the death event. This level of specificity is often possible when evaluating trauma to the soft tissues. Skeletal alterations, however, cannot usually be timed so precisely. Perimortem trauma to bone is best defined as those injuries that occur when the bone is in a biomechanically fresh state; that is, when it retains components and properties that make it fracture in the same mechanical manner as viable bone. This means that the perimortem interval for forensic anthropological assessments could be quite long and extend relatively far (months, for example) into the postmortem period, as long as the bone is still in a fresh state when the fracture occurred. Because of these different temporal meanings, when the term "perimortem" is used, it should be clearly explained and accompanied by a justification for the classification.

Various fracture characteristics are typical of biomechanically fresh bone. Evidence of perimortem trauma to bone includes plastic deformation (Figure 13.6), hinge fractures, and staining on the bone associated with a hematoma. The presence of small bone fragments adherent to adjacent fractured bone also suggests perimortem trauma (Ortner and Putschar, 1985). By comparison to antemortem fractures, perimortem fractures will lack evidence of healing or infectious response. Compared to postmortem fractures, fresh bone fractures are often more straight whereas dry bone fractures tend to have a more jagged appearance. Another indicator of

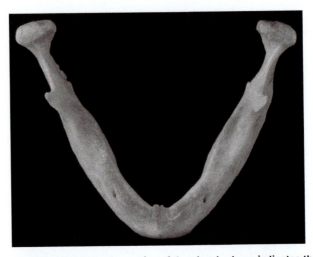

FIGURE 13.5 Edentulous mandible. Resorption of the alveolar bone indicates that tooth loss was an antemortem process

(Photo by Rebecca Meeusen; specimen courtesy of the National Museum of Natural History)

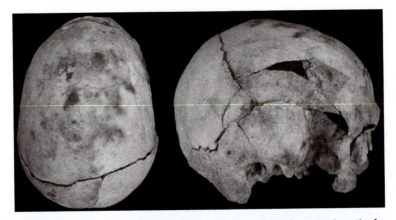

FIGURE 13.6 Perimortem trauma with associated plastic deformation; note how the fragments cannot all be refitted along their edges due to changes in bone shape

perimortem trauma is an overall fracture pattern that is characteristic of a terminal event (Scientific Working Group for Forensic Anthropology [SWGANTH], 2011; Moraitis et al., 2009) such as a gunshot wound or fall from a great height.

Postmortem damage refers to taphonomic alterations to bone that are produced after death and that are unassociated with the death event. In some cases, postmortem damage may be *related* to the death event (for example, mutilation or

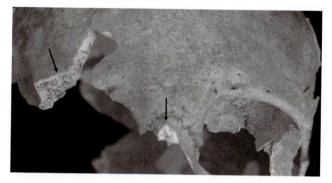

FIGURE 13.7 Postmortem damage to cranium; note the lighter color of the recently exposed surfaces

dismemberment inflicted by a perpetrator after a homicide), but in most cases, the analysis of postmortem bone alteration technically falls under taphonomic analysis (see Chapter 5). Postmortem damage can sometimes be distinguished from perimortem trauma by differential staining, such as where perimortem fracture edges are stained by hemorrhage, decomposition fluids, soil, or other materials. The fracture edges of postmortem damaged bones will often be lighter than the surrounding bone because these surfaces are exposed to the environment at a later time (Figure 13.7). Like perimortem trauma, postmortem damage will not show evidence of healing. An overall pattern of damage consistent with known postmortem causes such as animal scavenging patterns can also differentiate the damage from perimortem trauma. In long bones, postmortem breaks will tend to occur at right angles to the long axis of the bone. Although assessment of fractures can yield clues that can differentiate postmortem damage from perimortem trauma, several factors can complicate differentiation of postmortem and perimortem alterations. These include abrasive modification that can round fracture edges, sun exposure and bleaching which can alter previous coloration differences, and other destructive postmortem alterations such as scavenging that can obscure or destroy the perimortem trauma.

Biomechanically, the reason postmortem fractures differ is because dry bone responds to force differently than fresh bone. Living bone contains moisture and collagen, which give it greater elasticity. When bone dries, its elastic modulus and strength will actually increase, but its toughness will decrease (Turner and Burr, 1993). While the stress must be greater to cause dry bones to fracture, they can absorb less energy prior to failure. One study demonstrated that a dried human femur showed a 17% increase in Young's modulus and a 31% increase in tensile strength, but a 55% decrease in toughness (Evans and Lebow, 1951). In addition, fresh bone contains water, which acts to absorb and dissipate some energy (a property called **viscoelasticity**). When bone is dry, it no longer has this energy-absorbing quality, so the mechanical properties are altered and it behaves more like an inorganic material. This response is similar to the way a dried out branch or twig that has lost its moisture content will snap, while a green stick will have more flexibility.

13.4 Trauma mechanism

Trauma mechanism refers to the way force was applied to the bone, resulting in the alteration. Trauma mechanism is typically classified as being the result of blunt force, high velocity projectile, sharp force, thermal, or some combination, and is usually determined by examination of the overall pattern of alteration. It is important to note, however, that although these categories can be descriptive and helpful, the forces that produce skeletal trauma occur along a continuum and not in discrete categories. For example, the difference between blunt trauma and some types of sharp trauma is the area of impact, with sharp trauma resulting from a force applied by a tool with very small surface area. The difference between blunt trauma and high velocity projectile trauma is the rate at which the force is applied, with high velocity projectile trauma resulting from a force applied by an object moving at a very high rate of speed and impacting a small surface area. At their extremes, trauma mechanisms are often more apparent, but they can sometimes be difficult to discern. Reconstruction of fractured bone fragments (see Chapter 7) is frequently necessary in order to observe the overall pattern of trauma, especially in cases with a large amount of fragmentation.

Blunt force trauma

Blunt force trauma results from (relatively) slow load application to bone (Passalacqua and Fenton, 2012; Berryman and Symes, 1998) over a relatively large surface area. Such traumas may result from a blow from an object (such as a club, hammer, or fist), but also include deceleration injuries such as transportation accidents and falls from heights. Blunt force traumas are usually interpreted by their fracture patterns.

Fractures from blunt force trauma will follow the path of least resistance, propagating until the energy has dissipated. In the cranium, fractures will often terminate into one of the cranial sutures which dissipate the fracture energy; greater amounts of force are typically involved in fractures that continue through sutures. Certain parts of the skeleton, especially in the cranium, have areas that are more reinforced (a characteristic referred to as **buttressing**) which also helps redirect forces and dissipate stress. Certain fracture patterns of the facial skeleton are fairly well understood and documented in relation to these facial buttresses. The patterns are a product of relative strengths of certain areas of the facial skeleton (Rogers, 1982), and are characterized by LeFort fractures (Figure 13.8). LeFort I (or horizontal) fractures involve the alveolar portion of the maxillae and inferior nasal aperture, and typically result from force applied to the lower face. LeFort II (or pyramidal) fractures involve the nasal bridge, lower borders of the orbits, and posterior maxillae, and typically result from force applied to the midface. LeFort III (or transverse) fractures involve the medial walls of the orbits and the zygomatics, and typically result from force applied to the nasal bridge or upper maxilla.

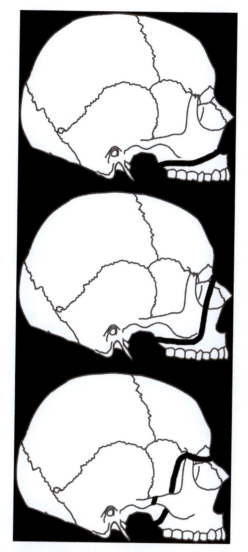

FIGURE 13.8 LeFort fractures: LeFort I (top), LeFort II (center), and LeFort III (bottom)

   In blunt force trauma to the cranial vault, the bone typically bends internally, creating tensile stress on the inner table. This internal tensile stress causes fractures which start at the inner table, but often continue through to the outer table and radiate outward from the impact site, creating a pattern of radiating fractures. If the object continues inward on the skull, concentric fractures (which are collapsing the bone inwardly) may also form, circumscribing the impact site (Figure 13.9).

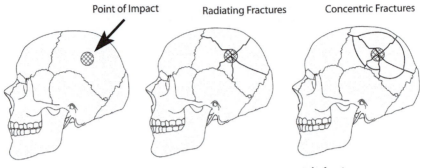

FIGURE 13.9 Blunt force trauma impact with radiating and concentric fractures

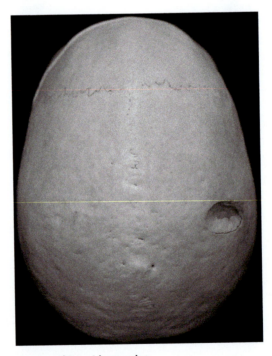

FIGURE 13.10 Blunt trauma with tool impression

Characteristics of blunt trauma include plastic deformation, **delamination**, patterns from known blunt causes (such as falls from heights), and tool marks or impressions (Scientific Working Group for Forensic Anthropology [SWGANTH], 2011) (Figure 13.10). Because of the slow loading nature of blunt force trauma, there is time for the bone to bend, which results in a permanent deformation of the material. When an implement or

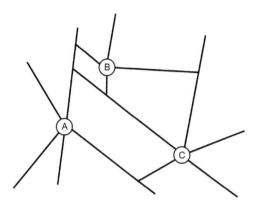

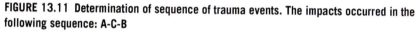

FIGURE 13.11 Determination of sequence of trauma events. The impacts occurred in the following sequence: A-C-B

tool is used to inflict blunt force trauma, the size and shape of the wound or impressions from tool features may give clues about the tool class and direction of impact.

In cases of multiple blunt impacts, it may be possible to determine the sequence in which the impacts occurred. Fractures from an impact will propagate until the energy has dissipated or until they encounter a discontinuity in the bone through which the energy is dissipated. This means that fractures from subsequent impacts will terminate into fractures from pre-existing impacts. In Figure 13.11, for example, the fractures originating from impact "A" do not terminate into any of the other fractures. The fractures from impact "B" terminate into fractures from impacts "A" and "C." Fractures from impact "C" terminate into fractures from impact "A." The sequence of the impacts is therefore A, then C, and then B.

Another form of blunt trauma is the slow application of force through compression of the neck as is seen in cases of strangulation (either manual or using a ligature) or hanging (which may be related to a suicide, homicide, or judicial hangings). Perimortem hyoid fractures (Figure 13.12) have been noted to indicate manual strangulation, although other forms of neck trauma cannot be excluded without further investigation (Ubelaker, 1992). Apparent hyoid fractures should be examined carefully, however, because unfused or incompletely ossified hyoids can easily be mistaken for traumatic separation. Hyoid fractures are more likely to occur in older individuals where ossification of the hyoid is more complete (Pollanen and Chiasson, 1996). Hyoids are not always fractured in cases of compressive trauma to the neck, and the absence of hyoid fractures does not mean that strangulation or neck compression can be excluded (Pollanen and Chiasson, 1996). Hangings, which usually produce more force on the neck than strangulation, can also result in fractures of the cervical vertebrae, especially the bilateral fracture of the pedicles of C2. These are referred to as a **hangman's fracture**, though these fractures do not always occur in judicial hangings (James and Nasmyth-Jones, 1992), and are also commonly associated with other causes such as motor vehicle accidents or sports-related injuries.

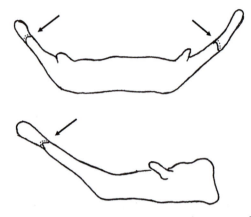

FIGURE 13.12 Fractures of the hyoid which likely resulted from strangulation or hanging; anterior (top) and lateral (bottom) views

High velocity projectile trauma

High velocity projectile trauma is characterized by a very rapid application of force over a relatively small surface area. Typically these wounds are produced by bullets from firearms (which travel at speeds of ~1100–4000 feet/second), but may also result from shrapnel from a blast or any other very fast-moving small object. This type of trauma is sometimes referred to as *ballistic trauma*, but the term **ballistic** technically refers to bullets in flight or the internal actions of firearms, and not to the actual force that resulted in the trauma. The term *high velocity projectile* is also more inclusive since not all high velocity projectile traumas are caused by bullets. Note that other projectiles such as thrown javelins or arrows (which travel at ~300 feet/ second), are not considered high velocity projectiles, and the resulting alterations would therefore be categorized as blunt force trauma. High velocity projectile trauma can usually be recognized by the fracture characteristics, and shape and size of the wound/s, as well as associated beveling and fractures.

Most high velocity projectile wounds are relatively round, but they may also be oval, keyhole-shaped, or irregularly shaped. Round wounds are commonly seen in cases where the impact of the projectile is roughly perpendicular to the surface of the bone. When the projectile trajectory is not perpendicular, the wounds are more likely to be oval or keyhole-shaped. The more extreme the angle (i.e., the more tangential the trajectory), the more likely a keyhole-shaped defect is to occur (Figures 13.13 and 13.14).

The size of the projectile wound is related to various factors, including characteristics of the projectile (its size, how it is constructed, and how fast it is moving) and characteristics of the bone (such as whether it is a flat or tubular bone). While the size of a projectile (such as the *caliber* or size of a bullet) is often roughly correlated with the size of the wound, bone is a material that deforms when force is applied, and the wound may not be a true representation of the projectile size. For bullets, for

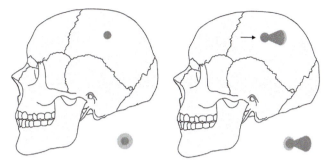

FIGURE 13.13 High velocity projectile defect shapes

Left: A round defect is typically produced when the projectile enters perpendicular to the bone. Right: A keyhole-shaped defect is typically produced when the projectile contacts the bone at an angle. Dark areas indicate missing bone and light areas indicated exposed diploë/beveling. Arrow indicates direction of projectile path; bottom wound patterns represent internal views.

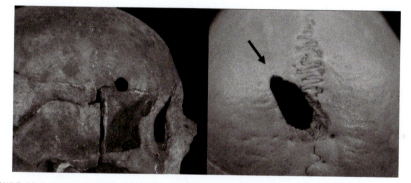

FIGURE 13.14 Round entrance defect (left) and keyhole entrance defect (right)

example, only the relative caliber size (i.e., large caliber versus small caliber) can usually be determined (Berryman et al., 1995; Ross, 1996).

One characteristic of high velocity projectile trauma is **beveling**, or angling of the alteration in the direction of the projectile, especially on flat bones such as those of the cranial vault. Beveling is the result of plug-and-spall fractures caused by fast-moving objects (Figure 13.15). As a high velocity projectile passes through bone, a plug of bone in the projectile's path is displaced. Spall refers to small flakes of bone that are broken off when the projectile penetrates the other side of the bone. The result is that the side of the bone where the projectile exits has a greater extent of missing bone than the side where the projectile enters. Entrance wounds are therefore typically internally beveled while exit wounds are externally beveled (Figure 13.16). The direction and path of a projectile can often be deduced from beveling characteristics.

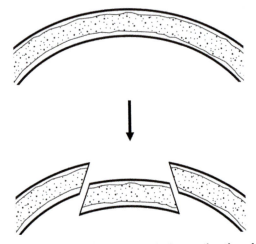

FIGURE 13.15 Beveling from plug-and-spall; arrow indicates direction of projectile

FIGURE 13.16 External beveling of a cranial projectile exit wound

(From Ross, n.d.)

Similarly to blunt trauma, high velocity projectile trauma occurring on the cranial vault often results in two common types of fractures, radiating and concentric (Figure 13.17). Radiating fractures are linear fractures that radiate out from the impact site, and concentric fractures are curved or circular lines that surround the impact site. In

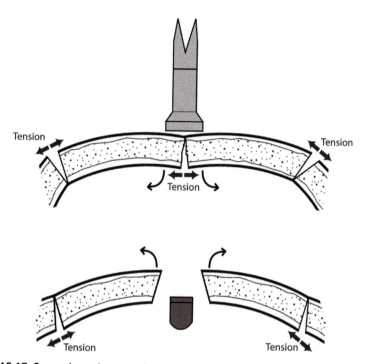

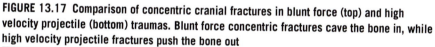

FIGURE 13.17 Comparison of concentric cranial fractures in blunt force (top) and high velocity projectile (bottom) traumas. Blunt force concentric fractures cave the bone in, while high velocity projectile fractures push the bone out

contrast to the collapsing concentric fractures produced in blunt force trauma, which tend to be internally beveled, the concentric fractures associated with high velocity projectile trauma tend to be externally beveled because they are heaving outward from intracranial pressure caused by the bullet passing through the brain (Smith et al., 1987).

Little or no plastic deformation is associated with high velocity projectile trauma because the force is applied so rapidly that the bone does not have time to bend and deform. Additionally, because of the magnitude of the force, high velocity projectile traumas also tend to result in a greater degree of fracturing and fragmentation than other traumas.

Even in the absence of a recognizable injury pattern, the involvement of a projectile may be evident from remnants of the projectile left behind and visible in radiographs (Figure 13.18). Recall from Chapter 3 that certain materials will stand out in radiographs due to their relative radiodensities. Projectiles are typically constructed of metals which are more radiodense than bone and will appear distinct from bone radiographically. In some cases, fragments of the projectile may be present within the cranium, and sometimes even if the projectile has passed all the way through the bone, small remnants of the projectile may have been deposited on the bone as they made contact (often called "lead wipe") which will also be visible in radiographs. Pellets

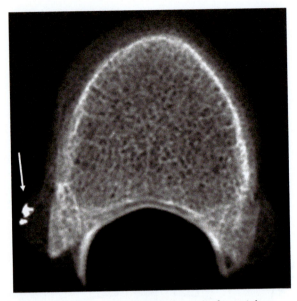

FIGURE 13.18 Projectile fragments visible in a radiograph of a vertebra

from shotgun wounds usually do not have enough remaining force to exit the body, and can often be located using radiography either within soft tissues or embedded in bone.

Multiple projectile wounds can often be sequenced similarly to blunt force trauma impacts on the basis of fracture patterns. It is important to note, however, that fractures can travel though bone at an extremely high speed, and it is possible for radiating fractures from an entrance wound to reach the other side of the cranial vault before the projectile exits the cranium.

Sharp force trauma

Sharp force trauma is characterized as trauma created by a tool with a point or beveled edge (Symes et al. 1998, 2002; DiMaio and DiMaio, 2001; Spitz, 1993). Sharp force trauma often occurs under loading conditions similar to blunt force trauma, but using a tool with a very small surface area (e.g., the edge of a blade). Sharp force traumas often leave distinctive marks (cuts) on the bone. While sharp force traumas can be caused by a wide variety of implements, two commonly utilized and heavily researched tools are knives and saws. Functionally, the purpose of a knife is to cut soft material, while a saw is designed to cut hard material and they therefore function rather differently. Knives typically have a narrow beveled edge which comes back to a wide **spine**. Saws have wide teeth which come back to a relatively narrow spine (Figure 13.19) so that they will not bind when cutting through hard material.

Knife cuts and stab wounds typically leave alterations such as straight line incisions, punctures, gouges, and clefts (Figure 13.20). There are two general classes of knives: serrated and non-serrated. Serrated knives have teeth built into the blade,

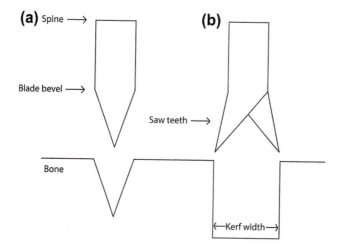

FIGURE 13.19 Cross-sections of a single bladed knife (a), and a cross-cut saw blade (b)

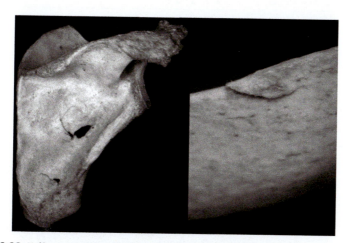

FIGURE 13.20 Knife puncture wounds in a scapula (left) and incised wound in a rib (right)

whereas non-serrated knives have smooth blades. The teeth on serrated blades create striations on bone that are distinctive from non-serrated blades, and can be used to determine the class of the knife used.

Saws consist of teeth which are designed to cut through hard material. As saws progress though material, they create a **kerf**, or groove (Figure 13.21). The marks created by saws can be analyzed to determine the class of the saw used. Class characteristics of saws include such traits as the blade and tooth size and shape, teeth-per-inch, blade and tooth set, cutting action, and saw power (i.e., hand vs. mechanical). The direction of the progress (of the saw cut) as well as the direction of the stroke can also be determined by examining the cut for exit chipping and breakaway spurs (Figure 13.22).

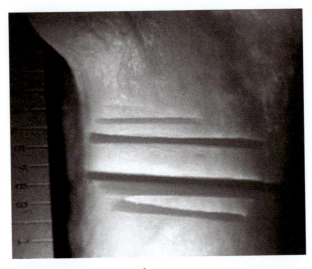

FIGURE 13.21 Kerf marks from a saw on a femur

(from Symes et al., 2010)

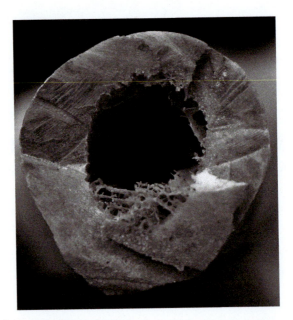

FIGURE 13.22 Saw cut marks on a bone

Dismemberment is almost always associated with sharp force trauma on bone. In many cases perpetrators attempt to dismember a body using knives, only to discover that the knives cannot easily cut through bone. It is therefore not uncommon to find both knife and saw marks on dismembered remains, or to have incomplete knife cuts in bones which are then broken at these weakened areas. Bodies are typically dismembered in order to prevent their detection and identification. Dismemberment generally occurs after death which is technically in the postmortem period (in relation to the death event), but is usually performed when bones are still in a biomechanically fresh state; alterations would therefore have the biomechanical properties of perimortem trauma.

It is common in cases of sharp force trauma for forensic anthropologists to work in conjunction with tool mark experts. Forensic anthropologists are typically the ones to discover and locate the trauma on the remains, and focus their examination primarily on classifying trauma type and timing and providing a general description of the skeletal alterations. Tool mark examiners are typically responsible for making more detailed conclusions about the class of tool used and comparing alterations to a particular tool to determine whether it is consistent with having created the alterations observed on the bone.

Thermal alterations

Thermal alterations result from exposure of the body to **fire** or other heat sources. Due to the nature of thermal reactions, the process can be very destructive to the organic material. Early stages of thermal alteration involve the burning of the fleshed human body. With the continued application of the thermal source, the bones may become exposed and damaged as the organic components become fuel for the continuing exothermic reaction. Although some studies have attempted to correlate certain bone alterations with particular temperatures, thermal alterations are a function of both time and temperature. In other words, similar alterations can be produced with high heat over a short period of time or lower heat over a longer period of time.

Understanding the normal burn pattern (e.g., that seen in an unobstructed body under typical burning conditions) can help with interpretations regarding whether any unusual circumstances were at play. The soft tissues are altered first, resulting in a loss of moisture which causes the muscles (typically the larger flexors) and ligaments to contract. As this occurs, the position of the body shifts, resulting is what is referred to as the pugilistic posture (Symes et al., 2008) (Figure 13.23). With continued exposure to heat, the soft tissues will continue to burn. The thickness of the soft tissues plays a large role in the exposure and heat alteration of bone. Skeletal regions with less overlying soft tissue will typically be exposed first, while those areas with more overlying soft tissue will burn last (Figure 13.24).

Understanding the cause and mechanism of the pugilistic posture and general body soft tissue thicknesses allows for burn patterns to be analyzed and abnormal

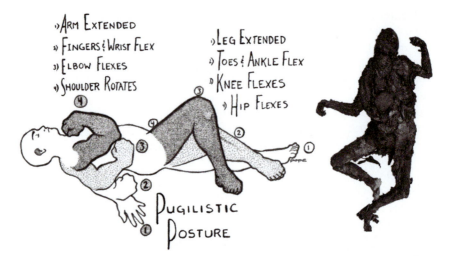

FIGURE 13.23 Pugilistic posture with flexion of the fingers, elbows, toes, knees, and hip

(Images courtesy of Elayne Pope)

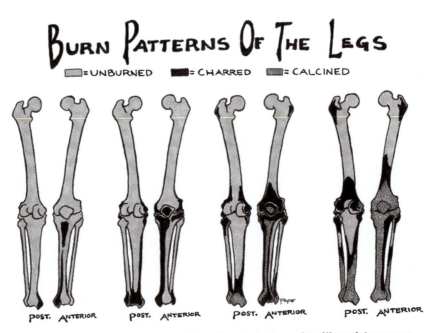

FIGURE 13.24 Burn patterns of the anterior and posterior legs with differential exposure sites of bone in areas of thin soft tissue protection, while other surfaces remain protected by muscle

(Image courtesy of Elayne Pope)

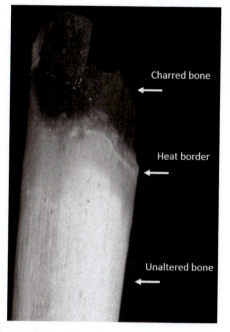

Charred bone

Heat border

Unaltered bone

FIGURE 13.25 Color changes in heat-altered bone

burn patterns to become apparent (Symes et al., 2008). For instance, if a body is burned using accelerants or placed in the trunk of a car, the burn patterns will often deviate from the normal pattern. Accelerants may result in a greater amount of burning to areas with thicker soft tissues, resulting in a greater degree of alterations in these areas than otherwise expected. Being placed in the trunk of a car or other confined space may limit the body's ability to assume the pugilistic posture. Thus careful documentation of the fire scene is important in order to fully interpret the burn pattern present on a set of remains (Dirkmaat, 2002).

Once the soft tissues have burned away, the bones become exposed to heat and flames, resulting in thermal alterations to the bone. Heat-altered bone is evident by color changes, shrinkage, fractures, and other physical alterations. Color changes are typically the first to occur in heat-altered bone, with these changes corresponding primarily to changes in the organic component (Figure 13.25). Normal, unheated bone is a pale yellow color. In the very early stages of heat alteration, occurring in areas that are still covered by soft tissues (such that the bone is exposed to heat but not to direct flame, resulting in loss of moisture and some molecular alteration), altered osseous tissue will first appear as a white color, sometimes referred to as the heat border. As thermal exposure continues, the bone becomes darkened in color, eventually becoming black, a condition referred to as **charred**. Charred bone has been directly exposed to fire, and is a result of the carbonization of the organic component of the bone. Eventually, the bone will become **calcined**. Calcined bone has been thermally altered to the extent that it has lost all organic content and moisture. At the calcined stage, the remains are simply a framework of the inorganic components of bone (i.e., hydroxyapatite) and are very fragile.

Table 13.2 Heat-induced fractures

Fracture type	Fracture characteristics
Transverse fracture	Fracture occurring transversely in long bone shafts as a function of the bone structure weakening and failing from heat alteration
Curved transverse fracture	Half-moon shaped fractures which occur in long bone shafts as the soft tissues shrink and pull back from the bone; these fractures are indicative of direction of fire progression
Step fracture	Fractures extending transversely from a longitudinal fracture across a long bone shaft
Patina	Superficial micro-fractures which often have a mesh or spider-web appearance

Thermally-altered bone also decreases in dimension, or shrinks. This shrinkage is a function of the combustion of the organic components of bone and evaporation of water, causing the bone to decrease in overall size. Shrinkage may also be associated with heat-related warping and deformation. These changes in dimensions and over-all shape should be considered in laboratory analysis since they could affect metric analyses such as those used to estimate sex and stature.

Another effect of heat on bone is fractures. Burned bone fractures share many characteristics with other postmortem dry bone fractures in that they have sharp (rather than smooth) margins and they often occur along the grain of the bone (longitudinally). Burned bone also fractures in response to soft tissue shrinkage and the direction of fire progression, resulting in fractures that are specific to heat-altered bone. Heat-induced fractures include transverse, curved transverse (thumbnail), step, and patina (Table 13.2 and Figure 13.26). Similar heat-induced fractures occur in the dentition as well (Schmidt, 2008). In crania, there is often delamination of the outer bone layer (Figure 13.27).

Heat alterations to skeletal tissues are also apparent at the microscopic level. With the application of heat of increasing temperatures, tissues (including both bones and teeth) first show an increase in surface roughness, then becoming glassy and smooth, then acquiring a frothy appearance, and finally protuberances coalesce into smooth-surfaced nodules (Shipman et al., 1984). Increasing temperature is also associated with an increase in mineral crystal size (Shipman et al., 1984).

Cremation is an extreme form of thermal alteration where the body is reduced to bone that is completely calcined and disintegrates to ash (Figure 13.28). Cremation can occur as a part of funerary practices, it may be performed intentionally as a criminal act to dispose of a body, or it may be accidental such as in a structure fire. In modern commercial cremation, remains are placed into a furnace called a **retort** where they are burned at high temperatures until they are calcined. The remains are then placed into mechanical pulverizers that reduce the remains to ashes. Whether funerary, accidental, or criminal, the analysis of cremated remains (often referred to as **cremains**) can be complex because there are typically few if any bones that retain any morphological features of value. In some cases, elemental analysis to determine the presence of bone may be the furthest extent of possible examinations (e.g., Gilpin, 2013).

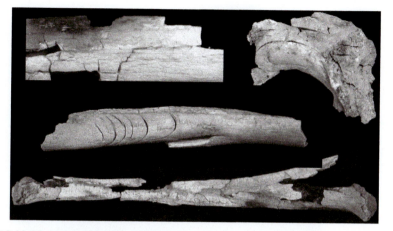

FIGURE 13.26 Heat-induced bone fractures

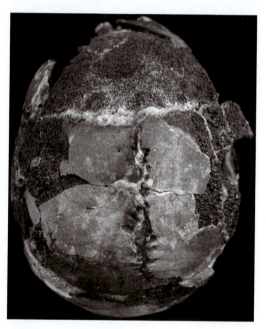

FIGURE 13.27 Delamination in a charred skull

Blast trauma

Blast traumas are complex and are often the product of mixed forces (compression, shearing, and bending) and mixed mechanisms (high velocity projectile, blunt, sharp, and thermal trauma). There is an abundance of literature on blast trauma in the medical and orthopedic fields, but it has been less frequently addressed in the anthropological literature. Most of the medical literature focuses on mortality and treatment of blast

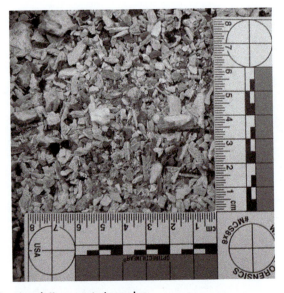

FIGURE 13.28 Commercially cremated remains

injuries, with few controlled studies aimed at investigating patterns of blast injuries, especially those relating to the skeleton. It has received a little more attention in the forensic anthropological literature recently, particularly as it relates to the involvement by anthropologists in humanitarian, conflict-related, and terrorism investigations (Kimmerle and Barabar, 2008; Christensen et al., 2012; Christensen and Smith, 2013).

Blast traumas were first described during World War I, and are categorized as primary, secondary, tertiary, and quaternary. Primary blast traumas are those resulting from barometric changes from the blast wave itself. These tend to affect primarily the hollow organs such as the eardrums, lungs, and bowels, but the blast wave, if strong enough, may also result in injuries affecting the skeleton such as amputation, decapitation, and skeletal fractures. Secondary blast traumas are those resulting from penetrating fragments and shrapnel. These too may affect the skeleton, producing sharp, blunt, or high velocity projectile trauma and associated radiating and concentric fractures. Tertiary blast traumas are the result of large objects falling onto a body, or a body being thrown into objects. Such forces may result in blunt traumas of the skeleton. Quaternary blast traumas include miscellaneous injuries such as burns and smoke inhalation.

Few patterns are recognized in relation to skeletal blast trauma, though blast events have been shown to produce extensively comminuted fractures with numerous small, displaced bone splinters (Christensen et al., 2012). In addition, butterfly fractures of the ribs with the fracture initiation on the visceral rib surface have been noted in association with ventrally-directed blasts and are believed to result from the blast wave expanding the ribcage and bending the ribs outward (Christensen and Smith, 2013) (Figure 13.29).

Fracture patterns from blasts may therefore differ in quality and extent from other types of skeletal trauma such that, if analyzing skeletal remains and the source of the

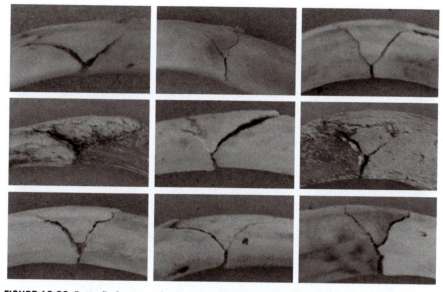

FIGURE 13.29 Butterfly fractures in ribs resulting from blast events

(From Christensen and Smith, 2013)

trauma in unknown, anthropologists may be able to differentiate between blast trauma and trauma from some other cause. Such a diagnosis, however, requires thorough analysis of the individual skeletal injuries and careful interpretation of the injury distribution over the entire skeleton. Much more research in the area of skeletal blast trauma is needed, especially considering the increasing frequency with which anthropologists are likely to encounter skeletal trauma resulting from explosive events.

13.5 Cause and manner of death

The **cause of death** (or "proximate cause of death") is the medically determined disease or injury responsible for the lethal sequence of events, or the factors that prompt these events to occur. Literally speaking, the cause of death is always the cessation of breathing and the heart beating, but practically speaking, the cause of death is etiologically specific, such as a particular disease, old age, malnutrition, or a gunshot wound. A term often used interchangeably with "cause of death," but which is subtly different, is "mechanism of death" or "immediate cause of death" which is not etiologically specific and refers to the physiological or biochemical alteration whereby the cause exerts its lethal effect (e.g., congestive heart failure, septicemia, etc.). The **manner of death** is a legal distinction for the way someone died, or how the cause of death occurred. While there are countless possibilities for the cause of death, there are only five generally accepted manners of death: homicide, suicide, accident, natural causes, or unknown.

While forensic anthropologists may provide conclusions and opinions regarding skeletal injuries, the determination of the cause and manner of death is the responsibility of the medicolegal authority (e.g., medical examiner or coroner) and not the forensic anthropologist. An anthropologist may discover evidence related to the mechanism of skeletal injury which may or may not have contributed to an individual's death, as well as other observations that may provide evidence pertaining to the manner of death. For example, a forensic anthropologist may conclude that a large caliber projectile entered the right side of the cranium and exited the left side. These conclusions often assist the medicolegal authority in making their determinations of cause and manner of death (i.e., they are the ones responsible for concluding that the previously described wound would have caused death).

Since not all death events leave alterations on the skeleton, however, forensic anthropological examinations may not always provide information relevant to the cause of death. Moreover, even if a mechanism of trauma can be identified by forensic anthropological analysis, it is usually not possible to distinguish based on the trauma pattern alone whether it resulted from, for example, an accident versus intentional violence; such determinations are often dependent on contextual and investigative information.

13.6 Case study – perimortem fall from a height

The University of Tennessee Forensic Anthropology Center (FAC) was contacted regarding a death that had occurred almost 25 years previously, in which decomposed remains of a female were discovered at the bottom of a cliff. The autopsy at the time indicated that no skeletal fractures were present. The family eventually requested another examination due to inconsistencies between the autopsy findings and the death certificate which indicated the cause of death was due to a fall. The remains were exhumed and transported to the FAC for a skeletal trauma analysis.

In contrast with the original autopsy findings, the anthropological analysis revealed extensive perimortem trauma to elements along the midline (Figure 13.30).

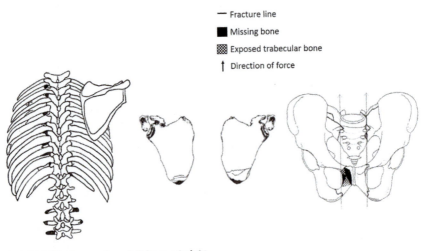

FIGURE 13.30 Trauma from fall from a height

Fractures (complete and incomplete) were found on the ribs, vertebrae, sacrum, teeth, scapulae, and os coxae. The overall pattern of fractures, which included numerous compression fractures of the axial skeleton, was consistent with vertical compression consistent with a fall from a height. The greater number of left-sided fractures further suggested that the individual was probably positioned toward the left side at impact.

13.7 Case study – antemortem and perimortem pediatric trauma

A two-year-old male was visiting his father's residence for six days, during which time the father reported that the child ate well and experienced no accidents or injuries. When the child was returned to his mother's residence, he played, ate, and went to bed. According to the mother, at 4:00am, the mother's boyfriend discovered the child in his room experiencing seizure-like activity. The child was taken to a local hospital but did not recover and was pronounced dead at around 5:30am.

The remains were examined by the Harris County Institute of Forensic Science, where irregularities were noted on several left and right ribs and the right radius and ulna (Figure 13.31). These skeletal elements were removed and processed for an anthropological trauma analysis. Antemortem trauma was noted in the form of fracture healing and subperiosteal new bone formation on six right ribs and three left ribs consistent with constriction of the chest. Additional antemortem trauma was present on the distal right radius and ulna consistent with axial compression. Perimortem

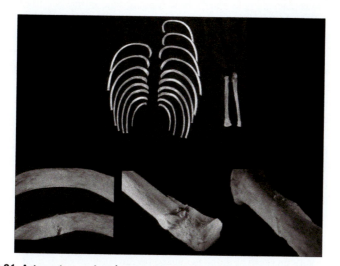

FIGURE 13.31 Antemortem and perimortem blunt trauma on a 2-year-old male

Top: Ribs and right radius and ulna, bottom left: Healing fracture and subperiosteal new bone formation on ribs, center: Healing fracture of the left ulna, and right: Perimortem fracture on rib.

(Images courtesy of Harris County Institute of Forensic Science)

trauma in the form of a torus fracture was noted on a right rib, consistent with anterior directed force to the lower right back. The fractures were concluded to represent a minimum of two traumatic events, one that occurred within three weeks of death and one that occurred very near the time of death. In addition, the autopsy revealed contusions, hemorrhages, and lacerations in various locations throughout the body. The death was determined to result from blunt force injuries.

13.8 Summary

- Skeletal trauma can be characterized by its timing in relation to the death event (antemortem, perimortem, or postmortem alteration) as well as the mechanism that caused the trauma (blunt force, high velocity projectile, sharp force, thermal, or mixed).
- Bones are objects that obey physical laws and understanding bone's response to force can help interpret how fractures may have occurred. The primary forces that cause skeletal fractures are compression, tension, bending, shear, and torsion.
- Fractures may be classified as incomplete or complete, and can be further categorized based on their morphology. Incomplete fractures include bow, greenstick, and depressed fractures. Complete fractures include transverse, oblique, spiral, and comminuted fractures.
- Antemortem trauma is an alteration that occurred prior to the death event, and is primarily evidenced by bone healing. Understanding the sequence and timing of fracture repair can help clarify how long ago the injury occurred, and may reveal trauma pattern histories.
- Perimortem trauma is an alteration that occurred when the bone was in a biomechanically fresh state. This typically includes trauma that occurred very near and is directly related to the death event, but may also include damage that occurred in the postmortem period.
- Postmortem damage refers to alterations to the bone after death and which are unassociated to the death event. These alterations may include taphonomic changes such as scavenging. Certain postmortem alterations may have a relationship to the death event such as dismemberment or thermal alterations.
- Blunt force trauma is caused by the application of relatively low speed force over a relatively large surface area. This may include blows from objects, falls from heights, and transportation accidents.
- Sharp force trauma is caused by the application of force by a tool with a pointed or beveled edge, typically a knife or saw. Sharp force traumas often leave clefts and striations that can be associated to a class of tool.
- High velocity projectile trauma is caused by the application of high-speed force over a small surface area. These injuries may include gunshot as well as shrapnel wounds, and can be recognized by their size, shape, beveling, and fracture pattern.
- Thermal trauma is caused by exposure of the bone to fire or heat resulting in alterations such as color changes, shrinkage, and fractures.

- Blast trauma is an example of a trauma pattern resulting from mixed forces and trauma mechanisms. Contextual information and certain fracture patterns may help identify trauma as resulting from a blast event.
- The results of forensic anthropological assessments of trauma may help the medicolegal authority in determining the cause and manner of death.

13.9 **Test yourself**

- Explain the relationship between elastic deformation, yield point, plastic deformation, and failure. How do these relate to a bone's strength and toughness?
- What type of directional force do you think might be involved in fractures resulting from a fall? A skiing accident? A collision between a car and a pedestrian? If you have ever fractured a bone, can you identify the directional force that caused it?
- A lawyer in a trial has asked you about an injury that you referred to in your report as a "perimortem fracture." How would you explain to the jury the meaning and significance of this conclusion?
- How would you categorize trauma created by the handle of a knife? Why? What alterations would you expect to see?
- You are presented with a cranium with two roughly circular defects, one on the right side and one on the left. What conclusions might you be able to draw and provide to investigators about these injuries? What would those conclusions be based on?
- Describe how you would go about locating, identifying, and analyzing alterations on remains which are reportedly from the victim of blunt trauma followed by dismemberment.
- You are presented with the contents of an urn which includes several small bone fragments along with a significant amount of ash. What types of analyses might you be able to perform? What conclusions might you be able to make?
- Besides blasts, what other events or scenarios might result in trauma from multiple forces?

Definitions

Alteration A change to the physical properties of skeletal material
Anisotropic Having different mechanical properties in different directions
Antemortem Before death
Ballistic Relating to projectiles and their flight and the internal actions of firearms
Bending A force that applies compression to one side of the bone and tension to the other
Beveling Angling of an alteration resulting from plug-and-spall fractures caused by fast-moving objects
Buttressing The reinforcement of the skeleton (typically in reference to the face or proximal femur) in order to transfer and dissipate forces

Calcined A condition of thermally-altered bone where the organic content and moisture have been lost, usually appearing as a white or gray color

Cause of death The disease or injury responsible for the lethal sequence of events or the factors that prompt these events to occur; also called "proximate cause of death"

Charred A condition of thermally-altered bone where the organic component has been carbonized, usually resulting in a blackened color

Complete fracture A fracture in which there is discontinuity between two or more bone fragments

Compression A force that acts to decrease the bone dimension in the direction of the applied force

Creep fracture Fracture occurring under stress levels less than the failure point due to relatively low static force applied over an extended period of time

Cremains Cremated remains

Cremation The process of thermally reducing remains to calcined bone and/or ash

Delamination Separation of the outer layer of bone of the skull

Dismemberment The act of taking something apart

Dynamic loading Force that is applied suddenly and at relatively high speed

Edentulous The antemortem loss of all teeth, accompanied by the resorption of the alveolar bone

Elastic deformation Temporary deformation in response to a force

Elastic modulus (Young's modulus) A measure of a material's intrinsic ability to resist deformation

Failure Cracking, displacement, or misalignment that results in a material no longer performing as it did previously

Fatigue fracture Fracture occurring under stress levels less than the failure point due to repetitive loading

Fire An exothermic oxidation reaction where fuel is consumed by an oxidizer, generating enough heat to be self sustaining

Force The action of one object on another

Fracture The loss of bone integrity due to mechanical failure

Fracture callus A new mass of bone in the fracture site which bridges the fracture gap

Hangmans's fracture Bilateral fractures of the pedicles of C2

Hematoma A localized collection of blood in the tissues that occurs as a result of broken blood vessels; also called a bruise

Incomplete fracture A fracture in which some continuity is retained between the fractured bone portions

Inflammation A reaction by organisms to injurious stimuli that initiates healing, often characterized by an influx of plasma and white blood cells to the injured area

Isotropic Having the same mechanical properties in all directions

Kerf The notch or groove made by a cutting tool, typically a saw

Load The application of force to an object

Magnitude The amount of force applied

Manner of death The way someone died, or how the cause of death arose; usually homicide, suicide, accidental, natural causes, or unknown

Mechanics The science that deals with the effects of forces on objects

Osteogenic reaction The formation of new bone

Perimortem At or around the time of death; anthropologically, when the bone is in a biomechanically fresh state

Plastic deformation Permanent deformation in response to a force

Postmortem After death

Retort A furnace where remains are cremated

Shear A force involving the sliding of two areas of bone relative to one other, parallel to the direction of force

Spine The thickest section of a knife; in single-bladed knives, this is typically along the opposite edge of the beveled portion of the blade

Static loading Force that is applied slowly

Stiffness The ability of a material to resist deformation when force is applied

Strain The change in dimension (deformation) of a loaded body

Strength A characteristic of a material that is related to the load or stress required to reach the failure point

Stress Load per unit area

Tension A force that acts to increase the dimension of the bone in the direction of the force

Torsion A force involving the combination of shear and twisting

Toughness A measure of the energy absorption capability of a material

Trauma Disruption of living tissue by an outside force

Viscoelastic A characteristic of materials that exhibit both viscous and elastic properties when force is applied, involving a molecular rearrangement when undergoing deformation

Yield point The load point after which material experiences plastic or permanent deformation

References

Agarwal, B.D., Broutman, L.J., 1980. Analysis and Performance of Fiber Composites. John Wiley and Sons, New York.

Barbian, L., Sledzik, P., 2008. Healing following cranial trauma. J. Forensic Sci. 53 (2), 263–268.

Berryman, H.E., Symes, S.A., 1998. Recognizing gunshot and blunt cranial trauma through fracture interpretation. In: Reichs, K.J. (Ed.), Forensic Osteology: Advances in the Identification of Human Remains. Charles C. Thomas, Springfield, pp. 333–352.

Berryman, H.E., Smith, O.C., Symes, S.A., 1995. Diameter of cranial gunshot wounds as a function of bullet caliber. J. Forensic Sci. 40, 751–754.

Caler, W.E., Carter, D.R., 1989. Bone creep-fatigue damage accumulation. J. Biomech. 22, 625–636.

Christensen, A.M., Smith, V.A., 2013. Rib butterfly fractures as a possible indicator of blast trauma. J. Forensic Sci. S1, S15–S19.

Christensen, A.M., Smith, V.A., Ramos, V., Shegogue, C., Whitworth, M., 2012. Primary and secondary skeletal blast trauma. J. Forensic Sci. 57 (1), 6–11.

Cowin, S.C. (Ed.), 2001. Bone Biomechanics Handbook. CRC Press, Boca Raton.

Currey, J.D., 1970. The mechanical properties of bone. Clin. Orthop. 73, 210–231.

DiMaio, D., DiMaio, V., 2001. Forensic Pathology, second ed. CRC Press, Boca Raton.

Dirkmaat, D.C., 2002. Recovery and interpretation of the fatal fire victim: The role of forensic anthropology. In: Haglund, W.D., Sorg, M. (Eds.), Advances in Forensic Taphonomy: Method, Theory, and Archaeological Perspectives. CRC Press, Boca Raton, pp. 451–472.

Evans, F.G., 1973. Mechanical Properties of Bone. Charles C. Thomas, Springfield.

Evans, F.G., Lebow, M., 1951. Regional differences in some of the physical properties of the human femur. J. Appl. Phys. 3, 563–572.

Galloway, A., 1999. The biomechanics of fracture production. In: Galloway, A. (Ed.), Broken Bones: Anthropological Analysis of Blunt Force Trauma. Charles C. Thomas, Springfield, pp. 35–62.

Gilpin, M., 2013. Elemental analysis of variably contaminated cremains using X-ray fluorescence spectrometry [MA Thesis]. George Mason University, Fairfax.

Gozna, E.R., 1982. Biomechanics of Musculoskeletal Injury. Williams & Wilkins, Baltimore.

Hooke, R.S., 1678. Lectures de potentia reflitutiva or of spring: Explaining the power of springing bodies. Royal Society, London.

James, R., Nasmyth-Jones, R., 1992. The occurrence of cervical fractures in victims of judicial hanging. Forensic Sci. Int. 54 (1), 81–91.

Kimmerle, E.H., Baraybar, J.P., 2008. Skeletal Trauma: Identification of Injuries Resulting from Human Rights Abuse and Armed Conflict. CRC Press, Boca Raton.

Martin, R.B., Burr, D.B., Sharkey, N.A., 1998. Skeletal Tissue Mechanics. Springer, New York.

Moraitis, K., Eliopoulos, C., Spiliopoulou, C., 2009. Fracture characteristics of perimortem trauma in skeletal material. Internet J. Biol. Anthropol. 3 (2).

Newton, I., 1687. Philosophiæ Naturalis Principia Mathematica. Royal Society, London.

Ortner, D.J., Putschar, W.G.J., 1985. Identification of Pathological Conditions in Human Skeletal Remains. Smithsonian Institution Press, Washington, DC.

Passalacqua, N.V., Fenton, T.W., 2012. Developments in forensic anthropology: Blunt force trauma. In: Dirkmaat, D.C. (Ed.), A Companion to Forensic Anthropology. Blackwell Publishing, Chichester, pp. 400–412.

Pollanen, M.S., Chaisson, D.A., 1996. Fracture of the hyoid bone in strangulation: Comparison of fractured and unfractured hyoids from victims of strangulation. J. Forensic Sci. 41 (1), 110–113.

Reilly, D.T., Burstein, A.H., 1975. The elastic and ultimate properties of compact bone tissue. J. Biomech. 8, 393–405.

Rogers, L.F., Malave Jr., White, H., Tachdjian, M.O., 1978. Plastic bowing, torus and greenstick supracondylar fractures of the humerus: Radiographic clues to obscure fractures of the elbow in children. Radiology 128, 145–150.

Ross, A.H., 1996. Caliber estimation from cranial entrance defect measurements. J. Forensic Sci. 41, 629–633.

Ross, A.H., 2013. Gunshot wounds: A summary. Retrieved August 30 http://www.southampt on.ac.uk/~jb3/bullet/gsw.html.

Schmidt, C.W., 2008. The recovery and study of burned human teeth. In: Schmidt, C.W., Symes, S.S. (Eds.), The Analysis of Burned Human Remains. Elsevier Ltd., Burlington, pp. 55–74.

Scientific Working Group on Forensic Anthropology, 2011. Trauma Analysis – Revision 0.

Shipman, P., Foster, G., Shoeninger, M., 1984. Burnt bones and teeth: An experimental study of color, morphology, crystal structure and shrinkage. J. Archaeol. Sci. 11, 307–325.

Smith, O.C., Berryman, H.E., Lahern, C.H., 1987. Cranial fracture patterns and estimate of direction from low velocity gunshot wounds. J. Forensic Sci. 32, 1416–1421.

Smith, O.C., Pope, E.J., Symes, S.A., 2003. Look until you see: Identification of trauma in skeletal material. In: Steadman, D.W. (Ed.), Hard Evidence: Case Studies in Forensic Anthropology, second ed. Pearson Education Inc, Upper Saddle River, pp. 138–154.

Symes, S.A., Berryman, H.E., Smith, O.C., 1998. Saw marks in bone: Introduction and examination of residual kerf contour. In: Reichs, K.J. (Ed.), Forensic Osteology: Advances in the Identification of Human Remains. Charles C. Thomas, Springfield, pp. 389–409.

Symes, S.A., Chapman, M.S., Rainwater, C.W., Cabo, L.L., Myster, S.M.T., 2010. Knife and saw toolmark analysis on bone: A manual designed for the examination of criminal mutilation and dismemberment. National Institute of Justice Report Document Number 232864.

Symes, S.A., Rainwater, C.W., Chapman, E.N., Gipson, D.R., Piper, A.L., 2008. Patterned thermal destruction of human remains in a forensic setting. In: Schmidt, C.W., Symes, S.S. (Eds.), The Analysis of Burned Human Remains. Elsevier Ltd., Burlington, pp. 15–54.

Symes, S.A., Williams, J.A., Murray, E.A., Hoffman, J.M., Holland, T.D., Saul, J.M., et al., 2002. Taphonomic context of sharp-force trauma in suspected cases of human mutilation and dismemberment. In: Haglund, W.D., Sorg, M. (Eds.), Advances in Forensic Taphonomy: Method, Theory, and Archaeological Perspectives. CRC Press, Boca Raton, pp. 403–434.

Spitz, W., 1993. Spitz and Fisher's Medicolegal Investigation of Death: Guidelines for the Application of Pathology to Crime Investigation. Charles C. Thomas, Springfield.

Turner, C.H., Burr, D.B., 1993. Basic biomechanical measurements of bone: A tutorial. Bone 14, 595–608.

Ubelaker, D.H., 1992. Hyoid fracture and strangulation. J. Forensic Sci. 37 (5), 1216–1222.

Personal Identification

14.1 Principles of personal identification

Personal identification is the process of linking an unknown personal object or material (which may be a whole body, a skeleton, a fingerprint, a biological fluid, etc.) back to an individual of known identity. Although personal identification is often applied in cases of living individuals (such as when associating someone with a crime or crime scene), the focus of this chapter is the identification of deceased individuals, since this is where forensic anthropologists are typically involved. Personal identification of an unknown deceased individual is important in our society for both legal and humanitarian reasons. Legally, many issues are dependent on the determination of identity. For example, matters related to wills, inheritance, insurance policies, prosecution of homicides, detection of fraudulent deaths, accident reconstruction, and remarriage all depend on the identification of the deceased. Morally, identification is usually important for closure and resolution by surviving relatives and friends. Identification may also be important in matters of humanitarian concern including investigations of armed conflict and human rights investigations (see Chapter 15).

Logistically, personal identification is a legal matter, and the final determination of identity is made by a legal authority. For deceased individuals, this is the responsibility of the local **medicolegal authority** – usually a **medical examiner** or **coroner** (see Box 14.1), or sometimes a justice of the peace or sheriff. The identification of the deceased becomes official with the signing of the individual's death certificate by the medicolegal authority. The determination of identity is often (and ideally) informed by many factors including contextual circumstances, investigative information, and the results of scientific comparisons such as fingerprints, DNA, dental records, or anthropological examinations, but there is currently no legal or scientific threshold for confirming or rejecting an identification.

While a forensic anthropologist *could* be a medicolegal authority (by appointment or election), forensic anthropologists do not typically have the authority to make a personal identification. The extent to which forensic anthropologists are utilized in the personal identification process differs based on jurisdiction, but in cases involving skeletal remains, they are often able to provide significant information in the personal identification process. The primary ways that forensic anthropologists contribute to the identification process are by estimating and detecting characteristics of the skeletal remains

Forensic Anthropology. http://dx.doi.org/10.1016/B978-0-12-418671-2.00014-8

> **BOX 14.1 MEDICOLEGAL AUTHORITIES – CORONER VERSUS MEDICAL EXAMINER**
>
> Both medical examiners and coroners are typically responsible for investigating suspicious deaths, identifying bodies, notifying next of kin, and signing the death certificate. The qualifications they have and the medicolegal systems in which they work, however, can be quite different. A medical examiner is a physician, preferably trained in forensic pathology, who is appointed to his or her position and performs autopsies. A coroner is an elected official who may or may not have training as a physician. Different jurisdictions (at the state or county level in the United States) may operate under a medical examiner or coroner system or some other medicolegal system. Some jurisdictions require coroners to be forensic pathologists, but others do not; in such cases, remains may need to be sent to a qualified medical examiner or forensic pathologist if an autopsy is required. Although sometimes contentious, many authorities advocate the medical examiner system over the coroner system, or support nationalizing the medical examiner system in the United States. It is advisable for forensic anthropologists to be cognizant of the medicolegal system in which they practice.

that may narrow the pool of potential matches, and by comparing postmortem skeletal information to antemortem information about a particular individual and assessing the likelihood that the skeletal remains belong to that individual. Many different techniques exist for facilitating a personal identification using forensic anthropological approaches, which depend on the condition of the remains as well as the availability of antemortem information about an individual with which to compare the evidence.

There are various systems and terms associated with the "strength" of a particular identification. These may include terms such as *tentative*, *presumptive*, *probable*, or *positive identification*. Tentative or presumptive identifications are typically those based on associations with personal effects (such as finding a body associated with a driver's license), but which require at least some additional investigation to confirm whether the remains actually belong to that person. While they do not usually provide conclusive evidence of identity, personal effects can provide useful leads in the identification process. A positive identification typically refers to the conclusion that the medicolegal authority is satisfied that all of the evidence supports that the correct identification has been made.

14.2 Narrowing the pool of potential matches

An anthropological analysis may be used to assess biological information about the individual including his or her age, sex, ancestry, and stature (see Chapters 8–11). This assessment, of course, is not itself an identification, but is very useful in narrowing the pool of potential candidates in the search for identity. The biological profile can be used by investigators (often law enforcement officials) to search missing persons records for individuals who share that biological profile and could therefore be included and further investigated as potential matches to the skeletal remains.

In addition to the biological profile, anthropologists may be able to identify conditions of the skeleton which may further narrow the search, such as antemortem skeletal trauma (see Chapter 13), or individual variants, pathological conditions, and

---

BOX 14.2 NATIONAL MISSING AND UNIDENTIFIED PERSONS SYSTEM (NamUs)

The National Missing and Unidentified Persons System (NamUs) is the first national repository of missing persons and unidentified decedent records, and was created with the assistance of the National Institute of Justice (NIJ). It is a free online system that can be accessed and searched by anyone (www.namus.gov), and consists of two primary portals: The Missing Persons Database and the Unidentified Persons Database. Missing persons information can be entered into the Missing Persons Database by anyone (pending verification). Medical examiners and coroners can enter unidentified deceased information into the Unidentified Persons Database. NamUs also provides information on access to free DNA, anthropology, and odontology services (NamUs, n.d.). This database has resulted in numerous associations of antemortem and postmortem records, and continues to be a useful resource for both recent and cold cases. A number of forensic anthropologists are trained to use NamUs in their casework, or to modify NamUs records with the results of anthropological examinations.

BOX 14.3 NATIONAL CRIME INFORMATION CENTER (NCIC)

The National Crime Information Center (NCIC) is a computerized index of criminal justice information, including criminal records, fugitives, stolen property, and missing persons, and is available to federal, state, and local law enforcement agencies. The system allows ready access for law enforcement officials to inquiries and prompt disclosures of information from other criminal justice agencies which can assist in apprehending fugitives, returning property, and locating missing persons (NCIC, n.d.). Unlike NamUs, NCIC is only searchable by law enforcement or other authorized personnel who have access to a designated NCIC terminal.

---

anomalies (see Chapter 12). In searching missing persons records, knowledge of a particular injury or condition may further narrow the pool of potential matches. Moreover, in the event that any of these conditions may have required medical diagnosis or treatment, it is likely that the individual will have an antemortem record available for comparison, and this information can be used in an identification comparison.

The estimation of the postmortem interval (see Chapter 5) can also be very useful in narrowing the pool of potential matches. The postmortem interval can be used to determine whether skeletal remains could belong to a potential match depending on whether the postmortem interval is consistent with the length of disappearance of a certain missing person. For example, skeletal remains determined to have a time since death of 5–10 years can be excluded as originating from an individual who was last seen several weeks ago.

Based on the fit with assessments such as the biological profile, other skeletal conditions, and the postmortem interval, particular individuals may be included or excluded from further consideration. The individuals to be considered in the identification process may be found in local missing persons records and registries, or may be included in one of several national missing persons databases such as the National Missing and Unidentified Persons System (Box 14.2) or the National Crime Information Center (Box 14.3). Not all anthropologists have appropriate authority to contribute results of analyses of unidentified individuals to these databases, but in some cases these permissions can be obtained from the appropriate authority, or anthropologists can collect and provide this information to an individual with authority to create or modify the record in the database.

14.3 Identification comparisons

Once a potential match has been located, the identification process moves to the identification comparison phase, and there are many comparison methods that can be employed. The objective of the personal identification process is to link an *unknown* item (for forensic anthropologists, usually an unidentified skeleton) to a person of *known* identity; methods of personal identification of deceased individuals therefore involve the comparison of antemortem (*known*) information with postmortem (*unknown*) information. Antemortem information is therefore required for comparison, which is usually obtained by law enforcement officials or medicolegal investigators through the next of kin or medical and dental facilities. The two sets of information are then examined, looking for consistencies and inconsistencies that may confirm or refute the hypothesis that they originated from the same person.

The comparison will typically result in one of several conclusions, which vary depending on the comparison approach used as well as the reporting requirements of the forensic anthropology laboratory. Results may include, for example:

- The two sets of information are consistent with originating from the same individual with no unexplainable differences (and therefore the presumed decedent should continue to be *included* as a possible source of the remains).
- The two sets of information are inconsistent with originating from the same individual (and therefore the presumed decedent can be *excluded* as the source of the remains).
- There is insufficient information to include or exclude the presumed decedent as the source of the remains.

It is also important to understand when differences or inconsistencies between the antemortem and postmortem information are explainable versus unexplainable. For example, a hip replacement that appears in the postmortem record but not in an antemortem record can be explained (the hip replacement could have been implanted sometime after that particular antemortem record was made); these two records could still be consistent with originating from the same individual. A hip replacement that is present in the antemortem record but absent in the postmortem record, however, would be an unexplainable difference, and the person from whom the antemortem data was collected can be excluded as the source of the postmortem record.

Common identification comparison methods which are *not* typically the purview of forensic anthropologists include visual examination, fingerprint comparison, dental comparison, and DNA comparison (although anthropologists occasionally have a role in some of these processes, which will be discussed further below). Visual examination and fingerprint comparison usually involve recent deaths with well-preserved

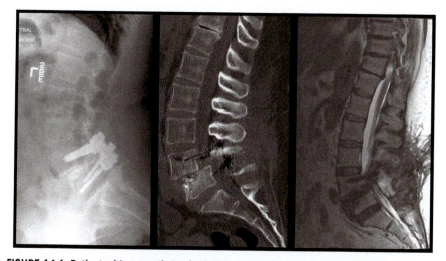

FIGURE 14.1 Patient with anterolisthesis, fusion, discectomy, and laminectomy who was imaged using standard x-ray (left), CT (center), and MRI (right)

(Images courtesy of Gary M. Hatch, MD, Radiology-Pathology Center for Forensic Imaging,
University of New Mexico School of Medicine)

bodies whose physical features have not been distorted by decomposition or injury. Visual comparisons rely on the recollections of relatives or friends of the deceased as compared to the postmortem viewing of the deceased body (usually facial features). Fingerprint comparisons are based on the premise that it is highly improbable that two individuals would share identical dermal ridge patterns. Dental comparisons are based on the numerous combinations of restorations, prosthetics, missing teeth, and lesions that an individual may possess, which are typically highly visible in radiographs, although even hand written notes and other non-radiographic records have been shown to be useful in the dental identification process (Adams, 2002; Adams, 2003). DNA comparison is a common identification procedure that relies on the fact that an individual's nuclear DNA is considered unique (except in the case of identical twins) and that the probability of two individuals sharing the same DNA sequence in the regions of the genome that are typically compared in DNA analysis is extremely small.

The most common identification comparison technique used by forensic anthropologists is **radiographic comparison**, which involves the comparison of antemortem (clinical) radiographic images with postmortem images. Historically, this approach involved the comparison of antemortem and postmortem plain film radiographs, but with advances in radiologic technology, the use of digital radiography, computed tomography (CT), multislice computed tomography (MSCT), and magnetic resonance imaging (MRI) have also become widely utilized (Figure 14.1). If an individual to whom the skeletal remains are believed to belong has a radiographic image from a clinical procedure taken during life, it may have captured skeletal features that can be compared to the skeletal remains and assessed for the likelihood of belonging to the same person. Less common features such as prosthetics, antemortem fractures, and congenital or traumatic deformities or abnormalities may be particularly helpful and can often provide the basis for a highly probable identification. The greater the number of skeletal features shared by the two sets of radiographs, and the more unusual the features, the greater the probability that they originated from the same individual.

The earliest suggestion of the use of radiology in the identification of unknown human remains was in 1921, when frontal sinus variability was suggested to have potential utility in this context (Schuller, 1921). The first identification obtained through radiographic comparison was in 1927 when radiographs of a skull were compared in the identification of an American who was discovered in a river in India and whose body had been disfigured by decomposition, precluding identification by other means (Culbert and Law, 1927). Radiographic comparison has also been used for authentication purposes in at least one high profile historical case (see Box 14.4). Comparative radiography for personal identification is now considered a well-established technique in forensic anthropology as well as forensic radiology (Brogdon, 2010). Moreover, radiology has become a common diagnostic tool for various medical investigations, thus increasing the potential availability of antemortem records for comparison. Radiographic identification is routinely used in the identification of decomposed, fragmented, and skeletonized human remains.

A radiographic comparison typically involves first locating a suitable antemortem radiograph of the presumed decedent. While a forensic anthropologist may be directly responsible for this task, it is normally done by (or with the assistance of) death investigators or law enforcement officials who will search for medical facilities possibly visited by the presumed deceased and request available radiographic records. Next, a radiographic image of the skeletal remains is taken with a similar scope, orientation, and magnification as the antemortem image. Not all forensic anthropologists have training in radiology and radiography, and those who do not have sufficient experience should consult with a radiologist. Finally, the two radiographs are compared by direct (side-by-side or superimposed) visual inspection (Figure 14.2). Depending on whether the radiograph is on film or in an electronic format, the comparison may be performed using a light box or computer screen.

Although features such as injuries and skeletal anomalies may be useful, the extent of normal anatomical detail revealed in radiographs of the skeleton can be equally if not more important in identification comparisons. Such details may include general bone morphology, trabecular pattern, skull features such as the paranasal sinuses (Figure 14.3), and cranial sutures, as well as dental features such as tooth morphology, pathological conditions, and antemortem tooth loss. Nearly every bone in the body could therefore potentially be used in the identification process.

There is a rather fine (and sometimes debated) line between those dental radiographic comparisons that can be conducted by a forensic anthropologist versus those that are more appropriately conducted by a forensic odontologist. The comparison of bone and tooth morphology in antemortem and postmortem radiographic records

---

BOX 14.4 AUTHENTICATION OF THE AUTOPSY RADIOGRAPHS OF PRESIDENT JOHN F. KENNEDY

When the authenticity of postmortem radiographs taken during the autopsy of President John F. Kennedy at the US Naval Hospital on November 22, 1963 was questioned by conspiracy theorists, two forensic anthropology consultants were contacted to assist. Dr. Ellis Kerley and Dr. Clyde Snow were asked by the House Select Committee on Assassinations (HSCA) in 1979 to examine the materials and, if scientifically possible, determine whether or not they were those of the late President. Kerley and Snow compared the radiographs allegedly taken at autopsy to antemortem clinical radiographs of President Kennedy taken at various times prior to his death. Based on comparisons of frontal and lateral skull views, they found that "the similarity in shape of the sinus print patterns in the ante mortem and post mortem films is sufficient to establish that they are of the same person on the basis of this trait alone." They also noted several other "strikingly similar" anatomical features including the nasal septum, orbital outline, sella turcica, cranial sutures, vascular grooves, and air cells of the mastoid (Kerley and Snow, 1979). The HSCA report concluded that the evidence indicated that the autopsy radiographs were taken of President Kennedy at the time of his autopsy (House Select Committee on Assassinations, 1979).

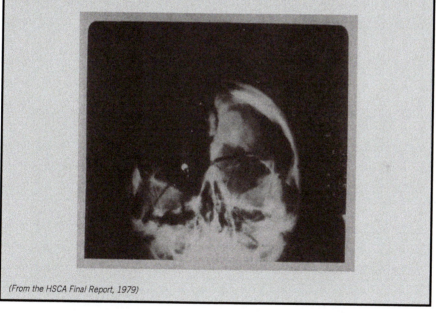

(From the HSCA Final Report, 1979)

---

is well within the expertise of most forensic anthropologists who are experienced in osteology and odontology and in assessing radiographic images (Figure 14.4). Descriptions and comparisons involving the identification and analysis of dental treatments such as restorations and implants (Figures 14.5 and 14.6), however, are beyond the scope of most education and training in forensic anthropology, and should be examined by a forensic odontologist when possible. Examinations by both experts will strengthen the probability of a correct identification or exclusion.

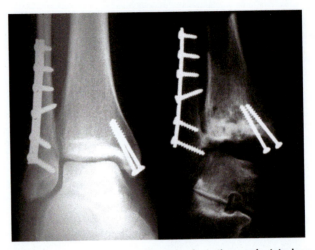

FIGURE 14.2 Radiographic comparison of ankle region including surgical devices – antemortem (left) and postmortem (right)

(From Christensen and Anderson, 2013)

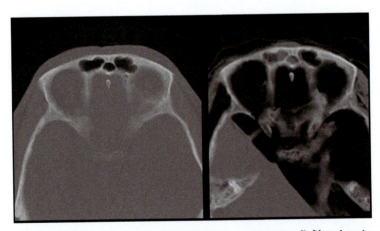

FIGURE 14.3 Frontal sinus comparison using CT scans – antemortem (left) and postmortem (right). The postmortem images are MPR (multiplanar reformatted) renderings from thin slice, soft tissue algorithm source images; the planes, W/L (window and level) and thickness are adjusted to match that of the antemortem images

(Images courtesy of Gary M. Hatch, MD, Radiology-Pathology Center for Forensic Imaging, University of New Mexico School of Medicine)

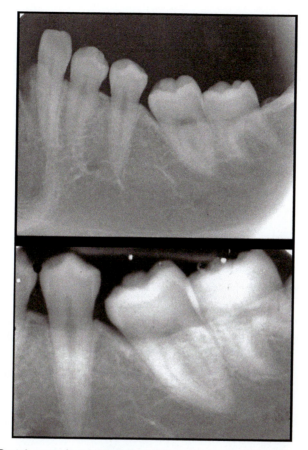

FIGURE 14.4 Dental comparison involving tooth and bone morphology. Correspondence can be seen in the contours of the teeth as well as the trabecular pattern of the alveolar bone

(From Brogdon et al., 2003)

An important caveat to consider is that the anatomy of adult bone is not static, but is being continually remodeled throughout life. Bone remodeling rates are affected by loading regimes as well as advanced age, which is associated with bone loss. It has been demonstrated, however, that those parts of the skeleton generally chosen to be compared for identification are quite stable, and the ability to facilitate identification may not diminish, even after two-and-a-half decades (Sauer et al., 1988). Nonetheless, in identification comparisons, consideration should be given to the time interval between the collection of the antemortem and postmortem information. Discrepancies between radiographs of the same person can often be explained by changes in bone morphology over time.

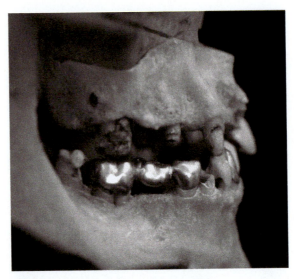

FIGURE 14.5 Dental prosthetic device (bridge) on a mandible

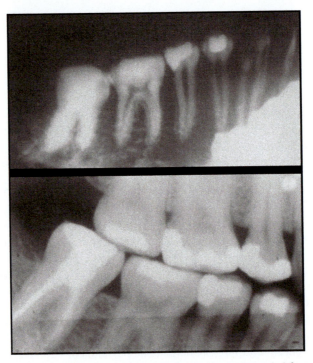

FIGURE 14.6 Dental comparison involving restorations and a root canal. A forensic odontologist should be consulted to assess the correspondence of type and placement of the dental treatments.

(From Brogdon, 2010)

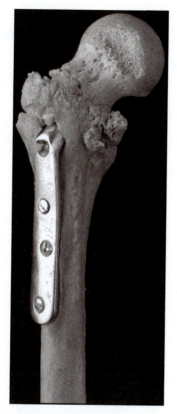

FIGURE 14.7 Femur with implanted surgical device

(Photo by Rebecca Meeusen; specimen courtesy of the National Museum of Natural History)

In addition to comparative radiography, forensic anthropologists occasionally encounter other skeletal evidence that may be useful for comparison to antemortem records. Sometimes skeletal remains have associated surgical implants or orthopedic devices (Figure 14.7). Although most forensic anthropologists are not experts in orthopedics, they may be able to provide information regarding surgical implants as part of their skeletal analysis (Scientific Working Group for Forensic Anthropology [SWGANTH], Personal Identification, 2011). Surgical implants (also called surgical implements, artifacts, or appliances) typically have a lot number, serial number, or insignia of the manufacturer stamped into them (Ubelaker, 1995; Wilson et al., 2011) (see Figures 14.8 and 14.9). Local or national registries or the manufacturer may be contacted for information associated with that device. In some cases it may be possible to link the device to a specific individual; in other cases, the devices may only be useful in narrowing the search, since not all devices have a unique serial number and registries may not necessarily provide adequate information to associate the device with a particular individual. Linking the device to an individual is more likely

FIGURE 14.8 Surgical implant with visible manufacturer information

(Image courtesy of Bruce Anderson)

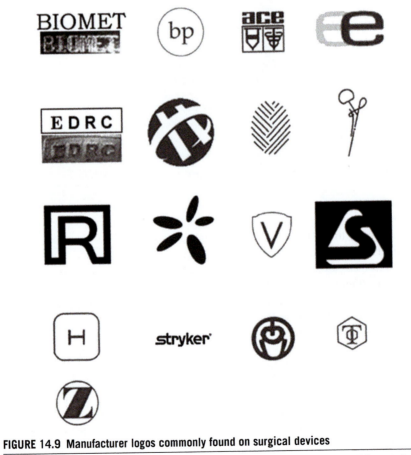

FIGURE 14.9 Manufacturer logos commonly found on surgical devices

(Modified from Wilson et al., 2011)

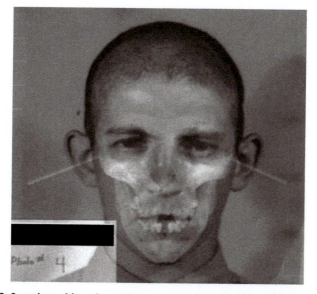

FIGURE 14.10 Superimposition of an unknown skull with a photograph of a presumed decedent

(Image courtesy of JPAC)

with more recently-implanted devices due to the Safe Medical Devices Act of 1990 (1989) which requires manufacturers, importers, and user facilities (e.g., hospitals) to be able to detect and correct any adverse effects of medical devices.

Craniofacial superimposition (also known as video superimposition or photographic superimposition) involves the superimposition of a photograph, video, or other image of a known individual with the skeletal remains (typically a photograph, negative, or drawing of the unidentified skull), and may be used if no other antemortem data are available (Ubelaker et al., 1992; Ubelaker, 2000). The ideal image for craniofacial superimposition is a close-up facial view with the teeth revealed. The skull is then imaged using comparable scaling, positioning, lighting, perspective, and angle as the original image. The two are then superimposed and examined for consistencies and inconsistencies in structures that are visible in both the antemortem and postmortem materials (Figure 14.10). Craniofacial superimposition is most often used to corroborate other identification methods or as a tool to include or exclude a possible identification, but strong associations are possible depending on the frequencies of the features observed (Ubelaker, 2000; Austin-Smith and Maples, 1994). Craniofacial superimposition should be conducted by experts with a thorough knowledge of human cranial anatomy and variation (Scientific Working Group for Forensic Anthropology [SWGANTH], Personal Identification, 2011), and practitioners should have the necessary training in the operation of the camera and software used in making comparisons.

Although much less frequent than cases involving deceased individuals, some forensic anthropologists assist in facilitating the identification or exclusion of living persons through forensic image analysis. Such cases may involve, for example, an individual filmed by a surveillance camera or other photographic or videographic means while robbing a convenience store or engaged in illegal sexual activities. An anthropologist may consult in these cases following a presumptive identification of the suspect made through police investigation. The comparison then involves analysis and/or superimposition of these captured images along with photographs of the suspect while looking for consistencies and inconsistencies (Figure 14.11). Like craniofacial superimposition, the approach is most effective when the two images are similar in terms of scale, position, and perspective.

14.4 Quantitative approaches

Most identification comparisons result in a largely subjective opinion as to whether the antemortem and postmortem information match in sufficient detail to conclude that they are consistent with originating from the same person. In order to provide more objective and quantitative results, however, the results of identification comparisons are ideally expressed as likelihood ratios. A **likelihood ratio** in the evaluation of evidence is the probability of the evidence supposing a hypothesis is correct divided by the probability of the evidence supposing the hypothesis is incorrect. In anthropological identification comparison terms, the likelihood ratio can be expressed as the probability of finding matching skeletal features given that the identification is correct over the probability of finding matching skeletal features given that the identification is incorrect, or:

$$\frac{P\,(skeletal\ match)\ |\ correct\ ID}{P\,(skeletal\ match)\ |\ incorrect\ ID}$$

This ratio is effectively a function of how common the particular matching feature is in the population at large. For example, in comparing a postmortem radiograph of a knee to an antemortem radiograph of a presumed match, both radiographs show a dorsal defect of the patella. This feature has been shown to occur in approximately 1% of the general population (Johnson and Brogdon, 1982). For the numerator, the probability that the skeletal features match given that the identification is correct would be 1; for the denominator, the probability that you would get a match of that feature with someone else (an incorrect identification) is 1 in 100 (or 1/100). The likelihood ratio would be 1/(1/100) or 100; it is therefore 100 times more likely that the skeletal information would match if the identification is correct than if it is incorrect. As another example, consider comparing a postmortem radiograph of a cranium to a presumed match, in which both radiographs *lack* a radiographically visible frontal sinus. This has been shown to occur in approximately 14% of the general population (Christensen, 2005). The likelihood ratio would be 1/(14/100) or 7.3; it is therefore 7.3 times more likely that the skeletal information would match if the identification is correct than if it is incorrect. A likelihood ratio greater than 1 is evidence in favor of the hypothesis that the two sets of data are from the same individual, while a likelihood ratio less than 1 is evidence against it, with exactly 1 being neutral (the

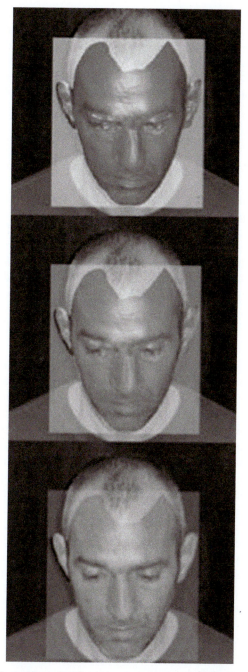

FIGURE 14.11 Superimposition of a 3D model of a suspect on a facial image captured in a surveillance video

(Image courtesy of Cristina Cattaneo)

two hypotheses are equally likely). The further from 1 the likelihood ratio is, the greater the probative value of the evidence. It can be seen from the two preceding examples that the rarer a shared feature is, the greater the likelihood ratio would be.

Even more relevant from an evidentiary perspective is the **posterior probability** (or posterior odds), which is derived using Bayes' Theorem (Bayes, 1763). Bayes' Theorem states that:

$$P(A|B) = P(B|A) \times P(A)/P(B)$$

or

$$\textit{Posterior Odds} = \textit{Likelihood Ratio} \times \textit{Prior Odds}$$

Prior odds represent a body of information which is used to logically update the belief that the hypothesis is correct. The likelihood ratio and prior odds are multiplied to estimate a final posterior probability, which represents the overall confidence that the hypothesis is correct. The posterior odds are what we really want to know – the overall degree of belief in the hypothesis that the identification is correct, or the probability that the identification is correct given that the skeletal information matches over the probability that the identification is incorrect given that the skeletal information matches, or:

$$\frac{P(\textit{correct ID}) \mid \textit{skeletal match}}{P(\textit{incorrect ID}) \mid \textit{skeletal match}}$$

The likelihood ratio and posterior probability will only be equal if the prior odds are 1, i.e., if the probability that the identification is correct is equal to the probability that it is incorrect. This is clearly not the case, however, since there is always some reason or evidence to suggest that the identification may be correct. Consider how it came to be that the two sets of skeletal data were being compared – antemortem radiographs were not randomly selected from the population at large for comparison. There is already other evidence to suggest that they belong to the same individual as the skeleton, such as the match in biological profiles and the person is presumed missing or deceased. Such evidence can logically update the belief in the hypothesis, and increase the confidence that the identification is correct (or incorrect).

One significant advantage of likelihood ratio approaches is that if the traits which are being compared are independent, each likelihood ratio can be multiplied (based on the product rule) and combined into a final likelihood ratio that represents the confidence in the identification after considering all available information. Take the two previous examples in which the likelihood ratios were 100 and 7.3. If these features were both present in the same individual, it is now 100×7.3 or 730 times more likely that the skeletal information would match if the identification is correct than if it is incorrect. This ratio can also be multiplied by ratios derived from other identification modalities (such as DNA or odontological comparisons) resulting in extremely robust statistical assertions of identity.

Although ideal, quantitative approaches to identification comparisons are not always straightforward in the evaluation of evidence. In order to calculate a likelihood ratio, the frequency of a feature in the population at large must be known or estimated, and such data do not exist for many features that forensic anthropologists use in identification comparisons. Moreover, the estimation of prior odds can be highly subjective. In practice, this can be similar to when a jury (often unknowingly) uses prior knowledge to evaluate the strength of a case, evaluating multiple lines of evidence in the course of a trial.

There are also practical and philosophical issues regarding determining whether features "match," particularly when the assessment is subjective such as a shape or other pattern comparison, although some studies have attempted to overcome this challenge by developing quantitative approaches to shape comparisons (e.g., Christensen, 2005; Stephan et al., 2011). Moreover, there is no legal or discipline-specific threshold for confirming or rejecting an identification, and it thus remains a matter of presenting the anthropological and other findings to the medicolegal authority who ultimately decides whether a convincing case has been made. For those interested in additional reading on this topic, Steadman et al. (2006) provide an excellent overview of how likelihood ratios and posterior probabilities can be calculated for a biological profile and other skeletal data using a real case example.

14.5 DNA analysis

The analysis of both nuclear and mitochondrial DNA has become a widely utilized tool in the identification of human remains (Box 14.5). Although few forensic anthropologists are experts in the extraction and analysis of DNA, unidentified remains

---

BOX 14.5 NUCLEAR AND MITOCHONDRIAL DNA COMPARISONS IN IDENTIFICATION

Nuclear DNA (nDNA) and mitochondrial DNA (mtDNA) are both used in forensic examinations for identification, each having advantages and disadvantages based primarily on the frequency of each type of DNA in the general population (and therefore its evidentiary value in identification), and copy numbers within the body's cells (which affects the ability to obtain a DNA profile from a sample).

nDNA is inherited from each parent and is considered to be unique to each individual (except for identical twins). In nDNA analysis, however, the entire genome is not examined. Most of the human genome is exactly the same in all individuals, with only a fraction of a percent of nDNA varying from person to person. Forensic scientists examine only these variable regions. Typically around 13 regions or **loci** that are highly variable are examined, and there is a very small chance that two people will have the same nDNA profile for all of these regions. mtDNA, on the other hand, is inherited only from the mother, and an individual therefore shares the same mtDNA with all maternal relatives. A particular mtDNA profile is therefore much more common in the general population than a nDNA profile. While not unique, mtDNA analysis can be very useful in missing persons investigations.

In order to perform a forensic DNA analysis, DNA must be extracted from the sample and amplified. There is only one full copy of nDNA in each cell, located within the nucleus, while mtDNA is located within the mitochondria of cells, and there may be thousands of mitochondria in each cell. An individual therefore has many, many more copies of mtDNA than nDNA. It is much easier to obtain a full mtDNA profile from smaller samples, and even from degraded or deteriorated samples including very old bones and teeth.

cases often involve both anthropological and DNA analysis, and the two approaches are frequently closely intertwined. Moreover, forensic anthropologists are in a good position to determine how DNA may be best utilized in skeletal remains cases and are often asked to collect samples or identify skeletal material that is potentially useful for DNA analysis (Christensen and Anderson, 2013). Knowledge of skeletal biology can be useful in selecting appropriate samples, especially in cases involving commingled remains (MacKinnon and Mundorff, 2006; Mundorff et al., 2009). The ability to identify duplicate skeletal elements (which are clearly from different individuals) can facilitate the personal identification process while also saving time and money.

During the World Trade Center victim identification effort, additional evidence of commingling was recognized through a second anthropological verification process (MacKinnon and Mundorff, 2006). This resulted in several new identifications as well as the re-association of remains to previously identified cases. It was also discovered through DNA testing that soft tissue remains often yielded contaminated results because taphonomic processes had resulted in the cross-transfer of genetic material. A significant DNA re-testing effort further demonstrated that sampling of weight-bearing elements (such as the femur and tibia) resulted in higher successful DNA yields than non-weight-bearing elements (Mundorff et al., 2009). This is likely due to differences in bone density caused by different biomechanical loads between weight-bearing and non-weight-bearing skeletal elements.

14.6 Facial approximation

Facial approximation (sometimes referred to as facial reconstruction or skull reconstruction) is an artistic reproduction of the soft tissue features of an individual (Komar and Buikstra, 2008). It involves the estimation and artistic reproduction of possible facial features on the basis of underlying skeletal structures (Figure 14.12). This approach is typically used when all scientific leads have been exhausted, with the goal of capturing public attention and seeing if anyone recognizes the approximation as possibly belonging to someone they know. Note that the term "facial approximation" is generally preferred to "facial/skull reconstruction" for two reasons: "approximation" is a more accurate term since the approach is indeed an estimation based on a combination of art and science and "reconstruction" in forensic anthropology is typically used to refer to the reassembly of fractured bone fragments (as in the case of trauma).

There are two generally accepted methods of facial approximation: the anatomical method and the tissue depth method. The anatomical method uses muscle origins and insertions to rebuild each muscle (Gerasimov, 1971), while the tissue depth method uses tissue depth markers at osseous landmarks followed by the building up of soft tissues (including muscles, connective tissues, and skin) upon the skull (Rhine and Campbell, 1980). The anatomical method requires more expertise in anatomy and is more time-consuming, which is likely why the tissue depth method is much more widely used today.

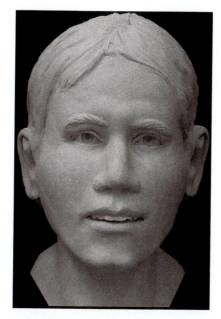

FIGURE 14.12 Facial approximation based on a skull estimated to belong to a 17–23-year-old Hispanic male

(Image used with permission of the Virginia Office of the Chief Medical Examiner)

In addition to knowledge of cranial and soft tissue anatomy, artistic ability is also naturally required for making successful facial approximations, and thus the best practice is a joint effort of anthropologists and anatomical or forensic artists (Scientific Working Group for Forensic Anthropology [SWGANTH], Facial Approximation, 2011). Anthropologists can provide the biological profile information, and because of their familiarity with skeletal landmarks, may also assist in placing tissue depth markers on the skull. Anthropological collaboration with the artist is also helpful in calling attention to details of the skull that may be useful for the artist to consider for the approximation such as size and shape of supraorbital ridges, shape characteristics of the nasal area, evidence of healed trauma, and unusual dental features (Ubelaker, 2000). While there are certain cranial structures that may be reliably reflected in the facial features (such as the breadth of the nose, the projection of the cheekbones, and the shape of the chin), there are many other features which necessarily require some artistic interpretation (such as the shapes of the ears and the style of the hair).

The ultimate goal of a facial approximation is for it to be publicized in order to potentially generate identification leads. If a visual recognition by a relative, friend, or acquaintance is made, the identification process must then proceed to comparative methods (such as DNA, dental records, medical radiographs, etc.). Although popular in the media and impressive to the public, facial approximations have often lacked scientific rigor, are associated with a high degree of error, and should be used for investigative leads only (Christensen and Anderson, 2013). Many anthropologists, in fact, are critical of the approach, and emphasize that, when used, statements regarding the power or value of facial imagery methods should be presented carefully (Stephan, 2003).

Facial approximations produced by sculpture historically involved applying clay directly onto the bony skull. Today, some laboratories use replicas of the skulls produced from laser scans or CT scans of the actual skull (see Box 7.3). This serves to better preserve the evidence as well as allow it to remain available for additional examinations such as DNA analysis. It also permits the skull to be used as a direct reference with which to compare and evaluate the approximation before release for public use.

14.7 Case study – radiographic comparison of foot

In 2010, a decomposed human body was found near the California coast. The remains were initially examined by a forensic pathologist, who was unable to identify the remains or determine the cause and manner of death. A forensic anthropologist estimated the decedent to be a White male, approximately 50 years of age. Analysis of the remains further revealed evidence of both blunt and sharp force trauma to the head and thorax. Following a possible missing persons lead, law enforcement officials submitted digital radiographs of the foot and ankle of a man reported missing from the area. Because adhering soft tissue on the lower limbs maintained the foot and ankle bones in anatomical position, it was possible to obtain digital postmortem radiographs in the same position as the antemortem images. Side-by-side comparison of the two sets of radiographs revealed no inconsistencies, and numerous points of similarities could be identified including similar bone morphology and degenerative changes (Figure 14.13). The comparison supported the identification of the presumed decedent, a White male reported missing from the area earlier that year.

14.8 Case study – exclusion based on cranial radiographs

Decomposed human remains were discovered by police in an abandoned drug house, and forensic anthropologists were requested to assist in their recovery, analysis, and identification. The remains were in a late stage of decomposition, being mostly skeletonized with some remaining desiccated soft tissue. Investigators had made a presumptive identification of the remains based on known visitors and occupants of the house. A radiograph of the head was obtained from a local medical center the presumed decedent had visited for prior medical treatments. Forensic anthropologists, along with a forensic radiologist, compared the antemortem record with a postmortem radiograph of the skull. Based on unexplainable differences in the size and shape of the frontal sinus, as well as differences in the contour of the nasal aperture, the eye orbits, and cranial vault, it was concluded that the presumed decedent could be excluded as the source of the skeletal remains (Figure 14.14). The remains were later identified as another missing person through dental records.

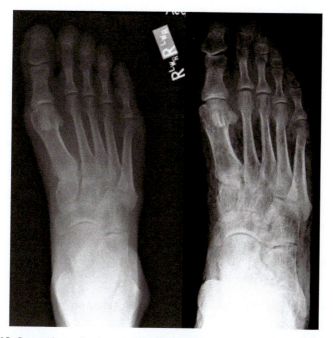

FIGURE 14.13 Comparison of antemortem (left) and postmortem (right) foot radiographs. Note the numerous similarities, suggesting that the individual imaged on the left cannot be excluded as the source of the skeletal remains imaged on the right

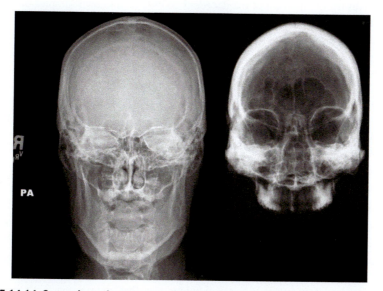

FIGURE 14.14 Comparison of antemortem (left) and postmortem (right) cranial radiographs. Note the discrepancies indicating that the individual imaged on the left can be excluded as the source of the skeletal remains imaged on the right

14.9 Summary

- Personal identification is the process of linking an unknown body or skeleton back to an individual of known identity, and is important for both legal and humanitarian reasons. Anthropologists assist in the identification process by helping to narrow the pool of potential matches, and by comparing antemortem and postmortem skeletal information.
- Forensic anthropologists use the biological profile as well as individual skeletal variation and the postmortem interval to narrow down the pool of missing persons to whom the skeletal remains might belong.
- Databases such as the National Missing and Unidentified Persons System (NamUs) and the National Crime Information Center (NCIC) are important tools used in the identification process. The widespread availability of programs like NamUs allow both the public and law enforcement community to work together in making possible matches of antemortem and postmortem records.
- Radiographic comparison has a long history in forensic science, and remains an important tool for facilitating identification by forensic anthropologists. Observations of radiographically visible skeletal features can be used for determining whether the remains are consistent with originating from a particular individual.
- Quantitative approaches incorporate information such as the frequency of skeletal features in the overall population to provide statistical support to an identification. The use of maximum likelihood ratios and Bayes' Theorem provide the foundation for statistically-based evaluations of identification hypotheses.
- Personal identification is routinely facilitated through DNA analysis, which involves the comparison of the decedent's DNA with known samples of the presumed deceased or living relatives.
- Typically used as a tool of exclusion rather than identification, craniofacial superimposition involves superimposing a photograph of a person taken during life with an image of a skull to observe anatomical points of similarity. A similar approach can also be applied to living persons using photographs and video footage.
- Facial approximation involves a combination of art and science and attempts to reproduce a likeness of an individual based on craniofacial characteristics. The method is subjective and often unsuccessful, but can be useful as a tool of last resort.

14.10 Test yourself

- Why is identification important, and why is it important that all available methods are used in order to arrive at the *correct* identification? Describe several situations in which problems could result from an *incorrect* identification.
- What features of the skeleton can be useful in the personal identification process? Are you aware of any skeletal features that you possess that might be useful in identifying your skeleton?

- Authorities have just notified you that, based on your report (which included an estimated biological profile and postmortem interval), they have narrowed their search down to two possible matches with the skeletal remains. Describe how you would proceed.
- In an identification comparison, why do you think is it important to look for consistencies *and* inconsistencies?
- If you knew you would be testifying in a trial regarding an identification comparison you made in the laboratory, why might it be especially helpful to use a quantitative approach?
- Describe the similarities and differences between identification approaches applied to the deceased and those applied to the living.
- Why is it important that forensic anthropologists and artists collaborate on facial approximations? What might be the consequences of involving only an artist? Only an anthropologist?

Definitions

Coroner An elected government official responsible for certifying death

Likelihood ratio In the evaluation of evidence, the probability that the evidence supposing a hypothesis is correct, divided by the probability that the evidence supposing the hypothesis is incorrect

Loci Locations of particular DNA sequences on a chromosome (singular: *locus*)

Medical examiner A medical expert who investigates deaths and performs autopsies

Medicolegal authority A person with the authority to make decisions or determinations pertaining to medical jurisprudence (such as determining the identity and cause and manner of death of the deceased); usually a coroner or medical examiner, or sometimes a justice of the peace or sheriff

Personal identification The process of linking an unknown personal object or material back to an individual of known identity

Posterior probability In the Bayesian evaluation of evidence, the likelihood ratio multiplied by the prior odds; the probability that the hypothesis is correct given the evidence, divided by the probability that the hypothesis is incorrect given the evidence

Radiographic comparison In the personal identification process, the practice of comparing antemortem (clinical) radiographic images with postmortem images to assess the likelihood that they originated from the same person

References

Adams, B.J., 2002. Personal identification based on patterns of missing, filled, and unrestored teeth [Dissertation]. The University of Tennessee. Knoxville.

Adams, B.J., 2003. Establishing personal identification based on specific patterns of missing, filled and unrestored teeth. J. Forensic Sci. 48 (3), 1–10.

Austin-Smith, D., Maples, W.R., 1994. The reliability of skull/photograph superimposition in individual identification. J. Forensic Sci. 39 (2), 446–455.

Bayes, T., 1763. An essay toward solving a problem in the doctrine of chances. Philos. Trans. R. Soc. Lond. 53, 370–418.

Brogdon, B.G., 2010. Radiological identification of individual remains. In: Thali, M.J., Viner, M.D., Brogdon, B.G. (Eds.), Forensic Radiology, second ed. CRC Press, Boca Raton, pp. 149–187.

Brogdon, B.G., Vogel, H., McDowel, J.D., 2003. A Radiologic Atlas of Abuse, Torture, Terrorism, and Inflicted Trauma. CRC Press, Boca Raton.

Christensen, A.M., 2005. Testing the reliability of frontal sinuses in personal identification. J. Forensic Sci. 50 (1), 18–22.

Christensen, A.M., Anderson, B.E., 2013. Personal identification. In: Tersigni-Tarrant, M.T., Shirley, N. (Eds.), Forensic Anthropology: An Introduction. CRC Press, Boca Raton, pp. 397–420.

Culbert, W.L., Law, F.L., 1927. Identification by comparison of roentgenograms of nasal accessory sinuses and mastoid processes. J. Am. Med. Assoc. 88, 1634–1636.

Gerasimov, M.M., 1971. The Face Finder. JB Lippincot, Philadelphia.

House Select Committee on Assassinations, 1979. Final Assassinations Report.

Johnson, J.F., Brogdon, B.G., 1982. Dorsal defect of the patella: Incidence and distribution. Am. J. Radiol. 139, 339–340.

Kerley, E.R., Snow, C.C., 1979. Authentication of John F. Kennedy's Autopsy Radiographs and Photographs. Final Report to the Select Committee on Assassinations, US House of Representatives. March 9.

Komar, D.A., Buikstra, J.E., 2008. Forensic Anthropology: Contemporary Theory and Practice. Oxford University Press, New York.

MacKinnon, G., Mundorff, A.Z., 2006. The World Trade Center: September 11th, 2001. In: Thompson, T., Black, S. (Eds.), Forensic Human Identification: An Introduction. CRC Press, Boca Raton, pp. 485–499.

Mundorff, A., Bartelink, E.J., Mar-Cash, E., 2009. DNA preservation in skeletal elements from the World Trade Center disaster: recommendations for mass fatality management. J. Forensic Sci. 54, 739–745.

National Crime Information Center (NCIC), n.d. http://www.fas.org/irp/agency/doj/fbi/is/ncic. htm. Accessed November 23, 2012.

National Missing and Unidentified Persons System (NamUs), n.d. www.namus.gov. Accessed November 23, 2012.

Rhine, J.S., Campbell, H.R., 1980. Thickness of facial tissues in American Blacks. J. Forensic Sci. 25, 847–858.

Safe Medical Devices Act of 1990, 1989. H.R. 3095–101st Congress. In GovTrack.us (database of federal legislation). http://www.govtrack.us/congress/bills/101/hr3095. Accessed November 23, 2012.

Sauer, N.J., Brantley, R.E., Barondess, D.A., 1988. The effects of aging on the comparability of antemortem and postmortem radiographs. J. Forensic Sci. 33 (5), 1223–1230.

Schuller, A., 1921. Das Rontgenogram der Stirnhohle: en Hilfsmittel fur die Identitatsbestimmung von Schadeln. Monatsschrift feur Ohrenheilkunde un Laryngo-Rhinologie 5, 1617–1620.

Scientific Working Group for Forensic Anthropology, 2011. Facial Approximation, Revision 1. http://www.swganth.org.

Scientific Working Group for Forensic Anthropology, 2011. Personal Identification, Revision 0. http://www.swganth.org.

Steadman, D.W., Adams, B.J., Konigsberg, L.W., 2006. Statistical basis for positive identification in forensic anthropology. Am. J. Phys. Anthropol. 131, 15–26.

Stephan, C.N., 2003. Anthropological facial reconstruction – Recognizing the fallacies, "unembracing" the errors and realizing method limits. Sci. Justice 43 (4), 193–200.

Stephan, C.N., Emanovsky, P.D., Tyrrell, A.J., 2011. The use of clavicle boundary outlines to identify skeletal remains of US personnel recovered from past conflicts: results of initial tests. In: Lestrel, P.E. (Ed.), Biological Shape Analysis: Proceedings of the 1st International Symposium. World Scientific, Hackensack, New Jersey, pp. 105–130.

Ubelaker, D.H., 1995. Identification of orthopedic device manufacturer. J. Forensic Sci. 40 (2), 168–170.

Ubelaker, D.H., 2000. A history of Smithsonian-FBI collaboration in forensic anthropology, especially in regard to facial imagery. Forensic Sci. Commun. 2 (4).

Ubelaker, D.H., Bubniak, E., O'Donnell, G.E., 1992. Computer-assisted photographic superimposition. J. Forensic Sci. 37, 155–162.

Wilson, R.J., Bethard, J.D., DiGangi, E.A., 2011. The use of orthopedic surgical devices for forensic identification. J. Forensic Sci. 56 (2), 460–469.

Contemporary Issues in Forensic Anthropology

15.1 Forensic anthropology and the broader forensic community

Forensic anthropology is a well-developed field, but it is not practiced in isolation. Rather, it is part of a larger scientific, legal, and forensic science community, and it is important to understand forensic anthropology's role within this broader framework. Most medicolegal investigations involve an **interdisciplinary** approach, and forensic anthropological examinations are typically just one component of a much larger investigation. It is important that forensic anthropologists be familiar with other complementary disciplines and investigative processes. Moreover, because forensic anthropology involves the intersection of physical anthropology, archaeology, and the law, an understanding of the relevant laws that govern how forensic anthropological evidence enters the legal system is critical. The potential sources of error and limitations of the science must be understood and properly conveyed to customers, jurors, and fellow scientists.

Forensic anthropologists are now taking on important roles in other legal and humanitarian efforts, including the investigation of human rights abuses such as genocide, as well as aiding in planning, response, and identification in mass disasters. Given recent changes in the legal and political landscape as well as the broadening scope of the field, it has become increasingly important for new methods to be continually re-examined and independently validated.

This chapter takes a broader view of contemporary forensic anthropology by providing overviews of more recent anthropological applications, examining the interrelationship of forensic anthropology with other disciplines and investigative approaches, discussing new research directions and challenges, and further exploring the future of the discipline.

15.2 Forensic anthropology in mass disaster response and disaster victim identification

Forensic anthropologists have recently begun to take on important roles in planning, response, and victim identification in disaster and mass fatality incidents. A **mass disaster** or **mass fatality incident** is an event that involves the deaths of multiple individuals, and can range from a relatively small-scale house fire to a large-scale

Forensic Anthropology. http://dx.doi.org/10.1016/B978-0-12-418671-2.00015-X

incident such as a plane crash or act of terrorism. Forensic anthropologists have responded to many recent mass fatality incidents including the 2010 Haiti earthquake, the 2004 Boxing Day tsunami in Thailand, Hurricane Katrina in 2005, and the World Trade Center and United Flight 93 incidents on September 11, 2001.

It has been noted that anthropologists are uniquely suited to contribute to disaster situations due to their broad training in human identification, anatomy, human biology, and taphonomy, supported by knowledge of cultural considerations including religion, death, and mourning (Sledzik, 2009). The roles of forensic anthropologists in mass disasters are highly varied. In the planning stages, forensic anthropologists are sometimes directly responsible for assisting with disaster planning protocols at the agency, regional, state, or national level. During a disaster situation, forensic anthropologists can serve roles in the disaster scene itself, the incident morgue, the victim information center, or disaster management.

Mass disasters typically represent a scenario where local facilities and resources are overwhelmed, and examinations and analyses are often not performed under ideal conditions. This may include having to perform examinations in limited timeframes and without the typical laboratory resources. Although based on the same scientific principles as the analysis of a single set of remains, the recovery and mapping procedures as well as **disaster victim identification** (often abbreviated DVI) follow a different workflow process to smaller scale incidents. The process varies so significantly from typical identification practices and requires such planning and organization that a separate SWG – The Scientific Working Group on Disaster Victim Identification (SWGDVI) – was created to advance the scientific basis for identification in DVI contexts (Scientific Working Group on Disaster Victim Identification, 2013).

Even in a mass disaster, the identification and determination of cause and manner of death are still the responsibility of the medicolegal authority in the jurisdiction in which the incident occurred. When overwhelmed by the influx of fatalities caused by a mass disaster, however, many agencies and individuals often work together to assist the local authority. Forensic anthropologists may become involved because they live or work within the vicinity of the disaster, because they are individually requested or volunteer to assist, or because they are part of a disaster response organization such as the Disaster Mortuary Operational Response Team (DMORT).

DMORT is one of the numerous response teams of the National Disaster Medical System (NDMS), a section of the US Department of Health and Human Services (HHS). The NDMS combines federal and non-federal resources into a unified response to federally declared disasters including natural disasters, major transportation accidents, technological disasters, and acts of terrorism including weapons of mass destruction events (NDMS, n.d.). DMORT is responsible for providing victim identification and mortuary services (Figure 15.1). Teams are composed of funeral directors, medical examiners, coroners, pathologists, forensic anthropologists, medical records technicians and transcribers, fingerprint specialists, forensic odontologists, dental assistants, X-ray technicians, mental health experts, computer professionals, administrative support staff, and security and investigative personnel (Public Health Emergency, n.d.). DMORT personnel are private citizens, but are expected to maintain appropriate certifications and licensures within their discipline.

FIGURE 15.1 Mock mass fatality morgue operation during a training exercise

(Image courtesy of Paul Sledzik)

Large-scale mass fatalities commonly involve citizens of multiple countries. Similar to the way deaths in the US are managed by the medicolegal authority in the jurisdiction in which the remains were recovered, the DVI operation in these cases is subject to the laws of the country in which the disaster occurred (INTERPOL, 2009). Disaster response, including recovery and identification efforts, may involve personnel only from the country where the disaster occurred, or may involve international efforts such as an INTERPOL Disaster Victim Identification Team.

INTERPOL, or the International Criminal Police Organization, is the world's largest international police organization with 190 member countries. INTERPOL's mission is to prevent and fight crime through enhanced international police cooperation, which it does through a framework of training, support, and data channels (INTERPOL, n.d.). One component of INTERPOL is disaster victim identification, including international DVI Teams. DVI Teams are composed of various units, teams, and commands with different responsibilities related to the DVI effort including emergency rescue, investigation, evidence collection, and victim identification. These teams involve a cooperative effort by member countries who are experts from various fields as needed, applying high standards of quality and respect in the effort to identify victims. In a typical Victim Identification Unit, a Recovery and Evidence Collection Team will collect remains, an Antemortem Team will collect antemortem data on possible victims, a Postmortem Team will collect relevant postmortem medical and forensic data from victims, and a Reconciliation Team will compare the antemortem and postmortem records and determine whether an identification can be submitted to the final Identification Board. Multinational DVI operations benefit from the use of international standards which are outlined in INTERPOL's Disaster Victim Identification Guide (2009).

Anthropologists are often involved in the recovery and mapping of remains at mass fatality scenes due to their experience organizing and maintaining spatial relationships using archaeological principles, and processing human remains in various states of preservation and degrees of commingling. Recovery efforts at mass fatality scenes are often very complex, requiring a great deal of organization and rapid recovery of evidence. Unlike smaller scale recoveries involving one or a small number of individuals, mass disaster scenes often do not require reconstructing the circumstances of death. Rather, these larger scale recoveries tend to focus on the systematic recovery of as much of the remains and evidence as possible. These larger scale recoveries may result in a loss of precision (such as mapping grid location of recovery only, rather than piece-plotting each item of remains or evidence), but a much larger area can still be accurately searched and excavated.

Following recovery of remains, anthropologists are often critical in the triage stage. Triage involves determining the identification potential of recovered remains, particularly since events such as plane crashes and explosions often result in severe fragmentation of bodies. For example, anthropologists can assist by determining whether recovered remains are human in origin, which bones or body segments are present and from which side of the body, and what biological information or identifying features may be gained from analysis. Identification strategies in mass fatalities differ depending on whether the victims represent a *closed population* or an *open population*. A **closed population** in a disaster is one in which a certain limited number of victims are known to be involved, such as passengers on a flight. An **open population** in a disaster is one in which the number of victims is initially unknown, such as a natural disaster. In a closed population, for example, exclusions can significantly narrow down the pool of possible matches for identification.

15.3 Forensic anthropology in conflict and human rights investigations

Forensic anthropologists have become increasingly involved in investigations of unidentified and missing persons as a result of armed conflict and human rights violations such as genocide (Doretti and Fondebrider, 2002). As with mass fatality incidents, forensic anthropologists and archaeologists are frequently utilized in search and recovery operations due to their expertise and training in scene detection and excavation. Skeletal analysis, including the estimation of the biological profile and assessment of individual skeletal variants, is used to facilitate personal identification of victims. Forensic anthropologists have been involved in a number of conflict and human rights operations in Bosnia and Herzegovina, Rwanda, East Timor, Cypress, Chile, Guatemala, and Argentina, many of which are still ongoing.

Since these cases are often investigated long after the incident and remains have become skeletonized, forensic anthropological training is very useful in the excavation, collection, and analysis stages. This is especially true given that these cases often involve **mass graves** containing commingled remains, sometimes representing hundreds of different individuals. Expertise in osteology is therefore critical in mapping and collecting remains, maintaining proper associations between skeletal elements, and determining the number of individuals represented. Trauma analysis in these cases can reveal valuable information regarding the circumstances of death, and often provides valuable evidence in the prosecution of crimes (Kimmerle and Baraybar, 2008). Wound patterns can also be used to provide prosecutors with a general description of execution events and unique patterns of wounds may facilitate identification based on surviving witness statements.

Working in conflict and human rights investigations, cultural awareness and sensitivity are often required in addition to professional experience and skill, and these are traits commonly possessed by trained forensic anthropologists. There are several organizations that work to coordinate various experts and resources to identify victims and prosecute crimes related to armed conflict and human rights violations, including the International Committee of the Red Cross (ICRC), the International Commission on Missing Persons (ICMP), and the Joint POW/MIA Accounting Command, Central Identification Laboratory (JPAC CIL).

The ICRC is a humanitarian organization that works on behalf of victims of war and armed violence. The ICRC's Mission Statement reads:

> "The International Committee of the Red Cross (ICRC) is an impartial, neutral and independent organization whose exclusively humanitarian mission is to protect the lives and dignity of victims of armed conflict and other situations of violence and to provide them with assistance. The ICRC also endeavors to prevent suffering by promoting and strengthening humanitarian law and universal humanitarian principles. Established in 1863, the ICRC is at the origin of the Geneva Conventions and the International Red Cross and Red Crescent Movement. It directs and coordinates the international activities conducted by the Movement in armed conflicts and other situations of violence."
>
> **(ICRC, n.d)**

The ICRC's Forensic Unit assists local authorities in carrying out their obligations under humanitarian law with regard to managing remains and disseminating information to families. It does this by providing support for the location, recovery, and analysis of human remains through the development of sustainable local forensic capacities, and by providing external assistance and training as needed.

The ICMP was established to ensure cooperation of governments in locating and identifying individuals who have disappeared during armed conflict or as a result of human rights violations (ICMP, n.d). The ICMP's Mandate reads:

> "ICMP endeavors to secure the cooperation of governments and other authorities in locating and identifying persons missing as a result of armed conflicts, other hostilities or violations of human rights and to assist them in doing so. ICMP also supports the work of other organizations in their efforts, encourages public involvement in its activities and contributes to the development of appropriate expressions of commemoration and tribute to the missing."

FIGURE 15.2 JPAC recovery operation of a WWII plane crash in Vanuatu

(Image courtesy of JPAC)

The JPAC CIL is a US government organization funded under the Department of Defense tasked with the humanitarian mission of accounting for the more than 83,000 Americans still missing from past conflicts (Emanovsky and Belcher, 2012). These primarily include World War II, the Korean War, and the Vietnam War, but individuals missing from World War I, the Cold War, and the Civil War have also been investigated by the JPAC CIL. This accounting effort is primarily achieved through recovery missions (see Figures 15.2 and 15.3), although the disinterment of unknown remains from cemetery burials for identification is also ongoing. Recovery missions are largely staffed by teams of military personnel stationed at JPAC, and all recovery efforts are directed and supervised by a CIL anthropologist or archaeologist (as of 2013, the JPAC CIL employs approximately 30 anthropologists, 17 archaeologists, including two who specialize in underwater recovery, and three forensic odontologists). Recovery missions typically last 35–60 days, with personnel working closely with local villages and authorities, often camping near the recovery scene. The types of scenes in which JPAC performs recoveries range from isolated burials to large aircraft crashes. The missions are primarily focused on maximizing the materials recovered, often working in 4 x 4 meter units because the scale is typically much larger than an isolated burial. Depending on the size of the recovery scene, multiple recovery missions may be required to fully excavate the area, and ensure that no additional remains can be recovered. Once a site is closed, the remains from the scene are analyzed at the CIL by an anthropologist and odontologist, following standard procedures for evidence handling and traceability. Identifications are typically made using radiographic dental comparison, chest radiograph comparison, or DNA. Remains recovered from a scene are not typically analyzed until the site

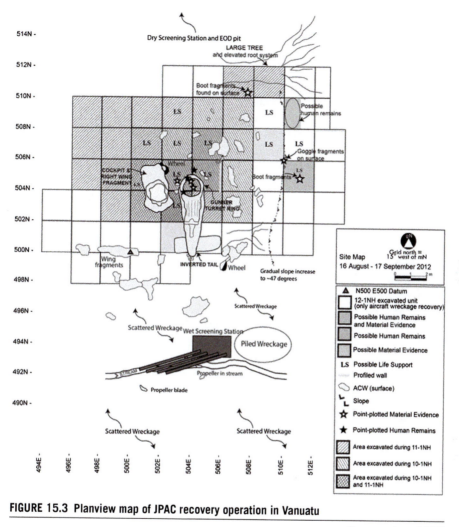

FIGURE 15.3 Planview map of JPAC recovery operation in Vanuatu

(Image courtesy of JPAC)

is fully excavated. In the work of the JPAC CIL, anthropologists and archaeologists play key roles in the recovery as well as analytical aspects of the investigation.

15.4 Forensic anthropology and human migration routes

People frequently migrate from one geographic location to another, often from one country to another, for the purpose of seeking a better quality of life (such as finding better work, health care, or education), taking refuge from conflict or a disaster, or in relation to illegal businesses such as smuggling, drug trading, or human trafficking. It is not uncommon for these migration routes to have disproportionate death rates, and forensic anthropologists have become increasingly involved in identifying remains from these contexts.

It is quite frequent, for example, for individuals to cross the border from Mexico into the United States (which shares a border with Mexico of approximately 2000 miles), particularly via the states of Texas, California, and Arizona. Migrants across the Mexico-US border are primarily of Mexican origin, but also include many other national origins including Brazil, Cuba, and Guatemala. The most common reason for border crossings in these regions is to seek work. Due largely to increased border enforcement by the US government and expansion of border fencing since the 1990s (and even greater since the September 11, 2001 terrorist attacks), migrants have been forced to seek out longer migration routes through much harsher areas to attempt to avoid detection and apprehension (Anderson and Parks, 2008). Crossings have therefore increased in areas such as the Sonoran Desert, where terrain is rugged, temperatures are high, and water is scarce. The leading cause of death in these cases is heat-related illness (Anderson and Parks, 2008; Anderson, 2008). In other regions, migration routes may include treacherous mountains and irrigation canals (Hinkes, 2008). Water crossing deaths often occur due to capsized overloaded rafts, though drownings have decreased in recent years as crossings have moved further inland (Hinkes, 2008). Another common cause of death is motor vehicle accidents, either from being struck by cars on poorly-lit roadways, or from overloaded vehicles fleeing authorities (Hinkes, 2008).

Identification of these individuals is complicated by a number of factors. The Pima County Office of the Medical Examiner (PCOME), which investigates the highest number of migrant deaths in the US, reports an identification rate of approximately 65% (Martinez et al., 2013). Remains are often not recovered immediately following death, and bodies tend to decompose very quickly in such warm environments. The remains are often scavenged by non-human animals, usually precluding identification by visual or fingerprint methods. Migrants may also carry false identification, or personal effects may be removed by subsequent migrants, even further confounding or reducing the available evidence for identification (Anderson, 2008).

The scarcity of antemortem medical and dental records for these individuals also hampers identification. Many migrants are likely to be from impoverished regions with poorer quality (or no available) medical and dental care. When available, records are more likely to be from a US facility where treatment was received during a prior visit to the country. Another hindrance to identification can be a lack of cooperation on the part of surviving family members. They may be afraid of confronting the possibility of the individual being deceased, they may fear that legal action will be taken against them, or they may fear the actions of human traffickers (Anderson, 2008).

Because of the prevalence of border crossing deaths, anthropologists have strived to improve methods for identification of these individuals. Offices that process a large number of undocumented border crossers such as the PCOME utilize an approach involving multiple information sources such as personal effects and the geographic location of recovery (together referred to as a "cultural profile") as well as biological characteristics (Anderson, 2008; Birkby et al., 2008) (Figure 15.4). Personal effects that may be useful include identification media (including voter registration cards and birth and marriage certificates), particular types or brands of clothing, food products, address books, foreign currency, and religious icons or amulets. The interpretation of these items in the identification process can be enhanced through knowledge of cultural anthropology. Geographic location of recovery can be informative, since certain routes are known corridors for trafficking migrants and drugs.

Much work has focused on improving the understanding of differences in biological characteristics of migrant groups of this region which can facilitate identification. The assessment of phenotypic traits such as hair form, facial morphology, dental restorations, and skeletal traits, as well as genotypic data from DNA profiling can help characterize the unknown individual and narrow down the likely region of origin. Of particular interest is a better understanding of the phenotypic differences from groups that are often collectively referred to as "Hispanic." As discussed in Chapter 9, the term Hispanic is a social construct with no precise genetic meaning and can refer to various population groups including those originating from Mexico, Puerto Rico, Cuba, South or Central America, or other Latino origins (Spradley et al., 2008). While individuals from Mexico and Central and Latin America are primarily derived from Spanish and Native American groups, Cubans are less likely to have Native American ancestry, and often more closely resemble American Blacks (Ross et al., 2004). The identification of Hispanic individuals can therefore be facilitated through regional research on various Hispanic populations and establishing population-specific morphological ancestry estimation criteria. Another promising

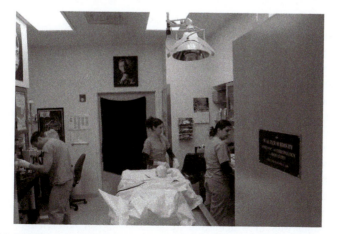

FIGURE 15.4 PCOME anthropologists in the WH Birkby Forensic Anthropology Laboratory examine the remains of suspected migrants, numbering over 2100 since 2001; despite their efforts, approximately 800 remain unidentified

(Photo courtesy of Bruce Anderson)

area of research is the use of isotopic analysis of dental enamel to identify the deceased's region of origin thereby narrowing the search to a particular geographic area (Juarez, 2008).

One effort that is helping to increase the identification rate of those recovered on the Mexican side of the border is the cooperation between US and Mexican authorities. NamUs databases are now available in Spanish, and accept the entry of foreign national missing persons reports. For individuals that remain unidentified, anthropological examinations should be performed including postmortem radiographs (including dental radiographs). Tissue samples for DNA should also be retained for possible future identification.

Similar to the United States, many European countries have increased border control measures to prevent migration, and this has also lead to increased migration-related deaths. For example, asylum-seekers and migrants from many African nations including Sudan, Nigeria, and Ethiopia frequently migrate by boat to southern Italy. The vessels, however, are often overcrowded and unseaworthy, resulting in deaths from capsizing and drowning. Many European countries are also seeing an influx of migrants seeking refuge from violence and civil wars in countries such as Iraq, Syria, Libya, and Palestine. Amnesty International encourages countries to avoid border management practices that put migrants, asylum-seekers, and refugees at risk by forcing them back to countries where they face human rights abuses (Amnesty International, n.d.). Identification efforts in these migration contexts present many of the same challenges for medicolegal systems and forensic anthropologists.

15.5 Forensic anthropology in the legal system

There are various ways that forensic anthropology interacts and interrelates with the legal system. The results of a forensic anthropological examination may facilitate legal determinations such as identity and cause and manner of death, or have relevance in terrorist or humanitarian rights investigations. Written reports should therefore clearly communicate the methods used, the conclusions reached, and the significance and limitations of those conclusions. In many cases, there may be no criminal investigation at all because no crime is suspected to have been committed. In these instances, the forensic anthropologist may simply be trying to assist in the identification process, and there may be no involvement beyond writing the report. In other cases, however, the results of a forensic anthropological examination may have bearing on whether a suspect is determined to be innocent or guilty of a crime. In these cases, it is much more likely that the anthropologist will receive a **subpoena** to testify in a trial in addition to issuing his or her report. Expert witness testimony is an important way in which forensic anthropologists' knowledge is utilized in the legal system, and testifying as an expert witness has become an important and increasingly frequent role of the forensic anthropologist.

Scientific testimony is generally thought of as somewhat novel, but the use of scientific evidence in court dates back nearly 500 years, with scientific testimony appearing increasingly frequently in the judicial system thereafter. Concurrent with this increase in expert testimony in the courts, debate in the legal community developed surrounding the standards for the admissibility of such evidence. As late as the middle of the 19th century, there was still an abundance of controversy and ensuing legal challenges. Since then, the standards for admitting scientific evidence in the US legal system have evolved significantly, due primarily to several Supreme Court rulings and Congressional Acts.

The first ruling regarding the admissibility of scientific evidence was issued in *Frye v. United States* (1923). James Alfonzo Frye was convicted of second degree murder after a lower court disallowed Frye from introducing evidence relating to the results of an earlier "lie detector" test as support of his "not guilty" plea. On appeal, the Court gave an opinion on the standard for the admissibility of scientific expert witness testimony. The Court's opinion stated that:

> *"[w]hile courts will go a long way in admitting expert testimony deduced from a well-recognized scientific principle or discovery, the thing from which the deduction is made must be sufficiently established to have gained general acceptance in the particular field in which it belongs."*

(Frye v. United States, 1923)

The court further concluded that the technique in question had not yet gained the required standing and scientific recognition among authorities in the field of physiology and psychology to be considered admissible under this new guideline.

This general acceptance test came to be known as the "***Frye* Rule**," and became the standard for determining the admissibility of scientific evidence in the majority of courts. Part of the attractiveness and popularity of the *Frye* Rule was that it was easy to apply and required little scientific sophistication on the part of the judges. Over time, however, many courts and legal commentators began to modify or ignore the *Frye* standard. One of the primary concerns was that new scientific techniques, though valid, often failed the *Frye* test. A key legal commentator on evidence indicated that while "general scientific acceptance" is a proper condition for taking judicial notice of scientific facts, it should not be a criterion for the admissibility of scientific evidence (McCormick, 1972).

In 1975, Congress enacted the first modern and uniform set of evidentiary rules for the trial of civil and criminal cases in US federal courts: *The Federal Rules of Evidence* (1975). *Rule 702* specifically addressed expert witness testimony, stating that:

> *"If scientific, technical or other specialized knowledge will assist the trier of fact to understand the evidence or to determine a fact in issue, a witness qualified as an expert by knowledge, skill, experience, training or education may testify thereto in the form of an opinion or otherwise."*

(Fed. R. Evid. 702, 1975)

The *Federal Rules of Evidence*, however, did not eliminate the confusion surrounding the admissibility of scientific evidence. Neither the text of the *Federal Rules* nor the legislative history mentioned the *Frye* standard, which led to a mixed use of *Frye*, the *Federal Rules of Evidence*, or some hybrid of the two. Since then, admissibility standards for expert testimony have been established and clarified through three United States Supreme Court decisions intended to ensure the reliability and relevance of scientific and technical testimony admitted as evidence in federal courts.

In 1993, a landmark decision was made in the case of *Daubert v. Merrell-Dow Pharmaceuticals, Inc.* (1993). The parents of Jason Daubert and Eric Shuller filed a suit against the pharmaceutical company Merrell-Dow, claiming that their children's birth defects were related to the mothers' ingestion of the prescription drug Bendectin (an anti-nausea drug) during their pregnancies. A well-credentialed physician and an epidemiologist who was considered a respected authority on health risks from exposure to chemical substances reviewed numerous published studies and concluded that Bendectin had not been shown to be a risk factor for human birth defects. Eight experts concluded that Bendectin can cause birth defects, but the Court ruled that the evidence did not meet the applicable "general acceptance" standard for the admission of expert testimony according to *Frye*. The case was appealed to the US Supreme Court who granted certiorari to resolve the issue of the proper standard for admission of expert testimony (*Daubert v. Merrell-Dow*, 1993).

The Supreme Court concluded that the *Federal Rules of Evidence* supersede *Frye* and should thus govern admissibility, and that a "rigid and absolute general acceptance test" should not be the standard in order that a reasonable minority opinion may be admitted into evidence, usually in the form of new and emerging research based on reliable, well-designed studies (*Daubert v. Merrell-Dow*, 1993). The Court also interpreted the language of *Rule 702* to set forth the standards of *reliability* and *relevance* for the admissibility of scientific evidence. The reliability standard requires that "scientific knowledge" be grounded in the methods and procedures of science and more than subjective belief or speculation. The relevance standard requires that the information facilitate the fact-finder in reaching a conclusion in the case (i.e., that there is a valid scientific connection to the pertinent inquiry). Furthermore, to assist trial judges, the Court identified several factors intended to assist in determining whether scientific evidence is reliable. These factors are often referred to as the "***Daubert* guidelines**" (see Table 15.1).

The scientific testing guideline is based upon the persuasions of two philosophers of science who have posited that the scientific status of a theory rests in its falsifiability, refutability, or testability (Popper, 1989), and that statements constituting a

---

Table 15.1 The *Daubert* guidelines

Has the technique been tested using the scientific method?

Has the technique been subjected to peer review, preferably in the form of publication in peer-reviewed literature?

What are the known or potential error rates of the technique?

Are there applicable professional standards for the technique?

Is the technique generally accepted within the relevant scientific community?

scientific explanation must be capable of empirical test (Hempel, 1966). Although publication is not required for admissibility, and in some cases may not ensure reliability, the review process associated with publishing in peer-reviewed literature is recognized as a means to increase the likelihood that the scientific community will detect errors or fundamental flaws that exist in the technique or its application.

Error rates are generally derived during the process of scientific testing and can help clarify the validity of the technique as well as any limitations of its application (note that the guideline does not state that the technique should be error-free, which is impossible). The court should also consider whether there are any applicable professional standards relevant to the technique. These standards are increasingly being addressed by organizations such as Scientific Working Groups (see Box 1.4). Finally, the Court noted that general acceptance may be considered, although it is not a necessary precondition for the admissibility of scientific expert evidence, and that pertinent evidence based on scientifically valid principles should be admissible.

In addition to providing the guidelines, the decision also instructed judges to be the "gatekeepers" in keeping "junk science" (i.e., nonscientific results, opinion, or speculations) out of the courtroom. It further indicated that judges should be flexible in conducting their inquiry, and focus on the principles and the methods used and not the conclusions that they generate. Given this focus on the methods themselves, a separate proceeding, called a *"Daubert* **hearing"** or "admissibility hearing," is sometimes held before or during the trial in which the expert has been asked to testify. The case study at the end of this chapter describes a *Daubert* hearing and trial in which a forensic anthropologist testified.

Since the *Daubert* ruling, additional flexibility in the application of the *Daubert* guidelines has been called for in two other cases which have supplemented and clarified the *Daubert* decision. In *General Electric Co. v. Joiner (1997)*, the Court argued that a technique's methodology and conclusions are not completely distinct, that there cannot be an analytical gap between the data and the opinion proffered, and the conclusion can be excluded in the event that valid reasoning does not support it. In *Kumho Tire Co. v. Carmichael (1999)*, the court ruled that the *Daubert* interpretation of *Rule 702* applies not only to "scientific" knowledge but also "technical and other specialized knowledge." Together with *Daubert*, these rulings are sometimes referred to as "the trilogy" of decisions which have set the current legal standard for scientific evidence admissibility.

In 2000, *Federal Rule 702* was amended to include the issues of reliability and relevance:

> *"If scientific, technical or other specialized knowledge will assist the trier of fact to understand the evidence or to determine a fact in issue, a witness qualified as an expert by knowledge, skill, experience, training or education may testify thereto in the form of an opinion or otherwise, if (1) the testimony is based upon sufficient facts or data, (2) the test is the product of reliable principles and methods, and (3) the witness has applied the principles and methods reliably to the facts of the case."*

(Fed. R. Evid. 702, 2000)

15.6 Error and uncertainty in forensic science and forensic anthropology

The *Daubert* guideline that has been the source of most confusion and the topic of most discussion is the one pertaining to "error rates." Forensic practitioners as well as the courts often misunderstand the meanings of scientific error, frequently confusing them with practitioner error (or "mistakes"). **Error** can be defined in a number of ways, including deviation from what is correct, having false knowledge, a mistake, or the difference between an observed value or measurement and the true value. Error can result from a number of different causes in forensic science, and the concept is often vague and subject to a variety of interpretations (Christensen et al., 2014).

In the *Daubert* decision and in the amended *Federal Rule 702*, the concept of "reliability" was heavily emphasized, but was perhaps somewhat improperly used. Scientifically, "**reliability**" refers to repeatability and consistency of observations – highly reliable observations show very low or no inter-observer variability and high repeatability. This is different, however, from **validity**, which has to do with how accurately results describe the real world (or the overall probability of reaching the correct conclusion), and this is probably what the Court had in mind when it empha-sized "reliability." Since the *Daubert* decision, method reliability (validity) has been the most frequently cited reason for excluding or limiting testimony involving foren-sic identification sciences (Page et al., 2011).

The known or potential error rate is one factor that can provide a measure of a method's reliability and validity, and this is likely why it was incorporated as part of the *Daubert* guidelines. Error rates, however, are not *known* in forensic science; they are *estimated* (the *potential* rate of error for any method is 100%), and it can be seen how this error rate guideline has often created confusion. The concept of error can perhaps be clarified and simplified by understanding the differences between several categories of error including practitioner error, instrument error, statistical error, and method (or technique) error (Christensen et al., 2014, 2011; Dror and Charlton, 2006).

Practitioner error refers to human error or mistakes. Practitioner errors may be unintentional and related to negligence or incompetence, such as blunders like trans-posing numbers when recording data, incorrect instrument use, selection of inap-propriate methods, or improper method application. In forensic anthropology, this might include incorrectly transcribing measurements or performing calculations, or selection of a particular age estimation method when another might be more appro-priate. Practitioner error may also be intentional, such as fraudulent behavior. Prac-titioner error is certainly a concern of practitioners and the courts, but it is not really error in the scientific sense, and can be reduced through quality assurance systems, training, proficiency testing, peer review, and adhering to validated protocols and discipline best practices such as those promulgated by Scientific Working Groups like SWGANTH (Christensen et al., 2014; Dror and Charlton, 2006).

Instrument (or technological) **error** is the difference between an indicated instrument value and the actual (true) value. Some acceptable amount of instrument error is generally recognized to exist (which has typically been determined by the instrument's manufacturer), but can be minimized largely by proper maintenance and calibration of instruments (Christensen et al., 2014; Dror and Charlton, 2006). Instruments used in forensic anthropology may include measurement tools such as calipers and osteometric boards, analytical instruments such as XRF and XRD, and diagnostic equipment such as radiology devices. All should be maintained properly and calibrated regularly to minimize instrument error.

Statistical error refers to random variation or deviation from actual and predicted values. Statistical error is generally represented by the standard error or the statistical probability of error, for example when a prediction interval with an explicit probability is specified (see Chapter 3). This "error," which often merely expresses normal variability, is inherent in measurements and estimates because they are based on the properties of a sample (Christensen et al., 2014). In forensic anthropology, this may be seen in calculations such as stature estimation. Regression formulae are based on the characteristics of a large sample which may or may not have the exact same properties as the case at hand; this is why these estimations are best expressed as intervals rather than point estimates.

Lastly, **technique** (or methodological) **error** relates to inherent limitations which are sources of potential error and which have nothing to do with practitioner error or breakdowns in technology (Christensen et al., 2014; Dror and Charlton, 2006). Method limitations in forensic anthropology are often a function of how measurements or traits overlap among different groups or to the frequency of the observed trait(s) in the population at large. While these limitations are not themselves "errors," they relate to the sensitivity or resolving power of the method. The more rare that a trait or suite of traits is in a population, the more sensitive that method is for associating the trait(s) to a particular individual, item, or group. For example, femoral head size may be used to estimate sex, but because there is some overlap between males and females (i.e., some males have small femoral heads, and some females have large ones), there is a chance that any given sex estimate based on femoral head size may be incorrect. There is no way to "minimize" these types of method limitations (with, for example, additional training or calibration) – they simply exist as a function of inherent limits in the material itself (in this case, inherent biological variation in femoral head size) (Box 15.1). Such limitations, however, should be acknowledged and communicated in reports and testimony. Moreover, the selection of good research designs and appropriate statistical models will assist in producing valid scientific methods with known or potential rates of error (Christensen et al., 2011).

Researchers in forensic anthropology are now using more sophisticated measurement techniques and statistical analyses to evaluate forensic evidence, and are also increasingly quantifying traits that had previously been difficult to address in this fashion (see Christensen 2005, for example). For the most part, contemporary anthropology research presents error values, but the term is often not defined and the potential effect on evidentiary examination is not addressed (Crowder and Ingvoldstad, 2009). In addition, anthropologists are increasingly engaging in measures to reduce error such as quality assurance programs and peer review.

> **BOX 15.1 "ZERO ERROR"**
>
> Some forensic practitioners have claimed that the error rate for their technique or method is zero; see US v. Mitchell (1998) for one example. The following testimony was provided by a fingerprint examiner explaining the reasoning behind the zero error rate claim:
>
> *"And we profess as fingerprint examiners that the rate of error is zero. And the reason we make that bold statement is because we know based on 100 years of research that everybody's fingerprints are unique, and in nature it is never going to repeat itself again."*
>
> **(People v. Gomez, 2002)**
>
> What this expert fails to understand is that despite the strength of the basis for fingerprint association (that there is a low probability for two identical fingerprint patterns to exist), error and limitations still exist in the comparison methodology. Error depends not only on how rare a particular trait is, but also on how reliable and valid the methods are for determining a match. There is always a non-zero probability of error, and to claim an error rate of zero is inherently unscientific. Reasons behind such misunderstandings of error range from improper training in statistics and the scientific method to concerns that current methods will be exposed as lacking an empirical footing.

Forensic anthropologists should be concerned with clarity, reliability, and validity of methods, and should also be cognizant of the concerns of the legal community, which includes understanding how the courts view and evaluate scientific evidence. This can best be accomplished by understanding, acknowledging, and communicating method limitations and potential sources of error in research and forensic analyses.

15.7 New research directions

Forensic anthropologists have traditionally been prolific academics, researchers, and publishers, continually striving to develop new methods of analysis and to improve on existing ones. Aspects of the biological profile have always been a rich area of research and are likely to continue to be. Secular change and the discoveries of new skeletal differences between geographic groups ensure that new models will need to be developed based on more recent and larger samples.

Trauma analysis has become a more frequent examination request of forensic anthropologists, and can have a significant impact on an investigation, especially those in which a crime is suspected to have been committed. Historically, studies often involved inflicting trauma to bones (often pig bones), usually manually, and then visually and microscopically assessing the alterations and looking for patterns. Today, advanced research approaches to evaluating trauma are more frequent, including sophisticated biomechanical tests using instruments that control force and measure strain (for example, Baumer et al., 2009) and provide a much more thorough understanding of the effects of certain forces on bone.

77.9°F

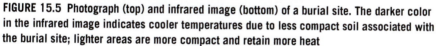

67.7°F

FIGURE 15.5 Photograph (top) and infrared image (bottom) of a burial site. The darker color in the infrared image indicates cooler temperatures due to less compact soil associated with the burial site; lighter areas are more compact and retain more heat

(Images courtesy of Richard Graf, Infrared Diagnostics, Inc.)

The analysis of taphonomy and time since death are also areas that are seeing increased attention. The biochemical processes involved in decomposition are still not well understood, and this is an area where more research is needed. For example, the number of outdoor taphonomic research facilities has dramatically increased within the last five years (as discussed in Chapter 5), and decomposition research has expanded into a more interdisciplinary science involving biochemists, microbiologists, entomologists, and anthropologists. Greater scientific rigor and larger sample sizes have resulted in a more comprehensive understanding of human decompositional sequences, as well as the myriad of contributing factors in different environments.

New technologies are also being explored for the detection of human remains and burial sites. **Infrared imaging** (also called *thermography*) can detect differences in the release of stored energy (heat) in soils due to differences in density/compaction (Figure 15.5). During the day, the sun heats objects and materials in the environment including soil. After the sun sets, these objects and materials retain heat differentially as a function of their density or compaction. Disturbed soil is less dense than undisturbed soil and will therefore lose heat at a faster rate. Infrared imaging utilizes this differential energy retention by imaging the temperature in the area of interest shortly after the sun has set (optimally, about 1.5 hours after sunset), and looking for localized areas of cooler soil. While not yet a widely used technique, and one that requires specialized photographic equipment and training, it shows promise as a useful tool in the detection of subsurface anomalies that may represent burial sites.

Another area that has seen increased attention in recent years is improved statistical analysis in forensic anthropological research and case analysis. Many of the traditional approaches as well as some of the current techniques used in forensic anthropology are relatively subjective, employing a combination of traditional scientific methodologies and less rigorous observational methodologies (Christensen and Crowder, 2009). This does not mean, however, that robust statistical approaches cannot be applied. In addition, Bayesian and other more complex statistical approaches are increasingly being applied to anthropological problems.

Other areas that have been identified as being in need of additional research include the collection of frequency data on skeletal and dental features for use in personal identification, trauma studies using human remains, the development of Postmortem Interval (PMI) estimation methods based solely on skeletal material, collection of additional isotope data on skeletal materials, increased collection of global population data to improve biological profile estimates, and the increased participation by forensic anthropologists in contributing case information to data repositories (SWGANTH, n.d.). It is very important that the aspiring forensic anthropologist is familiar not only with current methods and practice, but also continually evaluates and considers which approaches might require updating and why, understands how to design appropriate studies, and keeps an eye on where anthropology is heading in the future.

15.8 Future of forensic anthropology

Given the expanding scope of the field, there is little doubt that forensic anthropological methods and techniques will continue to be in great demand in crime laboratories, medical examiners' offices, and various other contexts. There are increasing numbers of, and more diversified employment opportunities for, forensic anthropologists, and new research in the area of forensic anthropology should be in continual supply. It is also important to keep abreast of developments in other relevant fields and to assess how they may affect current forensic anthropological methods. Moreover, the ever-changing legal and political landscape means that there are an increasing number of policies and requirements pertinent to the practice of forensic anthropology.

There has been speculation that advances in DNA technology for individual identification may obviate the need for forensic anthropological examinations to assist in the identification process, making some of the roles of the forensic anthropologist (such as determining the biological profile) obsolete. It is certainly the case that more sophisticated, sensitive, and timely approaches for extracting, amplifying, and analyzing DNA from skeletal remains are constantly being developed. A DNA profile, however, is only half of what is needed for an identification – it is also necessary to have something with which to compare it. In some cases, family members of missing persons may contribute DNA samples to be uploaded into databases such as the **National Missing Persons DNA Database** (NMPDD), a component of the **Combined DNA Index System** (CODIS), in the event of a potential match with a DNA sample from an unidentified person. In many cases, however, investigative information such as that provided by a forensic anthropologist's biological profile and assessment of other individualizing skeletal features is still necessary to narrow the search for a potential match, after which DNA samples can be collected for comparison.

One area that significantly complements the biological profile is the determination of sex from DNA. A set of proteins referred to as **amelogenin** (so called because they are involved in the development of dental enamel, or *amelogenesis*) shows differences in the X and Y chromosomes. Amelogenin analysis can therefore determine the sex of the source of unknown DNA samples. Such tests are already commonly used in forensic DNA analyses to determine whether the contributor of an unknown DNA sample was male or female, often from blood or other bodily fluids. Unknown DNA may also come from the bones or teeth of unidentified skeletal remains. The method, however, is not 100% accurate and results should therefore be considered to supplement forensic anthropological assessments rather than replace them. Some anthropological studies have examined the correlation between anthropological and amelogenin results regarding sex (Anderson, 2013).

There have also been recent advances in ancestry estimation from DNA, based largely on **Ancestry Informative Markers**, or AIMs. This approach is based on the fact that certain parts of human DNA show significant differences in allele frequencies due to an individual's geographic ancestral origin (typically at the continental level). Many of the AIMs are related to skin and hair pigment. This information can be used to determine the continental origin (or admixture thereof) of an unknown individual's DNA. This application has gained the most ground in developing the profiles of possible suspects in homicide or rape cases. The approach could, however, also potentially be used to facilitate the development of a biological profile from unidentified human remains. This application has not yet gained wide popularity, and it is cautioned that the approach, like metric analysis of cranial shape, is based on suites of genetic traits that tend to be shared by certain groups for evolutionary or adaptive reasons, and does not constitute a "diagnosis" of ancestry.

At the direction of the US Congress, the National Academy of Sciences was charged with conducting a study on forensic science to assess resource needs, make recommendations to maximize technologies and their implementation, recommend programs to increase the number of qualified scientists, disseminate best practices for collecting and analyzing forensic evidence, and other issues related to forensic science. The study culminated in a report issued in 2009 titled: *Strengthening*

Forensic Science in the United States: A Path Forward (National Research Council, 2009). The document outlined various scientific and technical challenges that needed to be met in order for the forensic science enterprise in the United States to operate at its full potential. In the opinion of the National Research Council, some disciplines (even some that were considered widely accepted) were found to lack scientific rigor, and systemic and scientific changes and advancements in the forensic sciences were determined to be necessary. The Council also recognized disparities among forensic science operations in various jurisdictions and agencies with respect to funding, access to analytical instrumentation, availability of trained personnel, certification, accreditation, and oversight.

The report outlined 14 specific recommendations including: establish a governing body to determine and enforce best practices; establish mandatory accreditation of laboratories and mandatory certification of forensic scientists; promote competitive research and technology development; establish a strategy to improve forensic research and educational programs; establish a strategy for efficient allocation of funds to support forensic science practices; provide funding to forensic science agencies, research projects, and educational programs; oversee education standards and accreditation; develop programs to improve understanding limitations; and assess new technologies.

Although forensic anthropology was not specifically targeted in the report, there are many anthropological methods and techniques that are based on principles similar to those identified in the report including approaches related to pattern matching and population frequencies. The report has prompted forensic anthropologists (and other forensic scientists) to take a critical look at the methods used including their reliability and validity, as well as how results are reported and how testimony is provided. In general, the National Academy of Sciences (NAS) report reminds us that forensic science needs to have a strong basis in reliable scientific testing, and that we also need to be cognizant of the concerns of the legal community.

In February 2013, the US Department of Justice and the US Department of Commerce's National Institute of Science and Technology (NIST) announced in a *Federal Registry* notice the formation of a new National Commission on Forensic Science (NCFS) and solicited applicants for its 30-member board. The board members will consist of forensic scientists, researchers, prosecutors, defense attorneys, and judges. The NCFS will be tasked with standardizing guidance for forensic science practitioners, developing unified codes for professional responsibility, and establishing requirements for training and certification. The Commission is expected to seek input from forensic practitioners and researchers who will develop discipline-specific best practice guidelines which will be considered by the Commission for policy recommendations to the Attorney General.

It is clear that scientific, legal, and political landscapes within which forensic anthropology is practiced are constantly evolving. It is therefore important to stay abreast of advances in practices and technology within forensic anthropology as well as related and complementary disciplines. It is also important to be aware of any legislative changes that affect the practice of forensic science, as well as the political climate as it relates to forensic issues.

15.9 Case study – the state of Tennessee v. David William Cosgrif, III

Seventy-six-year-old Kathleen Taylor mysteriously disappeared from her Harriman, Tennessee home in 2001. A friend of her grandson's who lived with Taylor, David William Cosgrif, III, aroused the suspicion of the police by remaining in the house after Taylor's disappearance, forging checks on her bank account, using her debit card and vehicle, and offering various accounts for her whereabouts and his presence on her property.

On December 27, 2003, a hunter noticed a human skull on the ground and notified the Roane County Sheriff's Department. The Sheriff's Department collected the bones, and with the assistance of a cadaver dog, located and collected additional remains on January 21 and 23, 2004. Cosgrif was charged with first degree premeditated murder and two counts of theft over $1000. The remains were turned over to Dr. Lee Meadows Jantz of the University of Tennessee's Forensic Anthropology Center for analysis.

In a pretrial admissibility hearing, the trial court ruled in favor of admitting Dr. Jantz's findings and testimony as an expert in forensic anthropology. Dr. Jantz testified that she determined that the bones came from a human female of European origin who was at least 60 years of age. She further noted the presence of healed nasal bone fractures, unhealed blunt trauma to the left side of the face and skull which occurred around the time of death, and estimated that the remains had been at the site for 1–5 years.

No dental records for Taylor were available for comparison, but Dr. Jantz was able to conclude that the bones had a high probability of being Taylor's by comparing the frontal sinus cavity of a clinical X-ray of Taylor's to that of the skull found in the woods (Figure 15.6). She testified that based on numerous studies published in

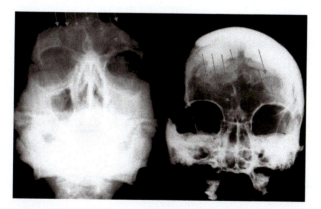

FIGURE 15.6 Radiographic comparison of an antemortem record from Kathleen Taylor (left) and skeletal remains discovered in Roane County, TN (right), with arrows indicating points of congruence

(Images courtesy of The Forensic Anthropology Center, University of Tennessee)

peer-reviewed literature, frontal sinuses of different individuals had been shown to be different at a highly significant level, making them a statistically reliable method of facilitating personal identification. Moreover, the nasal bone fractures were consistent with the radiologist's report regarding fractures which Taylor had sustained during a home invasion. Based on this and other evidence, Cosgrif was convicted of second degree murder and sentenced to 20 years in prison.

Cosgrif appealed the decision on three grounds, including a challenge that the trial court erroneously allowed Dr. Jantz's testimony with respect to the method used to identify the remains. Specifically, he argued that the testimony should have been disallowed because the frontal sinus identification method Dr. Jantz used did not meet reliability indicia for admission under Tennessee Law. In Tennessee, the admission of expert testimony is governed by the Tennessee Rules of Evidence 702 and 703, which are based to a large extent on the Federal Rules of Evidence. Tennessee Rule 702 states that:

> "[i]f scientific, technical, or other specialized knowledge will substantially assist the trier of fact to understand the evidence or to determine a fact in issue, a witness qualified as an expert by knowledge, skill, experience, training or education may testify in the form of an opinion or otherwise."
>
> **(Tenn R. Evid. 702)**

Rule 703 states that expert testimony shall be disallowed "if the underlying facts or data indicate lack of trustworthiness" (*Tenn. R. Evid. 703*). Further, *Tenn. R. Evid 702* in a 2001 note indicates that the *Frye* test no longer exists in Tennessee, and that factors taken largely from the *Daubert* ruling apply, including: whether scientific evidence has been tested and the methodology with which it has been tested; whether the evidence has been subjected to peer review or publication; whether a potential rate of error is known; whether, as formerly required by *Frye*, the evidence is generally accepted in the scientific community; and whether the expert's research in the field has been conducted independent of litigation (*Tenn R. Evid 702, 2001*).

Citing several precedents, the court ruled that Dr. Jantz was clearly qualified as an expert in forensic anthropology, and that apart from her testimony about the identification based on frontal sinus morphology, the biological profile and antemortem trauma history reported by Dr. Jantz were also consistent with Taylor. That evidence, combined with the fact that the remains were discovered in the same county from which the victim had disappeared, was sufficient for a jury to conclude that the remains were those of Taylor [*State v. David William Cosgrif, III, (2010)*]. The conviction was held on appeal, though the sentence was reduced to 15 years.

15.10 Summary

- Forensic anthropology is an evolving discipline that continues to broaden in both depth and scope.
- Forensic anthropologists work within an interdisciplinary framework in which a skeletal analysis is typically just one component of a much larger investigation.

It is important for forensic anthropologists to stay abreast of their field, as well as other relevant areas of study.

- In recent years, forensic anthropologists have expanded from domestic casework to international human rights investigations and mass disaster victim identification efforts. This has required broader knowledge of the legal system as well as an understanding of large-scale victim identification.
- Recent court rulings have changed the meaning of what information qualifies as admissible in regard to expert witness testimony. Forensic anthropologists must be aware of these legal requirements and also the scientific limitations and sources of error for different analytical methods.
- New research directions in contemporary anthropology include advanced technologies as well as more sophisticated analyses of skeletal biomechanics and secular change.
- Although DNA testing has become increasingly important in human identification, forensic anthropologists will continue to play a significant role in the identification process.

15.11 **Test yourself**

- What roles do forensic anthropologists have in human rights investigations? Mass disasters? What other disciplines are also important for identification in these contexts? Why is an interdisciplinary approach important?
- Discuss the differences between the *Frye Rule* and the *Daubert guidelines.* Why are these differences important? What is the standard for evidence admissibility in the state or jurisdiction where you live?
- Describe the differences between statistical, practitioner, technique, and instrument error. Can you think of additional examples of each type of error that may be encountered in forensic anthropological analyses? Explain why no expert can claim that his or her error rate is zero.
- What are some of the key implications for forensic anthropology based on the recommendations of the National Academy of Sciences' 2009 report?
- What new scientific areas do you believe will become more important for future forensic anthropologists?

Definitions

Amelogenin A set of proteins that can be used to determine sex due to differences on the X and Y chromosomes

Ancestry Informative Markers (AIMs) Allele frequency differences known to be related to geographic origin and often relating to skin and hair pigment

Closed population A certain limited number of victims known to be involved in a mass fatality event, such as passengers on a flight

Combined DNA Index System (CODIS) An FBI database and software containing DNA profiles contributed by federal, state, and local participating forensic science laboratories

***Daubert* guidelines** A series of guidelines offered in the ruling of the 1993 *Daubert v. Merrell-Dow Pharmaceuticals* case which is to be used by trial judges to determine whether expert witness testimony should be admissible

***Daubert* hearing** A hearing, usually held prior to a trial, in which the trial judge evaluates the testimony of an expert witness to determine whether it will be admissible in the trial

Disaster victim identification (DVI) A component of mass fatality management that involves the scientific identification of human remains

Error The difference between an estimated or observed value and the true value

The Federal Rules of Evidence A code of US law enacted in 1975 and revised in 2000 that governs the admissibility of evidence in the US federal court system

***Frye* Rule** A standard for admissibility of expert witness testimony based on a 1923 court ruling which required that the content of the testimony be generally accepted by the relevant scientific community

Infrared imaging A technique that uses infrared radiation (which is differentially emitted from objects on the basis of their temperature) to make images instead of visible light; also called *thermography*

Instrument error The difference between an indicated instrument value and the actual (true) value

Interdisciplinary Involving two or more scientific or academic disciplines; the collaboration of scientists from multiple fields for a common goal

Mass disaster An event involving the deaths of multiple individuals; also called *mass fatality incident*

Mass grave A grave containing multiple individuals, often as part of a single event

National Missing Person DNA Database (NMPDD) A program to assist in the identification of missing persons and unidentified remains using CODIS

Open population An initially unknown victim population in a mass fatality event, such as those affected by a natural disaster

Practitioner error Human error; mistake

Reliability The ability to obtain the same result using the same methods and instruments

Statistical error Random variation or deviation from actual and predicted values, generally represented by the standard error or the statistical probability of error

Subpoena A formal request to appear in court and give testimony

Technique error Inherent limitations of a method or approach which are sources of potential error, often a function of how measurements or traits overlap among different groups or to the frequency of the observed trait(s) in the population at large

Validity The degree to which an observation or result reflects empirical reality

References

Amnesty International, n.d. www.amnesty.org. Accessed July 27, 2013.

Anderson, B.E., 2008. Identifying the dead: Methods utilized by the Pima County (Arizona) Office of the Medical Examiner for undocumented border crossers: 2001–2006. J. Forensic Sci. 53 (1), 8–15.

Anderson, B.E., 2013. Received wisdom vs. reality: Utilizing amelogenin profiles to evaluate the accuracy of skeletal morphologic and metric sex assessments in adults. Proceedings of the 65th Annual Meeting of the American Academy of Forensic Sciences, Washington, DC.

Anderson, B.E., Parks, B.O., 2008. Symposium on border crossing deaths: Introduction. J. Forensic Sci. 53 (1), 6–7.

Baumer, T.G., Fenton, T.W., Haut, R.C., Powell, B.J., 2009. Age dependent mechanical properties of the infant porcine parietal bone and a correlation to the human. J. Biomech. Eng. 131 (11), 111006: doi:10.1115/1.4000081.

Christensen, A.M., Crowder, C.M., 2009. Evidentiary standards for forensic anthropology. J. Forensic Sci. 546, 1211–1216.

Christensen, A.M., Crowder, C.M., Houck, M.M., Ousley, S.D., 2011. Error, error rates and their meanings in forensic science. Proceedings of the 63rd Annual Meeting of the American Academy of Forensic Sciences, Chicago, IL.

Christensen, A.M., Crowder, C.M., Ousley, S.D., Houck, M.M., 2014. Error and its meaning in forensic science. J. Forensic Sci. In Press.

Committee on Identifying the Needs of the Forensic Sciences Community, National Research Council, 2009. Strengthening Forensic Science in the United States: A Path Forward. National Academies Press.

Crowder, C.M., Ingvoldstad, M., 2009. Observer error trends in forensic anthropology. Proceedings of the 61st Annual Meeting of the American Academy of Forensic Sciences, Denver, CO.

Daubert v. Merrell Dow Pharmaceuticals, Inc., 509 US 579, 1993.

Doretti, M., Fondebrider, L., 2002. Science and human rights: Truth, justice, repatriation and reconciliation, a long way in Third World countries. In: Buchli, V., Lucas, G. (Eds.), Archaeologies of the Contemporary Past. Routledge, London, pp. 138–144.

Dror, I.E., Charlton, D., 2006. Why experts make errors. J. Forensic Identification 56 (4), 600–616.

Emanovsky, P.D., Belcher, W.R., 2012. The many hats of a recovery leader: Perspectives on planning and executing worldwide forensic investigations and recoveries at the JPAC Central Identification Laboratory. In: Dirkmaat, D.C. (Ed.), A Companion to Forensic Anthropology. Blackwell Publishing, Chichester, pp. 565–592.

Federal Rules of Evidence, 1975; 2000.

Frye v. United States, 54 App. D.C. 46, 293 F. 1013, 1923.

General Electric Co. v. Joiner, 522 US 136, 1997.

Hempel, C.G., 1966. Philosophy of natural sciences. Prentice Hall, Englewood Cliffs.

Hinkes, M.J., 2008. Migrant deaths along the California-Mexico Border: An anthropological perspective. J. Forensic Sci. 53 (1), 16–20.

International Committee for the Red Cross, n.d. www.icrc.org. Accessed August, 2012.

International Commission on Missing Persons, n.d. www.ic-mp.org. Accessed August, 2012.

INTERPOL, 2009. Disaster Victim Identification Guide. INTERPOL.

INTERPOL, n.d. INTERPOL Overview. www.interpol.int. Accessed July 8, 2013.

Juarez, C.A., 2008. Strontium and geolocation, the pathway to identification for deceased undocumented Mexican border crossers: A preliminary report. J. Forensic Sci. 53 (1), 46–49.

Kimmerle, E.H., Baraybar, J.P., 2008. Skeletal Trauma: Identification of Injuries Resulting from Human Rights Abuse and Armed Conflict. CRC Press, Boca Raton.

Kumho Tire Co. v. Carmichael, 5216 US 137, 1999.

Martinez, D.E., Reineke, R.C., Rubio-Goldsmith, R., Anderson, B.E., Hess, G.L., Parks, B.O., 2013. A Continued Humanitarian Crisis at the Border: Undocumented Border Crosser Deaths Recorded by the Pima County Office of the Medical Examiner, 1990–2012. The Binational Migration Institute. The University of Arizona.

McCormick, C.T., 1972. McCormick's Handbook of the Law of Evidence, second ed. West Publishing Company, St. Paul. Cleary EW (Ed.).

National Disaster Medical System, n.d. http://ndms.fhpr.osd.mil/. Retrieved June 20, 2013.

Page, M., Taylor, J., Blenkin, M., 2011. Forensic identification science evidence since Daubert: Part I – A quantitative analysis of the exclusion of forensic identification science evidence. J. Forensic Sci. 56 (5), 1180–1184.

People v Gomez, 99CF 0391, 2002.

Popper, K., 1989. Conjectures and refutations: The growth of scientific knowledge. Harper & Rowe, New York.

Public Health Emergency, n.d. http://www.phe.gov/Preparedness/responders/ndms/teams/Pages/dmort.aspx. Retrieved June 20, 2013.

Ross, A.H., Slice, D.E., Ubelaker, D.H., Falsetti, A.B., 2004. Population affinities of 19th century Cuban crania: Implications for identification criteria in south Florida Cuban Americans. J. Forensic Sci. 49, 1–6.

Scientific Working Group on Disaster Victim Identification, n.d. www.swgdvi.org. Accessed July 8, 2013.

Scientific Working Group on Forensic Anthropology, n.d. Current Needs in Forensic Anthropology. Accessed July 27, 2013.

Sledzik, P.S., 2009. Forensic anthropology in disaster response. In: Blau, S., Ubelaker, D.H. (Eds.), Handbook of Forensic Anthropology and Archaeology. Left Coast Press Inc, Walnut Creek, pp. 374–387.

Spradley, M.D., Jantz, R.L., Robinson, A., Peccerelli, F., 2008. Demographic change and forensic identification: Problems in metric identification of Hispanic skeletons. J. Forensic Sci. 53 (1), 21–28.

State of Tennessee v. David William Cosgrif, III, No. E2009–02547-CCA-R3-CD, 2010.

Tennessee Rules of Evidence, 1990; 2001.

United States v Mitchell 145 F.3d 572 3d Cir., 1998.

Index

Note: Page numbers followed by "f" denote figures; "t" tables; "b" boxes.